RETRACING THE PAST

Readings in the History of the American People

Volume II

Since 1865

Sixth Edition

Gary B. Nash

University of California, Los Angeles

Ronald Schultz

University of Wyoming

PEARSON

Longman

New York San Francisco Boston
London Toronto Sydney Tokyo Singapore Madrid
Mexico City Munich Paris Cape Town Hong Kong Montreal

For Sara, Tristan and Hanna

Executive Editor: Michael Boezi
Executive Marketing Manager: Sue Westmoreland
Production Manager: Denise Phillip
Project Coordination, Text Design, and Electronic Page Makeup: WestWords, Inc.
Cover Designer/Manager: Wendy Ann Fredericks
Cover Art: George Luks (1867–1933/American), *On the Steps*. Oil on wood panel. David David
    Gallery, Philadelphia. SuperStock, Inc.
Manufacturing Buyer: Roy Pickering
Printer and Binder: Courier Corporation
Cover Printer: Courier Corporation

For permission to use copyrighted material, grateful acknowledgment is made to the copyright holders on the first page of the respective selections, which are hereby made part of this copyright page.

Library of Congress Cataloging-in-Publication Data

Retracing the past : readings in the history of the American people / [edited by] Gary B.
  Nash, Ronald Schultz.—6th ed.
    p. cm.
    Contents: v. 1. To 1877—v. 2. Since 1865.
    ISBN 0-321-33379-9 (v. 1)—ISBN 0-321-33380-2 (v. 2)
    1. United States—History. I. Nash, Gary B. II. Schultz, Ronald

E178.6.R45 2005
973—dc22
                                                                    2005048910

Please visit out website at http://www.ablongman.com

ISBN 0-321-33380-2

1 2 3 4 5 6 7 8 9 10—CRS—08 07 06 05

CONTENTS

PART TWO   A Modernizing People   94

PART THREE   A Resilient People   208

PREFACE

This two-volume reader has been constructed as a supplement to the many American history survey textbooks currently in use in the United States and beyond. The essays have been selected with three goals in mind: first, to blend political and social history; second, to lead students to a consideration of the roles of women, ethnic groups, and laboring Americans in the weaving of the nation's social fabric; and third, to explore life at the individual and community levels. The book is also intended to introduce students to the individuals and groups that made a critical difference in the shaping of American history or whose experience reflected key changes in society.

Some of the individuals highlighted are famous, such as James Madison and Lyndon Johnson. A number of others, George Whitefield and John Muir for example, are historically visible but are not quite household names. Many will be totally unknown to students, such as George Robert Twelves Hewes, a Boston shoemaker who participated in some of the most important events of the American Revolution; Thomas Peters, who escaped slavery by fleeing to the British during the Revolutionary War and later led several thousand escaped slaves to a new homeland in Sierra Leone; and Lozen, an Apache women who functioned as an important war leader in the last decades of the nineteenth century. Often the focus is on groups whose role in history has not been adequately treated—the Chinese in the building of the transcontinental railroad, the grassroots black leaders during Reconstruction, and the rising African American middle and underclasses of the post–Civil Rights era.

Some of these essays take us inside American homes, farms, and factories, such as the essays on working women and their families in New York City before the Civil War and the people of Butte, Montana, who welcomed newly available radios into their homes during the 1920s and 1930s. Such essays, it is hoped, convey an understanding of the daily lives of ordinary Americans, who collectively helped shape their society. Other essays deal with the vital social and political movements that transformed American society: the debate over the Constitution in the 1780s; reform in the antebellum period; populism and progressivism in the late nineteenth and early twentieth centuries; and the rise of economic uncertainty and political conservatism in our own time.

Accessibility has been a guiding concern in preparing this edition of *Retracing the Past*. Consequently, we have continued with the significant changes made in the previous edition that were designed to make the readings more accessible and useful to student readers and more effective in the classroom. At the same time, we have replaced a third of the previous readings with new essays that better reflect current scholarship and current student interests. Especially important here is a new emphasis on the diversity of American society. For example, the first volume opens with James Axtell's depiction of the first encounters between Europeans and Native Americans in the sixteenth and seventeenth centuries, while the second volume brings the study of diversity into the present with Robin D.G. Kelley's portrayal of the simultaneous growth of poverty and middle-class prosperity in African American communities during the late twentieth century. We have edited each of the readings to make them more straightforward and understandable to students and, in addition, have included glossaries at the end of each reading to help students better identify the people and terms discussed in the essays.

One of the most important changes to the previous edition was the inclusion of thought-provoking questions at the end of each essay. These questions—**Implications**—ask students to move from the local and personal focus of the essays to consider the broader implications of what they have read, placing the essays in the wider perspective of the American past. We have continued these very successful questions in this edition. Another important change in the previous edition was the inclusion of primary documents to introduce each reading. These documents, often taken from sources used in the essays themselves, enliven the past, make the experiences of the American people more concrete, and set the stage for the readings that follow. These documents, too, have been continued in this edition. Finally, like its predecessors, this edition includes a brief introductory essay—**Sources and Interpretations**—that provides students with a strategy for reading these documents and the essays that follow in a way that is both efficient and effective. This strategy has been used at the University of Wyoming for a decade with excellent results, and we think this strategy will work equally well in any college or highschool classroom. In sum, we think these changes in the sixth edition of *Retracing the Past* will make this a more approachable and therefore more useful reader and will make the American past an engaging and rewarding subject for a new generation of students.

Acknowledgments

In developing this volume of readings, the editors have been well-advised by the following academic colleagues, who reviewed the previous edition and read preliminary tables of contents: Ginette Aley, Virginia Tech; James A. Zimmerman, Tri-State University; Anthony Gulig, University of Wisconsin-Whitewater; Catherine Candy, Raritan Valley Community College; Peter Murray, Methodist College; Robert Sawrey, Marshall University; and Jeff Pasley, University of Missouri-Columbia.

Gary B. Nash
Ronald Schultz

INTRODUCTION

Sources and Interpretations

People often think that history is mostly about facts: Who invented the cotton gin? Where was the nation's first capital? When did women secure the vote? But, while no historian would dispute the importance of facts, historical writers are much more concerned with interpretation, that is, with giving facts historical meaning. In practice, historians normally spend very little time debating the facts of a particular historical process or event; instead they typically differ about what those established facts mean. Take, for example, a letter written by an early nineteenth-century New England farmer outlining his plan to purchase land on the western New York frontier. One historian might recall what she has read about the family-centeredness of New Englanders and find in the letter a father's concern to place each of his sons on freehold land, thus allowing them to re-create his own life as an independent family farmer. On the other hand, the contents of the same letter might lead another historian to remember the economic position of early American farmers and conclude that the father was purchasing land for speculation, hoping to sell the land at a higher price once settlers entered the region. Or a third historian might integrate both of these views and infer from the letter that the farmer's main aim was family continuance but that he was not above a little speculation along the way. In all of these cases, the historians have no dispute with the source (the letter) itself but draw very different and potentially conflicting conclusions from it.

This example points to one of the fundamental features of historical interpretation: the essential ambiguity of sources. Like the farmer's letter, no document or physical artifact is ever perfectly clear to the reader or observer. Instead, it requires the exercise of historical judgment—re-creating the context in which the source was produced and making collateral connections between it and other sources from the same time and place—to give it meaning. It is the historian's job to interrogate a source by asking a series of questions, most importantly, Who produced the source? What was their purpose in doing so? For whom was the source intended? How was the source received and how was it used? Historians employ this basic arsenal of questions when analyzing a source, and only when the source has been internally scrutinized and these questions answered satisfactorily can the source be used to build an interpretation.

Facts and interpretations are thus closely linked and historians acknowledge this linkage by dividing their materials into two groups: primary sources and secondary interpretations. Primary sources are items produced during the time period being investigated. These items might be written documents—such as letters, diaries, travel accounts, or contemporary books—or they might be statistical compilations—such as census tabulations, business records, or tax lists. They might even be material artifacts—such as houses, home furnishings, or clothing—that have survived from the period in question. It is from the broad array of such primary sources that historians draw the facts they will use in constructing interpretations of past events and processes.

History is a discipline that builds on the work of others, and historians continually measure the primary source data they gather against existing interpretations of their subject. These interpretations (sometimes called secondary sources) most commonly appear as articles in professional journals and as monographs which deal with a specific aspect of the period in question, say an essay about agricultural change in the early republic or a book about the origin of Jim Crow laws in the post–Reconstruction South. Historians use secondary sources to help them place their primary materials in context and to give those materials a wider meaning. In turn, they use primary sources to question the conclusions drawn by other writers. By utilizing primary sources and secondary interpretations in this way, historians advance historical understanding through a process of successive interrogation and refinement. Written history is thus a continuous dialogue between the past and the present, a dialogue that is always ongoing and provisional and one that is never final or complete.

As you read each of the essays in *Retracing the Past*, you will first encounter "Past Traces," a brief selection of primary documents drawn from the time period of the essay. The purpose of these documents is two-fold: first, to give you a sense of the lives and concerns of ordinary people in a particular time period and, second, to involve you in the process of historical evaluation and interpretation. For example, in the opening essay of this volume you will find a letter written by a former slave, answering his exmaster's request that he return with his family to work as an employee on his old plantation. Read with care and imagination, the letter tells us much about the attitudes that slaves held about slavery and slave owners. We learn, for example, that slaves recognized the importance of their labor and the value it generated. If we look a little further, we also learn that slaves, like many other subordinate people, were adept at using irony as a symbolic assertion of their humanity and power. By offering to return to the South if properly compensated for his and his family's previous labor, this former slave assumes the upper hand and, at the same time, reminds his exmaster that he has not forgotten the fact of exploitation under the slave regime. These are just a few of the things that can be learned from the primary documents that follow; there are many others as you will discover. As you read the documents, you will begin to ask your own questions and form your own interpretations. Most importantly, in learning to read the documents for their diverse meanings, you will already be thinking like a historian.

Following the documents, you will find six essays of historical interpretation. In each, a historian has consulted primary and secondary sources and constructed an interpretation that explains what he or she thinks the sources reveal about an individual or group of people in the chronological period in question. Thus, in "Messenger of the New Age," Mary Murphy uses letters from listeners of radio station KGIR in Butte, Montana, to measure the impact that the new medium of radio had on one American community. In doing so, Murphy uses her sources to question historians who claim that during the Great Depression of the 1930s Americans were left with few national resources to cope with the disruptions that economic downturn brought to their lives. This, then, is the procedure of the working historian, a procedure that depends on the mutual interrogation of primary sources and secondary interpretations in the process of reaching historical conclusions.

Reading with Purpose

One of the unusual aspects of written history is that, like literature, it is often read by nonhistorians for no other purpose than simple relaxation and pleasure. Thus, while few people will spend their leisure hours reading a new book on the biochemistry of enzymes, many nonspecialists will read the latest book about the American Civil War. This difference between a work of chemistry and a work of history lays a trap that often snares student readers. The chemistry book will most likely be read pragmatically, that is, it will be read in order to gain specific information about enzymes that can be used later in an experimental or classroom application. The history book, on the other hand, will more likely be read without any expectation of future use or application.

Each of the historical essays that follow can be read as an interesting story in its own right, whether about southern slave resistance, the Populist critique of big business, or the youth culture of the 1960s. As such, each essay invites a casual rather than a pragmatic reading. Yet, most history courses will ask for exactly that: a purposeful, pragmatic, and analytical reading that goes beyond the story line and focuses instead on what the essay and its evidence tell us about a person (or group of people) and their times. In his essay about slave resistance, for example, Peter Wood uses newspapers and contemporary journals to reveal ways in which southern slaves contested the terms of their enslavement and put the lie to slaveholder attempts to dehumanize their bondsmen and women. It is a compelling story in its own right, but in a college classroom or discussion section you would be expected to gain more from Wood's essay than a casual reading would allow. At a minimum, you would be expected to recount the main and subsidiary points of his essay and be able to say something about how the essay adds to our understanding of southern society in the colonial period.

How, then, does one avoid the pitfalls of a casual reading of an essay and grasp its most salient points? One of the most effective ways to accomplish this is to read each essay with a structured set of questions in mind, that is, to read with a purpose. There are five basic questions you should ask yourself as you read the essays in *Retracing the Past*.

First, you should be able to identify the main subject of the essay and place that person or group in the context of their times. Some questions you might wish to ask include: Who are the most important people in the essay? Is the essay about an individual or group? What are the most important characteristics of this person or group for an understanding of the essay? What is their class? Their race? Their gender? Their occupation? Where did the events discussed in the essay take place? When?

Second, since history deals with human predicaments, you should be able to identify the major problem or problems faced by the subject of the essay. What did the subject hope to accomplish? What was the most important obstacle(s) or impediment(s) standing in the way of the fulfillment of the subject's desires? What was the source of this impediment(s)? Was it individual and personal or structural and impersonal?

Third, because people respond to their predicaments in many different ways, you should be able to locate major actions undertaken by the subject to solve the problem(s). How did the subject go about trying to solve the problem(s)? Does the person or group solve the problem alone? Who provides help? What help was given? Why was it given?

Fourth, since some actions lead to successful conclusions and others do not, make a judgment about the ultimate resolution of the actions taken by the people in the essay. Did they achieve what they set out to accomplish? Or did they realize only some of their goals? If they solved their problem(s), what allowed them to do this? If the problem remained unsolved, why wasn't it solved? What obstacles prevented a solution? What was the person's or group's response to the lack of a solution?

Lastly, since each essay in *Retracing the Past* is a case study of a larger historical process, you should be able to place the subject's problem and its resolution into the larger context of the historical period in question. What ideas do you think the author wanted to convey in his or her article? How does the essay relate to other course materials, such as lectures, multimedia presentations, or points made in your textbook and other readings? Do the points made in the essay agree or disagree with other interpretations you've heard or read about in the course? How do they agree or disagree? If they disagree, which interpretation do you accept? Why?

By asking these questions as you read the essays in *Retracing the Past*, you will be engaged in reading pragmatically. This purposeful way of reading will help you to understand and enjoy the essays more fully and, at the same time, will actively engage you in the process of historical interpretation, thus helping you draw your own conclusions and form your own arguments about the historical period in question.

RETRACING THE PAST

PART ONE

An Industrializing People

The post-Civil War decades witnessed the rapid expansion of heavy industry, large-scale immigration and urbanization, the effective completion of western settlement, and the continued subordination of African Americans not only in the South but in northern and western cities as well. But while the economic success of the late nineteenth century meant prosperity for some, it also meant wrenching changes in the lives of ordinary people, many of whom became disenchanted with the nation's new urban-industrial order.

The end of the Civil War posed one of the most critical questions in American social relations. The Thirteenth, Fourteenth, and Fifteenth Amendments to the Constitution had promised ex-slaves citizenship and civil rights and guaranteed freedmen the right to vote. But constitutional doctrine was one thing and social practice another. In "African Americans in Public Office during Reconstruction," Eric Foner reveals the vital role of African American leaders in shaping social and political relations in the postwar South. Much of the local character of southern politics before 1877, he argues, derived from the active participation of ex-slaves in the formal political process.

In 1865, the United States spanned some 3000 miles between its Atlantic and Pacific coasts, yet the cheapest and most effective form of transportation between East and West remained the arduous ocean route around the southern tip of South America. In 1863, the Civil War Congress sought to bind the nation together more effectively by authorizing the construction of a transcontinental railroad. Working feverishly from bases in California and Nebraska, Chinese and Irish immigrants forged a rail link that made rapid settlement of the western territories a practical possibility. In "The Chinese Link a Continent and a Nation," Jack Chen takes us into the world of Chinese workers who, using an unsurpassed knowledge of explosives learned in their native land, risked life and limb to blast a path for the Central Pacific Railroad through the granite mountains of the Sierra Nevada range.

One consequence of rapid economic growth at the close of the nineteenth century was growing unrest among the nation's family farmers. Finding themselves forced into cycles of overproduction to pay for mechanized farm implements and trapped by railroad conglomerates who overcharged to ship their goods to market, American farmers increasingly turned to politics for a solution to their problems. In "The Southern Populist Critique of American Capitalism," Bruce Palmer explores the ideas behind the Populist movement and its political arm, the Peoples' party. He discovers that, far from being a backward-looking movement, Populism combined traditional agrarian values with a modern acceptance of the marketplace. Populism, he shows, was a creative attempt to preserve long-held ideals in the face of the realities of the modern world.

Industrial growth at the close of the nineteenth century brought with it two linked phenomena: large-scale immigration of Europeans to work in the nation's new industries and the rise of large and crowded cities to house these new workers. In "First Encounters," Elizabeth Ewen recounts this decisive immigrant experience by focusing on the lives of immigrant women and the rigors of adjustment to New York City life. Adjustment to American industrial and urban life was difficult for these women, as it was for all immigrants, but the shared communities that flourished in New York's ethnic neighborhoods gave these women a sense of support and belonging as they developed new lives and relationships in their adopted homeland.

The rapidly changing world of the industrial Northeast introduced new stresses into the lives of all urban residents, but it also offered new forms of popular entertainment that made urban life exciting and enjoyable. For little more than a nickel or a dime, city residents could attend vaudeville shows, visit penny arcades, and watch the latest film clips in downtown amusement parlors. As David Nasaw reveals in "Talking and Singing Machines, Parlors, and Peep Shows," the joining of new machinery and new forms of entertainment created the first mass culture in modern America.

The closing decades of the nineteenth century witnessed the final phase of a century-long process of government-sponsored Indian removal. Employing an army composed of battle-hardened Civil War veterans, the federal government sought to clear the Great Plains and Southwest of its native residents and move them onto isolated reservations. Native American resistance to this process took many forms, ranging from cultural revitalization to armed conflict. In "Lozen: An Apache Woman Warrior," Laura Jane Moore shows that Native American resistance was complex and sophisticated and depended on female as well male leaders.

Past Traces

One of the most important results of the Civil War was the freedom gained by southern slaves. In the decade following the defeat of the Confederacy, hundreds of thousands of freed men and women migrated throughout the South searching for land, work, and relatives lost through prewar sale. Some former slaves, however, took an even bolder step, leaving the South altogether and traveling west in search of cheap farmland or north seeking industrial employment. While most faced difficult years adjusting to the world of free labor and white prejudice, none would have exchanged their life of freedom for the days of bondage.

In this document, a letter from an ex-slave to his former master, we can read the emotional force of freed people's hatred of slavery as well as the sharp mind and poignant wit of the author. Finding the tables turned, the former slave underlined his newfound status as a free man, using the pretext of a reply to his ex-master's offer of work, to point out the exploitation he and his wife endured under the slave regime.

As is often the case in reconstructing the history of ordinary people, we know little about the author of this letter beyond what can be inferred from the letter itself. He was literate, an unusual condition for slaves, but we don't know whether he became literate before or after he became free. Likewise, we don't know whether he was one of the thousands of ex-slaves who searched for their spouses and loved ones at the end of the Civil War, or whether he married after he became free. But, whatever his personal history might have been, we can be certain that he possessed crucial skills and abilities that his former master wanted very much to regain.

Jourdon Anderson, *A Letter "To My Old Master . . . ,"* (c. 1865) To My Old Master, Colonel P. H. Anderson Big Spring, Tennessee

Sir: I got your letter, and was glad to find that you had not forgotten Jourdon, and that you wanted me to come back and live with you again, promising to do better for me than anybody else can. I have often felt uneasy about you. I thought the Yankees would have hung you long before this, for harboring Rebs they found at your house. I suppose they never heard about your going to Colonel Martin's to kill the Union soldier that was left by his company in their stable. Although you shot at me twice before I left you, I did not want to hear of your being hurt, and am glad you are still living. It would do me good to go back to the dear old home again, and see Miss Mary and Miss Martha and Allen, Esther, Green, and Lee. Give my love to them all, and tell them I hope we will meet in the better world, if not in this. I would have gone back to see you all when I was working in the Nashville Hospital, but one of the neighbors told me that Henry intended to shoot me if he ever got a chance.

I want to know particularly what the good chance is you propose to give me. I am doing tolerably well here. I get twenty-five dollars a month, with victuals and clothing; have a comfortable home for Mandy—the folks call her Mrs. Anderson—and the children—Milly, Jane, and Grundy—go to school and are learning well. The teacher says Grundy has a head for a preacher. They go to Sunday school, and Mandy and me attend church regularly. We are kindly treated. Sometimes we overhear others saying, "Them colored people were slaves" down in Tennessee. The children feel hurt when they hear such remarks; but I tell them it was no disgrace in Tennessee to belong to Colonel Anderson. Many darkeys would have been proud, as I used to be, to call you master. Now if you will write and say what wages you will give me, I will be better able to decide whether it would be to my advantage to move back again.

As to my freedom, which you say I can have, there is nothing to be gained on that score, as I got my free papers in 1864 from the Provost-Marshal-General of the Department of Nashville. Mandy says she would be afraid to go back without some proof that you were disposed to treat us justly and kindly; and we have concluded to test your sincerity by asking you to send us our wages for the time we served you. This will make us forget and forgive old scores, and rely on your justice and friendship in the future. I served you faithfully for thirty-two years, and Mandy twenty years. At twenty-five dollars a month for me, and two dollars a week for Mandy, our earnings would amount to eleven thousand six hundred and eighty dollars. Add to this the interest for the time our wages have been kept back, and deduct what you paid for our clothing, and three doctor's visits to me, and pulling a tooth for Mandy, and the balance will show what we are in justice entitled to. Please send the money by Adam's Express, in care of V. Winters, Esq., Dayton, Ohio. If you fail to pay us for faithful labors in the past, we can have little faith in your promises in the future. We trust the good Maker has opened your eyes to the wrongs which you and your fathers have done to me and my fathers, in making us toil for you for generations without recompense. Here I draw my wages every Saturday night; but in Tennessee there was never any pay-day for the Negroes any more than for the horses and cows. Surely there will be a day of reckoning for those who defraud the laborer of his hire.

In answering this letter, please state if there would be any safety for my Milly and Jane, who are now grown up, and both good-looking girls. You know how it was with poor Matilda and Catherine. I would rather stay here and starve—and die, if it come to that—than have my girls brought to shame by the violence and wickedness of their young masters. You will also please state if there has been any schools opened for the colored children in your neighborhood. The great desire of my life now is to give my children an education, and have them form virtuous habits.

Say howdy to George Carter, and thank him for taking the pistol from you when you were shooting at me.

From Your Old Servant,
Jourdon Anderson

—Source: L. Maria Child, *The Freedmen's Book* (1865).

1

African Americans in Public Office During the Era of Reconstruction: A Profile

Eric Foner

The end of the Civil War in 1865 raised the question of the position of freedpeople in American society. Now that they were no longer slaves, would black Americans be allowed the same rights as white citizens? Should black males be allowed to vote? To serve on juries? To hold office? To own property? The Fourteenth and Fifteenth Amendments to the Constitution provided one answer to these questions: They gave to freedmen all of the rights of American citizenship, including the right to vote.

But constitutional principle was one thing and southern practice another. Through intimidation and violence, southern whites sought to maintain the old system of racial domination and white supremacy that had prevailed in the prewar South. Throughout the region, blacks were beaten for attempting to vote, black political leaders were assassinated, and the Ku Klux Klan was organized with the object of keeping blacks "in their place." By the late 1860s it was clear that white southerners were determined to prevent any change in their system of racial privilege and power.

The history of Reconstruction was not only a story of black suppression and white domination, however. Wherever they could, freedpeople reestablished the family and kinship ties they had lost during slavery. Meanwhile, thousands of ex-slaves flocked to urban areas in search of employment, and others purchased land and livestock in order to establish their economic independence. Most importantly, with citizenship rights guaranteed by the Constitution and the Union Army, southern blacks eagerly embraced politics as a means to gain an equal place for themselves in American society. From a series of black political conventions held in the early years of Reconstruction emerged a group of black officeholders who spoke for the rights of freedmen to not only economic opportunity and political and legal equity, but also the possession of confiscated Confederate land. In this essay, Eric Foner tells the story of these political leaders and in the process reveals the hopes and dreams of freedpeople as well as the limits of black Reconstruction.

....

Reconstruction, which began during the Civil War and ended in 1877, was a time of momentous change in American political and social life. In the aftermath of slavery's demise, the federal government guaranteed the equality before the law of all citizens, black as well as white. In the South, former masters and former slaves struggled to shape the new labor systems that arose from the ashes of slavery, and new institutions—black churches, public schools, and many others—redefined the communities of both blacks and whites and relations between them. But no development during the turbulent years that followed the Civil War marked so dramatic a break with the nation's traditions, or aroused such bitter hostility, as the appearance of large numbers of black Americans in public office only a few years after the destruction of slavery.

Before the Civil War, blacks did not form part of America's "political nation." Black officeholding was unknown in the slave South, and virtually unheard of in the free states. Four years before the outbreak of civil war, the Supreme Court decreed in *Dred Scott v. Sanford* that no black person could be a citizen of the United States. In 1860, only five Northern states, all with tiny black populations, allowed black men to vote on the same terms as white.

During Presidential Reconstruction (1865–67), when President Andrew Johnson gave the white South a free hand in governing the region, voting and elective office in the South continued to be restricted to whites, although a handful of blacks were appointed to local offices and federal patronage posts. Black officeholding began in earnest in 1867, when

Congress, in the Reconstruction Act, ordered the election of new Southern governments under suffrage rules that did not discriminate on the basis of race. This inaugurated the era known as Radical Reconstruction. The right to vote for black men was extended throughout the nation in the Fifteenth Amendment, ratified in 1870. By 1877, when the last Radical Reconstruction governments were overthrown, approximately 2,000 black men had held federal, state, and local public offices, ranging from member of Congress to justice of the peace. Although much reduced after the abandonment of Reconstruction, black officeholding continued until the turn of the century, when most Southern blacks were disenfranchised. The next large group of black officials emerged in urban centers of the North, a product of the Great Migration that began during World War I. Not until the passage of the Voting Rights Act of 1965 did significant numbers of black Southerners again hold public office.

Although blacks held office in every part of the old Confederacy during the Reconstruction (as well as in Missouri and the nation's capital), the number varied considerably from state to state. Factors that explain the pattern of black officeholding include the size of a state's black population, the length of time that Reconstruction survived, attitudes of white Republicans toward blacks exercising political power, and the structure of state and local government. Of the eleven former Confederate states, blacks in 1870 comprised nearly 60 percent of the population in South Carolina; over half in Mississippi and Louisiana; between

40 and 50 percent in Alabama, Florida, Georgia, and Virginia; over one third in North Carolina; and between one quarter and one third in Arkansas, Tennessee, and Texas. Since in most states there were few white Republican voters, and these in any case often proved reluctant to vote for black candidates, almost all black officials represented localities with black majorities. Thus, it is not surprising that South Carolina, Mississippi, and Louisiana had the largest number of black officeholders, and Arkansas, Tennessee, and Texas relatively few. South Carolina was the only state where blacks comprised a majority of the House of Representatives throughout Reconstruction, and about half of the state Senate between 1872 and 1876. South Carolina and Louisiana, in addition, possessed large communities of free blacks, many of them educated, economically independent, and well-positioned to demand a role in government from the outset of Reconstruction. Mississippi's black leadership took longer to demand a significant share of political power, but by the early 1870s, blacks there had significantly increased their representation in the legislature and on county boards of supervisors throughout the plantation belt. Black officials in these three states account for more than half of those elected during Reconstruction.

Nowhere in the South did blacks really control state government, and nowhere did they hold office in numbers commensurate with their proportion of the total population, not to mention the Republican electorate. Nonetheless, the fact that over 1,400 blacks occupied positions of political authority in the South represented a stunning departure in American government. Moreover, because of the black population's concentration, nearly all these officials served in or represented plantation counties, home of the wealthiest and, before the Civil War, most powerful Southerners. The spectacle of former slaves representing the South Carolina rice kingdom and the Mississippi cotton belt in state legislatures, assessing taxes on the property of their former owners, and serving on juries alongside them, epitomized the political revolution wrought by Reconstruction.

Black officials served at every level of government during Reconstruction. Two sat in the United States Senate (Hiram Revels and Blanche K. Bruce of Mississippi) and 14 in the House of Representatives. For the first time in American history, the nation had black ambassadors: Don Carlos Bassett in Haiti, and J. Milton Turner in Liberia. Blacks also held numerous federal patronage appointments, including postmaster, deputy U.S. Marshall, treasury agent, and clerks in federal offices.

In December 1872, P. B. S. Pinchback became governor of Louisiana when he succeeded Henry C. Warmoth, who had been suspended because of impeachment proceedings. Pinchback served until the inauguration five weeks later of William P. Kellogg. A century and a quarter would pass until C. Douglas Wilder of Virginia, elected in 1989, became the next black American to serve as governor. Twenty-five major state executive positions (lieutenant governor, treasurer, superintendent of education, secretary of state, and state commissioner) were occupied by blacks during Reconstruction, and one, Jonathan J. Wright of South Carolina, sat on a state supreme court. Of the approximately 1,000 delegates to the constitutional conventions of 1867–69 that created new structures of government for the Southern states, 267 were black (they comprised a majority of the delegates in South Carolina and Louisiana). And during Reconstruction, 683 black men sat in the lower house of state legislatures (four serving as Speaker of the House), and 112 in state senates.

In virtually every county with a sizable black population, blacks held some local office. At least 110 served as members of the boards that governed county affairs, variously called the county commission, board of supervisors, board of police, or police jury; of these, the largest number served in Mississippi, South Carolina, and North Carolina. There were at least 41 black sheriffs (most in Louisiana and Mississippi), and 25 deputy sheriffs. Five held the office of mayor, and 132 served on city councils and boards of aldermen. Among the other important county and local offices occupied by blacks were 17 county treasurers, 31 coroners, and 35 tax collectors. At least 78 blacks served on local school boards, 109 as policemen or constables, and 228 as justice of the peace or magistrate.

The backgrounds of black officeholders reflect the often neglected diversity of the black population in mid-nineteenth century America. Nearly half (324) of those for whom information is available had been born free. Another fifty-four were former slaves who, by manumission, purchase, or escaping to the North, gained their liberty before the Civil War. Fewer than 300,000 free blacks lived in the South in 1860. But they clearly enjoyed far greater opportunities to obtain education, accumulate property, and observe public affairs. South Carolina and Louisiana were the homes of the South's wealthiest and best-educated free black communities, and about half the officeholders known to have been free served in these two states. In Louisiana, where the New Orleans free community had agitated incessantly for civil rights and the vote from the moment federal forces occupied the city during the Civil War, the freeborn far outnumbered former slaves in political office.

Many of the freeborn officeholders were men of uncommon experiences and abilities. Andrew J. Dumont, born free in Louisiana, had emigrated to Mexico, and served there as an army officer under Emperor Maximillian, before returning home, where he was elected to the state house and senate. Ovid Gregory of Alabama, a member of the constitutional convention and legislature, was fluent in Spanish and French and had traveled widely in the United States and Latin America before the Civil War. Deputy Sheriff James H. Jones of Wake County, North Carolina, had worked as coachman and personal servant for the Confederacy's President, Jefferson Davis,

during the Civil War. Jones helped the Confederate president escape from Richmond in April 1865, and three decades later drove the funeral car when Davis' body was interred in a Virginia cemetery.

Many of these freeborn officeholders had held themselves aloof from the plight of slaves before the Civil War. Twenty-two had themselves been slaveholders, nearly all in South Carolina and Louisiana. A few held slaves by necessity, owning a relative who, according to state law, could not be freed without being compelled to leave the state. Others were craftsmen whose slaves worked in their shops, or entrepreneurs who purchased slaves as an investment. One, Antoine Dubuclet, Louisiana's Reconstruction treasurer, was a sugar planter who had owned over 100 slaves.

On the other hand, a number of free blacks who became officials had placed themselves in considerable danger before the war by offering clandestine assistance to slaves. James D. Porter, a member of Georgia's legislature during Reconstruction, had operated secret schools for black children in Charleston and Savannah. Although a slaveholder himself, William Breedlove, who served in Virginia's constitutional convention, had been convicted during the Civil War of helping slaves escape to Union lines. Another freeborn Virginian, William Hodges, who served as superintendent of the poor for Norfolk county during Reconstruction, had been arrested around 1830 for providing slaves with forged free papers, leading to the persecution of his entire family and their flight to the North.

No fewer than 138 officeholders lived outside the South before the Civil War. Most were born in the North (where about 220,000 free blacks lived in 1860), but their numbers also included free Southerners whose families moved to the North, free blacks and privileged slaves sent North for education, a few immigrants from abroad, and fugitives from bondage. A majority held office in Louisiana, Mississippi, or South Carolina where opportunities were greatest for aspiring black political leaders from outside the state. Although these black "carpetbaggers" have received far less attention from historians than their white counterparts, they included individuals with remarkable life histories. Mifflin Gibbs, for instance, a native of Philadelphia, traveled to California in 1850 as part of the gold rush, established the state's first black newspaper, moved to British Columbia in 1858 to engage in railroad and mining ventures, and eventually made his way to Arkansas, where he became a judge, attorney, and longtime power in the Republican party.

Ten black officials are known to have escaped from slavery before the Civil War. Half had been born in Virginia, where proximity to the North made flight far easier than from the Deep South. Fugitive slaves who returned South during or after the Civil War included some of Reconstruction's most militant black leaders. Daniel M. Norton, who, with his brother Robert (also a Reconstruction office-holder) escaped from Virginia around 1850, returned to the Hampton area in 1864. The following year, he was "elected" as local blacks' representative on a Freedmen's Bureau court but denied his place by the Bureau. Embittered by this experience, Norton formed an all-black political association that became the basis of a career in York county politics lasting forty years. Another Virginia fugitive was Thomas Bayne, who failed in one escape attempt in 1844, and finally reached the North in 1855. Returning to Norfolk at the end of the Civil War, Bayne immediately became involved in the movement for black suffrage, and chaired a mass meeting one of whose resolutions declared, "traitors shall not dictate or prescribe to us the terms or conditions of our citizenship." Described by one newspaper as an "eloquent and fiery orator," Bayne became the most important black leader at the Virginia Constitutional Convention of 1867, advocating, among other things, an overhaul of the state's antiquated taxation system to shift the tax burden from the poor to large landowners.

Among the most radical of all black office-holders was Aaron A. Bradley, once the slave of Francis Pickens, South Carolina's Civil War governor. Born around 1815, Bradley escaped during the 1830s to Boston, where he studied law and became an attorney. He returned to Georgia in 1865, and emerged as an articulate champion of black suffrage and land distribution. Early in 1866, after helping to organize freedmen who resisted the restoration of land to their former owners, and delivering a speech containing disparaging remarks about Abraham Lincoln and Secretary of War Edwin M. Stanton, Bradley was expelled from Georgia by the Freedmen's Bureau. He soon returned, however, and in 1867 held a "confiscation-homestead" meeting in Savannah. He went on to serve in the constitutional convention and state senate.

Despite the prominence of those born free or who in one way or another acquired their freedom before 1860, the majority of black office-holders had remained slaves until sometime during the Civil War. A number had occupied positions of considerable privilege, enabling them to have access to education, despite laws barring such instruction. Several were sons of their owners and treated virtually as free; others, even when not related by blood, were educated by their masters or other whites. Blanche K. Bruce, the future Senator from Mississippi and possibly his owner's son, was educated by the same private tutor who instructed his master's legitimate child. Alabama legislator John Dozier had been owned by a Virginia college president and acquired an extensive education, including a command of Greek. Théophile L. Allain, who served in both houses of the Louisiana legislature, accompanied his planter father on a trip to Europe and was educated by private tutors. Ulysses S. Houston, a member of Georgia's legislature, was taught to read by white sailors while working as a slave in Savannah's Marine Hospital.

Some black officials had previously been allowed to sell their own labor and accumulate property, like Reconstruction Congressman Benjamin S. Turner, who operated a hotel and livery stable in Selma, Alabama, while still a slave. William A. Rector, a Little Rock city marshall had been owned by Chester Ashley, U. S. Senator from Arkansas, and as a youth played in "Ashley's Band," a traveling musical troupe composed of the Senator's slaves. (Rector was the only one to escape death when a steamboat on which the band was sailing exploded.)

In a few cases, the actions of privileged slaves and their owners reflected a shared sense of mutual obligation. Walter F. Burton, a Texan sheriff and tax collector during Reconstruction, remained devoted to his owner, who had taught him to read and write and sold him several plots of land after the Civil War. Mississippi legislator Ambrose Henderson, who had been able to sell his own labor as a slave barber, rescued his owner when the latter was wounded in the Confederate army. Meshack Roberts, who later served in the Texas House of Representatives, protected his master's family while the owner fought in the Civil War, and later received from him a gift of land in appreciation for his loyalty.

As the experience of a number of black Reconstruction officials illustrates, however, the status of even the most privileged slave was always precarious. The death of a paternalistic owner was often a time of disruption for his slaves, even those he had fathered. Future Florida constitutional convention delegate and Senator Robert Meacham was the son of his owner. According to Meacham, his father "always told me that I was free." But after his father's death, Meacham was forced to work as a slave for his own aunt. Especially when the inheritance of property (including property in slaves) was involved, the master's sense of obligation frequently followed him to the grave. John Carraway, who served in Alabama's constitutional convention and legislature, was the son of a planter and a slave mother, and was freed in his father's will. Yet, according to Carraway, white "guardians" sold

his mother "all for the purpose of getting possession of the property left us by my father." Carraway remained free but was forced to leave the state. Reconstruction Congressman John R. Lynch's Irish-born father arranged in his will for the freedom of Lynch and his slave mother. But the white trustee in charge of the arrangement forced Lynch to remain in bondage. Thomas M. Allen, a Charleston slave, was freed along with his mother and brother in the will of his owner-father. But, as Allen later related, his father's relatives "stole" the members of his family, sold them to Georgia, and seized the money bequeathed to them. Allen remained a slave until the end of the Civil War. During Reconstruction, he served in Georgia's legislature.

Some Reconstruction officials had experienced first hand the worst horrors of slavery. Congressmen Jeremiah Haralson and John A. Hyman had both been sold on the auction block, where, as Hyman put it, he was treated "as a brute." Richard Griggs, Mississippi's Commissioner of Immigration and Agriculture, was sold 18 times while a slave; at one point, Griggs was owned by Nathan B. Forrest, the Confederate general responsible for the murder of black soldiers in the Fort Pillow massacre, and a founder of the Ku Klux Klan. William H. Heard, a deputy United States marshall and a bishop in the African Methodist Episcopal church, was sold twice before the Civil War, and saw his mother used as a "breeder." Florida legislator John Proctor was the son of a free black man who had bonded himself to purchase the freedom of his slave wife, defaulted, and had his wife and children repossessed. Virginia constitutional convention delegate John Brown, a slave in Southampton county, saw his wife and two daughters sold to Mississippi, and the sister, two daughters, and a son of Charles L. Jones, who held the same position in South Carolina, were sold at auction in Charleston. It should not be surprising that in the black political ideology that emerged after the Civil War, slavery was remembered not as a time of mutual rights and responsibilities, but as a terrible injustice, a stain upon the conscience of the nation.

The 1,465 blacks who served as officials during Reconstruction followed a wide range of occupations, from apothecary to woodfactor, chef to gardener, insurance agent to "conjurer." Taken together, the black officials present a picture that should be familiar to anyone acquainted with the political leadership that generally emerged from nineteenth-century lower-class communities in times of political crisis—artisans, professionals, small propertyholders, and laborers. For some, their prominence in Reconstruction was an extension of leadership roles they had occupied in the slave community. Henry W. Jones, a slave preacher and later a delegate to the South Carolina constitutional convention of 1868, had been "a ruling spirit among his race before the war," according to a Charleston newspaper. T. Thomas Fortune later explained how the political role of his father, Emanuel Fortune, a Florida constitutional convention delegate and legislator, was rooted in events antedating the Civil War:

> It was natural for him to take the leadership in any independent improvement of the Negros. During and before the Civil War he had commanded his time as a tanner and expert shoe and bootmaker. In such life as the slaves were allowed and in church work, he took the leader's part. When the matter of the Constitutional Convention was decided upon his people in Jackson County naturally looked to him.

Like Fortune, a large number of black officeholders had been enslaved artisans whose skill and relative independence (often reflected in command over their own time and the ability to travel off the plantation) accorded them high status in the slave community. Others were free blacks who had followed skilled trades before the Civil War. Among artisans, carpenter (125), barber (50), blacksmith (47), mason (37), and shoemaker (37) were the crafts most frequently represented.

Another large occupational grouping consisted of professionals. There were 237 minis-

ters among the Reconstruction officials (many of whom held other occupations as well, since it was difficult for black congregations to support their pastors). Most were Methodists and Baptists, with a handful of Presbyterians, Congregationalists, and Episcopalians. "A man cannot do his whole duty as a minister except he looks out for the political interests of his people," said Charles H. Pearce, who had purchased his freedom in Maryland as a young man, served as an African Methodist Episcopal preacher in Canada before the Civil War, came to Florida as a religious missionary, and was elected to the constitutional convention and state senate.

Many of Reconstruction's most prominent black leaders not only emerged from the church, but had a political outlook grounded in a providential view of history inspired by black Christianity. The cause of the Civil War, declared James D. Lynch, a minister and religious missionary who became Mississippi's secretary of state during Reconstruction, was America's "disobedience," via slavery, to its divine mission to "elevate humanity" and spread freedom throughout the globe. Justice for the former slaves, Lynch continued, could not be long delayed, because "Divine Providence will wring from you in wrath, that which should have been given in love."

Teachers accounted for 172 officeholders, some of whom not only established schools for black children on their own initiative immediately after the Civil War, but used their literacy to assist the freed people. William V. Turner, a former slave, established a school in Wetumpka, Alabama, served as agent in northern Alabama for the black-owned Mobile *Nationalist*, and brought cases of injustice against blacks in the local courts to the attention of the Freedmen's Bureau. Turner went on to serve as a registrar and member of the state legislature. Other educators included Francis L. Cardoza, the Reconstruction secretary of state and treasurer of South Carolina, who had lived in the North and Europe before the war, and returned to his native Charleston where he served as a teacher for the American Missionary Association and helped to establish the Avery Normal Institute. The training of black teachers, Cardoza wrote, was "the object for which I left all the superior advantages and privileges of the North and came South."

Of the 83 officials who edited and published newspapers, a few, like South Carolina trial justice Martin R. Delany and Isaac D. Shadd, Speaker of the House in Mississippi, had acquired journalistic experience in the North before the Civil War. (Delany published *The Mystery* in Pittsburgh during the 1840s, and Shadd, with his sister Mary Ann, edited the *Provincial Freeman* in Canada in the following decade.) Those who operated newspapers during or after Reconstruction included Florida Congressman Josiah T. Walls, owner of the Gainesville *New Era*; Richard Nelson, a Texas justice of the peace, who established the Galveston *Spectator*, the state's first black newspaper; and James P. Ball, clerk of the district court in Concordia parish, Louisiana, who edited the *Concordia Eagle*. Sixty-nine black officeholders were attorneys, seven were musicians, five were physicians, and one practiced dentistry.

Businessmen comprised another large group of officeholders, the majority (104) of whom were small shopkeepers and grocers. Fifty-two earned their livings as merchants, and there was a scattering of building contractors, saloonkeepers, and hotel owners. Not surprisingly, farmers constituted the largest occupational category, accounting for 294 officials. Unfortunately, the census of 1870 did not distinguish between farm owners and tenants, so it is not known how many worked for their own land. An additional 32 were planters, who owned a significant amount of acreage. Finally, there were 115 laborers, most of whom worked on farms, but a few worked as factory operatives and unskilled employees in artisan shops and mercantile establishments.

Information about ownership of property is available for 928 black officials. Of these, 236 were propertyless, while 352 owned real estate

and personal property amounting to under $1,000. Three hundred thirty-nine held property valued at over $1,000, a considerable sum at a time when the average non-farm employee earned under $500 per year and Southern farm wages ranged between $10 and $15 per month. Of these wealthiest black officials, a majority had been born free or became free before the Civil War. Nearly half held office in South Carolina and Louisiana, states with relatively large populations of propertied freeborn blacks. At least 94, however, had remained slaves until the Civil War and acquired their wealth during Reconstruction. Holding office, for many blacks, was a surer way to advance their economic standing than laboring in the postwar Southern economy. The thirteen dollars per diem earned by members of the Louisiana constitutional convention, or the seven dollars per day plus mileage paid to North Carolina legislators, far outstripped the wages most blacks could ordinarily command, and offices like sheriff garnered far higher rewards in commissions and fees.

The black political leadership included a few men of truly substantial wealth. Antoine Dubuclet owned over $200,000 worth of property on the eve of the Civil War. Florida Congressmen Josiah T. Walls, a former slave, prospered as a planter during Reconstruction, and Mississippi Senator Blanche K. Bruce acquired a fortune in real estate. When he died in 1898, Bruce was worth over $100,000. Ferdinand Havis, a former slave who served on the Pine Bluff, Arkansas board of aldermen and in the state legislature, owned a saloon, whiskey business, and 2,000 acres of farm land. Toward the end of the century, Havis described himself in the city directory simply as a "capitalist." William J. Whipper, a South Carolina legislator and rice planter, was said to have lost $75,000 in a single night of poker. Pinckney B. S. Pinchback, who served briefly as Louisiana's governor, operated a commission brokerage and parlayed inside information about state expenditures into a fortune in government bonds. (Despite earlier historians' charges of widespread corruption during Reconstruction, Pinchback is one of relatively few black officials against whom charges of malfeasance in office can in fact be documented.)

Most black propertyholders, however, were men of relatively modest incomes, and often precarious economic standing. Like their white counterparts, black small farmers, tenants, artisans, and small businessmen were subject to the vagaries of the post-Civil War economy. Among Reconstruction officeholders, at least 24 black entrepreneurs, mostly grocers and small merchants, are known to have gone out of business during the depression of the 1870s. Even Dubuclet suffered financial reverses; when he died in 1887, his estate was valued at only $1,300. Black professionals often found it difficult to make ends meet, since whites shunned them and few blacks were able to pay their fees. Talented professionals like Robert B. Elliott, a congressman and lawyer from South Carolina, sometimes had to request small loans from white politicians to meet day-to-day expenses. Unlike white counterparts, moreover, black officials who operated businesses found themselves subjected to ostracism by their political opponents, often with devastating effect. Georgia Congressman Jefferson Long, a tailor, had commanded "much of the fine custom" of Macon before embarking on his political career. But as another black official recalled, "Long's stand in politics ruined his business with the whites who had been his patrons chiefly." Most truly wealthy blacks avoided politics, and black politicians, even those who owned property, relied heavily on office for their livelihood.

Ridiculed by their opponents as incompetent and corrupt, most black officials proved themselves fully capable of understanding public issues and pursuing the interests of their constituents and party. To be sure, slavery, once described by its apologists as a "school" that introduced "uncivilized" Africans into Western culture, was hardly intended as a training ground for political leaders. Looking back on the post-emancipation years, James K. Green, who served in Alabama's constitutional convention and legislature, remarked:

> I believe that the colored people have done well, considering all their circumstances and surroundings, as emancipation made them. I for one was entirely ignorant; I knew nothing more than to obey my master; and there were thousands of us in the same attitude . . . but the tocsin of freedom sounded and knocked at the door and we walked out like free men and met the exigencies as they grew up, and shouldered the responsibilities.

As Green suggested, there was something remarkable about how men, who until recently had been excluded from the main currents of American life, "shouldered the responsibilities" of Reconstruction lawmaking. It would be wrong, however, to assume that the black officials were mainly unschooled.

Remarkably, in a region where before the Civil War it was illegal to teach slaves to read and write, and where educational opportunities for free blacks were in many areas extremely limited, the large majority of black officials were literate. Of the 1,126 for whom information is available, 933, or 83 percent, were able to read and write. Of these, 339 had been born or become free before the Civil War, and 273 were former slaves. Some slaves, as has been related, were educated by their owners or sympathetic whites. Others were taught to read and write by a literate slave, often a relative, or, like George W. Albright, a Mississippi field hand who went on to serve in the state Senate, became literate "by trickery." Albright listened surreptitiously as his owner's children did their school lessons in the kitchen, where his mother worked. A number of literate officials learned to read and write in the Union army, and others studied during and after the Civil War in schools established by the Freedmen's Bureau or Northern aid societies. Albright himself attended a Reconstruction school for blacks run by a Northerner, married a white instructor from the North, and became a teacher.

However acquired, the ability to read and write marked many black officials as community leaders. Former slave Thomas M. Allen explained how he became a political organizer in rural Jasper county, Georgia, and was chosen to sit in the legislature:

> In all those counties of course the colored people are generally very ignorant; . . . but some know more about things than the others. In my county the colored people came to me for instructions, and I gave them the best instructions I could. I took the New York Tribune and other papers, and in that way I found out a great deal, and I thought they had been freed by the Yankees and Union men, and I thought they ought to vote with them; go with that party always.

Those officials who could not read relied on associates or relatives who could. "I have a son I sent to school when he was small," said Georgia legislator Abram Colby. "I make him read all my letters and do all my writing. I keep him with me all the time."

At least 64 black officeholders attended college or professional school either before or during their terms of public service. Thirty-four studied in the South: 25 at the black colleges established immediately after the Civil War, including Howard, Lincoln, Shaw, and Straight Universities, and Hampton Institute, and nine at the University of South Carolina when it admitted black pupils between 1873 and 1877. Twenty-seven received their higher education in the North, 14 at Oberlin College. Four officials had studied abroad: Francis L. Cardoza, who received a degree from the University of Glasgow; Louisiana legislator Eugéne-Victor Macarty, a musician who graduated from the Imperial Conservatoire in Paris; James W. Mason, an Arkansas sheriff whose father, a wealthy planter, sent him to college in France; and Martin Becker, a native of Surinam and member of South Carolina's constitutional convention, who appears to have attended college in Holland or Germany. Black college graduates included Mifflin Gibbs, who received a degree from Oberlin's law department in 1870, and his brother Jonathan, who graduated from Dartmouth College in 1852 after being refused

admission to 18 colleges in the North because of his color. Among other officeholders who had at least some higher education were Benjamin A. Boseman, a member of South Carolina's legislature, who had graduated from the Medical School of Maine; John W. Menard, who attended Iberia College in Ohio before the Civil War and went on to hold several posts in Florida Reconstruction; and Louisiana officials C. C. Antoine, Robert H. Isabelle, Joseph Lott, Louis A. Martinet, and Victor Rochon, all of whom attended Straight University during the 1870s.

Given the almost universal prohibition on blacks voting and holding office before the Civil War, few Reconstruction officials had experience in public service. Two, John M. Langston and Macon B. Allen, had held public office in the North before the Civil War. Allen was appointed justice of the peace in Middlesex county, Massachusetts in 1848, and Langston in 1855 apparently became the first black American to hold elective office when he was chosen township clerk in Brownhelm, Ohio, a stronghold of abolitionism. Immediately after the war, Thomas Bayne was elected to the New Bedford, Massachusetts, city council, and beginning in 1866, Mifflin Gibbs served two terms on the city council of Victoria, British Columbia. William H. Grey, the leading black spokesman at the Arkansas constitutional convention, had learned legislative procedures while attending sessions of Congress with his antebellum employer, Virginia Congressman Henry A. Wise. Among other Reconstruction officials with experience in public affairs were the nine who had worked at newspapers before or during the Civil War.

Thirty-one officials, either natives of the North or men who had migrated or escaped from the slave South, were involved in the movement for the abolition of slavery and equal rights for Northern blacks before the Civil War. Fugitive slaves Thomas Bayne and Aaron A. Bradley worked with the antislavery movement in Massachusetts, and the freeborn

Hodges brothers—Charles, William, and Willis, whose family had been forced to flee Virginia—were active in the abolitionist crusade and the movement for black suffrage in New York State. John and Matthew Leary, North Carolina officeholders, had a brother, Lewis S. Leary, who was killed in 1859 while fighting alongside John Brown at Harper's Ferry. O. S. B. Wall, the first black justice of the peace in the nation's capital, and Andrew J. Chestnutt, a town commissioner in Cumberland county, North Carolina, had participated in violent encounters in Ohio that prevented fugitive slaves from being returned to the South. Five officials, including brothers Abraham and Isaac Shadd, had been active in the abolitionist movement while living in Canada, and eight, including the "father of black nationalism," Martin R. Delany, in the 1850s had advocated black emigration from the United States. Delany traveled to Africa seeking a homeland for black Americans, and George T. Ruby, born in New York City and brought up in Portland, Maine, had journeyed to Haiti as an emigration agent and newspaper correspondent before coming South to teach and work for the Freedmen's Bureau. Ruby went on to serve the Texas constitutional convention and senate.

At least 129 officeholders were among the 200,000 African American black men who served in the Union army and navy during the Civil War. Military service was a politicizing experience, a training ground for postwar black leadership. Many not only received schooling in the army, but for the first time became involved in political activism. Such men included several officers of Louisiana regiments who protested discriminatory treatment by white counterparts, and the nine Reconstruction officials who served in the famous 54th and 55th Massachusetts regiments, which for many months refused their salaries to protest the government's policy of paying black soldiers less than white.

Another stepping stone to office was the Freedmen's Bureau, the federal agency estab-lished in 1865 to oversee the transition from slavery to freedom, for which 46 black officials worked in some capacity immediately after the war. Another path to political prominence was organizational work with the Republican party. In 1867, the Republican Congressional Committee employed 118 speakers, 83 of them black, to lecture in the South. Of the blacks, 26 went on to hold Reconstruction office. Many other officials were members of black fraternal societies like the Masons, and emerged from the black church and other positions of leadership within the slave community.

It is difficult to gauge with precision how much political power black officeholders exercised. The phrase "Black Reconstruction" originated as a Democratic effort to arouse the resentments of white voters, even though political power generally remained in white hands. Even in Louisiana, with its articulate and well-organized black leadership, a group of prominent black officeholders, including the state's lieutenant governor and treasurer, complained in 1874 of their systematic exclusion from "participation and knowledge of the confidential workings of the party and government." Black officials never controlled Reconstruction. But, as DuBois indicated when he adopted the term "Black Reconstruction" to describe the era, blacks were major actors of the Reconstruction drama, and their ascent to even limited positions of political power represented a revolution in American government and race relations.

In the early days of Radical Reconstruction, blacks often stood aside when nominations for office were decided upon, so as not to embarrass the Republican party in the North or lend credence to Democratic charges of "black supremacy." In South Carolina, Francis L. Cardozo and Martin R. Delany, promoted, respectively, for the lieutenant governership and a Congressional seat in 1868, declined to run, citing the need for "the greatest possible discretion and prudence." In the first state governments established after the advent of black suffrage, blacks held no important positions in six states, and occupied only the largely ceremonial post of secretary of state in Florida, Mississippi, and South Carolina. In Louisiana alone, where Oscar J. Dunn was elected lieutenant governor in 1868 and Antoine Dubuclet treasurer, did blacks hold more than one major post from the beginning of Reconstruction.

It did not take long for black leaders, and voters, to become dissatisfied with the role of junior partners in the Republican coalition, especially since the first governors of Republican Reconstruction seemed to devote greater energy to attracting white support than addressing the needs of black constituents. By the early 1870s, prominent black leaders in many states were condemning white Republican leaders who, in the words of Texas state senator Matthew Gaines, set themselves up as "the Big Gods of the negroes." Gaines organized a Colored Men's Convention to press for more black officeholders. By this time, black officeholding was already waning in Virginia and Tennessee, where coalitions of Democrats and conservative Republicans had come to power in 1869, and in Georgia, where Democrats overthrew Republican rule in 1871. Elsewhere, however, black leaders not only assumed a larger share of offices, but led successful efforts to repudiate the conservative policies of the early governors, often engineering their replacement by men more attuned to blacks' demands. During the 1870s, blacks in five states occupied powerful executive positions as lieutenant governors, treasurers, and superintendents of education. Blacks served, moreover, as Speakers of the House in Mississippi and South Carolina.

Even more remarkable was the growing presence of blacks in county and local offices scattered across the South. Most local officials were white, but the high concentration of the black population, a legacy of the plantation system, meant that most former slaves encountered at least some local black officials during Reconstruction. (The Mississippi counties and Louisiana parishes that elected black sheriffs,

for example, accounted for a considerable majority of these states' black populations.) John R. Lynch later recalled how, when he served as a justice of the peace, freedmen "magnified" his office "far beyond its importance," bringing him cases ranging from disputes with employers to family squabbles. With control over such matters as public expenditures, poor relief, the administration of justice, and taxation policy, local officials had a real impact on the day to day lives of all Southerners. On the Atlanta city council, William Finch pressed for the establishment of black schools and the hiring of black teachers, and lobbied effectively for street improvements in black and poor white neighborhoods. Other officials tried to ensure that blacks were chosen to serve on juries, and were employed, at the same wages as whites, on public projects.

Only a handful of black officials, including former slave Aaron A. Bradley, were actively involved in efforts to assist freedmen in acquiring land, or advocated confiscation of the land of ex-Confederates. Many black officials fully embraced the prevailing free labor ethos, which saw individual initiative in the "race of life," not public assistance, as the route to upward mobility. Free blacks from both North and South, many of whom had achieved astonishing success given the barriers erected against them, expressed most forcefully the idea of competitive equality. "Look at the progress of our people—their wonderful civilization," declared freeborn North Carolina registrar George W. Brodie. "What have we to fear in competition with the whites, if they give us a fair race?"

A considerable number of black officeholders made efforts to uplift the conditions of black laborers in other ways. William H. Grey of Arkansas purchased a plantation in order to sell it in small plots to sharecroppers. Benjamin S. Turner introduced a bill in Congress for the sale of small tracts of land to Southern freedmen, and several officials, including Matthew Gaines of Texas and Abraham Galloway, who served in the constitutional convention and state senate of North Carolina, urged heavy taxation of unoccupied land, to force it onto the market. At least 58 black officials attended statewide labor conventions, encouraged the formation of agricultural labor unions, or sponsored legislation to assist farm laborers. Other local officeholders, as planters persistently complained, sided with employees in contract disputes, failed to enforce vagrancy laws, and refused to coerce freedmen into signing plantation labor contracts.

Even the most powerful African American officials were not immune to the numerous indignities and inequalities to which blacks were subjected in the post-Civil War South. Despite national and state civil rights laws, many common carriers and places of business either refused to serve blacks, or relegated them to inferior accommodations. A common experience was being refused service in a first class railroad car or steamboat cabin, and being forced to ride in the "smoking car" or on deck. Edward Butler, a member of Louisiana's Senate, was beaten and stabbed by a riverboat crew while seeking admission to the first class cabin. In speeches supporting Charles Sumner's Civil Rights Bill in 1874, black Congressmen related the "outrages and indignities" to which they had been subjected. Joseph Rainey had been thrown from a Virginia streetcar, John R. Lynch forced to occupy a railroad smoking car with gamblers and drunkards, Richard H. Cain and Robert B. Elliott excluded from a North Carolina restaurant, James T. Rapier denied service by inns at every stopping point between Montgomery and Washington. Such incidents were not confined to the South. In 1864, Robert Smalls, a military hero soon to become a major political leader in Reconstruction South Carolina, was evicted from a Philadelphia streetcar, provoking a mass protest that led to the desegregation of the city's public transportation.

Like Smalls, many black officials resisted their exclusion from access to public facilities. Mifflin Gibbs and Arkansas legislator W. Hines Furbush successfully sued a Little Rock saloon for refusing to serve blacks, and in Louisiana, Charles S. Sauvinet, the sheriff of Orleans parish, took a saloonkeeper to court after being denied service, and was awarded $1,000. South Carolina Supreme Court Justice Jonathan B. Wright won $1,200 in a lawsuit after being ejected from a first-class railroad car. When Eugéne-Victor Macarty was refused a seat at the New Orleans Opera House in 1869, he sued and organized a black boycott, which lasted until the theater was integrated in 1875.

Given such experiences, and the broad aspiration widely shared in the black community to construct a color-blind society from the ashes of slavery, black officials devoted considerable effort to the passage of national and state civil rights legislation. "Sir," North Carolina legislator Thomas A. Sykes wrote Charles Sumner, "if I am a free citizen of this 'grand Republic,' why am I denied privileges which are given to my white brother, although he might be the basest culprit on earth?" It was the insistence of black legislators that led Florida, Louisiana, Mississippi, South Carolina, and Texas to enact laws during Reconstruction requiring equal treatment by railroads and places of public accommodation.

The frequent denial of equal access to public facilities, however, was hardly the most serious danger confronting black officials during Reconstruction. It is difficult to think of any group of public officials in American history who faced the threat of violence as persistently as Reconstruction's black officeholders. No fewer than 156 officials—over ten percent of the total—were victimized by violence, generally by the Ku Klux Klan, White League, and other paramilitary criminal organizations allied with the Democratic party. Their number included 36 officials who received death threats, 45 of whom were driven from their homes, and 41 shot at, stabbed, or otherwise assaulted. Thirty-four black officeholders were actually murdered, most during Reconstruction, but a few after the South's "Redemption."

Violence was an endemic feature of post-Civil War Southern society, directed against anyone who challenged inherited norms of white supremacy. The targets included laborers who refused to work in a disciplined manner or sought to acquire their own land, teachers and others who worked to uplift the former slaves, Union League officials, and Republican party organizers. No state was immune from political violence, but the targeting of public officials was concentrated in four states—Georgia, Louisiana, Mississippi, and South Carolina—which together accounted for nearly 80 percent of the known victims. All were centers of Klan or White League violence in the late 1860s and early 1870s and all except Georgia were the scene of exceptionally violent Redemption campaigns as Reconstruction drew to a close.

From constables and justices of the peace to legislators and members of constitutional conventions, no black official was immune from the threat of violence. Those murdered included eight constitutional convention delegates and twelve legislators, the most prominent of whom was Benjamin Randolph, killed in 1868 while serving as chairman of the Republican state executive committee in South Carolina. Numerous Mississippi officials were threatened or driven from their homes during the 1875 campaign in which Democrats regained control of the state, and at least five were murdered, including state senator Charles Caldwell, who was lured to his assassination by a white "friend" a few weeks after the election. Andrew J. Flowers, a justice of the peace in Tennessee, was whipped by the Ku Klux Klan because, in his words, "I had the impudence to run against a white man for office, and beat him. . . . They said they had nothing particular against me . . . but they did not intend [to allow] any nigger to hold office in the United States."

Abram Colby, a member of Georgia's legislature, was beaten "in the most cruel manner" by Klansmen in 1869. His offense, reported the local agent of the American Missionary Association, was that he had gone to Atlanta to request protection for the former slaves, "and [they] had besides . . . many old scores against him, as a leader of his people in the county." Richard Burke, a minister and teacher in Sumter county, Alabama who served in the state House of Representatives, was murdered in 1870. Burke, his former owner told a Congressional committee, "had made himself obnoxious to a certain class of young men by having been a leader in the Loyal League and by having acquired a great influence over people of his color," but the immediate cause of his death was a report that he had delivered a speech stating that blacks had the same right to carry arms as whites.

In Edgefield county, South Carolina, violence was pervasive throughout Reconstruction. Local political leader Lawrence Cain in 1868 appealed to Governor Robert K. Scott for protection: "If we cannot get this we will all be killed or beat . . . to death. There cannot pass a night but what some colored man are killed or runned from his house." Eight years later, during South Carolina's violent Redemption campaign, threats of murder prevented Cain himself from campaigning. One letter warned him: "If you want to rule a country, you must go to Africa." The roster of black officials victimized by violence offers a striking insight into the personal courage required to take a position of prominence in Reconstruction politics, and the corruption of public morality among those who called themselves the region's "natural rulers."

Southern black officeholding did not end immediately with the overthrow of Reconstruction. Although the Redeemers in several states moved to restrict black voting, gerrymander districts, and reduce the number of elective positions in predominantly black counties, blacks continued to serve in state legislatures and local positions, and a handful even managed to win election to Congress. Many others occupied patronage posts distributed by Republican administrations in Washington.

The nation's longest-serving black official was Joseph H. Lee, a Reconstruction legislator who served as customs collector at Jacksonville, Florida from the 1880s until 1913. The number of black officeholders was reduced substantially after Reconstruction, but until disfranchisement had been completed around the turn of the century, enclaves of local black political power existed in most of the Southern states. Ferdinand Havis remained the "boss" of Jefferson county, Arkansas long after Reconstruction, and Norris W. Cuney was the most powerful black politician in late nineteenth-century Texas, his machine resting on his post as collector of customs at Galveston. Daniel M. Norton's political organization in Hampton, Virginia survived into the twentieth century, as did his tenure as justice of the peace. Robert Smalls won election to Congress in the 1880s, served as collector of customs at Beaufort until 1913, and represented his county in South Carolina's constitutional convention of 1895, where he spoke out eloquently against the disfranchisement of black voters.

Of Reconstruction's black officials, 285 are known to have occupied some public office, elective or appointive, after Redemption. But if black officeholding survived the end of Reconstruction, it did so in a profoundly altered context. Local officials confronted hostile state governments and national administrations at best indifferent to blacks' concerns, and black lawmakers found it impossible to exert any influence in Democratic legislatures. Most black officials now depended for their influence on the goodwill of prominent Democrats, connections with white Republicans, and the patronage largess of the federal government, rather than the backing of a politically mobilized black community.

One indication of the limiting of options after Reconstruction was the revival of interest in emigration among Southern blacks. "Let us go where we can grow lawyers, doctors, teachers," said Davidson county commissioner Randall Brown after Democrats ended Tennessee's brief period of Reconstruction. Let us go "where we can be representatives, Congressmen, judges and anything else." Twenty-nine Reconstruction officials supported post-Reconstruction emigration projects, particularly the Liberia movement that flourished in South Carolina in 1877 and 1878, and the Kansas "Exodus" of 1879. Harrison N. Bouey, a probate judge in Edgefield county during South Carolina's Reconstruction, concluded "that the colored man has no home in America," and helped organize the Liberia emigration movement. Bouey himself left for Liberia in 1878, returned to the United States as a Baptist religious missionary a few years later, and then sailed again for Africa, where he died in 1909. Aaron A. Bradley, the militant spokesman for Georgia's freedmen, helped publicize the Kansas Exodus, and died in St. Louis in 1881.

Many officeholders, although not involved in emigration projects, left the South after the end of Reconstruction. A number, including Pinchback, Bruce, and John R. Lynch, moved to Washington, D.C., where they held federal appointments and became part of the city's black elite. Legislator Thomas Walker, driven from Alabama during the state's violent election campaign in 1874, ended up in Washington, where he became a successful lawyer and real estate broker. William Thornton Montgomery, who had been treasurer of Warren county, Mississippi, moved to Dakota territory, where he lived among Scandinavian immigrants and became the largest black farmer in the northwest. His enterprise failed, however, and he died in poverty in 1909. Alabama Congressman Jeremiah Haralson farmed in Louisiana and Arkansas, and engaged in coal mining in Colorado. In 1916, he was reported to have been "killed by wild beasts."

Many black "carpetbaggers" returned to the North. After being ousted from the legislature and jailed by Georgia's Redeemers, Tunis G. Campbell moved to Boston, where he devoted his remaining years to church work. James P. Ball left Louisiana for Montana and then Seattle, where he worked as a photographer, newspaper editor, and lawyer.

The majority of Reconstruction officials remained in the South, many seeking careers in the black church, education, and journalism. Edward Shaw, the militant county commissioner of Shelby county, Tennessee, who had fought for more positions for blacks from the white political machine of Memphis, left politics in disgust and devoted the remainder of his life to the black Masons and church work. Former South Carolina Congressman Richard H. Cain became president of Paul Quinn College in Waco, Texas, and then a bishop of the African Methodist Episcopal church. After Reconstruction, William E. Johnson, a South Carolina legislator, helped to found the Independent A. M. E. Church, and preached that Christ, Mary, and Joseph were black Africans. Joseph T. Wilson edited a number of newspapers and published a volume of poetry and other books. Jeremiah J. Hamilton, a Reconstruction legislator in Texas, published until the twentieth century a succession of newspapers in Austin.

A number of Reconstruction officials prospered in business and the professions after leaving politics. Former Speaker of South Carolina's House Samuel J. Lee was the state's leading black lawyer until his death in 1895. Matthew M. Lewey, a Reconstruction postmaster and mayor, became president of the Florida State Negro Business League, and James C. Napier, who had been Davidson county claims commissioner, headed the National Negro Business League and became a friend and political ally of Booker T. Washington. Alabama senator Lloyd Leftwich acquired an Alabama plantation that remained in his family's hands into the 1960s.

Other officeholders found their economic standing severely diminished by the elimination of politics as a livelihood. Henry Turpin, former Virginia legislator, worked as a sleeping car porter, and his Louisiana counterpart

Moses Sterrett was employed as janitor of the Caddo parish court house. Alonzo Ransier, who had been South Carolina's lieutenant governor, was employed as a night watchman at the Charleston Custom House and as a day laborer for the city. His Reconstruction successor, Richard H. Gleaves, spent his last years as a waiter at the Jefferson Club in Washington, D.C. Prince Rivers, a member of South Carolina's Reconstruction constitutional convention and legislature, worked as a coachman, as he had while a slave. Robert B. Elliott, unable to earn a living as a lawyer "owing to the severe ostracism and mean prejudice of my political opponents," held minor patronage posts and died penniless in New Orleans. Former fugitive slave Thomas Baynes abandoned politics after Reconstruction and in 1888 entered Virginia's Central State Lunatic Asylum, where he died. In the asylum's records, his disease was said to have been caused by "religion and politics."

While many black officeholders scattered after the end of Reconstruction, some continued in various ways to work for the ideals of civil rights and economic uplift that had animated the post-Civil War era. Lewis Lindsay, an advocate of land confiscation while serving in the Virginia constitutional convention in 1868, became a leader in Richmond's Knights of Labor, and Cyrus Myers, a member of the Mississippi constitutional convention, became prominent in the effort to have Congress provide pensions to former slaves, at one point bringing a petition with 6,000 signatures to the nation's capital. J. Milton Turner, who had served as Missouri's assistant superintendent of education, devoted his career to winning for Cherokee freedmen a share of the funds appropriated by Congress to the Cherokee nation, finally winning his prolonged court battle in 1895.

A number of Reconstruction officeholders reemerged in the Populist movement. When a Populist Republican coalition in the mid-1890s ousted the Democrats in North Carolina from power, Reconstruction officials J. P. Butler, formerly mayor of Jamesville, and Richard Elliott, who had served in the legislature, were again elected to office. John B. Rayner, who held several local posts in Tarboro, North Carolina during Reconstruction, became the leading black Populist of Texas, and at the end of his life collected "Wise Sayings," intending to publish them, including "When wealth concentrates, poverty radiates," and "God does not intend for one part of his people to feel that they are superior to another part."

When the Southern states, around 1890, began to enact laws mandating racial segregation, veterans of Reconstruction were involved in opposition. Winfield Scott, who had served on Little Rock's city council, took part in an 1891 protest meeting against an Arkansas law requiring segregation in transportation, and in Louisiana, several former Reconstruction officials helped to create the New Orleans Citizens Committee, which filed the court challenge that gave rise to *Plessy v. Ferguson*. The civil rights impulse of Reconstruction also survived in other careers. Daniel A. Straker, a customs collector in Charleston during the 1870s, moved from South Carolina to Detroit, where he served as an attorney in civil rights cases, won election as a municipal judge, and took part in the movement that led to the formation of the NAACP. George W. Albright, who moved with his wife, a white teacher, to Chicago, Kansas, and Colorado after the end of Reconstruction in Mississippi, lived into the 1930s. At the age of 91, he was interviewed by the *Daily Worker*, and praised the Communist party for nominating a black man, James W. Ford, for vice president. Former Mississippi Congressman John R. Lynch wrote *The Facts of Reconstruction* and a series of articles exposing the shortcomings of historical scholarship of the early twentieth century. At a 1930 Negro History Week celebration in Washington, Lynch said, "we must make paramount the enforcement of the Fifteenth Amendment."

Today, of the nation's approximately 350,000 elected officials, some 7,000 (or two percent) are black Americans, including 436 state legislators (the majority in states of the North and West), and mayors of some of the nation's largest cities. It is safe to say, however, that nowhere do black officials as a group exercise the political power they enjoyed in at least some Southern states during Reconstruction.

Reconstruction's black leaders, to be sure, faced political dilemmas in some ways similar to those of their counterparts today. With the black vote concentrated in a single party, it could essentially be taken for granted by white allies, while opponents saw no need to address black concerns. Neither during the first Reconstruction nor the civil rights era, often called the Second Reconstruction, did black officials find a way to translate political equality into meaningful long-term economic advancement for the mass of the black community. Nonetheless, the overthrow of Reconstruction was a disaster for black America. It delayed for nearly a century the nation's effort to confront the social and racial agenda generated by the destruction of slavery.

The accomplishments of this nation's first generation of black officeholders were a remarkable part of America's first experiment in interracial democracy. The nation's failure to make good on the promise of equality reminds us that rights, once won, may be taken away, that even when rights are enshrined in the Constitution and laws, their survival requires continuing struggle.

GLOSSARY

Freedmen's Bureau: The Bureau of Freedmen, Refugees, and Abandoned Lands, a federal agency charged with reconstructing American society following the Civil War, especially concerned with integrating ex-slaves into postwar society.

Redeemers: Southern Democratic politicians who used their power to end Reconstruction in their individual locales.

Carpetbagger: A Northerner who went into the South after the Civil War to seek political or financial advantage.

Populist Party: Political party that sought to represent the interests of farmers and laborers in the 1890s, advocating increased currency issue, free coinage of gold and silver, public ownership of railroads, and a graduated federal income tax.

IMPLICATIONS

In this essay, Foner provides a profile of African American officeholders following the Civil War and recounts their attempts to use the political arena to address the problems faced by freed people during Reconstruction. Why do you think these African American politicians had only limited impact on postwar politics? What were the limits of their power in Reconstruction America?

Past Traces

No sooner had word of the 1848 California gold strikes reached the southern Chinese port of Guangzhou than thousands of young men left their homes in the surrounding countryside and booked passage on merchant ships bound for the United States. Their aim was to work the gold mines for a few years, save money, and return to their homes and families richer for the experience. Once in California, however, the Chinese found themselves driven from the gold fields by white racism and forced to seek whatever employment they could find. By the 1860s, many had found work building the western half of the transcontinental railroad. In this document, Lee Chew, one of these immigrants, recounts his life as a Chinese immigrant. Like most of his cohorts, Chew's brief sojourn in America turned into a life-long stay.

Lee Chew, *Life of a Chinese Immigrant (1903)*

The village where I was born is situated in the province of Canton, on one of the banks of the Si-Kiang River. It is called a village, altho it is really as big as a city, for there are about 5,000 men in it over eighteen years of age—women and children and even youths are not counted in our villages. . . .

. . . I heard about the American foreign devils, that they were false, having made a treaty by which it was agreed that they could freely come to China, and the Chinese as freely go to their country. After this treaty was made China opened its doors to them and then they broke the treaty that they had asked for by shutting the Chinese out of their country. . . .

The man had gone away from our village a poor boy. Now he returned with unlimited wealth, which he had obtained in the country of the American wizards. After many amazing adventures he had become a merchant in a city called Mott Street, so it was said. . . .

Having made his wealth among the barbarians this man had faithfully returned to pour it out among his tribesmen, and he is living in our village now very happy, and a pillar of strength to the poor.

The wealth of this man filled my mind with the idea that I, too, would like to go to the country of the wizards and gain some of their wealth, and after a long time my father consented, and gave me his blessing, and my mother took leave of me with tears, while my grandfather laid his hand upon my head and told me to remember and live up to the admonitions of the Sages, to avoid gambling, bad women and men of evil minds, and so to govern my conduct that when I died my ancestors might rejoice to welcome me as a guest on high.

My father gave me $100, and I went to Hong Kong with five other boys from our place and we got steerage passage on a steamer, paying $50 each. . . .

. . . Of the great power of these people I saw many signs. The engines that moved the ship were wonderful monsters, strong enough to lift mountains. When I got to San Francisco, which was before the passage of the Exclusion act, I was half starved, because I was afraid to eat the provisions of the barbarians, but a few days' living in the Chinese quarter made me happy again. . . .

The Chinese laundryman does not learn his trade in China; there are no laundries in China. . . . All the Chinese laundrymen here were taught in the first place by American women just as I was taught.

When I went to work for that American family I could not speak a word of English, and I did not know anything about house work. The family consisted of husband, wife and two children. They were very good to me and paid me $3.50 a week, of which I could save $3. . . .

In six months I had learned how to do the .work of our house quite well, and I was getting $5 a week and board, and putting away about $4.25 a week. I had also learned some English, and by going to a Sunday school I learned more English and something about Jesus, who was a great Sage, and whose precepts are like those of Kong-foo-tsze.

It was twenty years ago when I came to this country, and I worked for two years as a servant, getting at least $35 a month. I sent money home to comfort my parents. . . .

When I first opened a laundry it was in company with a partner, who had been in the business for some years. We went to a town about 500 miles inland, where a railroad was building. We got a board shanty and worked for the men employed by the railroads. . . .

We were three years with the railroad, and then went to the mines, where we made plenty of money in gold dust, but had a hard time, for many of the miners were wild men who carried revolvers and after drinking would come into our place to shoot and steal shirts, for which we had to pay. One of these men hit his head hard against a flat iron and all the miners came and broke our laundry, chasing us out of town. They were going to hang us. We lost all our property and $365 in money, which a member of the mob must have found.

Luckily most of our money was in the hands of Chinese bankers in San Francisco. I drew $500 and went East to Chicago, where I had a laundry for three years, during which I increased my capital to $2,500. After that I was four years in Detroit. I went home to China in 1897, but returned in 1898, and began a laundry business in Buffalo.

The ordinary laundry shop is generally divided into three rooms. In front is the room where the customers are received, behind that a bedroom and in the back the work shop, which is also the dining room and kitchen. The stove and cooking utensils are the same as those of the Americans. . . .

I have found out, during my residence in this country, that much of the

Chinese prejudice against Americans is unfounded, and I no longer put faith in the wild tales that were told about them in our village, tho some of the Chinese, who have been here twenty years and who are learned men, still believe that there is no marriage in this country, that the land is infested with demons and that all the people are given over to general wickedness.

I know better. Americans are not all bad, nor are they wicked wizards. Still, they have their faults, and their treatment of us is outrageous. . . .

The reason why so many Chinese go into the laundry business in this country is because it requires little capital and is one of the few opportunities that are open. . . .

There is no reason for the prejudice against the Chinese. The cheap labor cry was always a falsehood. Their labor was never cheap, and is not cheap now. It has always commanded the highest market price. But the trouble is that the Chinese are such excellent and faithful workers that bosses will have no others when they can get them. If you look at men working on the street you will find an overseer for every four or five of them. That watching is not necessary for Chinese. They work as well when left to themselves as they do when some one is looking at them. . . .

From *The Independent*, 54 (2818), February 19, 1903, 417–423.

2

The Chinese Link a Continent and a Nation

Jack Chen

It is a historical commonplace that America is a nation of immigrants. From the original settlers of Jamestown in 1607 to the Hispanic and Asian immigrants of the 1990s, new Americans have loomed large in the national experience. But while immigration has always played an important role in American life, its impact was perhaps greatest during America's industrial revolution of the nineteenth century. From the 1820s, when 100,000 men, women, and children entered the United States, to the first decade of the twentieth century, when 8.2 million landed on American shores, more than thirty-three million immigrants came to the United States and helped build it into the world's premier industrial power.

Among these millions of immigrants, one group has received scant attention—the Chinese peasants, almost entirely males, who came to America as contract laborers to provide agricultural labor for California's central valley and to build railroads and levees in the West. Unlike European immigrants who arrived as free men and women in New York and other eastern cities, the Chinese who landed in San Francisco were bound to the mercantile companies that acted as labor contractors and had advanced them the cost of their fare. Under this contract system, one of the Six Companies in San Francisco negotiated with an employer to provide workers at an agreed-upon rate. The Companies were then responsible for the supply, supervision, and discipline of the contract laborers.

As Jack Chen shows in this essay, these Chinese contract laborers braved the harshest of conditions to fulfill their contract to build America's first transcontinental railroad. Employing skills in excavation and the use of explosives, which they had brought from China, these Chinese workers carved a path through the solid granite of the Sierra Nevada range that opened the West to the remainder of the nation.

The expansion of the railroad system in the United States was astonishingly swift. England had pioneered the building of railways and for a time was the acknowledged leader in the field, but from the moment the first locomotive was imported into the United States in 1829 the farsighted saw railways as the obvious solution for transport across the vast spaces of the American continent. By 1850, 9,000 miles of rails had been laid in the eastern states and up to the Mississippi. The California Gold Rush and the opening of the American West made talk about a transcontinental line more urgent. As too often happens, war spurred the realization of this project.

The West was won. California was a rich and influential state, but a wide unsettled belt of desert, plain, and mountains separated it and Oregon from the rest of the states. As the economic separation of North and South showed, this situation was fraught with danger. It could lead to a political rift. In 1860, it was cheaper and quicker to reach San Francisco from Canton in China—a sixty-day voyage by sea—than from the Missouri River, six months away by wagon train. The urgent need was to link California firmly with the industrialized eastern states and their 30,000 miles of railways. A railway would cut the journey to a week. The threat of civil war loomed larger between North and South over the slavery issue. Abraham Lincoln's Republican administration saw a northern transcontinental railway as a means to outflank the South by drawing the western states closer to the North. In 1862, Congress voted funds to build the 2,500-mile-long railway. It required enormous resourcefulness and determination to get this giant project off the drawing boards. Not much imagination was required to see its necessity, but the actual building presented daunting difficulties. It was calculated that its cost would mount to $100 million, double the federal budget of 1861.

It was Theodore Judah, described by his contemporaries as "Pacific Railroad Crazy," who began to give substance to the dream. An eastern engineer who had come west to build the short Sacramento Valley Railroad, he undertook a preliminary survey and reported that he had found a feasible route crossing the Sierra by way of Dutch Flat. But the mainly small investors who supported his efforts could not carry through the whole immense undertaking. With rumors of civil war between North and South, San Francisco capitalists, mostly Southerners, boycotted the scheme as a northern plot, and pressed for a southern route. Then the Big Four, Sacramento merchants, took up the challenge: Leland Stanford as president, C. P. Huntington as vice-president, Mark Hopkins as treasurer, and Charles Crocker, in charge of construction, formed the Central Pacific Railway Company. Judah was elbowed out.

The Big Four came as gold seekers in 1849 or soon after but found that there was more money to be made in storekeeping than in scrabbling in the rocks in the mountains. As Republicans, they held the state for the Union against the secessionists. Leland Stanford, the first president of the Central Pacific, was also the first Republican governor of California.

The beginnings were not auspicious. The Union Pacific was building from Omaha in the East over the plains to the Rockies, but supplies had to come in by water or wagon because the railways had not yet reached Omaha. The Civil War now raged and manpower, materials, and funds were hard to get. The Indians were still contesting invasion of their lands. By 1864, however, with the Civil War ending, these problems were solved. The UP hired Civil War veterans, Irish immigrants fleeing famine, and even Indian women, and the line began to move westward.

The Central Pacific, building eastward from Sacramento, had broken ground on January 8, 1863, but in 1864, beset by money and labor problems, it had built only thirty-one miles of track. It had an even more intractable manpower problem than the UP. California was sparsely populated, and the gold mines, homesteading, and other lucrative employments offered stiff competition for labor. Brought to the railhead, three out of every five men quit immediately and took off for the better prospects of the new Nevada silver strikes. Even Charles Crocker, boss of construction and raging like a mad bull in the railway camps, could not control them. In the winter of 1864, the company had only 600 men working on the line when it had advertised for 5,000. Up to then, only white labor had been recruited, and California white labor was still motivated by the Gold Rush syndrome. They wanted quick wealth, not hard, regimented railway work. After two years only fifty miles of track had been laid.

James Strobridge, superintendent of construction, testified to the 1876 Joint Congressional Committee on Chinese Immigration: "[These] were unsteady men, unreliable. Some would not go to work at all. . . . Some would stay until pay day, get a little money, get drunk and clear out." Something drastic had to be done.

In 1858, fifty Chinese had helped to build the California Central Railroad from Sacramento to Marysville. In 1860, Chinese were working on the San Jose Railway and giving a good account of themselves, so it is surprising that there was so much hesitation about employing them on the Central Pacific's western end of the first transcontinental railway. Faced with a growing crisis of no work done and mounting costs, Crocker suggested hiring Chinese. Strobridge strongly objected: "I will not boss Chinese. I don't think they could build a railroad." Leland Stanford was also reluctant. He had advocated exclusion on the Chinese from California and was embarrassed to reverse himself. Crocker, Huntington, Hopkins, and Stanford, the "Big Four" of the Central Pacific, were all merchants in hardware, dried goods, and groceries in the little town of Sacramento. Originally, they knew nothing about railroad building, but they were astute and hard-headed businessmen. Crocker was insistent. Wasted time was wasted money. The CP's need for labor was critical.

The men they already had were threatening a strike. Finally fifty Chinese were hired for a trial.

BUILDING THE TRANSCONTINENTAL RAILROAD

In February 1865, they marched up in self-formed gangs of twelve to twenty men with their own supplies and cooks for each mess. They ate a meal of rice and dried cuttlefish, washed and slept, and early next morning were ready for work filling dump carts. Their discipline and grading—preparing the ground for track laying—delighted Strobridge. Soon fifty more were hired, and finally some 15,000 had been put on the payroll. Crocker was enthusiastic: "They prove nearly equal to white men in the amount of labor they perform, and are much more reliable. No danger of strikes among them. We are training them to all kinds of labor: blasting, driving horses, handling rock as well as pick and shovel." Countering Strobridge's argument that the Chinese were "not masons," Crocker pointed out that the race that built the Great Wall could certainly build a railroad culvert. Up on the Donner Pass today the fine stonework embankments built by the Chinese are serving well after a hundred years.

Charles Nordhoff, an acute observer, reports Strobridge telling him, "[The Chinese] learn all parts of the work easily." Nordhoff says he saw them "employed on every kind of work. . . . They do not drink, fight or strike; they do gamble, if it is not prevented; and it is always said of them that they are very cleanly in their habits. It is the custom, among them, after they have had their suppers every evening, to bathe with the help of small tubs. I doubt if the white laborers do as much." As well he might. Well-run boarding-houses in California in those days proudly advertised that they provided guests with a weekly bath.

Their wages at the start were $28 a month (twenty-six working days), and they furnished all their own food, cooking utensils, and tents.

The headman of each gang, or sometimes an American employed as clerk by them, received all the wages and handed them out to the members of the work gang according to what had been earned. "Competent and wonderfully effective because tireless and unremitting in their industry," they worked from sun-up to sun-down.

All observers remarked on the frugality of the Chinese. This was not surprising in view of the fact that, with a strong sense of filial duty, they came to America in order to save money and return as soon as possible to their homes and families in China. So they usually dressed poorly, and their dwellings were of the simplest. However, they ate well; rice and vermicelli (noodles) garnished with meats and vegetables; fish, dried oysters, cuttlefish, bacon and pork, and chicken on holidays, abalone meat, five kinds of dried vegetables, bamboo shoots, seaweed, salted cabbage, and mushroom, four kinds of dried fruit, and peanut oil and tea. This diet shows a considerable degree of sophistication and balance compared to the beef, beans, potatoes, bread, and butter of the white laborers. Other supplies were purchased from the shop maintained by a Chinese merchant contractor in one of the railway cars that followed them as they carried the railway line forward. Here they could buy pipes, tobacco, bowls, chopsticks, lamps, Chinese-style shoes of cotton with soft cotton soles, and ready-made clothing imported from China.

On Sundays, they rested, did their washing, and gambled. They were prone to argue noisily, but did not become besotted with whiskey and make themselves unfit for work on Monday. Their sobriety was much appreciated by their employers.

Curtis, the engineer in charge, described them as "the best roadbuilders in the world." The once skeptical Strobridge, a smart, pushing Irishman, also now pronounced them "the best in the world." Leland Stanford described them in a report on October 10, 1865, to Andrew Johnson:

As a class, they are quiet, peaceable, patient, industrious, and economical. More prudent and economical [than white laborers] they are contented with less wages. We find them organized for mutual aid and assistance. Without them, it would be impossible to complete the western portion of this great national enterprise within the time required by the Act of Congress.

Crocker testified before the congressional committee that "if we found that we were in a hurry for a job of work, it was better to put on Chinese at once." All these men had originally resisted the employment of Chinese on the railway.

Four-fifths of the grading labor from Sacramento to Ogden was done by Chinese. In a couple of years more, of 13,500 workers on the payroll 12,000 were Chinese. They were nicknamed "Crocker's Pets."

APPRECIATING CHINESE SKILLS

The Chinese crews won their reputation the hard way. They outperformed Cornish men brought in at extra wages to cut rock. Crocker testified,

They would cut more rock in a week than the Cornish miners, and it was hard work, bone labor. [They] were skilled in using the hammer and drill, and they proved themselves equal to the very best Cornish miners in that work. They were very trusty, they were intelligent, and they lived up to their contracts.

Stanford held the Chinese workers in such high esteem that he provided in his will for the permanent employment of a large number on his estates. In the 1930s, some of their descendants were still living and working lands now owned by Stanford University.

The Chinese saved the day for Crocker and his colleagues. The terms of agreement with the government were that the railway companies would be paid from $16,000 to $48,000 for each mile of track laid. But there were only so many miles between the two terminal points of the projected line. The Union Pacific Company, working with 10,000 mainly Irish immigrants and Civil War veterans, had the advantage of building the line through Nebraska over the plains and made steady progress. The Central Pacific, after the first easy twenty-three miles between Newcastle and Colfax, had to conquer the granite mountains and gorges of the Sierra Nevada and Rockies before it could emerge onto the Nevada-Utah plains and make real speed and money. The line had to rise 7,000 feet in 100 miles over daunting terrain. Crocker and the Chinese proved up to the challenge. After reaching Cisco, there was no easy going. The line had to be literally carved out of the Sierra granite, through tunnels and on rock ledges cut on the side of precipices.

Using techniques from China, they attacked one of the most difficult parts of the work: carrying the line over Cape Horn, with its sheer granite buttresses and steep shale embankments, 2,000 feet above the American River canyon. There was no foothold on its flanks. The indomitable Chinese, using age-old ways, were lowered from above in rope-held baskets, and there, suspended between earth and sky, they began to chip away with hammer and crowbar to form the narrow ledge that was later laboriously deepened to a shelf wide enough for the railway roadbed, 1,400 feet above the river.

The weather, as well as the terrain, was harsh. The winter of 1865–1866 was one of the severest on record. Snow fell early, and storm after storm blanketed the Sierra Nevada. The ground froze solid. Sixty-foot drifts of snow had to be shoveled away before the graders could even reach the roadbed. Nearly half the work force of 9,000 men were set to clearing snow.

In these conditions, construction crews tackled the most formidable obstacle in their path: building the ten Summit Tunnels on the twenty-mile stretch between Cisco, ninety-two miles from Sacramento and Lake Ridge just west of Cold Stream Valley on the eastern slope of the summit. Work went on at all the tunnels simultaneously. Three shifts of eight hours each worked day and night.

The builders lived an eerie existence. In *The Big Four*, Oscar Lewis writes,

> Tunnels were dug beneath forty-foot drifts and for months, 3,000 workmen lived curious mole-like lives, passing from work to living quarters in dim passages far beneath the snows surface. . . . [There] was constant danger, for as snow's accumulated on the upper ridges, avalanches grew frequent, their approach heralded only by a brief thunderous roar. A second later, a work crew, a bunkhouse, an entire camp would go hurtling at a dizzy speed down miles of frozen canyon. Not until months later were the bodies recovered; sometimes groups were found with shovels or picks still clutched in their frozen hands.

On Christmas Day, 1866, the papers reported that "a gang of Chinamen employed by the railroad were covered up by a snow slide and four or five [note the imprecision] died before they could be exhumed." A whole camp of Chinese railway workers was enveloped during one night and had to be rescued by shovelers the next day.

No one has recorded the names of those who gave their lives in this stupendous undertaking. It is known that the bones of 1,200 men were shipped back to China to be buried in the land of their forefathers, but that was by no means the total score. The engineer John Gills recalled that "at Tunnel No. 10, some 15–20 Chinese [again, note the imprecision] were killed by a slide that winter. The year before, in the winter of 1864–65, two wagon road repairers had been buried and killed by a slide at the same location."

A. P. Partridge, who worked on the line, describes how 3,000 Chinese builders were driven out of the mountains by the early snow. "Most . . . came to Truckee and filled up all the old buildings and sheds. An old barn collapsed and killed four Chinese. A good many were frozen to death." One is astonished at the fortitude, discipline, and dedication of the Chinese railroad workers.

Many years later, looking at the Union Pacific section of the line, an old railwayman remarked, "There's an Irishman buried under every tie of that road." Brawling, drink, cholera, and malaria took a heavy toll. The construction crew towns on the Union Pacific part of the track, with their saloons, gambling dens, and bordellos, were nicknamed "hells on wheels." Jack Casement, in charge of construction there, had been a general in the Civil War and prided himself on the discipline of his fighting forces. His work crews worked with military precision, but off the job they let themselves go. One day, after gambling in the streets on payday (instigated by professional gamblers) had gotten too much out of hand, a visitor, finding the street suddenly very quiet, asked him where the gamblers had gone. Casement pointed at a nearby cemetery and replied, "They all died with their boots on." It was still the Wild West.

It is characteristic that only one single case of violent brawling was reported among the Chinese from the time they started work until they completed the job.

The Central Pacific's Chinese became expert at all kinds of work: grading, drilling, masonry, and demolition. Using black powder, they could average 1.18 feet daily through granite so hard that an incautiously placed charge could blow out backward. The Summit Tunnel work force was entirely composed of Chinese, with mainly Irish foremen. Thirty to forty worked on each face, with twelve to fifteen on the heading and the rest on the bottom removing material.

The Donner tunnels, totaling 1,695 feet, had to be bored through solid rock, and 9,000 Chinese worked on them. To speed the work, a new and untried explosive, nitroglycerin, was used. The tunnels were completed in November 1867, after thirteen months. But winter began before the way could be opened and the tracks laid. That winter was worse than the preceding one, but to save time it was necessary to send crews ahead to continue building the line even while the tunnels were being cut. Therefore, 3,000 men were sent with 400 carts and horses to Palisade Canyon, 300 miles in advance of the railhead. "Hay, grain and all supplies for men and horses had to be hauled by teams over the deserts for that great distance," writes Strobridge. "Water for men and animals was hauled at times 40 miles." Trees were felled and the logs laid side by side to form a "corduroy" roadway. On log sleds greased with lard, hundreds of Chinese manhandled three locomotives and forty wagons over the mountains. Strobridge later testified that it "cost nearly three times what it would have cost to have done it in the summertime when it should have been done. But we shortened the time seven years from what Congress expected when the act was passed."

Between 10,000 and 11,000 men were kept working on the line from 1866 to 1869. The Sison and Wallace Company (in which Crocker's brother was a leading member) and the Dutch merchant Cornelius Koopmanschap of San Francisco procured these men for the line. Through the summer of 1866, Crocker's Pets—6,000 strong—swarmed over the upper canyons of the Sierra, methodically slicing cuttings and pouring rock and debris to make landfills and strengthen the foundations of trestle bridges. Unlike the Caucasian laborers, who drank unboiled stream water, the Chinese slaked their thirst with weak tea and boiled water kept in old whiskey kegs filled by their mess cooks. They kept themselves clean and healthy by daily sponge baths in tubs of hot water prepared by their cooks, and the work went steadily forward.

Crocker has been described as a "hulking, relentless driver of men." But his Chinese crews responded to his leadership and drive and were caught up in the spirit of the epic work on which they were engaged. They cheered and waved their cartwheel hats as the first through train swept down the eastern slopes of the Sierra to the meeting of the lines. They worked with devotion and self-sacrifice to lay that twenty-odd miles of track for the Central Pacific Company in 1866 over the most difficult terrain. The cost of those miles was enormous—$280,000 a mile—but it brought the builders in sight of the easier terrain beyond the

Sierra and the Rockies. Here costs of construction by veteran crews were only half the estimated amount of federal pay.

By summer 1868, an army of 14,000 railway builders was passing over the mountains into the great interior plain. Nine-tenths of that work force was Chinese. More than a quarter of all Chinese in the country were building the railway.

By September 1868, the track was completed for 307 miles from Sacramento, and the crews were laying rails across the plain east of the Sierra. Parallel with the track layers went the telegraph installers, stringing their wires on the poles and keeping the planners back at headquarters precisely apprised of where the end of the track was.

THE GREAT RAILWAY COMPETITION

On the plains, the Chinese worked in tandem with all the Indians Crocker could entice to work on the iron rails. They began to hear of the exploits of the Union Pacific's "Irish terriers" building from the east. One day, the Irish laid six miles of track. The Chinese topped this with seven. "No Chinaman is going to beat us," growled the Irish, and the next day, they laid seven and a half miles of track. They swore that they would outperform the competition no matter what it did.

Croaker taunted the Union Pacific that his men could lay ten miles of track a day. Durant, president of the rival line, laid a $10,000 wager that it could not be done. Crocker took no chances. He waited until the day before the last sixteen miles of track could be laid and brought up all needed supplies for instant use. Then he unleashed his crews. On April 28, 1869, while Union Pacific checkers and newspaper reporters looked on, a combined gang of Chinese and eight picked Irish rail handlers laid ten miles and 1,800 feet more of track in twelve hours. This record was never surpassed until the advent of mechanized track laying. Each Irishman that day walked a total distance

of ten miles, and their combined muscle handled sixty tons of rail.

So keen was the competition that when the two lines approached each other, instead of changing direction to link up, their builders careered on and on for 100 miles, building lines that would never meet. Finally, the government prescribed that the linkage point should be Promontory, Utah.

On May 10, 1869, the two lines were officially joined at Promontory, north of Ogden in Utah. A great crowd gathered. A band played. An Irish crew and a Chinese crew were chosen to lay the last two rails side by side. The last tie was made of polished California laurel with a silver plate in its center proclaiming it "The last tie laid on the completion of the Pacific Railroad, May 10, 1869." But when the time came it was nowhere to be found. As consternation mounted, four Chinese approached with it on their shoulders and they laid it beneath the rails. A photographer stepped up and someone shouted to him "Shoot!" The Chinese only knew one meaning for that word. They fled. But order was restored and the famous ceremony began; Stanford drove a golden spike into the last tie with a silver hammer. The news flashed by telegraph to a waiting nation. But no Chinese appears in that famous picture of the toast celebrating the joining of the rails.

Crocker was one of the few who paid tribute to the Chinese that day: "I wish to call to your minds that the early completion of this railroad we have built has been in large measure due to that poor, despised class of laborers called the Chinese, to the fidelity and industry they have shown." No one even mentioned the name of Judah.

The building of the first transcontinental railway stands as a monument to the union of Yankee and Chinese-Irish drive and know-how. This was a formidable combination. They all complemented each other. Together they did in seven years what was expected to take at least fourteen.

It was heroic work. The Central Pacific crews had carried their railway 1,800 miles through the Sierra and Rocky mountains, over sagebrush desert and plain. The Union Pacific built only 689 miles, over much easier terrain. It had 500 miles in which to carry its part of the line to a height of 5,000 feet, with another fifty more miles in which to reach the high passes of the Black Hills. With newly recruited crews, the Central Pacific had to gain an altitude of 7,000 feet from the plain in just over 100 miles and make a climb of 2,000 feet in just 20 miles.

All this monumental work was done before the age of mechanization. It was pick and shovel, hammer and crowbar work, with baskets for earth carried slung from shoulder poles and put on one-horse carts.

For their heroic work, the Chinese workmen began with a wage of $28 a month, providing their own food and shelter. This was gradually raised to $30 to $35 a month. Caucasians were paid the same amount of money, but their food and shelter were provided. Because it cost $0.75 to $1.00 a day to feed a white unskilled worker, each Chinese saved the Central Pacific, at a minimum, two-thirds the price of a white laborer (1865 rates). Chinese worked as masons, dynamiters, and blacksmiths and at other skilled jobs that paid white workers from $3 to $5 a day. So, at a minimum, the company saved about $5 million by hiring Chinese workers.

When the task was done, most of the Chinese railwaymen were paid off. Some returned to China with their hard-earned savings, and the epic story of building the Iron Horse's pathway across the continent must have regaled many a family gathering there. Some returned with souvenirs of the great work, chips of one of the last ties, which had been dug up and split up among them. Some settled in the little towns that had grown up along the line of the railway. Others took the railway to seek adventure further east and south. Most made their way back to California

and took what jobs they could find in that state's growing industries, trades, and other occupations. Many used their traditional and newly acquired skills on the other transcontinental lines and railways that were being swiftly built in the West and Midwest. This was the start of the diaspora of the Chinese immigrants in America.

Ironically, the great railway soon had disastrous results for the Chinese themselves. It now cost only $40 for an immigrant to cross the continent by rail and a flood of immigrants took advantage of the ease and cheapness of travel on the line the Chinese had helped to build. The labor shortage (and resulting high wages) in California turned into a glut. When the tangled affairs of the Northern Pacific line led to the stock market crash of Black Friday, September 19, 1873, and to financial panic, California experienced its first real economic depression. There was devastating unemployment, and the Chinese were made the scapegoats.

The transcontinental lines on which [the Chinese] worked "more than any other factor helped make the United States a united nation," writes the *Encyclopaedia Britannica* ["Railways"]. They played a major role in building the communications network of iron roads that was the transport base of American industrial might in the twentieth century.

Speaking eloquently in favor of the Chinese immigrants, Oswald Garrison Villard said,

> I want to remind you of the things that Chinese labor did in opening up the Western portion of this country. . . . [They] stormed the forest fastness, endured cold and heat and the risk of death at hands of hostile Indians to aid in the opening up of our northwestern empire. I have a dispatch from the chief engineer of the Northwestern Pacific telling how Chinese laborers went out into eight feet of snow with the temperature far below zero to carry on the work when no American dared face the conditions.

And these men were from China's sun-drenched south, where it never snows.

In certain circles, there has been a conspiracy of silence about the Chinese railroadmen and what they did. When U.S. Secretary of Transportation John Volpe spoke at the "Golden Spike" centenary, not a single Chinese American was invited, and he made no mention in his speech of the Chinese railroad builders.

GLOSSARY

California Gold Rush: Discovery of gold in 1849 that brought a flood of migrants to California, whose population mushroomed from 15,000 to nearly 300,000 between 1849 and 1856.

Irish "terriers": Irish railroad workers known for their speed in track-laying.

Iron Horse: Railroad locomotive.

IMPLICATIONS

Chen's account of Chinese railroad workers raises the issue of racism and financial interest in nineteenth-century America. Do you think Crocker's decision to employ Chinese workers to build his portion of the transcontinental railroad shows him to be less racist than most of his fellow white Californians? What does this essay say about the relationship between self-interest and racism?

The economic changes that swept through American society at the close of the nineteenth century disrupted the lives of urban and rural residents alike. On America's farms, mechanization, competition, monopoly, and overproduction made agrarian life ever more precarious. Faced with the decline of their long-established way of life, farmers throughout the country joined the Populist movement and its political arm, the People's party. In this document, the national platform of the People's party, we see a clear statement of the wrongs felt by American farmers and their plan to restore their traditional independence and security.

The Omaha Platform of the Populist Party (1892)

Preamble

The conditions which surround us best justify our cooperation; we meet in the midst of a nation brought to the verge of moral, political, and material ruin. Corruption dominates the ballot-box, the Legislatures, the Congress, and touches even the ermine of the bench. The people are demoralized; most of the States have been compelled to isolate the voters at the polling places to prevent universal intimidation and bribery. The newspapers are largely subsidized or muzzled, public opinion silenced, business prostrated, homes covered with mortgages, labor impoverished, and the land concentrating in the hands of capitalists. The urban workmen are denied the right to organize for self-protection, imported pauperized labor beats down their wages, a hireling standing army, unrecognized by our laws, is established to shoot them down, and they are rapidly degenerating into European conditions. The fruits of the toil of millions are boldly stolen to build up colossal fortunes for a few, unprecedented in the history of mankind and the possessors of these, in turn, despise the Republic and endanger liberty. From the same prolific womb of governmental injustice we breed the two great classes—tramps and millionaires. . . .

Assembled on the anniversary of the birthday of the nation, and filled with the spirit of the grand general and chief who established our independence, we seek to restore the government of the Republic to the hands of the "plain people," with which class it originated. We assert our purposes to be identical with the purposes of the National Constitution; to form a more perfect union and establish justice, insure domestic tranquillity, provide for the common defense, promote the general welfare, and secure the blessings of liberty for ourselves and our posterity. . . .

Platform

We declare, therefore—

First.—That the union of the labor forces of the United States this day consummated shall be permanent and perpetual; may its spirit enter into all hearts for the salvation of the Republic and the uplifting of mankind.

Second.—Wealth belongs to him who creates it, and every dollar taken from industry without an equivalent is robbery. "If any will not work, neither shall he eat." The interests of rural and civil labor are the same; their enemies are identical.

Third.—We believe that the time has come when the railroad corporations will either own the people or the people must own the railroads. . . .

FINANCE.—We demand a national currency, safe, sound, and flexible issued by the general government only, a full legal tender for all debts, public and private. . . .

1. We demand free and unlimited coinage of silver and gold at the present legal ratio of 16 to 1.
2. We demand that the amount of circulating medium be speedily increased to not less than $50 per capita.
3. We demand a graduated income tax.
4. We believe that the money of the country should be kept as much as possible in the hands of the people, and hence we demand that all State and national revenues shall be limited to the necessary expenses of the government, economically and honestly administered.
5. We demand that postal savings banks be established by the government for the safe deposit of the earnings of the people and to facilitate exchange.

TRANSPORTATION.—Transportation being a means of exchange and a public necessity, the government should own and operate the railroads in the interest of the people. The telegraph and telephone, like the post-office system, being a necessity for the transmission of news, should be owned and operated by the government in the interest of the people.

LAND.—The land, including all the natural sources of wealth, is the heritage of the people, and should not be monopolized for speculative purposes, and alien ownership of land should be prohibited. All land now held by railroads and other corporations in excess of their actual needs, and all lands now owned by aliens should be reclaimed by the government and held for actual settlers only.

Expressions of Sentiments

1. RESOLVED, That we demand a free ballot, and a fair count of all elections, and pledge ourselves to secure it to every legal voter without Federal intervention, through the adoption by the States of the unperverted Australian or secret ballot system.
2. RESOLVED, That the revenue derived from a graduated income tax should be applied to the reduction of the burden of taxation now levied upon the domestic industries of this country.
3. RESOLVED, That we pledge our support to fair and liberal pensions to ex-Union soldiers and sailors.
4. RESOLVED, That we condemn the fallacy of protecting American labor under the present system, which opens our ports to the pauper and criminal classes of the world and crowds out our wage-earners; and we denounce the present ineffective laws against contract labor, and

demand the further restriction of undesirable emigration.

5. RESOLVED, That we cordially sympathize with the efforts of organized workingmen to shorten the hours of labor, and demand a rigid enforcement of the existing eight-hour law on Government work, and ask that a penalty clause be added to the said law.

6. RESOLVED, That we regard the maintenance of a large standing army of mercenaries, known as the Pinkerton system, as a menace to our liberties, and we demand its abolition. . . .

7. RESOLVED, That we commend to the favorable consideration of the people and the reform press the legislative system known as the initiative and referendum.

8. RESOLVED, That we favor a constitutional provision limiting the office of President and Vice-President to one term, and providing for the election of Senators of the United States by a direct vote of the people.

9. RESOLVED, That we oppose any subsidy or national aid to any private corporation for any purpose.

3

The Southern Populist Critique of American Capitalism

Bruce Palmer

The last decade of the nineteenth century was a time of upheaval in a century marked by unprecedented change. In the Northeast, mammoth factories and the immigrants who labored in them dominated the cities of America's industrial heartland. Throughout the country, an ever-growing network of railroads connected even outlying regions to the burgeoning metropolises of the nation. And in these metropolises, financial and industrial cartels, monopolies, and holding companies exercised an economic and political influence unparalleled in American life.

Facing these changes were workers and farmers. American workers responded to the growing power of industrial capitalism with the collective power of their numbers and struggled with their employers over control of the workplace and the process of production itself. For their part, the small farmers of the South, Midwest, and Far West responded by forming local organizations to fight discriminatory railroad freight rates and to challenge the power of eastern banks to yoke them to a cycle of unending indebtedness.

Beginning in the late 1880s, these farm protests took on a national political focus. Dissatisfied with inaction and outright hostility on the part of both national parties, southern and midwestern farmers created a series of Farmers' Alliances and eventually the Populist or People's Party. The Populists quickly became one of the greatest social and political reform movements in American history. At the heart of the movement was their belief in the importance of small family farms and their concern about the threat that an eastern "moneyed interest" posed to this agrarian institution. Their rallying cry became "man over money," and by 1892, the People's party had elected governors in Kansas and North Dakota and dominated all levels of politics in Colorado. Although the Populists met the fate of all third parties in American politics—being absorbed into the easy-credit, free-silver wing of the Democratic party represented by William Jennings Bryant—their protest served notice to both parties that the needs of American family farmers could not be ignored.

In this study of populism, Bruce Palmer investigates the ideas behind the movement. He finds that both traditional agrarian ideals and a modern appreciation of the marketplace animated the thoughts of Populist leaders, rank and file members, and the platform of the People's party.

....

For the Southern Populists any properly ordered society required what might best be called balance, though they most often used the words "harmony," "equilibrium," and sometimes "homogeneity." "When He multiplied the loaves and the fishes," wrote a North Carolina Allianceman, "none went away hungry. God does not create disparities." Despite their positions at opposite ends of the Populist political spectrum in the South, North Carolina Populist Senator Marion Butler and radical Texas organizer H. S. P. "Stump" Ashby could agree that in a society properly ordered "the merchant and farmer, lawyer and artisan . . . [would] dwell together, not as warring enemies, but as kind friends, joining willing hands in the beneficent work of production." Rather than serve as a battleground on which selfish people fought each other for personal advantage, society should be the arena in which everyone worked together for what most benefited each—the production of tangible wealth.

The distance between the ideal and the actual social order, those real disparities which existed in America, made this idea pivotal in the Southern Populist demand for reform. L. L. Polk, president of the National Farmers' Alliance and Industrial Union for a little less than three years, noted that the country had not witnessed the "peace, contentment and plenty" that should have been expected from America's tremendous post-1865 expansion in railroads, manufacturing, towns, and cities. Instead, the result had been hard times. "The greatest industrial revolution of the ages" had one more goal to reach: "To restore and maintain that equipoise between the great industrial interests of the country which is absolutely

essential to a healthful progress and to the development of our civilization." A balanced and harmonious development did not mean America's thousands of homeless and hungry families, thousands dressed in rags. America's social development, concluded Helen W. Post, a *People's Party Paper* contributing editor, "is deformity, monstrosity; it is not symmetry; it is dropsy and not good healthy substance; and it means premature death."

At the center of the Southern Populists' notion of social balance lay their concept of the "middle class": "the great and noble middle farming and laboring class" to which a Georgia Populist declared the southern reformers themselves belonged. This class consisted solely of the producers of tangible wealth and drew its members neither from the rich nor the poor. These people provided "the bone and sinew of the country," those who supported the government, "the bulwark of any social system." But in America these people of "moderate means" were fast disappearing, wrote a Texas Populist, "leaving only the two classes, the two extremes, the very rich, who live in idleness, extravagance and luxuriousness, and the destitute poor, who are compelled with their families to labor incessantly for a subsistence."

More clearly than anything else this growing imbalance signaled a major injustice in American society. God had made the bounty available and ruled that it be distributed properly, to all people. "Larger equity in the division of labor—in the distribution of the products of labor, must obtain," wrote a North Carolina Populist. "Anything short of this is contrary to the teachings of the Holy Writ." At issue were not the productive abilities of

American farmers and laborers. "There is plenty of wealth in this country," wrote a Georgia Populist. "It is not that we are kicking about. The trouble is that the people who produce all this great wealth are robbed of it by bad laws made in the interest of an idle, do-nothing class of people." To correct the situation the producers demanded enjoyment of the fruits of their own toil, fruits which heretofore the Rockefellers, Carnegies, Goulds, and others had stolen from them to create their gigantic fortunes.

The worsening depression of the 1890s substantiated the Southern Populists' fear that social and economic disaster would follow the growing injustice. Nor was the issue at hand purely secular. The wealthy few's accumulation of riches, stolen from the producers, flew in the face of a righteous and wrathful God. "False systems," created by "false legislation," meant that labor no longer enjoyed what it produced, millions of children starved, and thousands of women were forced into prostitution. It was the work of the Devil, and the millionaires were warned by Arkansas editor W. S. Morgan that "it is only a matter of time when [the people] will turn upon you and rend you. Again we say, beware. Get back to the righteousness of God." Whether the problem was a secular or a moral and religious one, however, the result was the same. "Millionaires make paupers," declared a Texas Populist; "paupers make anarchists and anarchists destroy nations."

Southern Populists often drew on a specific Biblical image, the Belshazzar story, to express their sense of outrage at the material and moral disaster they saw flowing from the growing maldistribution of wealth. One part of the image juxtaposed riches and poverty to emphasize the injustice of the widening chasm between rich and poor. Watson in early 1892, described a postelection dinner of the Georgia Democratic leaders in Atlanta using the image to make his point, contrasting the elaborate preparations and food inside the hotel with the "millions of toilers going to rest in their squalid homes, amid all the gloom, the cold and the hunger of their hard lot." The second element of the image made the threat to the wrongdoers explicit. Disaster awaited the rich who robbed and plundered the producing masses. Blind to what was happening, they wined and dined on their last evening, Watson wrote, "the tread of Cyrus and his Persians without. The pampered Aristocrats will listen to no warning, until Daniel strides into the Hall and the laugh of the voluptuary freezes on the lips of the quaking coward." The situation could not continue. Retribution would be had, justice be done.

The Southern Populists, however, did not always picture the danger from growing extremes of wealth in such stark terms. The maldistribution also caused disorders and immorality on a lower but increasing level of intensity. The extremes of wealth and poverty bred disease, vice, and sensuality—the extremes of human personal and social behavior. The producing middle class—quite literally in the middle between rich and poor, debauched and degraded, idler and slave—furnished the moderate virtues which sustained a harmonious and balanced society. The same class which concentrated wealth was destroying had, as Populists, to save the country from both the rich and poor by restoring the proper distribution of wealth. Politically this achievement required returning equality to the social order. Inherited from the Jacksonians, the motto which ran at the head of Watson's *People's Party Paper* from 1891 through 1896 read "Equal Rights to All, Special Privileges to None." His southern brethren agreed completely with him on his choice. They did not intend, as a North Carolina editor pointed out, an actual material equality for everyone, for "people are not born equals, neither physically, mentally nor morally." They did share "natural rights" to life, liberty, and happiness, however, which implied "a right to the means of comfortable existence, the right to the conditions that produce happiness."

To what area did this demand for equal rights refer? "The Omaha platform has but one principle," wrote a Georgia Populist, F. J. Ripley, "that wealth belongs to him who creates it, rather than to those who by chicanery, legislation and fortuitous circumstances manage to get possession of it." The platform favored the distribution of "wealth, prosperity and happiness," and opposed their concentration; it called for "such legislation as will give every man a fair chance to obtain and retain a competency." If that fair chance were provided, observed a North Carolina editor, there would be but one class, "those who do honest work and enjoy the fruits of their labor. Of course some of these will be richer than others in worldly goods, for God has given to some men more talents than to others, but all of this class will be equally as rich in contentment and happiness." No one who worked would be poor. The major problem of imbalance in society be solved, social and economic justice served.

Their religious experience gave the Southern Populists, like most Americans, a tool for explaining and understanding American society. One of the best examples of its usage appeared in the southern reformers' attempt to deal with their own relation to American politics in the 1890s. An Alabama Allianceman, in mid-1892, expressed his hopes and concern for the reform movement with an elaborately mixed metaphor built around the flight of the Jews from Egypt. "The children of Israel," he wrote, had at last escaped Egypt, and would regain the promised land if they did not hesitate at the Red Sea or linger to hear "the syren [sic] song of the money power Delilah, and the lying entreaties or menaces of the Benedict Arnolds of American Independence, and the Judases to the cause of justice, liberty and righteousness." Although they had turned toward the land of milk and honey, the reformers, open to the blandishments and threats of their enemies and faced with the seeming impossibility of defeating them, had yet to win their struggle. The metaphor served to define, in terms the Populists' listeners would understand, the difficulty of the reform struggle, the

enemies it confronted, and the promise victory held. And it gave all the importance that only the guiding hand of God could provide for the faithful.

Often their choice of terms indicated that the Southern Populists perceived the mission of their party as analogous to the task of religious salvation. Many believed, with one Georgia Populist, that "the People's Party is the political Savior of this country." The southern reformers often used Christ to link religious salvation with Populism. Their Christ was not, however, a savior who told people to repent of this world to win salvation in the next. "Christ did not come, as our theological quacks are so fond of saying, to prepare men for another world," wrote a Texas Populist, "but to teach them how to rightly live in this." Christ was a reformer and a radical. The Southern Populist demand for equal rights to all and special privileges to none urged nothing new. "Years ago the Man of Galilee used it," wrote Watson, "as the chief plank in His platform. 'Whatsoever ye would that I do unto you do ye even so unto them.'" Like the Populists, Christ was born a workingman, a producer, and His Sermon on the Mount, argued a North Carolina Populist editor, showed that He understood that "the unduly rich were the worst sort of criminals, because it is they who are responsible for the social conditions which make all other crimes possible or necessary."

The Southerners took their religion seriously. They took literally what they heard from the pulpit or read in their Bibles about the wrongs of oppression and the responsibility of all for their neighbors. The Populists, a Texas reformer asserted, "led mainly by men who are Christians in principle, but like the late Judge Nugent, not members of any so-called orthodox church," were "leading the industrial millions out of slavery into freedom. The church that professes to be the light of the world under Christ is not doing it. We plead for the rights of man and the old-fashioned gospel of the brotherhood of humanity as Christ preached it and lined [*sic*] it." In this real sense, for many southern reformers the Populist party obviously came very close to replacing the church, at least in this world. As the use of the religious metaphors and imagery indicated, for these the authority of the church in society belonged to the People's party.

While their own experience taught them about the injustice of a growing maldistribution of wealth, the Southern Populists often used religious metaphors and imagery to organize and articulate that experience, to give it more universal meaning, and to explain both the process and solutions they proposed utilizing to eradicate that social and economic injustice. The southern reformers, of course, had another frame of reference available—their Jeffersonian and Jacksonian intellectual and political heritage—which they often closely tied to their moral and religious referents. One Alabama editor called Populism "the morals of Christ and the politics of Thomas Jefferson." The religious framework lent divine sanction to the Jeffersonian and Jacksonian formulations, while Jeffersonian and Jacksonian ideas often served to particularize God's commandments as they affected politics, economics, and society.

The Southern Populists cited not only God's commandments but Jefferson's authority for the injustice of and solutions to the great inequalities of wealth in American society. Not only was equal rights to all and special privileges to none a Jeffersonian doctrine, but so was the idea to which the Southern Populists tied it, equal opportunities for each person in the race of life. The notion of Jeffersonian simplicity highlighted for the Southern Populists the evils of the growing extremes of wealth. Regarding the costly paraphernalia and the elaborate ceremony surrounding President Cleveland and his entourage, Populists in North Carolina, Georgia, and Texas could only regret the passing of the "days of Jeffersonian simplicity." The concentration of wealth from which this extravagance flowed threatened to destroy American society. The extravagance itself signaled impending destruction. Jeffersonian simplicity, in the same way, reflected the ideal society out of which it grew, a society balanced and homogeneous, where all enjoyed a relatively equal amount of the total wealth of the country.

The analysis of society based on the function of tangible production allowed the Southern Populists to elaborate an ideal society which consisted of the interaction of several groups—working people, manufacturers, bankers, merchants, and some professionals. Religious metaphors and images affected the range of this elaboration little, although they helped to explain some of it. The Southern Populists drew most of the content of this ideal society from their own rural and reform experience, although they often interpreted it through the metaphors and images their Jeffersonian and Jacksonian heritage provided them. While their background as post-Civil War southern farmers taught them, with the sharp lessons of experience, that the most central injustice in American society was the growing maldistribution of wealth, they used their religious heritage, and the metaphors and images offered, to explain the extent and import of this injustice, to predict what would happen if the wrong were not righted, and to explain the importance of the means to be used by the reform movement in correcting it. As their religious heritage had played a secondary role in their elaboration of a producer-oriented society, so their Jeffersonian and Jacksonian heritage, while it identified some of the more particular elements of society that needed change, played a secondary role in explaining what had gone wrong with America. It was contact with the specific society around them, however, that forced the Southern Populists to make the choices which ultimately governed their reform program.

As late nineteenth-century Southerners, the Populists encountered a conception of the proper economic and social order which owed little to Jefferson and Jackson. When the South emerged in the late 1870s from the turmoil of Reconstruction and depression, among some young urban Southerners talk began of a way to solve the problems of southern backwardness, poverty, and the region's burdens of race and sectional isolation. Henry Grady, Richard Edmonds, Henry Watterson, Daniel Tompkins, and others like them outlined a plan for sectional development which they called the New South and which Paul Gaston has noted "bespoke harmonious reconciliation of sectional differences, racial peace, and a new economic and social order based on industry and scientific, diversified agriculture—all of which would lead, eventually, to the South's dominance in the reunited nation."

In the 1880s a small but vigorous southern "new middle class" adopted this creed as its own, and as this commercial, professional, and land-owning class grew stronger in the cities and towns of the South, the New South gospel matured with it. Although in order to win political control in most southern states the new middle class had to wait for the Populists and the Redeemers to destroy each other, by the 1890s their creed of industrialization and urbanization had spread widely in the small towns and cities of the South. The New South advocates were the middle class regional representatives of America's maturing industrial society. They rode to sectional power on the direct penetration of American capitalism into the southern towns and countryside, and the New South creed furnished them with an ideology to explain and justify both their struggle and their victory. The Populists, challenging the Redeemers and the Redeemers' temporary middle-class allies in the 1890s, also had to confront the New South creed.

Although the New South advocates paid only spotty, and usually critical, attention to the farmers, Southern Populists did not remain entirely immune to the plans and promises of the new order. Walter Hines Page had a wider readership in North Carolina than many historians have credited him with. "We regret," wrote a North Carolina Allianceman, "that we have a good many old fogies in the State, but are glad that North Carolina is keeping up with what is known as the New South." They often supported the New South's largest advertising vehicle, the local, state, or regional fair. Almost every Southern Populist newspaper, and all the major ones, at one time or another carried a column from the *Manufacturers' Record*, a Baltimore-based paper and major exponent of the New South gospel, noting the start of manufacturing and other enterprises in their states, and sometimes in the whole South. On rare occasions editorial paragraphs distinctly reminiscent of the heyday of Grady and Dawson appeared in southern reform papers. In an otherwise critical response to an editorial in the Brooklyn *Eagle* praising the North, the *Progressive Farmer* in 1892 commented that Northerners were, in fact, "full of business; they read, they study, they plan. They put business into politics, where we of the South put sentiment. We must change. We must have some business ideas. Our people must read and get posted." The *Farmer* continued the advice, four years later urging farmers to visit "some prosperous manufacturing establishment" to learn techniques of regularity and efficiency.

Like most Southerners, the Populists uncritically accepted certain other accoutrements of the New South order which were often alien to their rural-centered life. The business college was one, and while the reformers frequently opposed them, even land development and town building schemes, close to the heart of the New South gospel of progress, could get support. Watson's paper in early March 1892 began carrying a full-page advertisement offering land for sale in Nantahala, a town planed for western North Carolina. Although he was careful to observe that such "town-booming" schemes could be risky, Watson also noted that "more fortunes have been made out of new built towns of late years than in any other way." Having found that the officers and stockholders were "substantial," "cautious," and "reliable" Georgia businessmen and that a demand existed for Nantahala's mineral and timber resources, Watson in an editorial praised it as "one of the very best investments now offered" and "a grand opportunity." Three years later he gave editorial support to a similar development in Atlanta, a "speculation" in town lots in Inman Park that would beat "even farm lands" for investment.

Nor was Watson alone in his advocacy. The county-city booster edition of the Dallas, Georgia, *Herald* could have been primed in any town or county weekly within the last ninety years. For the growth it promised, Populist editors in North Carolina and Texas urged their readers to fight for railroads through their counties and towns. The Ozark, Alabama, *Banner-Advertiser* mounted a two-year campaign of varying intensity, starting in early 1895, to get a cotton factory started in the town. W. S. Morgan constantly advertised benefits and desirability of Arkansas for farming and business. Progress, development, and town growth sometimes mattered as much to these Populist papers as they always did to their many Democratic, New South rivals.

But while they supported the New South goals of progress and prosperity—few Southerners would not have done so—and even some of that creed's techniques, the Southern Populists were never happy with the new society envisaged by the New South adherents. In the heart of the northern Alabama coalfields, location of one of the proudest examples of the New South, Birmingham, an Alabama Populist editor wondered whether the new era would blend with the old to prevent "the undesirable surroundings too often produced in a 'development' whose only object is the sordid desire for the accumulation of wealth." Even the *Progressive Farmer*, which generally responded more positively than other Populist papers to New South sentiments, knew the reality of the New South. "A few cities like Atlanta, Birmingham, Chattanooga and other smaller places have grown up quite rapidly, factories have multiplied with gratifying rapidity," wrote the editor in 1893, "but the great agricultural sections of the South have made no progress." A very few farmers had prospered, but most of them were worse off than in 1880. Until the farmers benefited the "New South" would remain "rather more vapor than anything else." The New South was an urban and industrial ideal, the ideology of a new southern small town and city merchant and professional class which led the opposition to the Alliance and later to Southern Populism.

The Southern Alliance and its Populist issue spoke, as much as any group in the late Nineteenth century, for the victims of the penetration of Northern industrial and finance capitalism into the South. The new southern middle class climbed to power on that penetration, and used the New South gospel of urban and industrial development to sell the new order and to justify their efforts toward political and social dominance. Despite some talk of making the farmer an efficiency expert, the Southern Populists knew that a victory for this class and its creed would come at their expense. They did not object to southern prosperity; they found advantage to the producers in the development of manufacturing and processing industries. But they wanted everyone to benefit, and had second thoughts about the effects of New South boosterism and development on the rural society to which they remained firmly attached. They wholeheartedly endorsed economic development for the South, objecting only to what now appear to be the necessary concomitants of that development. They never succeeded, however, in separating the one from the other. By accepting the same basic economic system which the New South advocates did, the Southern Populists chose to fight on territory not only far more familiar to their New South opponents, but also where they were outmanned and completely outgunned. The choice made, the reformers were bound to lose.

That they made this choice was evident whenever the Southern Populists discussed the kind of economic system America ought to have. Almost all of them accepted what they understood to be the basic American economic system—a simple market society with private property, profit, and economic competition among small producers. The Populists, wrote a Virginia Populist editor, were not "destroyers of private property" and did not desire "to uproot the existing order of things and start a brand new arrangement of our own." Populists elsewhere echoed his demurrer. At issue was not private ownership of wealth and property but their concentration in a few hands. A wider distribution of private property through equalization of opportunities would correct this basic injustice.

Since a chance to accumulate wealth remained important to their argument, most southern reformers, although they equivocated about it, could not spurn economic competition. The Populist party, stated Watson, "stands for the doctrine that the whole world's stock of wealth and opportunity belongs to all mankind—to be won or lost on the basis of merit and demerit." Accumulated wealth should not be permitted to protect itself from the risks of "competition" through legislation giving special privileges to the wealthy few. Other southern reformers agreed. Marion Butler, defending government ownership of the railroads, argued that the men who wrote the Constitution "took the position that any business that affected all or a great portion of the people, under circumstances where there could be no successful competition by men of small capital, was a *government function* and should be owned and operated by the government, at cost, for the benefit of all the people alike." He justified an apparent violation of America's economic system in terms of preserving one of its essential qualities. According to Judge Nugent, the Populists wanted a society where "strictly public or social functions shall be turned over to the government, and the private citizen left in undisturbed freedom to achieve

his own destiny in his own way by the exercise of his own individual skill and industry, and the legitimate investment of his own capital." The Southern Populists accepted competition between small, individual, relatively equal economic units and, within this context, the individual accumulation of wealth.

The southern reformers' attitude toward socialism provided a counterpoint to their adherence to a private enterprise market economy. When they spoke as producers or as landowners or aspiring landowners, most of them wanted no part of what they felt to be the socialists' commitment to ending private ownership of property and profits. This opposition was a good deal more vocal during the 1893 and 1896 debate between the right and left wings of the party, although so few reformers advocated socialism, before 1895 that there is little reason to suspect large numbers of Populists had suddenly deserted it. Certainly Watson had not. A committed though more articulate Lockean than most other Southern Populists, he maintained that the Populist party protected those who profited justly from their exertions and skills by supporting "the constitutional rights of the individual—individual liberty, individual enterprise, and individual property. She (the party) does not believe in Socialism, with all its collective ownership of land, homes, and pocketbooks." An Alabama Populist found communism "fascinating" but "impracticable" and "evidently unwise" because it was based on a yet unreachable "individual perfection." Without the incentive provided by profit and private ownership, people, no longer driven by their material self-interest, would stop working, production would cease, and society would collapse.

A just and equitable society did not require eliminating the existing economic order. While the unequal distribution of wealth was the "menacing evil of the times," the way to distribute it more evenly, argued Judge Nugent, was not to grant every person an equal share, but to give everybody "fair opportunities for the exertion of their faculties." The creation of a "community" with "no material waste, no check in production" and a general sharing among the producers of the wealth they created required only the destruction of "monopoly in these things which productive labor must have for practical use. Protect these things from the speculative greed of men, disembarrass trade of arbitrary legal interference, give free play to competition within the proper sphere of individual effort and investment, and steadily oppose those extreme socialistic schemes which ask by the outside pressure of mere enactments or systems to accomplish what can only come from the free activities of men—do these things and you will have achieved the real genuine and lasting reforms which labor and capital equally need, and which, in fact, are the only practicable reforms lying within range of party action." Socialism could not accomplish what control and reform of the existing economic system would. With the assurance of profits and private ownership and some governmental control, "individual effort and investment" would assure ceaseless production and a fair distribution to all who worked.

When not talking about practical political and economic problems, however, the Southern Populists, antimonopoly greenbackers and financial reformers alike, often had positive things to say about socialism. Many agreed with the Alabama editor who thought socialism too ideal to be a workable way of organizing society, with the qualification that "if the whole world should be converted to practical Christianity . . . thus rendering socialism possible, so much the better." Some even felt that there might be some good in the doctrine in the here and now. This was particularly true of the antimonopoly greenback Populists. One Texan maintained that although the People's party was not socialist, its platform did contain "a few of the underlying principles of socialism," a necessity for destroying "the infernal industrial monopolistic system which we have upon us." Such principles included demands for a national currency, an income tax, a postal savings bank, and government ownership of

the railroad, telephone, and telegraph systems. "There is socialism in all governments that are not purely despotic," stated the editors of the *Arkansaw Kicker*.

In fact, two Austin, Texas, Populist papers openly adopted socialism during the period— the *People's Advocate* and the *Argus*. Neither paper stopped backing Populist candidates. The editor of the *People's Advocate*, G. W. Mendell, in 1894 served as chairman of the Travis County (Austin) People's party executive committee. The call to socialism, the call to get rid of private property, proceeded from the same perceptions of the ills in existing society that other Populists held—millions unable to work, the growing chasm between the poor masses who produced the wealth and the wealthy few who consumed it, the same contrasts of poverty amid plenty, starvation alongside wealth. The *Argus*, discussing the Pullman strike and its lessons, shared with Watson, Marion Butler, Judge Nugent, and the rest of the Southern Populists the idea that government ownership would solve the railroad crisis. Unlike them, however, it extended the reasoning behind such a solution and came up with something a little different. If the government had owned and operated the coal mines, the railroads, the oil wells, the sugar refineries, and the banks, then coal millionaires, Pullman, Gould, Rockefeller, Havemeyer, a sugar Senate, and a financial panic would not have been possible. "The only remedy, the only means of abolishing wage-slavery, poverty, and the unendurable despotism of the money kings is the collective ownership of all the means of production and distribution." These papers, with a slight extension of Southern Populist ideas, became socialist, albeit very moderate. Both papers, however, continued to advocate the whole panoply of Populist reform, including the Omaha platform.

The ease with which it was ideologically possible to move to socialism meant that the Southern Populists often had to make a conscious decision to avoid it. In some cases political expediency helped draw the line. As Watson pointed out, "do you believe that the People's party in Georgia would have a corporal's guard left, if it were generally understood among Populists that the platform opposed individual ownership of homes and money?" There was, however, more to it, as Watson's statement itself hinted. Their desire for a better society could propel them in the opposite direction. "Every living man who has a spark of human sympathy in his chest is socialistic to some extent," wrote W. S. Morgan in the *National Reformer*. "Socialism, in its literal sense, means a better state of society, and as the world gets better it 'drifts' nearer to socialism." Their experience with poverty and exploitation, combined with a sense of human sympathy reinforced by their religious background and tradition, tended to push the Southern Populists toward some sort of socialism as the only decent and humane alternative to the society they found around them. But their political heritage and their class position as landowners or aspiring landowners suggested both the decency and possibility of a market society of independent producers. The latter influence, reinforced by political considerations of the kind Watson stated so bluntly, prevented them from moving into socialism, a move which would seem to have been an easy one for them to make, given their adherence to government ownership of various large industries and a basic commitment to a society made more decent by a more equitable distribution of wealth. Some of the Southern Populists, though, particularly the antimonopoly greenback radicals, came close.

Anarchy, socialism's nineteenth-century radical American counterpart, had no appeal at all, although the reformers used the term quite as often, applying it most frequently to those whom they regarded as the most serious enemies of the social order, the anarchistic politicians, plutocrats, and corporations." Their condemnation of anarchy or anarchists concentrated on the order imposed on society by its laws. The Southern Populists, believing as they did in the importance of private prop-

erty, had no reason to regard with equanimity the social upheaval anarchy promised. The producing middle classes, wrote a North Carolina Populist in 1892, "are not enemies of law and order, they do not envy or hate those who have acquired property by honest methods." The reformers carefully supported strict adherence to the law, good or bad, until it was changed. Walter E. Grant, running for Congress on the Populist ticket in Virginia's third congressional district, told the voters that despite inequitable laws his party did "not blame anyone for using the law to accumulate a large fortune;" the Populists would, if necessary, "aid him in keeping whatever he has lawfully acquired."

Because they associated the rule of law with a stable, orderly society, the Southern Populists often expressed concern over the violence of labor strikes. Few of them, however, censured strikes quite as completely as did the North Carolina Populists, who announced in their 1894 platform: "We sympathize with the oppressed everywhere, but we are opposed to all lawless combinations of men, whether representing capital or labor. We believe in peace and strict obedience to law." The platform urged that, instead, labor use the ballot to defeat monopoly peacefully. The political orientation of the Knights of Labor and its minimal strike activity in the state during the late 1880s and early 1890s, the financial reform stance of most of the state Populist leadership, and fusion with the Republicans had much to do with the attitude of the North Carolina party. In Texas, Alabama, and Georgia, Populists more often directed their antistrike hostility at the owners and the capitalists.

On the other hand, most Southern Populists advised laboringmen to vote right instead of striking. This was not the case usually only where the Populists had some contact with working people and strikes. In Alabama, in the Birmingham area, Populists worked in 1894 to keep the miners' strike going at least through the fall elections. In Texas the massive 1886 railroad strike played a role in energizing the

Alliance radicalism which led to the Omaha platform and the Populist party. Connections like these made the attitudes of some Southern Populists toward working people more complex.

In general, however, most Southern Populists regarded strikes and labor violence with concern. Part of the reason was their lack of contact with industrial labor and the absence of a thorough education in working class problems such as the mass of Texas Alliancemen received in 1886. They also differed with working people on how best to win the goals labor wanted. "Quicker than dynamite, more effective and more lasting than revolution, more far-reaching in its sweep than strikes, and more terrible to plutocracy than all is the ballot," argued the socialist editor of the Austin *Argus*. This advice had a strong element of practicality, for strikes often seemed to work badly for the strikers. Nevertheless, the Southern Populists, even those who had a better understanding than most of their brethren of the working people's lot, often failed to appreciate either the desperation of strikers like those at Pullman or the tactical pressures which labor union leaders like Debs faced when a strike broke out. In neither case did the participants have much choice. Certainly the option of ballot or strike was not available in the spring of 1894 to workers living in Pullman, Illinois.

Both of these commitments—to America's basic economic order and to a stable, orderly society—also revealed a side of Southern Populism about which we have not spoken. Their conception of themselves as the middle class was not rooted exclusively in their Jeffersonian-Jacksonian heritage. The economic revolution after the Civil War created, even in the South of the 1890s, a new kind of middle class. Ragged Dick and Andrew Carnegie often replaced the yeoman farmer and Daniel Boone as cultural heroes. Independence shaded into cleverness in the search for the main chance; simple abundance became the security of success, hard work acquired over-

tones of diligence and tenacity in search of profits; and a business education became more important than a farm upbringing for social mobility. This new urban middle class, a white-collar, professional, clerical, storekeeper, management middle class, had its own ethos of success and failure which the Southern Populists did not escape any more completely than they did other parts of the middle class' New South creed. While they questioned the actual existence of equal opportunity for success, the reformers shared with most other Americans a firm belief in the beneficial effect of such equal opportunity for all who would work. The concern for law and order, the careful opposition to socialist and anarchist, was more familiar in the late nineteenth century than in Jeffersonian or Jacksonian America. The yeoman farmer and artisan worried about threats to private property from anarchist and labor violence far less than did the new middle class, or the Southern Populists. Jeffersonians and Jacksonians would not have given corporations, finance capitalism, and town-booming quite as clean a bill of health as the Southern Populists sometimes did, even though the latter's certificate always contained many more qualifications than those handed out by most of their contemporaries.

At times the religious metaphors and imagery used by the Southern Populists reflected a more recent middle-class concern for purity than did the Biblically based religious morality of a younger America. An Alabama Populist spoke of the need for "wholesome" reform legislation. A favorite crusade of this new middle class, the prohibition movement, occasionally touched the Southern Populist party around its edges, although demon rum never became an important party issue. Another North Carolina man identified himself as a "Bryan Populist" for three reasons, the first being that, like himself, Bryan was a good moral man, affiliated with the church, and did not smoke, chew, swear, or drink. The Southern Populists rarely denied the propriety of prohibition. Many obviously felt that temperance might be a good, if not important, ingredient in a better society.

The Southern Populists' concern with respectability also disclosed some affinity with the new middle classes. The complaint against the influence of riches in society, especially in regard to personal integrity and character, was rather widespread. "Honest labor," blessed by God, and not the accumulation of money, made men "truly great," wrote a Texas reformer. "Therefore, men should seek rather to be upright, honest and true rather than to be rich." The increasing importance of money in determining one's respectability furnished another excellent example of the evils of the growing maldistribution of wealth. But the concern with this change, although rare, also reflected the impact on the Southern Populists of the social code of new middle class society, where men were respectable as often as independent, pure-minded as often as rational, and as virtuous in the service of blue laws as in the preservation of republican government. The Populist did "not wish to be rich," maintained a North Carolina reformer, "but only want a reasonable chance that we may be able to go decent and respectable and educate our children. Surely no enemy could say anything against such doctrine as this." No one could; the wish was only for a decent life. A more even distribution of wealth and the opportunity to enjoy the fruits of their toil, however, promised not only a more productive, harmonious, and balanced society, but also an increased portion of a new town and city middle class respectability.

Finally, the Southern Populists also shared with other nineteenth-century Americans, including their new middle class, success-oriented contemporaries, a belief in the social and personal value of industry and frugality. "Nothing in this life can be gained without hard work. . . . If you are industrious, your work, even though hard, will be a pleasure." But the Southern Populists, having experienced for a generation the seemingly inexorable advance of rural poverty, knew that the exist-

ing organization of society failed to reward properly hard work and frugality. A Georgia Populist speaker in 1892 pointed out that in the last twenty-five years Georgia farmers had grown millions of dollars worth of cotton, yet remained poor. The farmers were "intelligent, economical and industrious," but under the existing system these qualities went unrewarded. Since the seventeenth century hard work and saving had been supposed to guarantee at least a fair share of wealth to those who practiced them diligently. When the Southern Populists found this ideal at odds with reality, however, rather than question their own personal worth, as the success ethic and their middle class contemporaries told them to do, they questioned the organization of society and found it unbalanced and unjust, favoring not those who worked but those who were clever enough to get more than they needed without working.

The Southern Populists found themselves in a difficult situation in the 1890s. They and those around them were sliding quickly into a poverty and dependence from which it became more and more difficult to escape. At the same time certain aspects of the new world encroaching upon their lives—machinery, railroads, economic development, and new markets—seemed beneficial, apparently representing possible gains for them and their neighbors. In response to the unfavorable elements of this new American industrial society, the Southern Populists tried to elaborate a social order which would preserve what they wanted to keep and get rid of what they did not. In doing so they drew on the material available to them—their rural Southern experience, their evangelical Protestant heritage, and their Jeffersonian–Jacksonian tradition. Of course, these elements supplied the basis for their critique of the new world they faced as well as their response to it.

Sometimes the Southern Populists' and heritage distorted their perceptions of capitalist America, particularly when, as in the case of manufacturers or the new industrial labor, these two things gave them no way develop an accurate analysis of this new society. On the other hand, in some cases their class position or contemporary experience overrode the dictates of their heritage, as occurred in their response to the New South gospel or in their affinity for a socialist ideal of society. In the areas of conflict between their heritage and their experience lay the sources of change in the Southern Populists' response to American industrial and financial capitalism.

GLOSSARY

Farmers' Alliance: Organization of farmers created in 1880. By 1882, it counted 100,000 members in eight state alliances and 200 local alliances. The Alliance was the forerunner of the Populist Party.

People's Party: An alternative name for the Populist Party.

Panic of 1893:   Financial panic that led to one of the nation's worst economic depressions, 1893–1897.

IMPLICATIONS

In this essay, Palmer notes that while the Populists criticized the drift of modern capitalist society, they did not propose eliminating the marketplace or commercial transactions. What do you think was the true aim of the Populists? To restore the rural past? To limit the impact of industrial society? Or to reform American society?

Past Traces

Immigration has always been a difficult process. Leaving family, friends, and familiar places is, at best, a disorienting experience. The disruption of travel, followed by the arduous process of adjustment to new people, places, and ways of life, only adds to the psychological and emotional stress of relocation. Given the rigors of immigration, it is no wonder that many immigrants have thought of relocation as the defining experience of their lives. In this reminiscence, Rose Gollop Cohen, a young Jewish immigrant to New York City, reveals both the bewilderment and the quick process of readjustment that characterized the lives of European immigrants at the close of the nineteenth century.

Rose Gollop Cohen, *A Young Immigrant in New York City (1918)*

One day, it was the first of July, Aunt Masha and I stood in Castle Garden. With fluttering hearts yet patiently we stood scanning the faces of a group of Americans divided from us by iron gates.

"My father could never be among those wonderfully dressed people," I thought. Suddenly it seemed to me as if I must shout. I caught sight of a familiar smile.

"Aunt Masha, do you see that man in the light tan suit? The one who is smiling and waving his hand?"

"Why, you little goose," she cried, "don't you see? It's father!" She gave a laugh and a sob, and hid her face in her hands.

A little while later the three of us stood clinging to one another. . . .

From Castle Garden we drove to our new home in a market wagon filled with immigrants' bedding. Father tucked us in among the bundles, climbed up beside the driver himself and we rattled off over the cobbled stone pavement, with the noon sun beating down on our heads.

As we drove along I looked about in bewilderment. My thoughts were chasing each other. I felt a thrill: "Am I really in America at last?" But the next moment it would be checked and I felt a little disappointed, a little homesick. Father was so changed. I hardly expected to find him in his black long tailed coat in which he left home. But of course yet with his same full grown beard and earlocks. Now instead I saw a young man with a closely cut beard and no sign of earlocks. As I looked at him I could scarcely believe my eyes. Father had been the most pious Jew in our neighbourhood. I wondered was it true then as Mindle said that "in America one at once became a libertine"?

Father's face was radiantly happy. Every now and then he would look over his shoulder and smile. But he soon guessed what troubled me for after a while he began to talk in a quiet, reassuring manner. He told me he would take me to his own shop and teach me part of his own trade. He was a men's coat finisher. He made me understand that if we worked steadily and lived economically we should soon have money to send for those at home. "Next year at this time," he smiled, "you yourself may be on the way to Castle Garden to fetch mother and the children." So I too smiled at the happy prospect, wiped some tears away and resolved to work hard.

From Mrs. Felesberg we learned at once the more serious side of life in America. Mrs. Felesberg was the woman with whom we were rooming. A door from our room opened into her tiny bedroom and then led into the only other room where she sat a great part of the day finishing pants which she brought in big bundles from a shop, and rocking the cradle with one foot. She always made us draw our chairs quite close to her and she spoke in a whisper scarcely ever lifting her weak peering eyes from her work. When she asked us how we liked America, and we spoke of it with praise, she smiled a queer smile. "Life here is not all that it appears to the 'green horn,'" she said. She told us that her husband was a presser on coats and earned twelve dollars when he worked a full week. Aunt Masha thought twelve dollars a good deal. Again Mrs. Felesberg smiled. "No doubt it would be," she said, "where you used to live. You had your own house, and most of the food came from the garden. Here you will have to pay for everything; the rent!" she sighed, "for the light, for every potato, every grain of barley. You see these three rooms, includ-ing yours? Would they be too much for my family of five?" We had to admit they would not. "And even from these," she said, "I have to rent one out."

Perhaps it was due to these talks that I soon noticed how late my father worked. When he went away in the morning it was still dark, and when he came home at night the lights in the halls were out. It was after ten o'clock. I thought that if mother and the children were here they would scarcely see him.

One night when he came home and as he sat at the table eating his rice soup, which he and Aunt Masha had taught me to cook, I sat down on the cot and asked timidly, knowing that he was impatient of questions, "Father, does everybody in America live like this? Go to work early, come home late, eat and go to sleep? And the next day again work, eat, and sleep? Will I have to do that too? Always?"

Father looked thoughtful and ate two or three mouthfuls before he answered. "No," he said smiling. "You will get married."

So, almost a week passed and though life was so interesting, still no matter where I went, what I saw, mother and home were always present in my mind. Often in the happiest moments a pain would rise in my throat and my eyes burned with the tears held back. At these moments I would manage to be near Aunt Masha so that I could lean against her, touch her dress. . . .

On the following day father came home at noon and took me along to the shop where he worked. We climbed the dark, narrow stairs of a tenement house on Monroe Street and came into a bright room filled with noise. I saw about five or six men and a girl. The men turned and looked at us when we passed. I felt scared and stumbled. One man asked in surprise:

"Avrom, is this your daughter? Why, she is only a little girl!"

My father smiled. "Yes," he said, "but wait till you see her sew."

He placed me on a high stool opposite the girl, laid a pile of pocket flaps on the little narrow table between us, and showed me how to baste.

All afternoon I sat on my high stool, a little away from the table, my knees crossed tailor fashion, basting flaps. As I worked I watched the things which I could see by just raising my eyes a little. I saw that the girl, who was called Atta, was very pretty.

A big man stood at a big table, examining, brushing and folding coats. There was a window over his table through which the sun came streaming in, showing millions of specks of dust dancing over the table and circling over his head. He often puffed out his cheeks and blew the dust from him with a great gust so that I could feel his breath at our table.

The machines going at full speed drowned everything in their noise. But when they stopped for a moment I caught the clink of a scissors laid hastily on a table, a short question and answer exchanged, and the pounding of a heavy iron from the back of the room. Sometimes the machines stopped for a whole minute. Then the men looked about and talked. I was always glad when the machines started off again. I felt safer in their noise.

Late in the afternoon a woman came into the shop. She sat down next to Atta and began to sew on buttons. Father, who sat next to me, whispered, "This is Mrs. Nelson, the wife of the big man, our boss. She is a real American."

She, too, was pretty. Her complexion was fair and delicate like a child's. Her upper lip was always covered with shining drops of perspiration. I could not help looking at it all the time.

When she had worked a few minutes she asked father in very imperfect Yiddish: "Well, Mr. ———, have you given your daughter an American name?"

"Not yet," father answered. "What would you call her? Her Yiddish name is Rahel."

"Rahel, Rahel," Mrs. Nelson repeated to herself, thoughtfully, winding the thread around a button; "let me see." The machines were going slowly and the men looked interested.

The presser called out from the back of the room: "What is there to think about? Rahel is Rachel."

I was surprised at the interest every one showed. Later I understood the reason. The slightest cause for interruption was welcome, it broke the monotony of the long day.

Mrs. Nelson turned to me: "Don't let them call you Rachel. Every loafer who sees a Jewish girl shouts 'Rachel' after her. And on Cherry Street where you live there are many saloons and many loafers. How would you like Ruth for a name?"

I said I should like to be called Ruth. . . .

I liked my work and learned it easily, and father was pleased with me. As soon as I knew how to baste pocket-flaps he began to teach me how to baste the coat edges. This was hard work. The double ply of overcoat cloth stitched in with canvas and tape made a very stiff edge. My fingers often stiffened with pain as I rolled and basted the edges.

Sometimes a needle or two would break before I could do one coat. Then father would offer to finish the edge for me. But if he gave me my choice I never let him. At these moments I wanted so to master the thing myself that I felt my whole body trembling with the desire. And with my habit of personifying things, I used to bend over the coat on my lap, force the obstinate and squeaking needle, wet with perspiration, in and out of the cloth and whisper with determination: "No, you shall not get the best of me!" When I succeeded I was so happy that father, who often watched me with a smile, would say, "Rahel, your face is shining. Now rest a while." He always told me to rest after I did well. I loved these moments. I would push my stool closer to the wall near which I sat, lean my back against it, and look about the shop. . . .

4

First Encounters: Immigrant Women in the City

Elizabeth Ewen

Immigration has always been a difficult undertaking. Uprooting themselves from familiar surroundings and traveling to strange and unfamiliar places, once there confronted with people whose languages and customs were often shocking and unintelligible, immigrants have always faced daunting tasks in adjusting to life in their new world.

America has witnessed nearly four centuries of this immigrant story but none so poignantly as during the great tide of European migration at the turn of the twentieth century. Flocking to the United States to take their places in the nation's newly developed industries and offices, more than seven million southern and eastern Europeans passed through New York City's Ellis Island and other immigrant reception centers before the National Origins Act of 1924 slowed legal immigration to a trickle. Often rural with little formal education and limited urban experience, these men and women met America with a full range of emotions. Some marveled at the size and complexity of the nation's cities, others feared the fetid and unhealthy slums in which they lived. Many found in their newly adopted land commodities and amenities that were unthinkable in their former lives. Mostly, however, these immigrants worked to rebuild their everyday lives and to fashion a workable accommodation to American life.

In this essay, Elizabeth Ewen recounts the first encounters of turn-of-the-century European immigrants with life in New York City's Lower East Side. She shows that while some came with dreams of finding a utopia, most immigrants found a much grittier way of life. Most foreign-born New Yorkers, like immigrants before and since, attempted to maintain familiar aspects of their old lives by maintaining Old World languages, family structures, and collective cultures. It was often only the children of these immigrants—who attended public schools and grew up immersed in American culture—who truly made the transition from immigrant to acculturated American.

On a sizzling hot day in the summer of 1895 Maria Ganz and her mother walked off the boat onto a New York City pier. They had left their comfortable farmhouse in Galicia to join Lazarus Ganz, who had recently rented a rear tenement apartment in the Lower East Side. For weeks he had been busy preparing their new home; he was flushed with anticipation. Maria's mother walked into her new apartment, looked around slowly, turned to her husband and cried: "So, we have crossed half the world for this?" Maria recreated the scene in her memoirs:

> I can see her now as she stood facing my father, her eyes full of reproach. I am sure it had never occurred to poor, dreamy, impractical Lazarus Ganz that his wife might be disappointed with the new home he had provided for her. The look of pain as he saw the impression the place made on her filled me with pity for him, young as I was. A five-year-old child is not apt to carry many distinct memories from that age of life, but it is a scene I have never forgotten.

On an autumn day in 1896 Leonard Covello, his brothers, and their mother landed in New York, worlds away from their native Avigliano, Italy. They had spent twenty days aboard ship. When the sea became rough, Leonard's mother held her sons close to her heart; the ocean storms mirrored the fear and torment locked inside her body. As Leonard reported later:

> And when finally we saw the towering buildings and rode the screeching elevated train and saw the long, unending streets of the metropolis that could easily swallow a thousand Aviglianese towns, she accepted it with the mute resignation as *la volonta di Dio* [the will of God], while her heart longed for the familiar scenes and faces of loved ones and the security of a life she had forever left behind.

A story by novelist Anzia Yezierska captured a mother's lament: "*Oi Veh!* my mother cried in dismay, where is the sunshine in America? She went to her tenement window and looked at the blank wall of the next house. Like a grave so dark. To greenhorns it seemed as if the sunlight had faded from their lives and buildings like mountains took its place." In another mother's story, a question: "Where are the green fields and open spaces in America? A loneliness for the fragrant silence of the woods that lay beyond my mud hut welled up in my heart, a longing for the soft, responsive earth of our village streets. All about me was the harshness of brick and stone, the stinking smell of crowded poverty."

Leonard Covello voiced a similar despair:

> The sunlight and fresh air of our mountain home . . . were replaced by four walls and people over and under and on all sides of us. Silence and sunshine, things of the past, now replaced by a new urban montage. The cobbled streets. The endless monotonous rows of tenement buildings that shut out the sky. The traffic of wagons and carts and carriages, and the clopping of horses' hooves which struck sparks at night. . . . The clanging of bells and the screeching of sirens as a fire broke out somewhere in the neighborhood. Dank hallways. Long flights of wooden stairs and the toilet in the hall.

Nothing prepared people for the immediacy of this experience. America, as myth or image, may have been the Big Rock Candy Mountain, a utopian dream, a piece of heaven, but this heaven turned out to be a concrete prison, a vast wall of steel that blocked out the familiar world of nature, replacing the sunshine with the gray stare of stone and brick and changing silence into an omnipresent screeching tune. Even in Eastern European cities, the woods were a walk away—a place to gather food or sneak away, a space to hide from the pogroms or hold secret revolutionary meetings. New York abolished the forests forever, leaving them retrievable only in memory or in the pictorial reproductions that hung on the walls of tenement apartments as reminders of a world lost but not forgotten.

Not only were the woods lost, but city life seemed to transform the natural rhythms of life, turning night into day. This is how two Italian immigrants put it: "Our first impressions of the brightly lit streets of New York at night time suggested that such excessive illumination was for the prevention of the commission of theft. In Italy, there was no need for street lighting because when it was dark, every good person was supposed to be asleep." For women, the loss of nature also meant a loss of space. An Italian homeworker summed this up when she responded to a question posed by an American social worker in 1911. Did she like America?

> Not much, not much. In my country, people cook out-of-doors, do the wash out-of-doors, tailor out-of-doors, make macaroni out-of-doors. And my people laugh, laugh all the time. In America, it is *sopra, sopra* [up, up, with a gesture of going upstairs]. Many people, one house; work, work all the time. Good money, but no good air.

Anna Kuthan, an immigrant from Czechoslovakia, described her first year in New York in much the same way: "I didn't smile for a long time. Why? Because this was a different country. Everybody was for himself, and there was always money, money, money; rush, rush, rush."

How many first-generation mothers experienced their new environment, with its density of people, filthy crowded streets, and small apartments, as the negation of their previous poor but more natural life? How many times did they compare past and present as they paced the floors of their new homes, thinking, as Yezierska put it: "In America were rooms without sunshine, rooms to sleep in, to eat in, to cook in, but without sunshine." How many asked, "Could I be satisfied with just a place to sleep and a door to shut people out to take the place of sunshine?"

For many, the loss of sunshine was a metaphor that described feelings of alienation and unfamiliarity, an image of mourning for a world left behind, a plaintive moan of entry into the unknown. The abrupt separation from the immediate past was probably hardest on the older generation, whose lives had been shaped in other worlds and different cultures. This separation also spoke to a primary difference between themselves and their children. After all, as Leonard Covello noted, "a child adapts to everything. It was the older people who suffered, those uprooted human beings who faced the shores of an unknown land with quaking hearts."

In the cultures from which these women came, mothers existed within the confines of the home, but that home was the "center of the world, at the heart of the real." For women with small children, pulling up the foundations of a known life was a severe shock, a shock that penetrated to the core of experience and the ways in which experience becomes codified as culture. The loss of the natural, as perceived by the first generation, also meant the loss of familiar social rituals that had given life meaning and value.

As the concrete walls of the tenement apartment closed in, announcing the new environment, the home itself changed irrevocably. It no longer looked out to nature but to thousands of other crowded rooms that opened to the urban street, to dirty hallways, to endless clotheslines, to fear and isolation. Some women never recovered. Jane Addams recorded the following incident one of her first encounters with an immigrant woman:

> We were also early impressed with the curious isolation of many of the immigrants: an Italian woman once expressed her pleasure in the red roses that she saw at one of our receptions, in surprise that they had been "brought so fresh all the way from Italy." She would not believe for an instant that they had grown in America. She said that she had lived in Chicago for six years and had never seen any roses, whereas in Italy she had seen them in great profusion. During all that time, of course, the woman had lived within ten blocks of a florist's window; she had not been more than a five-cent ride away from a public park; but she had never dreamed of faring farther forth for herself and no one had taken her. Her conception of America had been the untidy street in which she lived and had made her long struggle to adapt herself to American ways.

The street, however, held a promise. In the spaces of American life carved out for immigrants the only "roses" were other people, family, relatives, friends. Italian and Jewish settlement patterns on the Lower East Side reflected the absolute necessity for family and ethnic cohesion. Italians settled between Pearl and Houston streets, east of the Bowery, while Jewish immigrants inhabited the Tenth Ward, west of the Bowery. Italians moved into the old Irish sections of the Lower East Side; Jews inherited the old German sector. The new immigrants lived and worked huddled together in tenement houses within easy reach of the garment district, surrounded by peddler stands and shops where language was not a barrier. If all America allowed its immigrants was a few city blocks, the blocks themselves were transformed to meet the needs of their inhabitants.

Caught in the margins between old and new, the neighborhoods were simultaneously an enclave of old-world custom and new-world adaptation, a curious admixture of tradition and change. For the first generation, a great deal of comfort was derived from this partial reconstruction of the old country: they nestled in communities of common language, bound by ties of custom, ritual, and institutions—a world not lost, but rebuilt.

For some old-world children, finding "America" was difficult. Rose Cohen, in her autobiography *Out of the Shadow*, described how it took her almost five years to find the New World:

> For though I was in America, I had lived in practically the same environment which we brought from home. Of course, there was a difference in our joys, in our sorrows, in our hardships, for after all this was a different country; but on the whole we were still in our village in Russia. A child that came to this country and began to go to school had taken the first step into the New World. But the child that was put into the shop remained in the old environment with the old people, held back by the old traditions.

Yet even in old-world neighborhoods there were signs of change, glimpses into the elusive promise of American life. Greenhorns who shopped in the market streets saw bananas for the first time, in addition to new kinds of mops, pots, and kitchenware. Advertisements showed new products: canned food, soap, toothpaste, modern sewing machines, furniture, and clocks of all varieties. For the fact was that industrial urban America was busy transforming material life, substituting machine-made products for those once produced by hand. While Maria Ganz's mother was reproaching her husband with a broken dream, Simon Patten, an American economist, was developing a theory to explain the effects of industrialization on immigrant women. In the Old World, he argued, women had primarily been "mothers and the makers of commodities." In the New, the relationship between women and production changes: here factory-made goods aroused and reinforced the economic motive, and this, Patten believed, would bring about a fundamental change. The immigrant working class would now, through wage labor, "spend its current wealth on commodities as formerly it spent the current wealth of womanhood." Thus, the loss of nature and of home production was a gain for women: for Patten, the progressive apostle of consumption, progress was measured by the access to new modes of life made possible by industry and commerce. It touched women's lives in two decisive ways: industry called women out of the home into the factory, and new factory-made goods transformed the home itself. If the Lower East Side appeared to its inhabitants as the underside of progress, to Patten this was mere appearance; under the surface were social forces that would alter women's lives as they moved from a patriarchal past to a progressive future.

Lazarus Ganz was upset by his wife's reaction to her new home. One day he came home with a sewing machine, a present to his wife that he had bought on the installment plan. According to his daughter:

> The machine he presented to my mother in the hope of making her more contented, for she had never been able to reconcile herself to the American tenement and had spent much time lamenting the more cheerful and comfortable home she had left behind in Galicia. It was a marvelous machine . . . I had never seen my mother so happy and enthusiastic.

Lazarus Ganz had hesitated for a long time, deciding between a sewing machine and a bronze clock for the mantelpiece: in his neighborhood, recently arrived immigrants purchased either one or the other as a sign of their Americanization. Each in its own way was an intervention into the rhythm of daily life. It took, however, eighteen years to pay for the sewing machine, raising questions as to whether Patten's belief in the power of economic arousal was not a condemnation to economic bondage as well.

Leonard Covello's father had preceded his family to America and had spent six years "trying to save enough for a little place to live and money for *l'umburco* [the voyage over]." During those six years he boarded with the Accurso family. As was customary, "it was Carmella, wife of his friend, Vito, who saved his money for him until the needed amounts accu-

mulated. It was Carmella Accurso who made ready the tenement flat and arranged the welcoming party." And when Leonard Covello's mother was upset when she arrived, and cried her way through the party, "it was Mrs. Accurso who put her arm comfortably upon my mother's shoulders and led her away from the party and into the hall and showed her the water faucet. 'Courage! You'll get used to it here. See. Isn't it wonderful how the water comes out.' Through her tears my mother managed to smile." In southern Italy, carrying water was one of the worst domestic chores. Mrs. Accurso offered running water as a miraculous compensation for Mrs. Covello's felt loss. For the first time since her arrival, Mrs. Covello was pleased: "Water, which to my mother was one of the great wonders of America—water with just a twist of the handle and only a few paces from the kitchen. It took her a long time to get used to this luxury. Water and a few other conveniences were the compensation the New World had to offer."

In another variation of this experience, Anna Kuthan recounted her understanding of new possibilities. During World War I she had worked as a domestic servant in the home of a wealthy woman in Vienna where one of her responsibilities had been to pick up the Red Cross packages sent from America. She was impressed with the packaging of Hecker's flour, Nestlé's cocoa, and Carnation evaporated milk: "I saved all the labels, even from the Hecker's flour. I says, oh my God, they must have everything so good if they pack everything so good. If I could only come to this country." Although she was allowed to save the labels, she was not allowed to taste any of the products:

> The lady locked everything up. I wanted to get a taste of the sweet condensed milk. One day she forgot to lock it up. She went into the bathroom. You know what I did? I just put the can in my mouth and it was dripping the milk like honey right in my mouth. And one, two, three, she opened the door. I says it's inside already, you can't get it out of me. I got a taste for it. I never forgot it.

When Anna Kuthan came to the United States right after the war, this experience of denial and theft was constantly in her mind:

> When I came to this country, the first thing I see is those big stores, I said there is the Hecker's flour . . . there is the condensed milk! When I was married . . . one day I was shopping and I came home crying; he says what happened to you. All the things I bought in the stores, what I got in Vienna and I could only dream about, not even taste it. And here I see it on the shelf. I bought everything and I'm gonna go there every day and I'm gonna buy it.

As a domestic servant in Vienna, Anna Kuthan saw the consumer products of American society as magical objects, the fruits of the land sealed mysteriously in shiny vessels, with beautiful painted scenes gracing their outsides. Yet what was magic for her had become for others—those of the Viennese upper classes—part of everyday life. Already, among the elites of Europe, American exports were beginning to make their mark on daily existence. "Luxury" came in cans. For Anna Kuthan, these cans thus took on great significance as concrete embodiments of her own deprivation, and stealing a taste was part of her attempt to break through a world of denial and assert her own needs. Anna Kuthan's self—before she ever set foot in America—intertwined with the brand names and products of a young and burgeoning consumer economy.

In the United States being able to buy Hecker's flour and Carnation evaporated milk symbolized Anna Kuthan's new social position: a "free consumer" in the universal marketplace, where money could free one from the class-bound world of European society. The ability to buy goods in the American marketplace was not simply an act of consumption; it was also an act of transcendence, the realization of a new social status.

If immigrant mothers were consumed by the realities of home life, some of their daughters were quick to notice the new world that swirled around their tenement apartments. The Lower East Side presented an audiovisual montage of possibilities: women dressed in ready-made American clothes, women running to work, billboards and posters graced with women in the latest styles, women carrying schoolbooks under their arms, women in the streets and in restaurants, women speaking openly to men on the street. While the mothers attempted to reassemble the terms of a known life, their daughters were busy decoding the messages, disassembling the old life, stepping into the present.

And the contrast between the greenhorns and the Americans was ever present. As social worker Josephine Roche put it:

> Inevitably, the influence of the new life in which she spends nine hours a day begins to tell on her. Each morning and evening as she covers her head with an old crocheted shawl and walks to and from the factory, she passes the daughters of her Irish and American neighbors in their smart hats, their cheap waists in the latest and smartest style, their tinsel ornaments and their gay hair bows. A part of the pay envelopes goes into the personal expenses of those girls. Nor do they hurry through the streets to their homes after working hours, but linger with a boy companion "making dates" for a movie or an affair.

Through observation and contact, through friends and relatives, immigrant daughters learned the vital importance of shedding their pasts. To be a greenhorn was to inhabit a region on the margins of modern life; to overcome being green was a metamorphosis. Gino Speranza wrote with patriarchal dismay in *Charities* magazine:

> Industrially it is the Italian woman that has suffered most. The Italian daughters or sisters, who in Italy used to work around the house or in the fields, never receiving compensation, sees the "girl on the lower floor" [Irish or American working girl] go out every day and earn good money that gives her, what appears to the newcomer, not only splendid independence, but even the undreamed of joy of wearing Grand Street millinery. The home becomes hateful.

Millinery in Italy was reserved, by custom and class, for the upper classes; the peasants wore shawls on their heads. Yet here Italians saw women of their own class donning hats as an everyday occurrence, an incitement to transgression and transformation.

David Blaustein, writing of the experience of Jews in America, echoed similar sentiments: "The woman finds women in public life. She finds it cheaper to eat in restaurants and to buy ready-made clothing."

Immigrant mothers brought large quantities of clothing with them, "representing sometimes their accumulations for a dowry—heavy linen underwear, thick, heavily lined waists, clumsy shoes and wide, bright skirts. A colored scarf or shawl completes the wardrobe." These costumes were discarded in the United States: "Only some of the older women have the courage to appear at their factories in the garments they brought. The first year in this country frequently means much skimping and saving to get new clothes, especially among the younger women who want to look American."

One of the first acts of initiation was to purchase new clothes. Sophie Abrams, a Jewish garment worker, recreated this experience:

> I was such a greenhorn, you wouldn't believe. My first day in America I went with my aunt to buy some American clothes. She bought me a shirtwaist, you know, a blouse and a skirt, a blue print with red buttons and a hat, such a hat I had never seen. I took my old brown dress and shawl and threw them away! I know it sounds foolish, we being so poor, but I didn't care. I had enough of the old country. When I looked in the mirror, I couldn't get over it. I said, boy, Sophie, look at you now. Just like an American.

In another variation, one young immigrant woman who came to the United States in 1911 had been taken by her relatives for new clothes. She also bought "the wherewithal to fix her hair in an American fashion. When asked why, she responded quite proudly: 'Yes, I'm almost an American. I have a rat for my hair. The essential thing in America is to look stylish.'"

If immigrant and American mothers grew up in an era of home production, where clothing was made to last, their daughters, caught up in the whirl of ready-made clothing, valued it for its symbolic power—style above durability or comfort. Sophinisba Breckenridge, in *New Homes for Old*, captured this change:

> In her [daughter's] main contention that if she is to keep up with the fashions she need not buy clothing that will last more than one season, she is probably right. It is also natural that this method of buying should be distressing to her mother, who has been accustomed to clothes of unchanging fashions which were judged entirely by their quality.

Style was not only alluring; it was also necessary for employment. One woman from Russia explained that in the old country, "the dresses we wore were made out of sack, old sheets or table cloths that did not need much style. It was not a question of style, but of how to cover one's body in those days." What she desired most in Russia was "the leather jacket that came with the Revolution"; the jacket to her was a "symbol of both Revolution and elegance." As soon as she got here she bought a leather jacket, but it brought her a lot of trouble. When she tried to get a job, the door was slammed in her face or she was asked if she belonged to a union. Finally, one employer made clear his understanding of her jacket: "I am sorry, miss, we don't like Bolsheviks." She asked why he thought she was one. He replied: "Never mind. I can see it at once. These leather jackets and bushy hair. I know them well." For a year she endured but, finally, faced with starvation, she decided to get rid of the jacket. "I dressed myself in the latest fashion with lipstick in addition, although it was so hard to get used to at first that I blushed, felt foolish and thought myself vulgar. But I got a job."

Some middle-class moralists were upset at the displays of finery; in their minds, the poor should *look* poor. Home economist Ellen Richardson was shocked to discover that tenement girls were not dressed in rags:

> Did you ever go down to one of the city settlements full of the desire to help and lift up the

poor shop girl? There must be some mistake, you thought. These could not be poor girls earning five or six dollars a week. They looked better dressed than you did. Plumes on their heads, a rustle of silk petticoats, everything about them in the latest style.

Jane Addams had a more realistic approach to the issues involved: "The working girl, whose family lives in a tenement . . . , who has little social standing, knows full well how much habit and style of dress has to do with her position. . . . Her clothes are her background and from them she is largely judged."

The daily press was fond of using the stylish look of working women as a weapon against their claims of poverty. In 1914 Lillian Wald, angered by one such editorial, decided to get to the bottom of the matter. She went to a young acquaintance "whose appearance justified the newspaper description" and discovered that she lived on $5 a week. She kept up her appearance by purchasing

> stockings from pushcart venders, seconds of off-colors but good quality for ten cents; boys' blouses, as they were better and cheaper. These cost twenty-five cents. Hats (peanut straw) cost ten cents. Having very small feet, she was able to take advantage of special sales, when she could buy a good pair of shoes for fifty cents.

Yet even with all this careful planning "there was practically nothing left for carfare, for pleasures, or the many demands made upon the meager purse but she looked good."

Some women made their own clothes. One newspaperman, for instance, reported an encounter with an East Side girl who showed up for their appointment all dressed up. He was taken aback: "One who did not know East Side girls would have said uncharitably that the heartless young woman was spending on clothes the money needed to buy bread for her old mother and small sisters." But then the truth came out:

> The waist, thin and charmingly cool-looking, she had made herself, buying the material from a Hester Street pushcart for twenty cents. Its style

came from the really handsome neck arrangement . . . she worked at neckware and the boss allowed her to take the odds and ends from which she fashioned the pretty thing. The skirt, her brother-in-law who works in skirts, made at odd times. Her hats, her chum made. To the uninitiated, the costume represented an outlay of twenty dollars at least, although she had achieved it at an expense of $3.30, and was able to go out without proclaiming to the world the dire poverty of her home.

Most bought their clothes, however, although they could do that on an installment plan:

> To solve the clothing problem many of these women have to steer between the dangers of Scylla and Charybdis. If they buy only what they can pay for it with ready money, without going into debt, they must get the cheapest qualities which give poor wear. Of course on the other hand, they appreciate the economy of buying a better grade of goods, they must pay the high prices of the installment plan and incur debt to be paid out of future wages.

For greenhorns, the change in dress and hair was an essential part of adaptation. Yet these acts concealed a secret. As Leonard Covello put it: "To all outward appearances I was an American, except that I didn't speak a word of English."

It was a good idea to shop with relatives, since it was a common practice for shopkeepers to take advantage of newcomers unskilled in the practices of the marketplace. Anna Kuthan, for example, described her first attempt to buy new clothes:

> My first expense when I came to this country was paying back money I owed from my trip. Then I decided I had to dress myself a little bit decent. All the stores had signs showing what language was spoken inside. I went into a Czech clothing store and I didn't have experience [bargaining]. I paid whatever was asked. The store owner said: "I have a coat for you, you're going to look like a million dollars." I paid forty dollars for this coat, but I found out the next day it was worth less than eighteen dollars.

The America contained in the Lower East Side did not just define new possibilities in terms of goods and products. It also presented to new immigrants new forms of pleasure and recreation. Greenhorns were often taken out to new forms of entertainment: the nickelodeon, the soda shop, and the candy store.

A common form of introduction, reported by *Survey* magazine, was to be "taken to the nickel show." There the newly arrived Jewish woman hears Yiddish jokes and American popular music and "marvels at the wonders of the motion picture." After being shown this magical new medium, she is taken to an ice cream parlor where she has her first ice cream soda. Magic for the eyes, sweets for the taste, a little piece of unheard-of luxury in the new world of concrete and steel.

Movies, soda shops, and candy stores were luxuries either unavailable or unknown in the older European world. In terms reminiscent of Anna Kuthan, Leonard Covello described his family's ecstatic encounter with an American candy store:

> There was a counter covered with glass and all manner and kinds of sweets such as we had never seen. Candy, my father told us, grinning. This is what we call candy in America. We were even allowed to select the kind we wanted. I selected some little round cream-filled chocolates which tasted like nothing I had ever eaten before. The only candy I knew was confetti, which we had on feast days or from the pocket of my uncle, the priest, on some special occasion.

While certain changes spoke to new possibilities, others widened the gulf between parents and children. The children, more plastic than their parents, often formed the advance guard: they were the first to learn English, the first to demand changes in those old-world cultural practices thought dishonorable by the older generation, the first to incorporate forms of American culture into their daily lives. A Jewish woman whose daughter had come to the United States before her wrote to the *Jewish Daily Forward* in dismay:

> During the few years she was here without us she became a regular Yankee and forgot how to talk Yiddish. . . . She says it is not nice to talk Yiddish and that I am a greenhorn. . . . She wants to make a Christian woman out of me. She does not like me to light the Sabbath candles, to observe the Sabbath. When I light the candles, she blows them out. Once I saw her standing on the stoop with a boy so I went up to her and asked her when she would come up. . . . She did not reply, and later when she came up she screamed at me because I had called her by her Jewish name. But I cannot call her differently. I cannot call her by her new name.

The changing of names was thought of as demeaning by the older generation, robbing the family of its history and honor. Leonard Covello's name had been changed in school from Coviello to Covello—the teacher thought it was easier to pronounce. His parents found this out when he brought home his report card. His father exploded: "In America anything can happen and does happen. But you don't change a family name." Leonard tried to explain. His mother intervened, defining the difference between external and basic change: "A person's life and honor is in his name. *A name is not a shirt or a piece of underwear.* . . . Now that you have become Americanized you understand everything and I understand nothing." The child, upset, fled the house feeling that "somehow or other the joy of childhood had seeped out of his life." An older female friend of the family who had witnessed the scene came up to him, and when he protested that they did not understand, replied: "Maybe some day you will realize that you are the one who doesn't understand."

Immersion in the public schools, in the language and manners of urban America, sometimes made the children carriers of culture and information. Whether by necessity or desire, the children broke through the barriers of language and custom, yet this changed the traditional conventions of the parent/child relationship.

For example, Lawrence Veiller, the noted tenement-house reformer, was working on a project to disseminate tuberculosis information to Italian immigrants. He conceived of a leaflet that combined a picture of an Italian pastoral scene on the top and rules about prevention on the bottom. He first thought to print the rules in Italian, but decided to consult the respected Italian doctor Antonio Stella. Dr. Stella advised him that "the majority of adult Italians do not read any language, either Italian or English. On the other hand, most of the children read English, but few read Italian. If you want your plan to be successful, print your poster in English. The children will then read it and translate it for their parents." Since the majority of immigrant parents did not have enough interaction with American institutions to require knowledge of the English language, the child often "stood between the new life and its strange institutions, he is the interpreter . . . he becomes the authority."

Despite the attractions of the new world of consumerism, many recognized its other side. Israel Friedlander, writing in *Survey* magazine, remarked that the immigrant Jew

> quickly notices those negative features which live on the surface of American life: the hunt after the dollar, the drift towards materialism, and he is forced to the dangerous and cynical conclusion that America—and here I repeat what one may frequently hear from the lips of Jewish immigrants—is the land of bluff, that religion, morality, politics and learning are a sham and the only thing of value in this country is almighty Mammon.

Whatever way one looked at the promise of America, it started and ended with money.

Underneath the consumer marketplace, the myth of money, and the image of the good life was a reality that was not completely different from the experience of life back home. Anna Kuthan spoke to the contradiction between image and reality. When she was seven years old, she had worked in a textile factory in Czechoslovakia. Her job was to unload bales of cotton sent to the factory from Texas. She remembered those cotton bales vividly, for they formed her first impression of America:

> Those big plantations they have big beautiful picture [on the bales] from their factories and the plantation and the colored people, you know how they work, and we [the children] always got it off nicely and we decorate everything. Oh my God, we save every picture and I was always saying I wish I could get to this country. I was dreaming already about this country. It's something you can't even picture until I came to this country and worked with the colored people and hear about and read about the history about the slaves and everything. Then I realize that, oh my God, how they have to work on the big plantation in the cotton fields, all those black people and the children almost for nothing . . . you know, like slaves, So you see, this is all real history, no matter where you live, no matter where you come from.

GLOSSARY

Bolsheviks: A member of the Russian Social Democratic Workers' Party that seized power in that country in November 1917.

Yiddish: The language of Ashkenazic Jews who immigrated from Central and Eastern Europe. Yiddish was a fusion of medieval German dialects, Hebrew and Aramaic, various Slavic languages, and Old French and Old Italian.

Mammon: Material wealth regarded as having an evil influence. In the New Testament, Mammon was a false god of riches, avarice, and worldly gain.

IMPLICATIONS

Immigrant experiences in America have often centered around a clash between the ideal images of American life that prompted immigration and the harsher and less idealistic realities encountered in the United States. Some, like the Jewish writer Israel Friedlander, quoted in this article, have even concluded that the sole value to be found in America was the making of money. What aspects of the immigrant experience do you think might account for Friedlander's conclusion?

The final decades of the nineteenth century saw the development of large-scale industry, immense foreign immigration, and the rise of complex, densely populated cities in many parts of the United States. These closely connected processes radically altered the American way of life, accelerating the pace of life and making social contacts increasingly impersonal. This same period also witnessed the rise of a mass entertainment industry that sought to create in peep shows and vaudeville a brief release from the stress and anonymity of modern life. One of the earliest of these escapes was Coney Island, a beachfront resort near New York City that catered to working- and middle-class families seeking respite from the pressures of city life. As the following excerpt from a popular Coney Island travel guide reveals, mass leisure did not come naturally and each activity had to be learned to be enjoyed.

Richard K. Fox, *Coney Island Frolics (1883)*

There are various ways of bathing at Coney Island. You can go in at the West End, where they give you a tumbledown closet like a sentry box stuck up in the sand, or at the great hotels where more or less approach to genuine comfort is afforded. The pier, too, is fitted up with extensive bathing houses, and altogether no one who wants a dip in the briny and has a quarter to pay for it need to go without it.

If a man is troubled with illusions concerning the female form divine and wishes to be rid of those illusions he should go to Coney Island and closely watch the thousands of women who bathe there every Sunday.

A woman, or at least most women, in bathing undergoes a transformation that is really wonderful. They waltz into the bathing-rooms clad in all the paraphernalia that most gladdens the feminine heart. The hair is gracefully dressed, and appears most abundant; the face is decorated with all that elaborate detail which defies description by one uninitiated in the mysteries of the boudoir; the form is moulded by the milliner to distracting elegance of proportion, and the feet appear aristocratically slender and are arched in French boots.

Thus they appear as they sail past the gaping crowds of men, who make Coney Island a loafing place on Sundays. They seek out their individual dressing-rooms and disappear. Somewhere inside of an hour, they make their appearance ready for the briny surf. If it were not for the men who accompany them it would be impossible to recognize them as the same persons who but a little while ago entered those diminutive rooms. . . .

The broad amphitheatre at Manhattan Beach built at the water's edge is often filled with spectators. Many pay admission fees to witness the feats of swimmers, the clumsiness of beginners and the ludicrous mishaps of the never-absent stout persons. Under the bathing-house is a sixty horse-power engine. It rinses and washes the suits for the bathers, and its steady puffing is an odd accompaniment to the merry shouts of the bathers and the noise of the shifting crowd ashore. . . .

A person who intends to bathe at Manhattan or Brighton Beach first buys a ticket and deposits it in a box such as is placed in every elevated railroad station. If he carries valuables he may have them deposited without extra charge in a safe that weighs seven tons and has one thousand compartments. He encloses them in an envelope and seals it. Then he writes his name partly on the flap of the envelope and partly on the envelope itself.

For this envelope he receives a metal check attached to an elastic string, in order that he may wear it about his neck while bathing. This check has been taken from one of the compartments of the safe which bears the same number as the check. Into the same compartment the sealed envelope is put. When the bather returns from the surf he must return the check and must write his name on a piece of paper. This signature is compared with the one on the envelope. Should the bather report that his check has been lost or stolen his signature is deemed a sufficient warrant for the return of the valuables. The safe has double doors in front and behind. Each drawer may be drawn out from either side. When the throng presses six men may be employed at this safe.

5

Talking and Singing Machines, Parlors, and Peep Shows: Popular Amusements in Turn-of-the-Century America

David Nasaw

Before the Civil War, amusements and entertainments were largely private affairs, conducted for the most part in the home with fellow family members. Political campaigns and religious revivals were the major forms of popular recreation that brought large numbers of unrelated people together in a public venue.

This situation changed dramatically in the half-century following the Civil War as rapidly expanding commerce and industry drew people from the American countryside and from abroad to work in the nation's urban factories, sweatshops, offices, and retail stores.

This process of urban industrialization transformed most aspects of everyday life for these urban migrants, exposing them to new experiences that ranged from new and unfamiliar work routines to crowded neighborhoods and human and animal congestion. As David Nasaw shows in this essay, leisure and entertainment, too, changed under the pressures of industrial expansion and urban growth. Intending to profit from the business use of his newly invented "talking machine," Thomas Edison soon found that his phonograph was too difficult to use in a typical office setting. Some of his investors, however, had another idea: if the machine could talk, it could also sing.

Thus began the early recording industry. Although it began as a nickel arcade curiosity, the phonograph, followed shortly by the kinetoscope, an early form of motion picture viewer, transformed urban entertainment. By simply walking from the street into an amusement parlor and dropping a nickel into a machine, anyone could listen to the latest tune or marvel at the novelty of moving images. Before long, these devices moved from the city to county fairs, small towns, and circuses—anywhere people congregated for leisure and enjoyment. As Nasaw shows, ordinary men and women worked hard in the new industrial society, but they also escaped the rigors of their work lives with even greater enthusiasm.

....

The first of the automatic amusement machines, the phonograph or "talking machine," was patented by Thomas Alva Edison in 1877. Edison, who early in his career had determined "not to undertake inventions unless there was a definite market demand for them," believed that his phonograph could have multiple uses as a business machine. It would, he predicted in an 1878 article for the *North American Review,* be the perfect dictation machine and record-keeper. It could also be used to record phonographic books for blind people; teach elocution; record the "last words" of aged family members; preserve dying languages; teach rote lessons to schoolchildren; transmit and preserve "permanent and invaluable" business records; and, when perfected, "be liberally devoted to music" and used in "music boxes, toys," and talking dolls.

Although the first machines were quite primitive and able to record and play back less than a minute of barely audible sounds, Edison was impatient to see a return on his investment. His plant produced about 500 phonographs that were exhibited by trained lecturers on the lyceum circuit to whet the public's appetite and attract investors and capital. When, after only a few months, the novelty of hearing thirty seconds of scratchy sound wore off for audiences and investors alike, Edison turned his attention to inventions with more practical and immediate applications, like the incandescent light bulb.

In 1886, Edison returned to his phonograph. Alexander Graham Bell, who with associates had been working on his own dictating machine cleverly named the graphophone (reversing the syllables of Edison's machine), suggested that the two inventors combine their talents and organizations. Edison, angered by what he considered to be Bell's theft of his invention but stimulated by the competition (Bell's machine apparently worked better than his), turned down the offer and returned to the laboratory to improve his phonograph.

By the spring of 1888, Edison and his assistants were ready to display their new dictating machine to investors and the public. When the initial demonstrations, however, failed to attract investment capital, Edison, again short of funds, sold the rights to market his machine to Jesse Lippincott, a venture capitalist who had already bought the rights to Bell's graphophone. With Edison's imprimatur, Lippincott enlisted investors across the country to buy state franchises to exploit the Wizard's latest discovery. The first phonographs and graphophones were designed as business instruments for taking dictation. Unfortunately, the machines were too complicated to run without extensive training and did not talk at all, but produced instead what one user described as "but a parody of the human voice." Court reporters, a potentially lucrative market, found the machines unworkable, stenographers lobbied against them, and the business firms that had been expected to lease them were discouraged by the poor sound reproduction and the constant maintenance required.

Only as it became obvious that the phonograph was a failure as a "talking" machine did a few adventurous (and probably desperate) investors begin to reconfigure it as a "singing" machine. Louis Glass of San Francisco sounded one of the only bright notes at the 1890 inaugural convention of the phonograph company executives when, on the last day of the meeting, he addressed the group on the subject of "public exhibitions." Glass began his talk with the simple, yet powerful, statement that "all the money" the San Francisco company had "made in the phonograph business" came from what he called "the-nickel-in-the-slot machine." He explained how he had fitted his phonographs with four listening tubes attached to four slots for coins and placed them in local saloons. Customers deposited nickels in the slots to start the machines, put the tubes to their ears, and heard the muffled but recognizable sound of music accompanied by scratches, clicks, and strange whirring noises. Glass's company had, he claimed, already made almost $2,000 from the two machines it had placed in the Palais Royal Saloon in San Francisco.

Mr. Chadbourne: Two machines in the same saloon?
Mr. Glass: Yes.
Mr. Chadbourne: Did they do as well?
Mr. Glass: Yes, and I will state right here, that we seem to have the same patrons all the time. We change the cylinders every two days, and if a man puts a nickel in one and hears a piece of band music, he almost invariably goes over and hears a second one.

Additional machines had been placed in the waiting room of the Oakland–San Francisco ferry and in other saloons—and all, Glass asserted, had made money. "We have fifteen machines out. . . . We have taken in altogether from those machines, eight of which were placed in April and May $4,019.00; figure out the details yourself."

The executives from the other companies questioned Glass about patents, operating expenses, and where and for how much they could purchase the rights to coin-operated phonographs. Although all appeared to be astonished by the amount of money the San Francisco company was taking in, none was completely surprised by the ease with which the business instrument had been turned into an entertainment machine. Each local company had already had some experience with what the director of the Georgia and Florida companies called "the social uses and amusement part of the instruments." Edison, always the wizard at attracting publicity for his inventions, had recorded a number of musical cylinders to demonstrate how the phonograph worked. For a modest price, local companies bought copies of these demonstration cylinders with opera singers, classical musicians (including the piano prodigy Josef Hoffman), brass bands, and "darky" songs whistled by a man Edison claimed to have met on a ferry ride into New York City, but who was in fact, George W. Johnson, a fairly well-known African-American minstrel.

Everywhere they were played, the demonstration musical cylinders attracted crowds. In Atlanta, Georgia, the director of the local company found that the demonstration phonographs were "daily amusing great numbers of people, the majority of whom never had an idea of using the instrument practically or otherwise." The same thing had happened in Texas, where dozens of businessmen had visited the phonograph company offices not to lease dictating machines but to listen to "a very nice musical exhibition."

Instead of capitalizing on the phonograph's ability to amuse customers by singing, as Glass had in San Francisco, most company executives banned the demonstration cylinders from their offices, fearful that customers, having been entertained by the machines, would regard them as toys instead of serious business tools. As the opening editorial in the *Phonogram*, the industry's trade journal, warned company executives, "The exhibition of the phonograph for amusement purposes [is] liable to create a wrong impression in the minds of the public as to its actual merits for other purposes."

The advocates of the phonograph as a business machine were fighting a losing battle. Before their first business year was out, most of the phonograph companies had bowed to the inevitable and converted their dictating machines into nickel-in-the-slot amusement machines. The Texas Phonograph Company opened a separate office in Dallas where customers who wanted to hear recorded music could do so—for a fee. The Spokane company abandoned its attempt to lease business machines and concentrated entirely on placing nickel-in-the-slot phonographs "in the most popular resorts in the city."

Salesmen on commission and independent exhibitors carried their phonographs into public spaces looking for crowds of passersby in a festive mood. The New England company put out machines at "all the summer resorts and beaches" in the Boston area. The New York Phonograph Company "placed a large number of these instruments at Saratoga." Machines were also exhibited at state, county, and world's fairs.

Wherever the phonographs were displayed—on fair midways, in train stations, in hotel lobbies, and at summer resorts—they were greeted with enthusiasm by first-time users who thrilled to the novelty of hearing machines sing or play music. Recorded music appealed, as a *Phonogram* writer insisted in late 1891, "to all classes and conditions of the human race, from the millionaire in his opera box to the bootblack with his grimy hands and his harmonica—all love music."

The demand of exhibitors for new recordings pushed the phonograph companies to expand their inventories. Because band music was popular with almost every type of audience, the larger companies entered into exclusive recording contracts with the better-known bands. The New York Phonograph Company recorded and distributed cylinders of Cappa's Seventh Regiment Band; the Columbia Phonograph Company entered into an exclusive contract with the United States Marine Band, which it proudly advertised as "in many respects, the most celebrated band in the world. It can play,

without notes, more than five hundred different selections." (Exhibitors who chose to purchase Marine Band cylinders were given display photographs of "the band in full uniform, as it appears when playing for the President of the United States at the White House, on state occasions, or in the grounds of the White House in pleasant weather.") Next in popularity to the bands were an assorted group of musicians, including artistic whistlers, the most famous of which was Mr. John Y. AtLee of Washington, D.C., cornet and clarinet soloists, and singers accompanied by orchestra in "Sentimental," "Topical," "Comic," "Negro," and "Irish" renditions. An increasing number of talking records, recitations, and humorous monologues, many in dialect, were also being produced.

Although most of the cylinders were distributed by the larger firms, the local companies continued to record, exhibit, and sell their own versions of the big hits of the day, such as "After the Ball" and "Daisy Bell." The Ohio company made money with cylinders of Dan Kelly, who recited mock Irish vaudeville monologues in the name of Pat Brady. In New York City, an independent record producer, Gianni Bettini, produced and marketed classical music, including many of the best-known opera stars of the 1890s.

Strangely enough given the fact that one of Edison's first musical cylinders had been of black performer George W. Johnson, African Americans were kept out of the early recording studios, although they were . . . featured performers in vandeville, musical comedy, and on the world's fair midways. The "darky" cylinders that were produced and widely circulated in the early 1890s were, for the most part, recorded by white impersonators. Before World War I, the Edison, Victor, and Columbia companies put out hundreds of "coon" song and parodies. The Ohio company boasted in 1891 that it had made up to $4.75 a day, more than it got from "some of the Marine Band" cylinders by hiring "a gentleman from an adjoining territory to sing a number of banjo songs" and advertising his cylinder as "an-old-time-before-the-war banjo song sung by a plantation darkey." The Louisiana Phonograph Company produced an entire "line of negro specialties . . . consisting of old plantation songs, darkey melodies, etc. Probably the most successful specialty is the work of 'Brudder Rasmus,' whose sermons, such as 'Charity ob de Heart,' 'Adam and Eve and de Winter Apple,' 'Sinners, Chicken Stealers, Etc.,' and 'De Lottery,' with the characteristic participation of his congregation are wonderfully realistic and attractive."

In addition to these officially recorded cylinders, there was a developing underground market for cylinders that indulged the amusement fantasies of the rougher elements of the male-only sporting crowd. To the dismay of phonograph company executives, "unscrupulous exhibitors had begun to record, collect, and exchange recordings of "jim-jam songs," profanities, vulgar conversations, and simulated sexual encounters. "A lively trade developed . . . in pornographic and obscene material, as for example the purportedly secret recording of a husband's dalliances with the maid." One exhibitor made a small fortune with such recordings at a Rhode Island state fair until a competing "lady exhibitor" who had "heretofore . . . always done an excellent business" with "clean" material complained about the unfair competition and had the scoundrel run "out of town."

While the traveling exhibitors were exhibiting phonographs during the warm weather on fair midways, at summer resorts, and in hotel lobbies, the parent companies had stumbled on what appeared to be an ideal—and permanent—exhibition site in the central business districts. They had found that by grouping several machines together in a downtown "parlor," with full-time attendants to service the machines and make change, they could attract large numbers of customers from the streams of pedestrians who passed by day and night.

These first phonograph parlors were unlike any other amusement sites or exhibition spaces. From the outside, they looked like retail stores, except for their full-size show windows that were lit and decorated not with items for sale but with framed posters and photographs of Edison, the current program of selections, and a sign inviting passersby to "walk in," admission free. Inside, the decor was somewhere between that of a fancy saloon and a hotel or theater lobby, with potted palms, ceiling fans, and quasi-Oriental rugs. The lighting was theatrical, with a separate "incandescent electric light [over each machine] bringing out plainly the likeness of Edison and the name of the selection to be heard." The phonographs themselves were encased in "handsome oak automatic cabinets." As the Ohio Phonograph Company explained, "a magnificent piece of mechanism like the phonograph deserves a fine setting." More to the point, the oak cabinets, "specimens of the finest woodwork that can be secured," upgraded the image of what were still slot machines only recently transported from barrooms and ferry terminals.

The show windows and lighting within signaled that these were establishments with nothing to hide. No one could be intimidated or frightened by the setting. No reputations would be risked by entering. Those who could not afford even a nickel or two of music were invited to "go partners" and share a listening tube with a friend. Those for whom money was no object could bring the whole family or spend a dollar or more listening once or twice to the selections on a dozen different machines. The parlors appealed, in particular, as the *Phonogram* suggested, to the large "number of travelers and visitors [who] come and go on business and pleasure" in the "great manufacturing and commercial centers." Customers did not have to plan in advance to visit the phonograph parlor. They merely "dropped in" on the way to or from lunch or appointments, or on their way home or to the theater.

Because the stream of pedestrians from whom the parlors drew their customers included a wide range of city folk, the parlor managers had to provide something for almost every taste: popular songs and perennial classics, military bands and comic whistlers, monologue such as "Brady's Election Speech," and special effects recordings such as "'Night Alarm,' a band record descriptive of a fire, with calls of the firemen, ringing of the bells, the clattering of horses' hoofs and the unwinding of the hose carriage reel." Mr. Ott of the Kansas company asked to describe his parlor at the fourth annual convention of the phonograph companies, emphasized the need to "keep a general assortment of good music" on hand. "All of them are more or less called for. There are some people who call for the talks, [like Shakespeare's] 'Seven Ages of Man' . . . and others call for sentimental songs but I believe that the greatest number of calls . . . is for such songs a 'After the Ball,' or 'After the Fair.' . . . They don't last like 'Down on the Farm,' or 'Home, Sweet Home,' but for the time that they are popular they are extremely so, and our experience has been that that class of songs has made the most money per cylinder for the exhibitor."

To bolster their receipts, the parlor owners surrounded their graphophones and phonographs with other "automatic" amusement novelties, machines that dispensed gum, candy, fruit, and miracle medicinals such as "Roy's Positive Remedy Curing Headache and Neuralgia in 15 Minutes—10¢ Per Package," and X-ray machines and fluoroscopes that displayed the bones in your hands and were all the rage until experimenters, including one of Edison's assistants, discovered that repeated exposure caused flesh to ulcerate, hair to fall out, and eventual death. The automatic dispensing machine industry had, the *Phonogram* reported in January of 1892, become "so valuable that companies are forming all over the country to cultivate it. . . . 'A penny in the slot.' This doesn't look like a heavy investment, but its earning capacity is great. . . . Few people realize the result of an accumulation of pennies or nickels."

The parlor owners were turning a profit by exhibiting the new amusement machines to a larger more "respectable" slice of the urban population than had encountered them in the

saloons or on the fair midways. Outside the larger cities, another group of amusement entrepreneurs were attempting to assemble similar audiences of "respectable" folk in small-town lecture halls and church auditoria. By the 1890s, the lecture-hall—or lyceum—circuit had grown in size and profitability until it had become a viable alternative to the vaudeville and live theater circuits. In almost every city and town with a vaudeville theater, there were church and school auditoria, libraries, lecture rooms, and rented halls where local religious, civic, charitable, educational, and fraternal associations sponsored special evening events for those who continued to regard the theater and commercial amusements as sinful at worst, indecent at best.

The phonograph, properly exhibited, was an ideal "attraction" on the lecture-hall circuit because it was as entertaining as it was educational. Lyman Howe, the most prominent and successful of the phonograph exhibitors to travel the circuit, had in the 1880s, made his living exhibiting a model coal mine, complete with a coal breaker, as an "educational" exhibit in small towns and cities in Pennsylvania, Maryland, and Ohio. In 1890, he exchanged his coal mine for a phonograph. The phonograph not only was easier to transport from town to town but also had much greater drawing power.

Howe billed his new attraction as Edison's latest scientific marvel, "the miracle of the nineteenth century," a photographer of sound that could break through the barriers of time and space, bring back the dead, and convey messages from thousands of miles away. While other traveling exhibitors ballyhooed their machines like sideshow barkers introducing dog-faced boys, Howe adopted the persona of the "professor" or "lecturer." As he explained in his advertising, "*his* entertainment would be 'Clean, Scientific, Amusing and Elevating—nothing like the Ordinary Phonograph that is seen on the Streets, in Hotels and at the Fairs.'" Howe mixed popular songs by quartets with banjo and cornet solos, comic parodies, recitations, sounds of babies crying, and lots of band music. His concerts also included demonstrations of music recorded live on stage and then played back for the audience. In large part as a result of Howe's commentary and his live demonstrations, audiences left his "concerts" entertained but feeling that they had learned something about science and mechanics as well.

Although Howe was the first and most successful, he was not the only exhibitor on the lyceum circuit to offer his audiences full-length phonograph "concerts." Technical improvements, including huge new "concert horns" several feet in diameter, had by early 1893 liberated the singing machine from its coin-slots and listening tubes. A remaining problem was solved in the middle 1890s when phonographs with spring motors instead of cumbersome, leaky batteries appeared on the market, meeting—in the words of the D. E. Boswell catalog—"the long expressed demand for a single, light, inexpensive, compact, portable, talking machine for exhibition." With the new traveling kits, lecturers and showmen could put together their own entertainments, skillfully combining brief talks on the "science" of the phonograph, live demonstrations, and musical selections. The most successful "concerts" were those that presented a wide variety of recordings. "As to selections," a *Phonogram* article advised, "a mixture of both serious and humorous should be made, the latter predominating, as the phonograph adapts itself to the humorous more readily than to the serious. . . . Monotony is the bugbear of the phonograph. In order to escape it, tact must be exercised, and all the inventive powers of which the exhibitor is possessed should be used to vary the selections as they follow one another. The entire exhibition should be an animated, shifting kaleidoscope, presenting new features at every turn."

Arrayed in tastefully decorated parlors or presented in lecture halls with "concert horn" attachments, the phonograph's chief attraction remained its novelty. Exhibitors such as Howe who traveled from city to city, seldom appear-

ing in the same place more than once a year, had less trouble with this than the parlor owners who were tied to fixed locations. When, in the middle 1890s, word came out of Menlo Park that the Wizard was experimenting with a device that would record visual images as the phonograph had sound, parlor owners across the country lined up to secure these machines for their storefronts.

Thomas Lombard, the president of the North American Phonograph Company, was in early 1893 among the first civilians admitted to a private exhibition of the new moving-picture machine, the kinetoscope. Through a peephole, he saw tiny, yet distinct, moving pictures of John Ott, one of Edison's assistants, doing an impromptu "skirt dance" and "going through all the phases of a prolonged sneeze." Entranced by the commercial possibilities of the peephole machines, Lombard formed a syndicate to exhibit them at the upcoming Chicago World's Fair, where he had already arranged to exhibit his phonographs.

In April of 1894, over a year late, the first shipment of kinetoscopes was delivered to Lombard's syndicate, which, the world's fair having long since closed, installed them in a vacated shoe store remodeled as an amusement parlor on 27th Street and Broadway in the heart of New York's entertainment district.

The first kinetoscope parlor looked and functioned much like the phonograph parlors, with one important exception. In the phonograph parlors, admission had been free and the minimum price of entertainment had been five cents for two minutes of song. In the kinetoscope parlors, customers were required to buy twenty-five-cent tickets at the door, which entitled them to peer into the peepholes of five different machines. For a second twenty-five cents they could see five more films in the remaining five kinetoscopes.

In setting the minimum price at a quarter rather than a nickel, the owners signaled their intention to attract a comparatively upscale audience, one that could afford to spend fifty cents for two and half minutes of flickering images. An early drawing of the parlor shows a room tastefully decorated with potted palms on the perimeter, incandescent lamps shaped like dragons on either side, a life-size bronzed bust of Edison in front, carpets and waxed floors, and the type of audience the owners hoped to attract: three elegantly dressed ladies and three men, one of whom was obviously a "gentleman" outfitted in top hat and cane.

The *Phonoscope*, the voice of the new industry, reproduced this drawing in its first issue as it offered advice to prospective parlor owners. "In all exhibitions, the neater and the more attractive the show, the greater is also the financial success. . . . The above cut represents an exhibition parlor which it would be well to study in order to use it as a model, wherever practicable. . . . Nobody would ever hesitate to enter such a parlor; it invites and attracts all."

Almost all of the early kinetoscope parlors were situated in downtown locations (State Street and Wabash Avenue in Chicago, Canal Street in New Orleans, Market Street in San Francisco, Tremont Street in Boston), where the business and entertainment districts intersected. In Chicago, a parlor was opened "in the Masonic Temple building, then Chicago's prided skyscraper." In San Francisco, Peter Bacigalupi, one of the more successful owner/operators of phonograph parlors, opened a kinetoscope parlor in the Chronicle Building on Market Street.

Everywhere they were exhibited, the kinetoscopes drew crowds at once—and did so without much advertising. Edison's name and word of mouth were sufficient to lure customers inside. By the summer of 1895, new kinetoscope parlors had been opened in the nation's larger cities and in smaller cities—from Binghamton, New York, and Riverside, Rhode Island, in the Northeast, to Nashville, Tennessee, and Augusta, Georgia, in the South, to Olympia, Washington, and Cyrene, Wyoming, in the West. The new amusement machines appeared to have so much commercial potential that the New York Security and Trust Company in January of 1896 issued $200,000 in mortgage bonds to an upstate New York company to manufacture and sell an improved version of the moving-picture camera and peep-show machine. The only security the company offered in return for the bonds were the patent rights to its machines.

We don't know much about the audience at these early parlors, although we do know that it was large enough to provide the owners with a profit and new investors with the incentive to buy into the business. A glimpse at the content of the early films suggests that the parlors probably attracted more sporting men than family groups or the well-dressed ladies in bustles pictured in the *Phonoscope* drawing of the well-run amusement parlor. According to the film historian Gordon Hendricks, the films distributed to the parlors included moving pictures of *Sandow* (the strongman stripped to the waist flexing his muscles): *Horse Shoeing; Barber Shop* (a slapstick skit); *Wrestling; Blacksmiths; Highland Dance; Trapeze* (probably with a lady acrobat in tights): *Roosters* (a cockfight): *Organ Grinder; Trained Bears;* and two turns by a contortionist, Mme. Bertholdi, intriguingly entitled *Mouth Support* and *Table Contortion.*

The major problem with these early films was not the content, which, though heavy on exotic dancers, was still varied enough to appeal to many tastes. It was the lack of new films. Raff and Gammon, the sole authorized distributors for Edison's moving pictures and machines, complained continually to Edison and his subordinates about the lack of decent films for their kinetoscopes. Those that were available were, as often as not, defective, faded, fuzzy, or flickering beyond repair.

The parlor owners and investors who had placed individual machines in drugstores, hotel lobbies, and in and around the summer resorts had little trouble getting them to peek in the peepholes. The difficulty was enticing them to return for a second look. Within a year of the opening of the first kinetoscope parlor, Raff and Gammon reported to their board of directors that business was "rather quiet." By the fall, the demand for new machines had fallen to a trickle. Raff and Gammon tried to sell the company but found no takers.

There were by this time more than 900 machines and thousands of films already in distribution and enough parlor owners to support a new trade journal, the *Phonoscope*. But it had become apparent that the downtown amusement parlors were not going to survive on ladies and gentlemen customers alone. The future of the business appeared to be the sporting men and boys who had initially come to the parlors to see the boxing matches and the hootchi-kootchi dancers.

No matter how brightly lit or tastefully decorated, the kinetoscope parlors operated as "drop in" centers that, like saloons, offered amusements in five- to ten-minute packages and, not surprisingly, drew a large portion of their customers from the sporting crowd. The parlor owners' decision to concentrate on cultivating a male-only crowd was reinforced by the invention and marketing of the mutoscope by the Biograph Company in 1897. Like the first automatic amusement machine, the phonograph, the mutoscope had been designed as a business machine for traveling salesmen to exhibit their wares. It was reconfigured as an amusement machine when company executives recognized that by substituting moving pictures of "Little Egypt" for pictures of loom-weaving machines, they could increase sales and profits. "*Little Egypt* . . . the first Mutoscope success . . . was followed by *Serpentine Dancers, How Girls Go to Bed, How Girls Undress*, and similar tidbits," including the first commercial film to exhibit partial nudity, "*The Birth of the Pearl*, showing a girl in white tights and bare arms crouching in an oversized oyster shell."

What made the mutoscope the perfect instrument for viewing such subjects was its mechanical crank. Unlike the kinetoscope that ran automatically when the switch was turned on or a coin dropped in the slot, the mutoscope was operated by hand. As an 1897 advertising brochure explained, "In the operation of the Mutoscope, the spectator has the performance entirely under his own control by the turning of the crank. He may make the operation as quick or as slow as fancy dictates . . . and if he so elects, the entertainment can be stopped by him at any point in the series and each separate picture inspected at leisure; thus every step, motion, act or expression can be analyzed, presenting effects at once instructive, interesting, attractive, amusing and startling."

By the time the mutoscopes reached the market in 1897, most of the phonograph and kinetoscope parlors had closed their doors and sold their machines secondhand to "tenderloin" arcades and shooting galleries. Although their rise and fall had been telescoped into only a few years, the parlors had opened a new phase in the history of urban amusements. Located in the heart of the city's business districts and offering entertainment in compact packages measured in minutes, not hours, they stretched the map of the entertainment world in new directions. They entertained customers—if only for a few minutes at a time—in drugstores, theater lobbies, railway and ferry terminals, department and general stores, resort hotels, boardwalks and midways, tents erected on vacant lots, small-town and city lecture halls, and parlors in the central business districts. Everywhere they were exhibited, they attracted an enthusiastic crowd of onlookers and customers willing to take a chance and buy a concert ticket or deposit a nickel in the slot for a few minutes of automatic entertainment.

Part of the attraction of the machines was their newness. They entered the public arena without a knowable past. They belonged neither to Fifth Avenue nor to the Bowery. They could present opera singers, vaudeville clowns, ballet dancers, or prize fighters. They were large enough to accommodate every taste and appeal to every audience.

The show businessmen were so enchanted by the amusement machines' potentially universal drawing power that they began to articulate their own psychology of amusements. Human beings, they were now convinced, were born with an inherent, inalienable need to be amused. As *Billboard* magazine explained in the spring of 1895, "Everybody knows that there is always an aching longing for diversion in the human heart. The public must, and will be amused." Or as the *Phonoscope* proclaimed in its inaugural editorial in 1896, "There is one great desire which animates all mankind, from the cradle to the grave, encompassing all:—the desire for amusement and entertainment."

While individual projects might fail and fail again, the show businessman's faith was ever renewed by the crowds each machine attracted before the novelty wore off. The public had demonstrated its hunger for cheap amusements. The showmen would find a way to satisfy it, even if it meant carrying the new amusement machines on their backs from place to place.

GLOSSARY

Thomas Alva Edison (1847–1931): American inventor who patented more than a thousand inventions, among them the microphone (1877), the phonograph (1878), and an incandescent lamp (1879).

Alexander Graham Bell (1847–1922): Scottish-born American inventor of the telephone in 1876. Bell also invented the audiometer, an early hearing aid, and improved the phonograph.

Fluoroscope: A device equipped with a fluorescent screen on which the internal structures of the human body may be continuously viewed as shadowy images formed by the differential transmission of x-rays through the object.

Menlo Park: Site of the New Jersey laboratory where Thomas Edison perfected the incandescent light bulb in 1879.

IMPLICATIONS

In this essay, Nasaw points out that the showmen who developed the mass entertainment industry were convinced that human beings possessed an inherent need for public amusement. Do you think this was simply self-serving rhetoric or a basic human truth?

Past Traces

Following the Civil War, the main focus of army activities turned to the western plains, where the army's new mission was to "protect" white immigrants and settlers and to move the 150,000 remaining Plains Indians onto government reservations. That Native Americans did not passively accept Washington's strategy is attested to by the numerous movements of cultural resurgence that punctuated the last decades of the nineteenth century. This reading is introduced by two documents, one stating the Native American position regarding ancient tribal lands and a second recalling the infamous army massacre of 300 Sioux men, women, and children following a cultural revival at Wounded Knee, South Dakota, in 1890.

Red Cloud (1890) and Flying Hawk (1936) on Wounded Knee

Red Cloud (1890)

I will tell you the reason for the trouble. When we first made treaties with the Government, our old life and our old customs were about to end; the game on which we lived was disappearing; the whites were closing around us, and nothing remained for us but to adopt their ways,—the Government promised us all the means necessary to make our living out of the land, and to instruct·us how to do it, and with abundant food to support us until we could take care of ourselves. We looked forward with hope to the time we could be as independent as the whites, and have a voice in the Government.

The army officers could have helped better than anyone else but we were not left to them. An Indian Department was made with a large number of agents and other officials drawing large salaries—then came the beginning of trouble; these men took care of themselves but not of us. It was very hard to deal with

the government through them—they could make more for themselves by keeping us back than by helping us forward.

We did not get the means for working our lands; the few things they gave us did little good.

Our rations began to be reduced; they said we were lazy. That is false. How does any man of sense suppose that so great a number of people could get work at once unless they were at once supplied with the means to work and instructors enough to teach them?

Our ponies were taken away from us under the promise that they would be replaced by oxen and large horses; it was long before we saw any, and then we got very few. We tried with the means we had, but on one pretext or another, we were shifted from one place to another, or were told that such a transfer was coming. Great efforts were made to break up our customs, but nothing was done to introduce us to customs of the whites. Everything was done to break up the power of the real chiefs.

Those old men really wished their people to improve, but little men, so-called chiefs, were made to act as disturbers and agitators. Spotted Tail wanted the ways of the whites, but an assassin was found to remove him. This was charged to the Indians because an Indian did it, but who set on the Indian? I was abused and slandered, to weaken my influence for good. This was done by men paid by the government to teach us the ways of the whites. I have visited many other tribes and found that the same things were done amongst them; all was done to discourage us and nothing to encourage us. I saw men paid by the government to help us, all very busy making money for themselves, but doing nothing for us. . . .

The men who counted (census) told all around that we were feasting and wasting food. Where did he see it? How could we waste what we did not have? We felt we were mocked in our misery; we had no newspaper and no one to speak for us. Our rations were again reduced.

You who eat three times a day and see your children well and happy around you cannot understand what a starving Indian feels! We were faint with hunger and maddened by despair. We held our dying children and felt their little bodies tremble as their soul went out and left only a dead weight in our hands. They were not very heavy but we were faint and the dead weighed us down. There was no hope on earth. God seemed to have forgotten.

Some one had been talking of the Son of God and said He had come. The people did not know; they did not care; they snatched at hope; they screamed like crazy people to Him for mercy they caught at the promise they heard He had made.

The white men were frightened and called for soldiers. We begged for life and the white men thought we wanted theirs; we heard the soldiers were coming. We did not fear. We hoped we could tell them our suffering and could get help. The white men told us the soldiers meant to kill us; we did not believe it but some were frightened and ran away to the Bad Lands. The soldiers came. They said: "don't be afraid—we come to make peace, not war." It was true; they brought us food. But the hunger-crazed who had taken fright at the soldiers' coming and went to the Bad Lands could not be induced to return to the horrors of reservation life. They were called Hostiles and the Government sent the army to force them back to their reservation prison.

Flying Hawk (1936)

This was the last big trouble with the Indians and soldiers and was in the winter in 1890. When the Indians would not come in from the Bad Lands, they got a big army together with plenty of clothing and supplies and camp-and-wagon equipment for a big campaign; they had enough soldiers to make a round-up of all the Indians they called hostiles.

The Government army, after many fights and loss of lives, succeeded in driving these starving Indians, with their families of women and gaunt-faced children, into a trap, where they could be forced to surrender their arms. This was on Wounded Knee creek, northeast of Pine Ridge, and here the Indians were surrounded by the soldiers, who had Hotchkiss machine guns along with them. There were about four thousand Indians in this big camp, and the soldiers had the machine guns pointed at them from all around the village as the soldiers formed a ring about the tepees so that Indians could not escape.

The Indians were hungry and weak and they suffered from lack of clothing and furs because the whites had driven away all the game. When the soldiers had them all surrounded and they had their tepees set up, the officers sent troopers to each of them to search for guns and take them from the owners. If the Indians in the tepees did not at once hand over a gun, the soldier tore open their parfleech trunks and bundles and bags of robes or clothes,—looking for pistols and knives and ammunition. It was an ugly business, and brutal; they treated the Indians like they would torment a wolf with one foot in a strong trap; they could do this because the Indians were now in the white man's trap,—and they were helpless.

Then a shot was heard from among the Indian tepees. An Indian was blamed; the excitement began; soldiers ran to their stations; officers gave orders to open fire with the machine guns into the crowds of innocent men, women and children, and in a few minutes more than two hundred and twenty of them lay in the snow dead and dying. A terrible blizzard raged for two days covering the bodies with Nature's great white blanket; some lay in piles of four or five; others in twos or threes or singly, where they fell until the storm subsided. When a trench had been dug of sufficient length and depth to contain the frozen corpses, they were collected and piled, like cord-wood, in one vast icy tomb. While separating several stiffened forms which had fallen in a heap, two of them proved to be women, and bugged closely to their breasts were infant babes still alive after lying in the storm for two days in 20° below zero weather.

I was there and saw the trouble,—but after the shooting was over; it was all bad.

6

Lozen: An Apache Woman Warrior

Laura Jane Moore

In 1893, Frederick Jackson Turner, a young historian at the University of Wisconsin, proclaimed the closing of the American frontier. The 1890 census, he argued, had revealed all of America to now be a settled land; the frontier that had defined America since the seventeenth century no longer existed. Turner advanced his thesis from the perspective of white America, making no connection in his thesis between the closing of the frontier and the final displacement of the Plains Indians, the last remaining large-scale contingent of Native Americans in the United States. What Turner had ignored was that the true meaning of the "closing" of the frontier had been the destruction through disease and warfare of the Plains and southwestern bands—the Sioux, Cheyennes, Crows, and Navahos—and their confinement on desolate and isolated reservations.

This, the final stage in a national program of western expansion and Native American displacement that had begun in the trans-Appalachian west during the 1780s, gained renewed force following the Civil War. In 1867, federal Indian policy turned increasingly toward forced segregation, federal supervision, and the forced education of children designed to suppress and eventually eradicate Indian culture and ways of life. Then, with the completion of the transcontinental railroad in 1869, settlers flooded the Plains and the Southwest, putting further pressure on the native residents. At the same time, the railroads also allowed soldiers to move rapidly and efficiently, enhancing their ability to enforce federal Indian policy. The arrival of the railroads and settlers dealt a final blow to the traditional Plains economy, as army-supported hunters nearly exterminated the buffalo, the Plains Indians' primary source of meat and leather. Where perhaps as many as 40 million buffalo had ranged the plains in the early nineteenth century, by 1895 fewer than a thousand remained.

Native American resistance had grown alongside this century-long program of displacement, beginning with the Miami and Shawnee defeat of General Josiah Harman's American army in 1790 and ending with the massacre at Wounded Knee,

South Dakota, in 1890. In those years, hundreds of young warriors had aggressively defended their people and their lands by a creative combination of military engagement and negotiation. In this essay, Laura Jane Moore tells the story of one of these warriors, the Apache war leader Lozen. Like most Native American warriors, Lozen chose the warrior's path early in life and endured privation and demanding training regimens in the process of becoming a full-fledged warrior. What made Lozen unusual—though not unique—was that she was a woman. As Moore shows, Native American conceptions of gender were flexible enough to incorporate woman warriors, shamans, and occasional chiefs into their communities.

....

During the waning days of the nineteenth-century Indian wars, five thousand American soldiers pursued a band of thirty-six Apache men, women, and children. Led by the chief Naiche and the shaman Geronimo, the group had holed up in the Sierra Madre mountains in northern Mexico. These Apaches never suffered a decisive defeat, but by the summer of 1886 they were tired of running and wanted to be reunited with their families back on the reservation. Two women assumed the dangerous mission of approaching United States troops in order to begin negotiations. While the American soldiers proudly recorded the names of the Apache men whom they met during these military campaigns, only Apache oral traditions identify Lozen and Dahteste as the "squaws" who played such an important role. Well suited to their task, the women were fighting members of the band, able to defend themselves and speak for their people. Each no doubt carried a knife, rifle, and cartridge belt, but since they were women, the soldiers did not assume that they posed much threat.

Both Lozen and Dahteste stepped outside the position usually occupied by Apache women, and both of them fought bravely in battles against U.S. and Mexican troops. Dahteste had found her way to warfare, as Apache women often did, by extending her role as a wife and accompanying her husband, Anandia, on raids and war expeditions. Lozen was more unusual. Probably in her forties in the 1880s, she had never married and had no children. Lozen's choice to opt out of the roles typically adopted by Apache women, however, did not lead to her marginalization or degradation within her Apache community. Rather, she became one of the most revered Apache warriors of the late nineteenth century. As a woman warrior, she possessed qualities that Apaches associated with both men and women that, in their eyes, made her especially powerful. Convinced that she was responsible for much of their success against their enemies, her comrades and kin celebrated her spiritual power and physical prowess. Geronimo and the rest of the group knew they could trust her to represent them to the American soldiers.

Lozen's life exemplifies the permeability of gender roles in a complex Native American culture even when those roles seem to be rigidly defined. Anthropologists describe Apaches as having strict divisions between men and women who performed different work and even occupied separate space in dwellings. "The feeling is," explained one Apache, "that a man should go his way with his friends and a woman her way with her friends." This separation of the sexes was extreme enough that it made men and women quite shy in the presence of each others. Unmarried women, in particular, refrained from spending time with men. Moreover, kin relations imposed further expectations of avoidance. Once grown, brothers and sisters dodged each other's company. Since Apaches considered people whom Euro-Americans call cousins to be siblings, avoidance often extended to many people. "If we even spoke" to the adolescent girls, recalled one Apache man of his own youth, "we could do so only with a bush between us, and back to back."

In contrast to these rules, Lozen was an unmarried woman who rode with male warriors by the side of her brother, the chief Victorio. She was an important enough member of the fighting force that Victorio called her "my right hand. . . . Strong as a man, braver than most, and cunning in strategy." By adopting the unusual but respected role of a woman warrior, Lozen stood in a powerful cross-gender position from which she could act as "a shield to her people."

Lozen and Victorio were Chiricahua Apaches, one of seven different Apachean tribes that lived in the southwestern United States. In the mid-nineteenth century the Chiricahuas occupied an area west of the Rio Grande, including what is now southwestern New Mexico, southeastern Arizona, and part of the Mexican borderlands. The Chiricahuas were highly decentralized and did not necessarily recognize each other as related, even if anthropologists have identified them as the same cultural group. Four major bands of Chiricahuas occupied this area: the Chihene, the Bedonkohe, the Chokonen, and the Nednai. These bands were composed of local groups that in turn each consisted of ten to thirty extended families. Most activities, including marriages, were carried out within the local group. Raiding and war parties, for example, usually were composed of members of a family or local group. Within a local group, a leader or "chief" gained prominence and influence through personal traits of generosity, bravery, integrity, eloquence, and ceremonial knowledge. By 1870, Victorio had assumed a leadership role in one of these local groups, the Warm Springs Apaches.

Apaches organized their society around a sexual division of labor embodied in the matrilocal extended family. That is, when a man married a woman, they lived near her mother. Generally property also followed a matrilineal line. The women of an extended family worked together gathering and processing the wild plants that were an essential food source. Meanwhile, men of the same family hunted in pairs or small groups, providing the game that supplemented their diet. Despite the disruptions of reservations and warfare in the late nineteenth century, Apaches living on reservations maintained this social organization. For example, Charlie Smith remembered that sometime in the 1880s his family received permission from the Indian agent to travel to an area where there was a good piñon crop. In the morning "usually by twos, the men left to hunt. . . . The women also divided into small groups." They brought the young children along and followed trails of pack rats to their dens, where they could sometimes gather as many as two gallons of nuts from one nest. They also placed skins under piñon trees and beat the lower branches to gather more nuts. "When the men returned in the evening, the women dressed the game" and began the process of tanning the hides.

The sexual division of labor did not put women in a subordinate position to men, but instead led to complementary roles for women and men. Women controlled a family's economic activities and managed its wealth; men, more mobile in their responsibilities for hunting and raiding, took command of relations with those outside the group. With marriage, a man assumed obligations not only to his wife but to her extended family as well, obligations that divorce or a wife's death did not automatically terminate. Though marriage for Euro-American women meant economic and legal dependence in this period, in many ways it was the opposite for Apache women. Marriage did, however, lead Apache women to be assigned certain roles within the community, roles that an unmarried woman such as Lozen could eschew, especially the domestic tasks of food preparation, child care, and house building.

Lozen's orientation toward more typically male activities probably emerged during her childhood. When they were small, girls and boys played together and competed in foot races. When they were about six, however, the community began to separate them. During puberty, girls were initiated into womanhood and boys into manhood, and they then avoided each other's company except within strict limits. Lozen apparently did not make this transition, but instead continued to participate in the boys' activities. She was not castigated for her seemingly masculine skills. After all, girls were "urged to be strong and fast. It is simply accepted," the anthropologist Morris Opler explained, that some individuals "have carried the requirement further than is strictly necessary. The attitude of those discussing them is never one of ridicule or condemnation but rather one of admiration." Eventually even girls who excelled at masculine pursuits usually married and entered into typically female roles. Lozen, instead, remained unmarried and became a warrior. That this was the right choice for her may well have been confirmed during puberty.

When a girl began to menstruate, it was a cause for celebration. A crowd of relatives, friends, and members of neighboring communities attended an elaborate four-day ceremony in her honor. During the ceremony the girl became "White Painted Woman," the central Chiricahua deity, and emerged at the end as a woman. No moment so definite as a girl's first period signaled when a boy was ready to make the transition to adulthood. Instead, once he was strong enough, perhaps when he was about fifteen, he volunteered to become an apprentice warrior. He then had to participate in four raids during which he followed special rules, used a special apprentice's language, and was called "Child of the Water" after the son of White Painted Woman. Once he had successfully joined four raids, he was considered a full-fledged warrior.

We can only speculate, based on what we know of Chiricahua culture, about Lozen's youth and how she chose the route of the woman warrior. Perhaps not long after her puberty ceremony Lozen volunteered to become an apprentice warrior, and the men in her family, recognizing her unusual talents with horses and hunting, agreed. It is also likely that she acquired the spiritual power that contributed to her skill as a warrior during adolescence, another sign, perhaps, that she was well suited for the alternative life of a woman warrior.

Both men and women had access to the supernatural world that infused nature. Apaches tapped into this power through visions that sometimes occurred in dreams but often were brought on by fasting in isolation during a "vision quest." In such a vision a supernatural force visited, usually in the guise of an animal, and taught the person a ceremony by which he or she could call on the force for aid. This ceremonial knowledge or "power" was an individual's own, and it normally could not be passed on or shared. Still, Apaches understood that their power was to be used for the good of their community. Those who did not were witches. Apaches might go on vision quests in order to make contact with the supernatural world, but they could not choose winch "power" would visit them. Most of these powers involved healing. Some Apaches also could call on the supernatural world to help them diagnose illness, find lost objects, even withstand bullets.

Ceremonial knowledge was an essential complement to a warrior's physical skills and intelligence. Geronimo based his leadership role, for example, on his abilities as a shaman. He had the power to foretell the result of a battle and to "handle men." Another chief, Chihuahua, had "the Power over horses" so that he "could gentle and ride the wildest" and "heal them of sickness or wounds." The chief Nana's "Power was over ammunition trains and rattlesnakes." Even when he was over eighty and crippled, he could make a successful raid for ammunition when younger men failed.

Lozen had the ability, through ceremony, to ask for supernatural aid in locating the enemy. The power that she received related to warfare, and so it may have helped confirm her special standing as a woman warrior. She summoned this power through a ritual in which she stood with arms outstretched and palms up. As she turned slowly in a circle, she sang a prayer such as:

Upon this earth
On which we live
Ussen has Power
This Power is mine
For locating the enemy
Which only Ussen the great
Can show to me.

During this ceremony a tingling in her palms indicated the direction and distance to the enemy. If the enemy were very near, her palms would turn purple.

Lozen's ceremony illustrates central aspects of the Apache worldview. Her power stemmed from her relationship with the supernatural, called in this case Ussen, the life-giver. Through her individual vision quest she had obtained the ability to manipulate this power, which she used to help her community. In another of her prayers she sang, "Ussen has Power. Sometimes He shares it. . . . This Power he has given me [f]or the benefit of my people. . . . This Power I may use [f]or the good of my people."

Shamans whose ceremonial knowledge related to warfare, such as Lozen's, always accompanied war expeditions, which departed only after certain ritualistic dances and singing were held. While both women and men had equal access to the supernatural world, traditionally warfare was strictly in the male domain, an extension of men's roles in hunting and raiding from which women were normally excluded. This exclusion stemmed from women's reproductive abilities, which made them especially powerful but also potentially dangerous to men, particularly men at war. Because menstruation was so powerful and so uniquely female, it could also cause harm. Boys learned early that contact with menstrual blood would make their joints swollen and painful and that sex with a menstruating woman could lead to deformity. The bodily discharge that accompanied childbirth was equated with menstrual blood, so men were well advised to avoid it. In other words, at the moments when a woman was most a woman, at menstruation and childbirth, she was also most dangerous to men. The rheumatism or

deformed joints that resulted from such contact would, in turn, hinder a man's ability to perform his duties as a warrior and hunter. The necessary separation of the sexes, however, could be bridged by a woman warrior such as Lozen. Her skills as a warrior would not be compromised by contact with women, for she shared their unique powers as well. Her powerful cross-gender position combined the most respected aspects of Apache femininity and masculinity.

As a warrior, Lozen displayed impressive talent at the masculine pursuits of hunting, raiding, and warfare. While raiding was a means to obtain supplies and, like hunting, an economic activity, a war party exacted revenge when a member of the group was killed. Apaches explained that "it is the duty of a man to avenge injury to his relatives." Moreover, "when the enemy does something, there have got to be consequences. If there aren't, things get out of balance. Pretty soon everything is upset." Apaches went to war, therefore, to preserve a necessary balance. War parties also reflected Apaches' kin-based social organization: "The relatives of the father of the dead person or of his wife get it started and try to enlist as many as possible."

Although women did not typically participate in war parties, they were as concerned as men were with the importance of exacting revenge. Sometimes women called for the organization of war parties. Sometimes married women followed the expedition in order to provide domestic services such as cooking or dressing wounds. And occasionally women who had accompanied their husbands found themselves participating in the fighting. If her husband were killed, for example, a wife might take his place and personally assume the task of avenging his death. Indeed, it was far easier for women to cross into the men's domain than for men to assume typically female tasks. Whether warriors or not, women needed to be prepared to participate in skirmishes, to handle weapons, and to defend themselves and their families. But even if respected for fighting bravely beside her husband, a woman observed the strict rules that governed relations between the sexes while raiding or warring. Warriors practiced strict sexual abstinence before and during war expeditions because a woman's strength could impede a man's. "Women could go with their husbands, but they could not live together," one Apache later explained.

Women's ability to participate in raids and war parties may have increased in the late nineteenth century. After the United States won the Southwest from Mexico at midcentury and increasing numbers of Angles began passing through and settling there, the U.S. military waged a campaign to move the various Native American residents onto reservations. The land set aside for reservations was often far from traditional homelands, overcrowded with a conglomeration of traditionally hostile Indian groups, and incapable of supporting the numbers expected to live there. During the last few decades of the century, various bands alternatively fought and negotiated with U.S. troops, agreeing to live on reservation lands for a time and then leaving when their situation became untenable.

Apache groups that resisted reservation life had to be increasingly mobile to elude capture. Warfare severely circumscribed life for Apaches on the run. If families were to stay together, women and children often had little choice but to accompany warriors. Constant movement and the possibility of attack and capture made it difficult for women to perform their normal productive roles as gatherers and processors of food. Raiding instead became the main means of obtaining food and other supplies, especially the all-important horses and ammunition that were necessary to keep up the fight. Not only did women participate in raids and skirmishes themselves but they dug trenches and acted as lockouts and scouts. It was not easy to keep warriors' activities within war parties separate from the activities of women and children. Charlie Smith remembered that frequently "Geronimo had the women and children along. . . . If pursued he, as did all Apaches, tried to pro-

tect them by sending them ahead; but ordinarily, when fighting occurred, it was because he laid an ambush, and every one of the band was there." He added that "some of the women were very good shots," Lozen most of all.

In 1870 the Warm Springs Apaches had agreed to live on a reservation called Ojo Caliente (Warm Springs) within their traditional lands in southwestern New Mexico. Because of bureaucratic complications between Washington, D.C., and the presiding military officers, along with the hostility of the local American and Mexican population, the site of the reservation kept changing. But the elder Warm Springs leader, Loco, and the younger and more hotheaded Victorio kept their bands settled and at peace with the American troops. Then in 1875 the American authorities began a new policy of trying to concentrate all Apaches on one reservation, called San Carlos, along the Gila River in eastern Arizona, far from where the Chiricahuas had agreed to live. Ace Daklugie, whose parents were Geronimo's sister, Ishton, and the Nednai chief, Juh, later claimed that it "was the worst place in all the great territory stolen from the Apaches." No one had lived there permanently before because there was no grass and no game, and the only vegetation was cacti. "The heat was terrible. The insects were terrible. The water was terrible. What there was in the sluggish river was brackish and warm. . . . Insects and rattlesnakes seemed to thrive there." James Kaywaykla, who was a few years younger than Daklugie, recalled the malaria, summer temperatures reaching well over a hundred degrees, and insects that "almost devoured the babies." At San Carlos, disease-ridden, inadequately supplied, and overcrowded with different Indian groups who were unfamiliar, suspicious, or even overtly hostile toward each other, Chiricahuas found themselves hungry, sick, and tense. The Warm Springs Apaches tried to live there for a time, but many found it intolerable. Loco and his followers, determined to pursue peace with the Americans, decided to remain, but at least three hundred others, including Victorio's band, left in 1877. Many of them were caught or killed; others made it across the border into Mexico.

Victorio's band eventually returned to their old reservation, Ojo Caliente, which the military had shut down, and indicated their willingness to surrender but not to live at San Carlos. Some of the Warm Springs group, following another chief, Nana, registered at the Mescalero reservation in New Mexico, while Victorio continued to pressure American officials to honor their promise of the Ojo Caliente land. Meanwhile, other Chiricahua leaders, including Juh and Geronimo, were arrested and imprisoned at San Carlos. In July 1879 the Warm Springs band heard a rumor that Victorio was to be arrested too, and the group again left the reservation and fled into the mountains. While family members hid in caves, Victorio and about sixty warriors attacked a contingent of cavalrymen near their old reservation. This battle opened a bloody war in which the Warm Springs Apaches fought to avenge the deaths of their kin and to live where they chose.

When the Apaches fled from the reservations, they left quietly at night in small scattered groups in order to evade pursuit. Their means of escape reflected their gender organization. Women took charge of helping young boys and girls and moved separately from the warriors. Kaywaykla's grandmother woke him one night and told him they were leaving. He had his emergency rations handy. At first she carried the sleepy boy on her back as they ran, and then they crawled slowly. Shielded from sight by mesquite and cactus, they froze when they heard a jingle of metal indicating that soldiers were nearby. They traveled carefully for a few days before they rendezvoused with the rest of their band on the banks of a swollen river.

While deeply ingrained ideas about the proper roles of women and men influenced this dangerous flight, the story also suggests the permeability of those roles. Kaywaykla's grandmother took charge of his safety because his mother accompanied her husband and the other warriors. When they reached the river, Kaywaykla's parents were there, as were the leaders Nana and Victorio. Kaywaykla spoke only briefly with his mother. When he later asked for her, his grandmother explained that "she rides with your father and Nana on another raid."

Meanwhile, the women and children needed to cross the river before the cavalry discovered them. Kaywaykla's grandmother tried to lead her horse into the water, but it balked. They seemed to be stuck in this dangerous position, between the rising water and the American soldiers who could find them there at any time. But then arrived "a magnificent woman on a beautiful black horse—Lozen, sister of Victorio. Lozen, the woman warrior!" She held her rifle over her head as she turned her horse into the torrent, and it began to swim against the current. The others followed across safely, with Lozen having to rescue just one horse and rider who began to wash downstream. On the other side of the river, Lozen gave Kaywaykla's grandmother instructions: "You take charge now," she said. "I must return to the warriors." She told the older woman to hurry to Salinas Peak, their "Sacred Mountain in the San Andres," taking only short stops along the way, and then to wait there for Nana. "We can spare no men," she explained, "but the young boys will obey your orders. . . . I go to join my brother." The success of this escape relied on Lozen's skill with horses, her physical strength, the trust that the other Apaches placed in her, and her ability to move between the worlds of women and warriors.

Normally only married women could ride with the warriors. But Lozen was not a normal woman. "No," Charlie Smith explained, "she never married. But to us she was as a Holy Woman and she was regarded and treated as one. White Painted Woman herself was not more respected." Kaywaykla agreed that although "she had not married, she went on the warpath with the men, which no woman other than the wives of warriors was permitted to do; and she was held in the greatest respect by them, much as though she were a holy person." He also remembered Lozen participating in the council of leaders as they deliberated about whether to return to the reservation or continue their fight. Lozen's position indicates that, even if men usually controlled politics, a person earned a place at the council fire not by one's biological sex, but by being a successful warrior, which required physical prowess, intelligence, and integrity. "No other woman" was "bidden to the council, but that was because no other had the skill as a warrior that Lozen did." Lozen's unusual position rested on a confluence to cultural, historical, and individual factors. Apache culture's flexibility allowed and even respected her unusual choice, and her physical and spiritual skills made her an asset to the beleaguered Chiricahuas, whose numbers in the 1870s and 1880s were depleted. Those skills were apparently extraordinary. "She could ride, shoot, and fight like a man; and I think she had more ability in planning military strategy than did Victorio," Kaywaykla recalled.

While Apache girls and boys, men and women, were expert riders, horses were especially associated with men and their roles in hunting, raiding, and warfare. Lozen was a renowned raider, thanks in large part to her skills with horses. She likely was the woman that cavalry officer John C. Cremony remembered "as one of the most dextrous horse thieves and horse breakers in the tribe, [who] seldom permitted an expedition to go on a raid without her presence." Ace Daklugie remembered her taking advantage of a melee between soldiers and Indians at San Carlos to grab some much needed ammunition. She and another warrior, Sanchez, "swooped down on the horse herd and drove a bunch off. They wanted especially the ammunition mules, for they had not yet been unloaded. . . . I do know that they got a good supply of ammunition." Kaywaykla, too, emphasized her ability to catch horses. She "was expert at roping. . . . No man in the tribe

was more skillful in stealing horses or stampeding a herd than she."

One particularly dramatic example of Lozen's talent, and how she chose to use it, occurred during the summer of 1880 while the Warm Springs band made its way into West Texas and then toward Mexico, pursued closely by American troops. Lozen dropped out of the main group in order to help a pregnant Mescalero Apache woman who had gone into labor. The two women hid just out of sight of the cavalry, and then Lozen helped the woman deliver her baby. They had not taken any horses, fearing that the soldiers would notice the tracks and realize that someone had separated from the group. They had limited food and no water, and the distance between water holes was too great to make on foot. When they spotted a herd of cattle, Lozen killed a longhorn with her knife, "a feat that few men would undertake," but they still could not travel far without water. They hid alongside the Rio Grande and observed a camp of Mexicans on the opposite bank. Lozen decided to steal one of their horses. She cut a strip from the longhorn's hide to fashion into a bridle, waited for nightfall, and swam across the rushing river. The men slept around the fire, while one guarded the horses hobbled not far away. She waited until the guard started toward the fire and then "crept softly" to the "powerful steed" she had selected. "When she bent to cut the hobbles it snorted and plunged. She leaped to its back and turned it toward the river. Bullets whizzed past her head as the horse slid down the bank and plunged into the water." She was scrambling up the opposite bank before the men could follow. By the time the sun rose, the two women, the infant, and their new horse were far away.

Their ordeal, however, had not yet ended. The American troops had received reinforcements, who were guarding every water hole and had inadvertently cut off the women's path back to their band. Lozen guided the woman and her newborn by a stealthy and circuitous route back to the Mescalero reservation, which took several more weeks and involved stealing another horse on the way.

Because Lozen was both a warrior and a woman, her cross-gender position made it possible for her to protect the Mescalero woman as a man normally would and to help her deliver her baby, which, because of the association with menstrual blood, would have been perilous for a man. Lozen, like many women, had ceremonial healing powers and may have known some of the ritual with which Apaches greeted a new life. At the same time, her skill as a warrior shielded the woman who was forced to give birth under particularly dangerous and unusual circumstances.

While Lozen and the new mother sneaked past enemy lines and made their way slowly to the Mescalero reservation, U.S. troops chased Victorio, Nana, and the rest of the band into Mexico. Previously, the Americans had not been able to follow them over the border, but Mexico and the United States had just instituted a treaty by which American troops were allowed to enter Mexican territory in pursuit of hostile Indians. The Apaches, low on ammunition, food, and water, camped on the slopes of a three-peak mountain range called Tres Castillos that rose out of the parched desert in the Mexican state of Chihuahua. Here their extraordinary ability to evade their pursuers finally failed. Mexican forces, who were the first to find them, attacked at dawn on October 15. At the end of this bloody battle, perhaps eighty Apaches lay dead and about seventy more, including Kaywaykla's grandmother, were captured and marched to the Mexican city, Chihuahua, where they were sold into slavery. Among the dead was Victorio.

"Many of the old Apaches," Ace Daklugie explained, "are convinced that, had [Lozen] been with Victorio at Tres Castillos, there would have been no ambush." She was missed not so much for her fighting skills—the band was outnumbered and trapped among the boulders on the mountain slope, an impossible situation for the best warrior—as for her ceremonial power to locate the enemy. If she

had been there, they believed, she would have anticipated the attack, and they could have escaped.

Lozen learned of her people's demoralizing defeat and her brother's death when she reached the Mescalero reservation. Leaving the mother and infant there, she headed south to find the remnants of the band, which was still unwilling to return to reservation life. An older chief, Nana, had been on a raid for ammunition during the battle and now led the group as it avenged Victorio's death.

Meanwhile, other Chiricahuas, including Geronimo, were living restlessly at San Carlos. There the "repugnant natural conditions" were exacerbated by "intrigue, intertribal rivalries, incompetent and corrupt agents, and conflict between civil and military officials." Moreover, land-hungry, Indian-hating white settlers ringed its boundaries. Tensions were already high when, in August 1881, the army tried to arrest a Western Apache shaman whose preaching seemed to the officials to have dangerously antiwhite overtones. Fighting broke out between the army and the shaman's followers, and the shaman, his wife, and several other Apaches were shot and killed. Lozen may have been visiting the reservation, as one Apache placed her theft of the ammunition laden mules at this time. About seventy Chiricahuas, including Geronimo and other leaders, broke out and headed for Mexico.

They arrived in the Sierra Madre mountains, where the elderly Nednai Apache leader, Juh, was now living. He welcomed straggling groups of recalcitrant Apaches including Nana's Warm Springs band. Juh, too, had given up his attempt, to live at San Carlos and had escaped to the Sierra Madres where his people had lived for generations. The mountains provided an impregnable natural fortress. Various leaders from different Apache bands, local groups, and tribes deferred to Juh. When he died suddenly, Naiche, the son of Cochise (a respected Apache leader who had been killed some years earlier), assumed the role of chief, but Geronimo, by virtue of his military leadership and stronger spiritual power, increasingly became the most important leader.

The Apaches used their natural fortress as a base from which to launch daring raids. In the spring of 1882 Geronimo led sixty warriors back to San Carlos where they killed the police chief and enticed several hundred more Chiricahuas to join them in Mexico. In response the American troops launched an all-out offensive, led by General George Crook, to recapture and subdue the last of the Apaches once and for all.

Crook was never able to administer a decisive defeat, but thanks to Apache scouts working for the U.S. army, he was able to keep the "hostiles" on the run. Constant pursuit and the coming winter made the reservation seem more appealing. It was the summers at San Carlos that the Chiricahuas feared the most, when the heat and malaria-carrying mosquitoes were most dangerous. Winter in the mountains could be harsh, especially when they were so short on supplies. And so, according to Apache memory, Lozen and Dahteste began the negotiations for their people's return. The Apaches reached a deal by which about three hundred of the renegade Chiricahuas moved to an area called Turkey Creek near Fort Apache, on much more appealing land north of San Carlos. Kaywaykla, now old enough to be a young warrior himself, remembered his people settling happily at Turkey Creek and planting successful crops.

But the old reservation tensions resurfaced almost immediately. The agents heard whisperings of insurrection, and the Indians heard rumors that their leaders were to be arrested and imprisoned at Alcatraz Island in San Francisco Bay. Moreover, the military took it upon themselves to interfere more than ever before in the Apaches' family life, policing domestic conflicts normally regulated through the 'kin-based community structure. In May of 1885, fearing arrest, Geronimo and Naiche fled the reservation once again with approximately 140 followers including Lozen and about forty other warriors. The majority of Chiricahuas

remained at San Carlos. Those who escaped leaded back to the fortress of the Sierra Madres. And once again, they left in small groups, the women leading the children. Most of the soldiers pursued the warriors, but a number of women and children were shot or recaptured. General Crook, with his Apache scouts, pursued them for almost a year until a woman, probably Lozen, brought word that again they were ready to negotiate.

Crook met with them on March 25, 1886. Once again, he had administered no decisive defeat so the Chiricahuas were in a strong negotiating position. The Apaches' desire to restore ties of kin and community motivated them to reach an agreement. According to the new deal, the renegades would go to prison in the east for two years, after which they would be permitted to live freely with their families at Turkey Creek. The Indians retained their arms as they began to move north toward the border, but they remained suspicious. While the majority of the group continued on with the troops, Geronimo and Naiche changed their minds and took off again with a handful of their followers. Lozen, as usual, was at their side.

As it turned out, Geronimo and his followers were right to be suspicious of the terms of their surrender. Crook's superiors, General Philip Sheridan and President Grover Cleveland, repudiated the arrangements that Crook had made. They had no intention of releasing these infamous Apache warriors after two years. In anger and embarrassment, Crook resigned, while his replacement, General George Miles, led an augmented force of 5,000 soldiers against the thirty-six men, women, and children who had returned once more to the Sierra Madres. And, again, the American troops, despite their numbers and constant replenishment of supplies, could not defeat the Apaches.

In late August 1886, Lozen and Dahteste, for the final time, assumed the task of opening negotiations. For several days, Lieutenant Charles B. Gatewood, with whom the Apaches had dealt before, and two Apache scouts called Martine and Kayitah followed the women into the mountains, toward the hidden camp. The scouts, carrying a white flag, went ahead up the steep and winding trail. The warriors observed the scouts climb, first with field glasses and then, as the two men got closer, with bare eyes, and they recognized them. The fugitives debated whether or not to shoot them, but decided to admit them to the camp only because Martine was a Nednai and related to one of the warriors.

Geronimo and Naiche's band thought they were in a strong position to negotiate their return to Turkey Creek to join their families, but they were stunned by the news that all the Chiricahuas had been rounded up and sent to Florida. The prisoners included those who had remained in good faith on the reservation the whole time and even the Apache scouts who had served in the U.S. army. The very scouts who had found their hiding place and who had been promised land at Turkey Creek would, it turned out, be imprisoned in Florida. No Chiricahuas would remain in the Southwest. If they wanted to rejoin their kin, this last free group had to go east as well. They agreed to surrender personally to General Miles and, on September 3, 1886, laid down their arms for the last time. Five days later they were train-bound for Florida, and the Indian wars ended.

On the way to Florida, the train stopped near the Nueces River in Texas where a photographer captured a group of the Apaches sitting in front of a railroad car. Naiche, as the chief, sits in the center of the front row, with Geronimo in the place of honor at his left. Lozen is there too, in the only photograph ever taken of her. She is to Geronimo's left, a place reserved for one's second in command, but behind him as well, with women and girls on either side of her. Her face is calm, although her brow is furrowed. None of the captives betray their feelings to the photographer, but Lozen's stance, leaning slightly forward, seems a ready and restless pose, as though she

remains prepared to protect either the girls who hide slightly behind her shoulders or to join the warriors in front of her.

Crowded into Florida's Fort Marion and Fort Pickens, accustomed to the dry climate of their homeland, the Chiricahuas suffered in Florida's heat and humidity. Tuberculosis, malaria, and smallpox took a heavy toll. By 1890, 119 of the 498 Chiricahuas who had been shipped to Florida had died. Their condition, especially the treatment of scouts who had served the American military faithfully, caused a public outcry led by General Crook. In 1887 and 1888, they were moved to the Mount Vernon barracks near Mobile, Alabama, which turned out to be just as miserable and unhealthy, and then, in 1894, to Fort Sill in Oklahoma. Finally, in 1913 the remaining Chiricahua Apaches were given their freedom and the choice of land near Fort Sill or a reservation in south-central New Mexico that they would share with the Mescalero Apaches. While some remained in Oklahoma, the majority returned to New Mexico, where their descendants still live. It was far too late, however, for Lozen. She had survived as far as Alabama, but there, like so many of those she had fought with and for, she succumbed to the "coughing sickness" and died of tuberculosis.

The story of the Apache Indian wars is often told as a heroic struggle among men with legendary names: Geronimo, Victorio, Crook, Miles. It is too easy to forget that at the heart of the wars lay the battle to preserve families, communities, and a culture—and that whole families and communities participated actively in the struggle and suffered immensely in the end. Apaches fought to live on land from which not only their sustenance but also their identity derived, an identity grounded in matrilocal extended families and a complementary sexual division of labor. Throughout this devastating period, Apache culture's strength lay in part in its flexibility. War parties continued to reflect traditional Apache social organization as they were structured around kin relationships and community bonds and called up in order to avenge the deaths of relatives. At the same time the all-out warfare of the late nineteenth century meant that women had difficulty practicing their normal economic roles and instead followed, and sometimes joined, their husbands at war. As wives these women brushed against a permeable gender boundary that Lozen, an unmarried woman warrior, was able to cross.

Lozen forswore Chiricahua gender norms. But although she did not marry, did not have children, did not perform women's typical tasks and instead excelled at masculine pursuits, her community perceived her as neither a threat nor a deviant. Quite the contrary, it celebrated her powerful cross-gender position.

Women warriors may have been unusual in Apache history, but they were also admired, even revered, and Lozen remains emblematic of that tradition. Almost invisible to the American authorities, her reputation and daring exploits survived in Chiricahua oral memory. That there was a place for such a woman within Apache society and that she was committed to using her exceptional position for the good of that society illustrate Apache culture's strength and complexity as it adapted to the dire circumstances of the late nineteenth century. When Lozen declined to live the life of a typical Apache woman, she did not deny the viability of her culture; instead, she spent her life defending it.

GLOSSARY

Apache: A Native American people inhabiting the southwest United States and northern Mexico. Various Apache tribes offered strong resistance to encroachment on their territory in the latter half of the nineteenth century. Present-day Apache populations are located in Arizona, New Mexico, and Oklahoma.

Alcatraz: A rocky island in San Francisco Bay. It was a military prison from 1859 to 1933 and a federal prison until 1963. It is now a tourist attraction.

IMPLICATIONS

Lozen's story raises important issues about Indian resistance and gender roles in Native American society. What do you think made it possible for women to assume such seemingly male roles as war leaders in Indian society? How do you think white Americans would have interpreted the existence of woman warriors such as Lozen?

PART TWO

A Modernizing People

Although the United States entered the twentieth century as one of the world's most advanced industrial nations, many Americans retained their traditional social and religious values and an isolationist view of the world. Between 1900 and 1940, however, intense social change and the worst economic depression in the nation's history forced many ordinary people to question these traditional values and brought others to embrace new, "modern" ways of life and thought. The tension between tradition and modernity thus became an integral part of everyday life in the early-twentieth-century world.

The early twentieth century witnessed the first sustained migration of African Americans from the rural South into the nation's northern and southern cities. Since there were few urban jobs for black men before World War I, the first wave of migrants was composed mostly of African American women, who moved to the cities in order to find work as domestics and laundresses. As Jacqueline Jones argues, these women formed "A Bridge of Bent Backs and Laboring Muscles" that linked their new urban lives with the lives of family members who remained in the rural South. The result was the creation of migration routes that would lead tens of thousands of African Americans to northern industrial centers in the second and third decades of the century.

While cities were the most obvious areas in need of reform during the early decades of the century, numerous problems also existed in rural areas and in the nation's rapidly vanishing wilderness. As the pressure of burgeoning population gradually transformed the natural landscape into farms, ranches, and cities, some reformers wondered about the health of nature itself. Would the heedless destruction of natural resources eventually strip the nation of its scenic resources? And would there be anything left of the country's magnificent wilderness for future generations to enjoy? As Peter Wild argues in "John Muir: The Mysteries of Mountains," it was to ensure the preservation of the nation's natural beauty that reformers such as John Muir fought for the creation of national parks and forests as places where the pristine beauty of nature would be left undisturbed by the consuming forces of modernization.

The largest number of immigrants who came to America in the early twentieth century came from Europe and Latin America to work in the nation's northeastern industrial enterprises. Yet hundreds of thousands of foreign workers also came from China, Japan, and the Philippines to work in West Coast factories and farms. While there were many similarities in the immigrant experience throughout America, Asian immigrants faced particular impediments because they were considered nonwhite and hence barred from citizenship and suffrage rights. In "Unbound Feet," Judy Yung looks at the experiences of Chinese women immigrants in San Francisco in the early days of the twentieth century. Despite the dual debilities of American racism and traditional Chinese gender roles, these women forged a path of adjustment that their daughters and granddaughters would follow to acceptance and integration at the close of the century.

The rapid social changes of the early twentieth century left many Americans feeling ambivalent about the modernity of American society. Reformers, pundits, and ordinary people alike felt the contradictory attractions of tradition and modernity in every aspect of their daily lives. In "Messenger of the New Age," Mary Murphy reveals the magnetic appeal of radio to ordinary citizens during the 1920s. Network entertainment programs, national and international news, and advertising spots opened new worlds to millions of listeners, who embraced the new medium with the same enthusiasm they showed for the motion picture theaters that had begun to appear in their local communities.

The Great Depression burned itself into the minds of all who lived through it. In "What the Depression Did to People," Edward R. Ellis captures the human meaning of the Depression and recounts the myriad ways in which ordinary people coped with this unprecedented crisis in their daily lives. Poverty and deprivation might have been the keynote of the Depression era, but the 1930s also witnessed the rise of new popular music forms, as young people embraced new, upbeat music and dances that added a note of fun and hopeful anticipation to an otherwise bleak period. In "The Crowd Goes Wild," Lewis A. Erenberg shows how American youth used Swing music and the Jitterbug to create a new and expansive youth culture in Depression-era America.

In the wake of the Civil War and Reconstruction, southern planters struggled to adjust to the changed circumstances of their lives. Foremost among these concerns was the supply of labor: now that slaves were free, who would work their fields and process their cotton? The answer throughout the South was to contain the social and political power of freedmen through the creation of Black Codes and the use of intimidation and to keep their former slaves as a usable labor force by trapping them in sharecropping contracts. This essay is introduced by Senate testimony describing the exploitative realities of the sharecropping system.

James T. Rapier, *The Agricultural Labor Force in the South (1880)*

A. Well, sir, there are several reasons why the colored people desire to emigrate from Alabama; one among them is the poverty of the South. On a large part of it a man cannot make a decent living. Another is their want of school privileges in the State: and there is a majority of the people who believe that they cannot any longer get justice in the courts; and another and the greatest reason is found in the local laws that we have, and which are very oppressive to that class of people in the black belt.

Q. State what some of them are.—A. First, we have only schools about three months in the year, and I suppose I need not say anything more on that head. In reference to the poverty of the soil, 33 to 40 per cent of the lands in Alabama is about all on which a man can make a living.

Q. Do you mean the parts that are subdued?—A. Yes, sir; the arable land.

The average is one-third of a bale of cotton to the acre, not making three bales to the hand; and a hundred bushels of corn to the hand, on an average. Then take the price of cotton for the last two years; it has not netted more than $45 to $47.50 to the bale; and I suppose it would not be amiss for me to state something of the plans of working the land in Alabama.

Mr. Vance. It will be very proper.

The Witness. The general plan is that the landlord furnishes the land and the teams and feed for the teams and the implements, for which he draws one half of the crop. I remarked that the three bales of cotton and a hundred bushels of corn is about all that you can make to a hand. We allow in Alabama that much, for that is as much as a man can get out of it, and that is not enough to support his family, including himself and the feed of his family; $95 to $100 is as much as a hand can make, and that is not enough to feed any man in a Christian country. . . .

A. . . . Now, it is very clear that a man cannot live on such terms, and hence the conclusion of many of these people, that there is not a decent living for them in that State. They are like the white people, and their living no better. Numbers of them, probably not less than 20,000 whites, have left Alabama since the war and gone to Texas to better their condition, and the blacks are doing the same thing, and that is the whole there is of it. So far as the negroes are concerned now they have a high desire to submit their fate to their own keeping in another country. Now here is one of the laws which also affects us, to which I will call attention. It is found in the acts of Alabama for 1878–79, page 63, act No. 57, section 1.

Section 1. *Be it enacted by the general assembly of Alabama*, That section 4369 of the Code be, and the same is hereby, amended so as to read as follows: Any person who shall buy, sell, receive, barter, or dispose of any cotton, corn, wheat, oats, pease, or potatoes after the hour of sunset and before the hour of sunrise of the next succeeding day, and any person who shall in any manner move, carry, convey, or transport, except within the limits of the farm or plantation on which it is raised or grown, any seed cotton between the hours of sunset and sunrise of the next succeeding day, shall be guilty of a misdemeanor, and, on conviction, shall be fined not less than ten nor more five hundred dollars, and may also be imprisoned in the county jail, or put to hard labor for the county, for not more

than twelve months. But this section shall not effect the right of municipal corporations to establish and regulate under their charters public markets within their limits for the sale of commodities for culinary purposes, nor the right of any proprietor or owner of any plantation or premises to sell on such plantation or premises the necessary grain and provisions for the subsistence of man and beast for the night to traveling or transient persons, or for the use of agricultural laborers in his own employment on such plantation or premises: *Provided*, That the provisions of such section shall not apply to any person carrying seed cotton to a gin for the purpose of having the same ginned.

Now, the effect of this upon the labor of the South is this: A great many laborers work by the month, but all of them are under contract. If I live three miles from a store, and I must work from sunup to sundown, I cannot go where I can do my trading to the best advantage. A man is prevented, no matter whether his family is sick from sundown to sunrise, from going and selling anything that he has, as the landlord will not give them time between sunrise and sundown.

Q. What was the purpose of this law?—A. It was, as appears from the debates, to keep the negroes from going to stores and taking off seed cotton from the plantation. Certainly it was to have that effect, but it goes further and prevents a man from selling what he has raised and has a right to sell. If a man commits a crime he ought to be punished, but every man ought to have a right to dispose of his own property.

Q. Is there any particular limitation of time to which this law applies?—A. No, sir.

Q. It runs all the year round?—A. Yes, sir.

Q. After the division of the crops as well as before?—A. Yes, sir; it operates so that a man cannot sell his crop at all in many cases.

Q. Do you say that the landlord will not let him sell his crop or that he can prevent it?—A. I say he will not let him do it, because the landlord will not let him take two or three hours out of the time due him in the day to sell it, and the law prevents him from selling at night.

Q. You say the effect of it is not to let him sell his crop at all?—A. I do; for if a man agrees to work from sunup to sundown he is made to do it. I work them that way myself, and I believe all the rest do. . . .

Q. It shall not be lawful to buy or sell seed cotton?—A. Yes, sir.

Q. At any time?—A. Yes, sir; night or day.

Q. From nobody?—A. From nobody.

Q. White or black?—A. White or black; but you see it applies wholly to black counties.

Q. But there are some white people there, are there not?—A. Yes, sir; but I do not know many who raise seed cotton.

Q. I thought something, may be, was left out of that act?—A. No, sir; that is to say, the gist of the matter is this: I may raise as much cotton as I please in the seed, but I am prohibited by law from selling it to anybody but the landlord, who can buy it because he has advanced to me on the crop. One of the rules is this: I have people working for me to day, but I give them an outside patch. If a man makes outside 1,200 pounds of seed cotton, which is worth $2.50 per 100 pounds, he cannot sell it unless to me. I may say I will give him $1.50 per 100 pounds for it, and he will be forced to take it; but I cannot sell it again unless I have a merchantable bale, which is 500 pounds, or 450 pounds by the cotton congress.

Q. Then the effect of that law is to place all the seed cotton into the hands of the landlord?—A. Yes, sir.

Q. He is the only purchaser who is allowed by law to buy it?—A. Yes, sir; nobody else can buy it. . . .

Q. I thought the law said that grand larceny should consist of as much as $235 worth?—A. No, sir; you have not got it right yet. Two ears or a stalk of corn is a part of an outstanding crop, and any man who sells any part of an outstanding crop can be prosecuted and convicted of grand larceny. . . .

The Witness. The point is this: Under the laws of Alabama the probate judge, the clerk, and the sheriff have had the drawing of jurors, and have had since Alabama was admitted as a State: but this bill comes in and covers those counties where the Republicans are likely to have a majority, and where they would draw the jurors. The proper heading of the law might have been, "An act to keep negroes off the juries." I want to state that it is the general opinion of the colored people in Alabama, and I will say of some of the judges, that it is a difficult matter for a colored man to get justice when there is a case between him and a white man. I will cite one of those cases: There was a case in Montgomery in which Judge J. Q. Smith presided. It was a civil suit. A white man had a black man's crop attached, and he had lost it. The colored man sued him on the attachment bond, and employed Judge Gardiner to defend or prosecute it for him. Soon after the case was given to the jury they brought in a verdict for the defendant. Judge Gardiner moved for a new trial, on the ground that the verdict was not in accordance with the facts; and the judge said, "I have observed that where an issue is between a white and a black man before a jury the verdict is almost invariably against the black man. The grounds on which the judge said he would not grant a new trial would be because he thinks the next verdict would not be different from that rendered, and as I do not think there would be a different verdict, I decline to give the new trial."

7

A Bridge of Bent Backs and Laboring Muscles: The Rural South, 1880–1915

Jacqueline Jones

In the years immediately following the Civil War, southern planters faced an uncertain future. The Union victory ended the slave labor system that planters had relied on since the seventeenth century, and while they were able to forestall a congressional attempt to dispossess former slave owners of their land, that land was useless without the labor necessary for growing and harvesting the cotton, sugar, and tobacco crops that were the source of planter profits. Faced with an immediate and pressing need for low-cost labor, between 1865 and 1880 landowners throughout the South turned to sharecropping and debt peonage as a means to secure a continued supply of agricultural labor. By the end of Reconstruction in 1877, the majority of former slaves, although legally free, were again under the control of white planters.

The working lives of these black sharecroppers were little different from their existence under slavery. This was especially true of freedwomen, who continued to be bound to the double duties of field and household labor long after the end of slavery. Until they abandoned sharecropping and moved northward to take up independent work as laundresses and domestics during World War I, these southern black women lived lives of toil and persistent expectation. Like every member of sharecropping households, women labored long hours to help families survive; but as Jacqueline Jones reveals in this essay, they also lived with the hope that their labor would permit their children to escape the economic and social bondage of postwar southern society.

For black women in the rural South, the years 1880 to 1915 spanned a period between the Civil War era and the "Great Migration" northward beginning with World War I. Although the physical dimensions of their domestic chores and field work had not changed much since slavery, women during this period toiled with the new hope that their sons and daughters would one day escape from the Cotton South. Maud Lee Bryant, a farm wife in Moncure, North Carolina, spent long days in the fields chopping cotton, wheat, and tobacco, and long nights in the house, washing dishes and clothes, scrubbing floors, and sewing, starching, and ironing. She later recalled, "My main object of working was wanting the children to have a better way of living, that the world might be just a little better because the Lord had me here of something, and I tried to make good out of it, that was my aim." Thus the substance of rural women's work stayed the same compared to earlier generations, while its social context was transformed by the promise, but not necessarily the reality, of freedom.

Black sharecroppers, with the "proverbial unacquisitiveness of the 'rolling stone,'" remained outside the mainstream of liberal American society during the years from 1880 to 1915. Their quest for household and group autonomy, like the heavy iron hoes they carried to the cotton fields, represented the tangible legacy of slavery. In an industrializing, urbanizing nation, the former slaves and their children were concentrated in the rural South, and their distinctive way of life became increasingly anomalous within the larger society. Caught in the contradiction of a cash-crop economy based upon a repressive labor system, black households achieved neither consumer status nor total self-sufficiency. Consequently, the lives of black women were fraught with irony; though many had planted, chopped, and picked their share of cotton over the years, they rarely enjoyed the pleasure of a new cotton dress. Though they labored within an agricultural economy, they and their families barely survived on meager, protein-deficient diets. Within individual black households, this tension between commercial and subsistence agriculture helped to shape the sexual division of labor, as wives divided their time among domestic responsibilities, field work, and petty moneymaking activities.

The postbellum plantation economy required a large, subservient work force that reinforced the racial caste system but also undermined the economic status of an increasing number of nonelite whites. By the end of the nineteenth century, nine out of ten Afro-Americans lived in the South, and 80 percent of these resided in rural areas, primarily in the formerly slave Cotton Belt. Blacks represented one-third of the southern population and 40 percent of its farmers and farm laborers, but by no means its only poverty-stricken agricultural group. Up-country yeomen farmers were gradually drawn away from livestock and food production and into the commercial economy after the Civil War. In the process they lost their economic independence to a burgeoning system of financial credit. Yet on a social hierarchy that ranged from planters at the top to small landowners in the middle and various states of tenancy at the bottom—cash renters, share tenants, sharecroppers, and wage laborers—blacks monopolized the very lowliest positions. In 1910 fully nine-tenths of all southern blacks who made their living from the soil worked as tenants, sharecroppers, or contract laborers. Most barely eked out enough in cotton to pay for rent, food, and supplies. They did not own their own equipment, nor could they market their crop independent of the landlord. As the price of cotton declined precipitously near the end of the century, landlords began to insist on a fixed amount of cash—rather than a share of the crop—as payment for rent. Thus individual black households had to bear the brunt of a faltering staple-crop economy.

The black women who emerged from slavery "knew that what they got wasn't what they wanted, it wasn't freedom, really." So they constantly searched for freedom, moving with their families at the end of each year to find better soil or a more reasonable landlord; or, bereft of a husband and grown sons, traveling to a nearby town to locate gainful employment; or raising chickens so they could sell eggs and send their children to school. These women partook of the uniqueness of rural, late-nineteenth-century Afro-American culture and at the same time bore the universal burdens and took solace from the universal satisfactions of motherhood. They were the mothers and grandmothers of the early-twentieth-century migrants to northern cities, migrants who as young people had been reared in homes with primitive hearths where women of all ages continued to guard the "embers of a smoldering liberty."

THE TRIPLE DUTY OF WIVES, MOTHERS, DAUGHTERS, AND GRANDMOTHERS

For black Americans, the post-Reconstruction era opened inauspiciously. According to Nell Irvin Painter, between 1879 and 1881 as many as twenty thousand rural blacks fled the "young hell" of the Lower South in search of the "promised land" of Kansas. Around this millenarian migration coalesced the major themes of Afro-American history from 1880 to 1915: the forces of terrorism and poverty that enveloped all rural blacks, and the lure of land, education, and "protection for their women" that made them yearn for true freedom. "Rooted in faith and in fear," the Kansas fever exodus consisted primarily of families headed by former slaves desperate to escape neoslavery. Together with their menfolk, then, black women did their best to minimize the control that whites sought to retain over their lives—a "New South" mandate succinctly summarized by the governor of North Carolina in 1883: "Your work is the tilling of the ground, . . . Address yourselves to the work, men and women alike."

In order to understand the roles of black women as workers and household members, it is necessary to examine the methods used by whites to supervise and restrict the options of the family as an economic unit. Although granted relatively more overall freedom than their slave parents, black men and women in the late nineteenth century had only a limited ability to make crucial decisions related to household and farm management. The nature of the sharecropping system meant that economic matters and family affairs overlapped to a considerable degree. Under optimal conditions, each family would have been able to decide for itself how best to use its members' labor, and when or whether to leave one plantation in search of better land or a more favorable contractual arrangement. These conditions rarely pertained in the Cotton South.

By the early twentieth century, some plantations were so large and efficiently managed they resembled agricultural industrial establishments with hired hands rather than a loose conglomeration of independently operated family farms. The degree to which a household was supervised determined its overall status in southern society, and blacks were systematically deprived of self-determination to a greater degree than their poor white counterparts. For example, in an effort to monitor their tenants' work habits, large cotton planters often employed armed "riders" who were "constantly traveling from farm to farm." As agents of the white landowner, these men kept track of the size of each black family and had the authority to order all "working hands" into the fields at any time. Riders dealt with recalcitrant workers by "wearing them out" (that is, inflicting physical punishment). Indeed, a government researcher noted that southern sharecroppers in general were "subjected to quite as complete supervision by the owner, general lessee or hired manager as that to which the wage laborers are subjected on large farms in the North and West, and indeed in the South." The more tenants a planter had, the larger his profit; hence he would more readily withhold food from a family of unsatisfactory workers, or deny its children an opportunity for schooling, than turn them off his land.

The planter thus sought to intervene in the black farmer's attempt to organize the labor of various family members. Usually the father assumed major responsibility for crop production, and he relied on the assistance of his wife and children during planting and harvesting. But, reported Thomas J. Edwards in his 1911 study of Alabama sharecroppers, if the father failed to oversee the satisfactory completion of a chore, then "the landlord compels every member of his family who is able to carry a hoe or plow to clean out the crops." Some very small households counted on relatives and neighbors to help them during these times; others had to pay the expense of extra laborers hired by the landlord to plow, weed, or chop the cotton on their own farms.

Ultimately a white employer controlled not only a family's labor, but also its "furnishings" and food. By combining the roles of landlord and merchant-financier, he could regulate the flow of both cash and supplies to his tenants. Annual interest rates as high as 25 percent (in the form of a lien on the next year's crop) were not unusual, and tenants had little choice but to borrow when they needed to buy seed, fertilizer, and clothes for the children. Some white men, like the planter who forbade sharecroppers on his land to raise hogs so that they would have to buy their salt pork from him, effectively reduced the opportunities for families to provide for their own welfare in the most basic way. To escape this vicious cycle of dependency required a good deal of luck, as well as the cooperation of each household member. The hardworking Pickens family of Arkansas, overwhelmed by debt in 1888, tried desperately to free themselves. Recalled William, the sixth of ten children: ". . . in the ensuing winter Mother cooked and washed and Father felled trees in the icy 'brakes' to make rails and boards [to sell]." Their landlord removed temptation by closing the neighbor-

hood school. Referring to that time, William Pickens remembered many years later that "very small children can be used to hoe and pick cotton, and I have seen my older sisters drive a plow."

Since tenant–landlord accounts were reckoned at the end of each year, sharecroppers had to remain on a farm until they received payment for their cotton (usually in December) or until they had discharged their debt to their employer. The tendency of families to move whenever they had the opportunity—up to one-third left for another, usually nearby, plantation at the end of any one year—caused apprehension among planters who wanted to count on a stable work force for extended periods of time. In the end the very measures used to subordinate black farmers served as an impetus for them to migrate—to another county, a nearby town, or, after 1916, a northern city. But until alternative forms of employment became available (the lack of free land and transportation halted the exodus to Kansas after a couple of years), most sharecroppers continued to move around to some extent within the plantation economy, but not out of it. Consequently, the annual December trek of sharecropping families from one plantation to another constituted a significant part of Afro-American community life. Some families "were ever on the move from cabin to cabin," prompting the story about the household whose chickens "regularly presented themselves in the dooryard at Christmastime with their legs crossed for tying up before the next morning. . . ." Within such a circumscribed realm of activity, even a neighboring plantation seemed to beckon with opportunity, or at least the possibility of change.

As productive members of the household economy, black women helped to fulfill the economic as well as the emotional needs of their families, factors to consider whenever a move was contemplated. These needs changed over the life course of individual families and clans. So too did the demands upon women fluctuate in the cabin and out in the cotton field, from season to season and from year to year. Thus the responsibilities of wives and mothers reflected considerations related to their families' immediate daily welfare, the fortunes of their kinfolk, and the staple-crop planting and harvesting cycle. Within this constantly shifting matrix of obligations, black women performed housekeeping and childcare tasks, earned modest sums of cash, and worked in the fields.

It is useful to begin a discussion of the farm wife's daily routine with the experience of a young married couple. She and her husband began their life together with very little in the way of material possessions, and they often had to make do with the "sorriest land"— "Land so doggone thin . . . 'it won't sprout unknown peas.'" At least for the first few years, each new baby (there would probably be five or six who would survive infancy) meant an extra mouth to feed and body to clothe while the number of available "hands" in the family stayed the same. Consequently a young wife had to divide her time between domestic tasks and cotton cultivation, the mainstay of family life; she did "a man's share in the field, and a woman's part at home." As Rossa B. Cooley reported of a South Carolina Sea Island family, "Occupation: Mother, farming and housework. Father, farming."

The primitive conditions under which these women performed household chores means that the term housework—when used in the traditional sense—is somewhat misleading. The size and rudeness of a sharecropper's dwelling made it extremely difficult to keep clean and tidy. Constructed by the white landowner usually many years before, the one- or two-room log or sawn-lumber cabin measured only fifteen or twenty square feet. It lacked glass windows, screens to keep out bugs and flies, running water, sanitary facilities, artificial illumination, cupboard and shelf space, and adequate insulation as well as ventilation. Most of the daily business of living—eating, sleeping, bathing— took place in one room where "stale sickly odors" inevitably accumulated. The ashes from

a smoky fire used to prepare the evening meal had barely cooled before the children had to "bundle themselves up as well as they might and sleep on the floor in front of the fireplace," while their parents shared a small bed in the same room. Each modest addition to the cabin increased a family's living space and relative comfort—a lean-to, chicken coop–like kitchen; a wooden floor; efficient chimney; sleeping loft for the children; closets and cupboards; or an extra bedroom.

Farm wives had little in the way of time, money, or incentive to make permanent improvements in or around a cabin the family did not own and hoped to leave in the next year or two anyway. One Alabama mother summed up her frustration this way: "I have done dug holes in de ya[r]d by moonlight mo' dan o[n]ce so dat whah I stay at might hab a rose-bush, but I nebber could be sho' whose ya[r]d it would be de nex' yeah." Yet many women remained sensitive to their domestic environment; if they could not always find time to clean up the mud tracked in from outside each day, still they rearranged the house "very nice to meet the great Easter morning," whitewashed it for a Christmas celebration, dug up flowers in the woods to plant in the yard, or attached brightly colored pictures to the inside walls.

Most families owned few pieces of heavy furniture; modest earnings were often invested in a mule, ox, plow, or wagon rather than domestic furnishings. In any case, a paucity of goods was appreciated when the time came to pick up and move on to another place. Sharecroppers' households also lacked artifacts of middle-class life, such as a wide variety of eating and cooking utensils, books, papers, pencils, bric-a-brac, and clocks. Black rural women relied on very few pieces of basic equipment in the course of the day; these included a large tub in which to bathe the youngsters and scrub the clothes, a cooking kettle, and a water pail. Their material standard of living was considerably lower than that of mid-century western pioneer families.

The round of daily chores performed by a sharecropper's wife indicates that the arduousness of this way of life bore an inverse relation to its "simplicity." She usually rose with the roosters (about 4 A.M., before other members) to prepare breakfast over an open fire—salt pork (sliced thin and then fried), molasses and fat on cornbread. She either served the meal in the cabin or took it out to family members who were by this time already at work in the field.

During the planting season she joined her husband and children outside at tasks assigned on the basis of sex and age. For example, a typical division of labor included a father who "ran furrows" using a plow drawn by a mule or oxen, a small child who followed him dropping seeds or "potato slips" on the ground, and "at each step the mother covering them with a cumbersome hoe or setting out the plants by piercing holes in the ground with a sharp stick, inserting the roots, and packing the earth with deft movements of the hand." Although she knew as much about the growing cycle as her husband, she probably deferred to his judgment when it came to deciding what she needed to do and when. More than one black person remembered a mother who "done anything my daddy told her to do as far as cultivatin a crop out there. . . ."

Harvest time consumed a substantial portion of each year; two to four cotton pickings lasted from August to December. Like planting techniques, picking had remained the same since the earliest days of slavery, and young and old, male and female, performed essentially the same task. During this period in particular, the Cotton South was remarkable for its resistance to technological innovations compared to the industrial section of the Northeast, or commercial agriculture in the Midwest, a fact that weighed heavily on the shoulders of rural black women. Cotton picking was still such a labor-intensive task, few tenant-farm wives could escape its rigors. The importance of this operation to the well-being of the family—the greater the crop, the more favor-

able their economic situation at the end of the year—necessitated the labor of every able-bodied person and took priority over all but the most vital household chores.

In the sharecropping family, children were a distinct economic asset. In 1880 nine out of ten southern black wives between the ages of twenty-one and thirty had at least one child aged three or under. Just as the agricultural system helped to influence family size, so the growing season affected an expectant mother's ability to refrain from field work. In 1918 a Children's Bureau report noted that "to some extent, the amount of rest a mother can have before and after confinement is determined by the time of year or by the stage of cotton crop upon which depends the livelihood of the family." The birth of a child represented the promise of better times in terms of augmenting the household's labor supply, but for the time being it increased the workload of other family members and placed additional physical demands on the new mother herself.

Compared to slave women, sharecroppers' wives had more flexibility when it came to taking care of their children during the day. Some women managed to hoe and keep an eye on an infant at the same time. But many, like the mother who laid her baby to sleep on a nearby fence rail, only to return and find "a great snake crawling over the child," found it difficult to divide their attention between the two tasks. Slightly older children presented problems of a different sort. For instance, the mother of five-year-old John Coleman had to choose between leaving him to his own devices while she worked in the field—he liked to run off and get into mischief in the creek—and coaxing him to help alongside her, "thinning the cotton or corn . . . picking cotton or peas." At the age of six or seven oldest siblings often remained at home to watch over the younger children while their mother labored "in the crop."

In preparation for the main meal of the day (about 11 A.M.), a woman left the field early to collect firewood (which she might carry home on her back) and fetch water from a stream or well. (If she was lucky, she had children to help her with water-toting, one of the worst forms of domestic drudgery; they would follow along behind her, carrying piggins, pails, or cups according to their size.) The noontime meal often consisted of food left over from breakfast, supplemented (if they were fortunate) by turnip or collard greens from the family garden during the months of summer and early fall. The additional time required to fish, hunt for wild game, and pick berries, and the money needed to purchase additional supplies, meant that many sharecropping families subsisted on a substandard, protein-poor diet of "meat, meal, and molasses," especially in the winter and spring. The decline in black fertility rates during the late nineteenth century and the strikingly high child mortality rates during the same period were probably due at least in part to the poor health of rural women and their families.

In the afternoon, work in the fields resumed. Once again, "the house was left out of order [as it was] in the morning, the cooking things scattered about the hearth just as they were used, and the few dishes on the old table . . . unwashed too." Indeed, travelers and social workers often remarked on the dirty dishes and unmade beds that were the hallmark of a sharecropper's cabin. Sympathetic observers realized that women who spent "twelve hours of the day in the field" could hardly hope to complete certain "homemaking" chores. The routine of meal preparation was repeated in the evening. After she collected firewood, brought up the water, and milked the cow, a wife began to prepare the final meal of the day. Once the family had finished eating, she might light a pine knot—"No lamps or oil are used unless some one is sick"—but usually family activity ceased around sunset. After a long day of physical labor, "nature overcomes the strongest and sleep is sought by all of the family"—for some, on mattresses stuffed with corn shucks and pine needles and pillows full of chicken feathers.

Few rural women enjoyed respite from the inexorable demands of day-to-day household tasks or the annual cycle of cotton cultivation. Nursing a newborn child and cooking the family's meals; digging, hoeing, and chopping in the fields—these chores dictated the daily and seasonal rhythms of a black wife's life. But they represented only the barest outline of her domestic obligations. On rainy days, or by the light of a nighttime fire, she sewed quilts and mended clothes. "I worked many hours after they was in bed," recalled one mother of nine; "Plenty of times I've been to bed at three and four o'clock and get up at five the first one in the morning." During the day she had to carve out time to grind corn for meal, bathe the children, weed the garden, gather eggs, and do the laundry. Periodically she devoted an entire day to making soap out of ashes and lard or helping with the hog butchering.

At this point, it is important to note that, unlike their slave grandmothers, most sharecropping women did not have the necessary equipment to spin cotton into thread and weave thread into cloth; the expense and bulk of spinning wheels and looms precluded household self-sufficiency in the area of textile production. Ironically, then, although the rural black family lived surrounded by raw cotton, its clothing had to be purchased from a local white merchant. A woman's freedom from the seemingly endless chores of spinning and weaving required a family's increased dependence on credit controlled by whites.

Her involvement with very poor women in the Alabama backcountry at the turn of the century convinced social worker Georgia Washington that "the mother has to hustle all through the winter, in order to get anything" for the family. The "wife and children are worked very hard every year" to pay for the bare necessities, but where "the family is large they are only half fed and clothed. . . ." As a result, most wives attempted to supplement the family income in a variety of ways, few of which earned them more than a few extra cents at a time. Some picked and sold berries or peanuts, while others marketed vegetables, eggs, and butter from the family's garden, chickens, and cow. A "midder" (midwife) found that her services were frequently in demand. Part-time laundresses took in washing and worked at home with the assistance of their older children.

Although modest in terms of financial return, these activities were significant because they yielded small amounts of cash for families that had to rely chiefly on credit. Furthermore, they allowed mothers to earn money and simultaneously care for their small children, and provided them with an opportunity to engage in commercial exchange on a limited basis and in the process gain a measure of self-esteem through the use of shrewd trading skills. This form of work contrasted with their husbands' responsibilities for crop production, which included not only field labor but also monthly and annual dealings with white landowner-merchants. Thus men's income-producing activities took place in the larger economic sphere of a regional cotton market, while women worked exclusively within the household and a localized foodstuff and domestic-service economy.

Husbands preferred that their wives not work directly for whites, and, if they had to, that they labor in their own homes (as laundresses, for example) rather than in a white woman's kitchen. Still, out of economic necessity, a mother's money-making efforts could periodically compel her to leave her house. Although relatively few Cotton Belt women worked regularly as servants for whites (4.1 percent in 1880; 9 percent in 1900), some performed day service during the slack season. In addition, if a black household was relatively large and productive (that is, if it included a sufficient number of "hands" to support itself), a woman might hire herself out to a local planter for at least part of the year. In 1910, 27 percent of all black female agricultural laborers earned wages this way. One Alabama mother managed to combine childcare with wage earning; she took her stepson along when she "went

and chopped cotton for white folks." He later recalled, "My stepmother wanted my company; but she also wanted to see me eat two good meals" provided each day by the landowner. As three-quarter hands, women could make about 35 cents per day for "full hours in the field."

Children often helped in and around the house; they supplied additional (though somewhat unpredictable) labor and supposedly stayed within their mother's sight and earshot in the process. Youngsters of five or six also worked in the fields, dropping seeds or toting water. As mentioned earlier, white planters often shaped a family's priorities when it came to the use of children as workers; as a general rule, landowners believed that "the raising of children must not interfere with the raising of cotton," and they advanced food to a household in proportion to its "working hands" and not its actual members. W. E. B. DuBois, in his 1899 study, "The Negro in the Black Belt," found sharecroppers' children to be "poorly dressed, sickly, and cross," an indication that poor nutrition combined with hard work took their toll at an early age. Parents at times hired out children to white employers in order to lessen the crowding at home and bring in extra money.

The sexual division of labor between boys and girls became more explicit as they grew older. For example, some families put all their children to work in the fields with the exception of the oldest daughter. Most girls served domestic apprenticeships under their mothers, but at the same time they learned to hoe and pick in the cotton fields and, in some cases, to chop wood and plow (these latter two were usually masculine tasks). In 1900 over half of all Cotton Belt households reported that at least one daughter aged sixteen or less was working as a field laborer. Still, girls probably worked in the fields less often, and in proportionately smaller numbers, than boys, and their parents seemed more willing to allow them to acquire an education; school attendance rates among black females remained higher than those among males throughout the period 1880 to 1915, producing an early form of the "farmer's daughter effect." In the fifteen-to-twenty-year age bracket, only seven black males attended school for every ten females. By 1910 literacy rates among young people revealed that girls had surpassed boys in literacy, although the situation was reversed among elderly men and women.

The financial imperatives of sharecropping life produced rates of prolonged dependency for both sexes compared to those of rural wage-earning economies. Black youths who worked on the sugar plantations of Louisiana often grew resentful of having to turn over their wages to their parents, and struck out on their own when they reached the age of fourteen or fifteen. As a result, it was economically feasible for "both boys and girls [to] mate early, take houses, and set up for themselves." On the other hand, sharecroppers' sons could draw upon little in the way of cash resources if they wanted to marry, forcing them "to wait for the home attractions." Men in the Cotton Belt married around age twenty-five, women at age twenty, reflecting, once again, the lessened demands made upon daughters as field workers.

The demographic and economic characteristics of rural black families demonstrate the continuous and pervasive effects of poverty. From 1880 to 1910 the fertility of black women declined by about one-third, due to disease and poor nutrition among females all over the South and their particularly unhealthful living conditions in urban areas. The life expectancy of black men and women at birth was only thirty-three years. If a woman survived until age twenty, she could expect to see one out of three of her children die before its tenth birthday and to die herself (around the age of fifty-four) before the youngest left home. Those women who outlived their husbands faced the exceedingly difficult task of trying to support a farm family on their own. Even women accustomed to plowing with a team of oxen and knowledgeable about the intricacies of cotton cultivation could find the process of bargaining with a white man for seed, supplies, and a sufficient amount of land to be an insurmountable barrier. Many widows relied on the assistance of an older son or other male relative, consolidated their own household with that of neighbors or kin, or moved to the city in search of paid work.

Women headed about 11 percent of all rural black southern households at any one time between 1880 and 1900, but not all of those who managed a farm or supervised the field work of their children were single mothers or widows. Some sharecropping fathers regularly left home to work elsewhere, resulting in a distinction between the "real" (that is, blood) family and the "economic" (cohabitating) household. In the Cotton Belt, men might leave their wives and children to till their land while they hired themselves out to a nearby planter. (In 1910 one-half of all southern black men employed in agriculture earned wages on either a year-round or temporary basis.) This pattern was especially common in areas characterized by noncotton local economies that provided alternative sources of employment for men.

For example, on the South Carolina coast, some black men toiled as day laborers in the rice industry, while others left their farms for Savannah or Charleston in order to earn extra money (usually only a few dollars each week) as stevedores or cotton-gin workers. Phosphate mining in the same area enabled husbands, fathers, and older sons to work together as "dredge han's" and to escape the tedium of rural life. A poor harvest or a natural disaster (like the great hurricane of 1896) affecting the Sea Islands prompted a general exodus of male household members old enough to work for wages; some went north, while most settled for indefinite periods of time in other parts of the South. Sugar plantations (in Louisiana), sawmills and coal mines (in Tennessee), lumbering and turpentine camps (along the Florida and Alabama coast), brickyards, and railroad construction projects provided income for men who sought to work for cash rather than "credit." While the "real" family never changed, then, the "economic" household responded to seasonal opportunities and to its own specific economic needs.

As older children began to leave a mature family, the economic gains achieved at the height of its productivity gradually slipped away. These established households sometimes took in boarders or relatives to offset the loss of departed offspring. There seemed to be no single pattern of either work or dependency among the rural elderly. For instance, DuBois noted of Black Belt communities in general, "Away down at the edge of the woods will live some grizzle-haired black man, digging wearily in the earth for his last crust; or a swarthy fat auntie, supported in comfort by an absent daughter, or an old couple living half by charity and half by odd jobs."

Widows throughout the South represented extremes of hardship and well-being. An elderly woman living alone sometimes took in a young "mudderless" or "drift" (orphan) for mutual companionship and support. Like Aunt Adelaide, who "received less and less when she needed more and more" once her children left home, some of these women lamented their loss of self-sufficiency: "I ben strong ooman," said Adelaide, "I wuk fo' meself wid me han'. I ben ma[r]sh-cuttin' ooman. I go in de ma[r]sh and cut and carry fo' myself." At the other end of the spectrum was the widow Mrs. Henry; she supported herself by farming and "peddling cakes" until her health failed—or rather, faltered. After that she made a comfortable living selling sweet potatoes, poultry, hogs, and vegetables with the aid of two other women and a child.

Regardless of their physical circumstances, these women formed a bridge of "bent backs and laboring muscles" between "the old African and slavery days, and the sixty difficult years of freedom" for their grandchildren and all younger people in the community. Although men headed individual households, it was not unusual to find an elderly woman presiding

over a group of people who in turn cared for her. In Charlotte, North Carolina, the former slave Granny Ann lived alone but "everybody respected" her and "they never would let her cook for herself." She served as spiritual advisor to the neighborhood. To cite another case, according to the 1900 census, Winnie Moore, aged eighty and mother of ten children, lived alone in Perry County, Alabama, with no visible means of support. But at least five nearby households included Moores. Among them was that of John (aged thirty-four) and his wife Sarah (thirty) who had a daughter of twelve named Winnie. Together grandmother and granddaughter Winnie reached from slavery into the twentieth century, and in their lives comingled the anguish of bondage and the ambiguity of freedom.

Despite the variations in these commercial economies, certain patterns of family organization remained characteristic of blacks in the rural South throughout the period from 1880 to 1915. For most households, a single, sudden misfortune—a flood, a summer drought, high prices for fertilizer, the death of a mule or cow—could upset the delicate balance between subsistence and starvation. Husbands and wives, sons and daughters, friends and kinfolk coordinated their labor and shifted their place of residence in order to stave off disaster—a process that was never-ending. Yet even the poorest families sought to preserve a division of labor between the sexes so that fathers assumed primary responsibility for the financial affairs of the household and mothers oversaw domestic chores first and labored as field hands or wage earners when necessary.

WOMEN'S WORK AND ASPIRATIONS

To outsiders, rural life, set within a larger framework of southern economic backwardness, seemed bleak indeed. DuBois himself asserted that the rural black person's "outlook in the majority of cases is hopeless." Perhaps on the surface the struggle for a living was waged "out of the grim necessity . . . without query or protest," as he suggested. But below that surface ran a deep current of restlessness among even the least fortunate. In St. Meigs, Alabama, Georgia Washington worked with farm wives who "looked pretty rough on the outside." She soon discovered that these mothers were "dissatisfied themselves and anxious to change things at home and do better, but had no idea how or where to begin." They especially wanted the time and resources "to mend or clean up the children before sending them to school in the morning." According to Washington, their "dissatisfaction" was a hopeful sign, proof that they had not succumbed to a paralyzing fatalism.

Two developments in late-nineteenth-century southern society—increasing literacy rates and a general urban in-migration among southern blacks—suggest that at least some families managed to wrench themselves from the past and look to the future. Neither books nor a home in the city would guarantee freedom, but they did afford coming generations a way of life that differed in important respects from the neoslavery of the rural South. Because black girls attended school in greater numbers than boys, and because southern towns had disproportionately large black female populations, it is important to examine the relevance of these developments in regard to Afro-American women and their aspirations for their daughters and sons.

It was not uncommon for sharecroppers' children who acquired some schooling later to credit their mothers with providing them with the opportunity to learn. Speaking from experience, William Pickens declared, "Many an educated Negro owes his enlightenment to the toil and sweat of a mother." The saying "chickens for shoes" referred to women's practice of using the money they earned selling eggs and chickens to buy shoes for their children so that they could attend school in the winter. Rossa B. Cooley pointed out that some black mothers were particularly concerned about rescuing

their daughters from a fate they themselves had endured. For example, born and raised in slavery, the Sea Island woman Chloe had "one idea" for her daughter Clarissa and that was "an education that meant going to school and away from all the drudgery, the chance to wear pretty clothes any day in the week, and as her utmost goal, the Latin and algebra offered by the early Negro schools in their zeal to prove the capacity of liberated blacks." Female college graduates who responded to a survey conducted by Atlanta University researchers in 1900 frequently mentioned the sacrifices of their mothers, who, like Job, were "patience personified."

Frances Harper, a black writer and lecturer, suggested that black mothers "are the levers which move in education. The men talk about it . . . but the women work most for it." She recounted examples of mothers who toiled day and night in the fields and over the washtub in order to send their children to school. One mother "urged her husband to go in debt 500 dollars" for their seven children's education. This emphasis on women's support for schooling raises the question of whether or not mothers and fathers differed in their perception of education and its desirability for their own offspring.

Although girls engaged in some types of field and domestic labor at an early age, we have seen that parents excused them more often and for longer periods of time (compared to their brothers) to attend the neighborhood school. For instance, the George C. Burleson family listed in the 1900 federal manuscript census for Pike County, Alabama, included four children. Ida May, the oldest (aged sixteen), had attended school for six of the previous twelve months. Her younger brother, Clifford (aged eleven) had worked as a farm laborer all year and had not gone to school at all. In 1910 the Bureau of the Census remarked upon higher female literacy rates among the younger generation by observing, "Negro girls and younger women have received at least such elementary school training as is represented by the ability to write, more generally than have Negro boys and men."

If literate persons prized their own skills highly, they might have felt more strongly about enabling their children to learn to read and write. Apparently, in some rural families the different experiences and immediate concerns of fathers compared to mothers prompted conflicting attitudes toward schooling. Perhaps the experiences of Martin V. Washington were not so unusual. Born in 1878 in South Carolina, Washington grew up in a household composed of his parents and ten siblings. His mother had received a grammar-school education, but his father had never gone to school. "Because of the lack of his education," explained Washington, "my father was not anxious for his children to attend school; he preferred to have them work on the farm." On the other hand, his mother, "who knew the value of an education," tried to ensure that all of her children acquired some schooling.

For blacks in the rural South, even a smattering of education could provoke discontent and thereby disrupt family and community life. Martin Washington's father might have feared that his children would move away; Martin himself eventually emigrated to New York City. Nate Shaw put the matter succinctly: "As a whole, if children got book learnin enough they'd jump off of this country; they don't want to plow, don't want no part of no sort of field work." He believed that the "biggest majority" of literate blacks sooner or later moved to town to find a "public job." If education was a means of personal advancement, then it could splinter families, as young people, eager to flee from the routine of rural life, abandoned the farms of their parents.

The Pickens family of South Carolina moved from the country to the village of Pendleton in the late 1880s. The various factors that shaped their decision revealed how considerations related to both work and schooling attracted people to the towns. (The 1880s represented the peak period of black urban in-migration between 1865 and 1915.) Mrs. Pickens had a great desire "to school the children," but they could hardly attend classes on a regular basis as long as the family's white landlord "would not tolerate a tenant who put his children to school in the farming season." Working together, the Pickenses just barely made ends meet in any case; cotton prices had fallen to the point where a hand earned only 35 or 40 cents a day for picking one hundred pounds.

In Pendleton, the children could attend a better school for longer stretches at a time. Their father relinquished the plow in order to become a "man of all work," and their mother found a job as a cook in a hotel. She preferred this type of employment over field work because it allowed her "somewhat better opportunities" to care for her small children (she probably took them to work with her). William Pickens believed that town life afforded a measure of financial independence for the family, compared to his experiences on a tenant farm where "my father worked while another man reckoned." The young man himself went on to become a scholar and an official of the early National Association for the Advancement of Colored People (NAACP).

By 1910 about 18 percent of the southern black population lived in towns of 2,500 inhabitants or more (an increase of 11 percent over 1860). Since emancipation, small but steadily increasing numbers of former slaves had made their way cityward. As wives, widows, and daughters, black women participated in this gradual migration in disproportionately large numbers. Some women accompanied their husbands to town so that the family as a whole could benefit from the wider variety of jobs available to blacks. Unmarried women—including daughters eager to break away from the "dreary drudgery" of the sharecropper's farm and widows desperate to feed and clothe their children—found an "unlimited field" of jobs, but only in the areas of domestic service and laundering. As a result, all of the major southern cities had an imbalanced sex ratio in favor of women throughout the late nineteenth century. The selection process at work in this population movement, like any other, indicates that black women possessed a spirit of "upward ambition and aspiration" at least equal to that of their menfolk.

Throughout this period, then, some black women demonstrated a restlessness of mind as well as body. In their willingness to move from cabin to cabin and from country to town, they belied the familiar charge that women were more "conservative" than men, less quick to take chances or to abandon the familiar. Perhaps even more dramatic were mothers' attempts to school their children, for in the process they risked losing them. Nate Shaw never went to school because, he thought, "my daddy was scared I'd leave him, so he held me down." Shaw's father had his own priorities, and at least he never had to share the pain felt by a Sea Island mother who read in a note from her self-exiled son, "It pays a man to leave home sometimes, my mother, and he will see more and learn more."

BLACK AND WHITE CULTURE AND MEN AND WOMEN IN THE RURAL SOUTH

Late-nineteenth-century middle-class white women derived their status from that of their husbands. Unproductive in the context of a money-oriented, industrializing economy, and formally unable to take part in the nation's political process, they enjoyed financial security only insofar as their spouses were steady and reliable providers. In contrast, black working women in the South had a more equal relationship with their husbands in the sense that the two partners were not separated by extremes of economic power or political rights; black men and women lacked both. Oppression shaped these unions in another way. The overlapping of economic and domestic functions combined with the pressures imposed by a surrounding, hostile white society meant that black working women were not so dramatically dependent upon their husbands as were middle-class white

wives. Within black families and communities, then, public–private, male–female distinctions were less tightly drawn than among middle-class whites. Together, black women and men participated in a rural folk culture based upon group cooperation rather than male competition and the accumulation of goods. The ways in which this culture both resembled and diverged from that of poor whites in the South helps to illuminate the interaction between class and racial factors in shaping the roles of women.

Referring to the world view of Alabama sharecropper Hayes Shaw, Theodore Rosengarten (the biographer-interviewer of Shaw's son Nate) observed that "righteousness consisted in not having so much that it hurt to lose it." Nate himself remembered that his father as a young man had passed up promising opportunities to buy land because "he was blindfolded; he didn't look to the future." Ruled by "them old slavery thoughts," Hayes Shaw knew that

> whenever the colored man prospered too fast in this country under the old rulins, they worked every figure to cut you down, cut your britches off you. So, it . . . weren't no use in climbin too fast; weren't no use in climbin slow, neither, if they was goin to take everything you worked for when you got too high.

Rural black communities that abided by this philosophy sought to achieve self-determination within a limited sphere of action. In this way they insulated themselves from whites and from the disappointment that often accompanied individual self-seeking. They lived like Nate's brother Peter; he "made up his mind that he weren't going to have anything and after that, why nothin could hurt him."

Rural folk relied on one another to help celebrate the wedding of a young couple, rejoice in a preacher's fervent exhortation, mark the annual closing of the local school, minister to the ill, and bury the dead. Women participated in all these rites and communal events. In addition, they had their own gender-based activities, as well as societies that contributed to the general good of the community. On the Sea Islands, young women would "often take Saturday afternoon as a time for cleaning the yard or the parlor, for ironing their clothes, or for preparing their hair." (Their brothers gathered at a favorite meeting place or organized a "cornfield baseball game.") Quilting brought young and old women together for a daylong festival of sewing, chatting, and feasting. Supported by the modest dues of their members, female voluntary beneficial societies met vital social-welfare needs that individual families could not always afford; these groups helped their members to pay for life insurance, medical care, and burial services. Even the poorest women managed to contribute a few pennies a month and to attend weekly meetings. In turn-of-the-century Alabama, "The woman who is not a member of one of these is pitied and considered rather out of date."

The impulse for mutual solace and support among rural Afro-Americans culminated in their religious institutions and worship services. At monthly meetings women and men met to reaffirm their unique spiritual heritage, to seek comfort, and to comfort one another. Black women found a "psychological center" in religious belief, and the church provided strength for those overcome by the day-to-day business of living. For many weary sharecroppers' wives and mothers, worship services allowed for physical and spiritual release and offered a means of transcending earthly cares in the company of one's friends and family. Faith created "a private world inside the self, sustained by religious sentiment and religious symbolism . . . fashioned to contain the world without." "Spiritual mothers" served as the "main pillars" of Methodist and Baptist churches, but they also exercised religious leadership outside formal institutional boundaries; elderly women in particular commanded respect as the standard-bearers of tradition and as the younger generation's link with its ancestors.

Of course, life in "places behind God's back" was shaped as much by racial prejudice as by black solidarity, and the "ethos of mutuality" that pervaded rural communities did not preclude physical violence or overt conflict between individuals. At times a Saturday night "frolic" ended in a bloody confrontation between two men who sought courage from a whiskey bottle and self-esteem through hand-to-hand conflict. Similarly, oppression could bind a family tightly together, but it could also heighten tensions among people who had few outlets for their rage and frustration. Patterns of domestic conflict reflected both historical injustices and daily family pressures. These forces affected black women and men in different ways.

On a superficial level, the roots of domestic violence are not difficult to recognize or understand. Cramped living quarters and unexpected setbacks provoked the most even-tempered of household heads. Like their slave parents, mothers and fathers often used harsh disciplinary techniques on children, not only to prepare them for life in a white-dominated world where all blacks had to act cautiously, but also to exert rigid control over this one vital facet of domestic life. If whites attempted to cut "the britches off" black fathers and husbands, then these men would try to assert their authority over their households with even greater determination. At times that determination was manifested in violence and brutality.

Hayes Shaw epitomized the sharecropping father who lorded over his wives (he married three times) and children. More than once the Shaw children watched helplessly as their father beat their mother, and they too were "whipped . . . up scandalous" for the slightest infraction. Hayes divided his time between his "outside woman"—an unmarried laundress in the neighborhood—and his "regular" family, and he made no effort to conceal the fact. The Shaw women-folk were hired out or sent to the fields like children, without daring to protest, while Hayes spent his days in a characteristically masculine fashion—alone, away from the house, hunting. According to Nate Shaw, his "daddy'd have his gun on his shoulder and be off on Sitimachas Creek swamps, huntin," after commanding his wife to "Take that plow! Hoe!" The son remembered with bitterness years later that his stepmother (who had borne his father thirteen children) "put part of a day's work in the field" before she died one night.

Hayes Shaw was undoubtedly an extreme example of a domestic tyrant, but he and other husbands like him inspired white and black women community leaders, educators, and social workers to formulate a critique of Afro-American family life in the late nineteenth century. Sensitive to the economic problems confronted by black marriage partners, these observers charged that black men enjoyed certain male prerogatives without the corresponding striving and ambition that those prerogatives were meant to reward. Juxtaposed with this "irresponsible" man was his wife—no doubt a "real drudge," but certainly "the greatest sufferer from the stress and strain attendant upon the economic conditions" faced by all Afro-Americans. The chief problem seemed to stem from the fact that black women played a prominent role in supporting the family in addition to performing their domestic responsibilities. In the eyes of their critics, black men as a group were not particularly concerned about "getting ahead" in the world and thus fell short of their wives' spirit of industry and self-sacrifice.

White teacher–social workers like Rossa Cooley and Georgia Washington and black writers and educators like Anna J. Cooper, Katherine Davis Tillman, Frances Harper, and Fannie Barrier Williams focused on the domestic achievements of poor women and with varying degrees of subtlety condemned their "worthless" husbands. Their critique of black womanhood marked the emergence of the "black matriarchy thesis," for they suggested that the main problem in Afro-American family life was an "irresponsible" father who took advantage of his "faithful, hardworking women-folks." By the mid-twentieth century sociologists had shifted public attention to the "irresponsible" father's *absence*; the relatively large number of single, working mothers in the nation's urban ghettos seemed to lend additional credence to an argument that originally purported to deal with the problems of rural women. Thus the image of the strong, overburdened black mother persisted through the years, and it was usually accompanied by the implicit assumption that women wielded authority over men and children in Afro-American families.

Yet Hayes Shaw's household was never a "matriarchy." Recent historians who have labeled the postemancipation rural black family "patriarchal" hardly help to clarify the issue. The difficulty in conceptualizing black male–female roles derives from the fact that most observers (whether writing in the nineteenth or twentieth century) have used as their basis for comparison the white middle-class model of family life. Black men headed the vast majority of southern rural families, and they self-consciously ruled their wives and children; hence the use of the term patriarchy to describe family relationships. But these households deviated from the traditional sexual division of labor in the sense that wives worked to supplement the family income, and fathers often lacked the incentive to try to earn money so that they could purchase property or goods and thus advance the family's status. These men worked hard—they had to, in order to survive the ruthlessly exploitative sharecropping system—but most realized that even harder work would not necessarily enable them to escape poverty. Those who confronted this dilemma hardly deserved the epithet "worthless manhood." Still, for the two sexes, relative equality of economic function did not imply equality of domestic authority.

Although a husband and wife each made an essential contribution to the welfare of the household, they were compensated in different ways for their labor. This reward differential

reflected their contrasting household responsibilities and produced contrasting attitudes
toward work and its personal and social value.
As a participant in a staple-crop economy, a
black father assumed responsibility for a crop
that would be exchanged in the marketplace
at the end of the year. He supposedly toiled
for future compensation in the form of cash.
However, not only did his physical exertion
gain him little in the way of immediate reward,
in fact he tilled the ground only to repay one
debt and to ensure that he would have another
in the coming year. Under such conditions,
most men took pride in their farming abilities,
but worked no more strenuously than was
absolutely necessary to satisfy white creditors
and keep their own families alive in the
process.

Their wives, on the other hand, remained
relatively insulated from the inevitable frustrations linked to a future-oriented, market economy. For example, women daily performed
discreet tasks that yielded tangible results upon
completion. Meal preparation, laundering, egg
gathering—these chores had finite boundaries
in the course of a day. Childcare was a special
case, but it had its own special joys. It was
an ongoing responsibility that began when a
woman had her first baby and ended only years
later when her youngest child left home. On a
more mundane level, childcare was a constant
preoccupation of mothers during their waking
hours, and infants' needs often invaded their
sleep. Yet a woman's exclusive authority in this
area of domestic life earned her emotional
gratification. Her husband hardly derived a
similar sense of gratification from his responsibility for the cotton crop; he "earned" only
what a white man was willing to pay him.
Hence the distinction between work patterns
simplistically labeled by some contemporary
writers as male "laziness" and female "self-
sacrifice" actually represented a complex phenomenon shaped by the different demands made
upon black men and women and the degree of
personal satisfaction resulting from the fulfillment of those demands.

Despite the transition in labor organization from slavery to sharecropping, the work
of black women in the rural South continued to
respond to the same human and seasonal
rhythms over the generations. By the early
twentieth century, they still structured their
labor around household chores and childcare,
field and wage work, and community welfare
activities. Moreover, emancipation hardly lessened the demands made upon females of all
ages; young girls worked alongside their mothers, and elderly women had to provide for
themselves and their families as long as they
were physically able. Although the specific
tasks performed by women reflected constantly
changing priorities (determined by the cotton-
growing cycle and the size and maturity of individual households), the need for a woman to
labor rarely abated in the course of a day, a
year, or her lifetime.

In its functional response to unique historical circumstances, the rural black household
necessarily differed from the late-nineteenth-
century middle-class ideal, which assumed
that men would engage in individual self-
aggrandizement. Furthermore, according to
this ideal, women were to remain isolated at
home, only indirectly sharing in the larger
social values of wealth and power accumulation. In contrast, rural black women labored in
harmony with the priorities of cooperation and
sharing established by their own communities,
even as their husbands were prevented from
participating in the cash economy in a way
that would answer to white-defined notions of
masculinity.

Despite the hard, never-ending work performed by rural women—who, ironically, were
labeled part of a "lazy" culture by contemporaries and recent historians alike—they could
not entirely compensate for the loss of both
a husband (through death or another form of
permanent separation) and older sons or male
relatives who established households on their
own. The sharecropping family strove to maintain a delicate balance between its labor
resources and its economic needs, and men,

as both negotiators in the public sphere and as field workers, were crucial to that balance. Therefore, during the latter part of the nineteenth century, when the natural selection process endemic to commercial crop agriculture weeded out "unfit" households, it forced single mothers, widows, and unmarried daughters to look cityward. Many of them would discover that while the southern countryside continued to mirror the slave past, in the towns that past was refracted into new shapes and images.

GLOSSARY

W. E. B. DuBois (1868–1963):   African American civil-rights leader and author. One of the first exponents of full and immediate racial equality, he cofounded the National Association for the Advancement of Colored People in 1910, edited the NAACP magazine, *The Crisis*, until 1932, and late in life promoted worldwide black liberation and Pan-Africanism.

New South: The ideal of industrial development in the southern states following the Civil War.

Millenarian: Relating to the doctrine of the millennium.

IMPLICATIONS

Jones' essay discusses the lives of African American women in the turn-of-the-century South. In what ways do you think the experiences of African American women were different from those of African American men? Do you think the lack of employment opportunities was the sole cause of these differences?

One of the most consequential responses to the economic changes and population growth of the late nineteenth and early twentieth centuries was the rise of a conservation movement that sought to preserve at least part of America's natural landscape. More than any other public figure, John Muir became the national symbol of this movement and the best-known spokesman for the preservation of America's wilderness. This essay is introduced by one of Muir's most influential essays, an account of his ascent of Mount Ritter in 1872.

John Muir, *Mount Ritter (1911)*

At a distance of less than 3,000 feet below the summit of Mount Ritter you may find tributaries of the San Joaquin and Owen's Rivers, bursting forth from the ice and snow of the glaciers that load its flanks; while a little to the north of here are found the highest affluents of the Tuolumne and Merced. Thus, the fountains of four of the principal rivers of California are within a radius of four or five miles.

Lakes are seen gleaming in all sorts of places round, or oval, or square, like very mirrors; others narrow and sinuous, drawn close around the peaks like silver zones, the highest reflecting only rocks, snow, and the sky. But neither these nor the glaciers, nor the bits of brown meadow and moorland that occur here and there, are large enough to make any marked impression upon the mighty wilderness of mountains. The eye, rejoicing in its freedom, roves about the vast expanse, yet returns again and again to the fountain-peaks. Perhaps some one of the multitude, excites special attention some gigantic castle with turret and battlement, or some Gothic cathedral more abundantly spired than Milan's. But, generally, when looking for the first time from an all-embracing standpoint like this, the inexperienced observer is oppressed by the incomprehensible grandeur, variety, and abundance of the mountains rising shoulder to shoulder beyond the reach of vision; and it is only after they have been studied one by one, long and lovingly, that their far-reaching harmonies become manifest. Then, penetrate the wilderness where you may, the main telling features, to which all the surrounding topography is subordinate, are quickly perceived, and the most complicated clusters of peaks stand revealed harmoniously correlated and fashioned like works of art eloquent monuments of the ancient ice-rivers that brought them into relief from the general mass of the range. The can~ons, too, some of them a mile deep, mazing wildly through the mighty host of mountains, however lawless and ungovernable at first sight they appear, are at length recognized as the necessary effects of causes which followed each other in harmonious sequence Nature's poems carved on tables of stone the simplest and most emphatic of her glacial compositions.

Could we have been here to observe during the glacial period, we should have overlooked a wrinkled ocean of ice as continuous as that now covering the landscapes of Greenland; filling every valley and canon with only the tops of the fountain-peaks rising darkly above the rock-encumbered ice-waves like islets in a stormy sea those islets the only hints of the glorious landscapes now smiling in the sun. Standing here in the deep, brooding silence all the wilderness seems motionless, as if the work of creation were done. But in the midst of this outer steadfastness we know there is incessant motion and change. Ever and anon, avalanches are falling from yonder peaks. These cliff-bound glaciers, seemingly wedged and immovable, are flowing like water and grinding the rocks beneath them. The lakes are lapping their granite shores and wearing them away, and every one of these rills and young rivers is fretting the air into music, and carrying the mountains to the plains. Here are the roots of all the life of the valleys, and here more simply than elsewhere is the eternal flux of Nature manifested. Ice changing to water, lakes to meadows, and mountains to plains. And while we thus contemplate Nature's methods of landscape creation, and, reading the records she has carved on the rocks, reconstruct, however imperfectly, the landscapes of the past, we also learn that as these we now behold have succeeded those of the pre-glacial age, so they in turn are withering and vanishing to be succeeded by others yet unborn.

But in the midst of these fine lessons and landscapes, I had to remember that the sun was wheeling far to the west, while a new way down the mountain had to be discovered to some point on the timber-line where I could have a fire; for I had not even burdened myself with a coat. I first scanned the western spurs, hoping some way might appear through which I might reach the northern glacier, and cross its snout; or pass around the lake into which it flows, and thus strike my morning track. This route was soon sufficiently unfolded to show that, if practicable at all, it would require so much time that reaching camp that night would be out of the question. I therefore scrambled back eastward, descending the southern slopes obliquely at the same time. Here the crags seemed less formidable, and the head of a glacier that flows north-east came in sight, which I determined to follow as far as possible, hoping thus to make my way to the foot of the peak on the east side, and thence across the intervening can~ons and ridges to camp.

The inclination of the glacier is quite moderate at the head, and, as the sun had softened the ne, I made safe and rapid progress, running and sliding, and keeping up a sharp outlook for crevasses. About half a mile from the head, there is an ice cascade, where the glacier pours over a sharp declivity and is shattered into massive blocks separated by deep, blue fissures. To thread my way through the slippery mazes of this crevassed portion seemed impossible, and I endeavored to avoid it by climbing off to the shoulder of the mountain. But the slopes rapidly steep-ened and at length fell away in sheer precipices, compelling a return to the ice. Fortunately, the day had been warm enough to loosen the ice-crystals so as to admit of hollows being dug in the rotten portions of the blocks, thus enabling me to pick my way with far less difficulty than I had anticipated. Continuing down over the snout, and along the left lateral moraine, was only a confident saunter, showing that the ascent of the mountain by way of this glacier is easy, provided one is armed with an axe, to cut steps here and there.

The lower end of the glacier was beautifully waved and barred by the outcropping edges of the bedded ice-layers which represent the annual snow-falls, and to some extent the irregularities of structure caused by the weathering of the walls of crevasses, and by separate snowfalls which have been followed by rain, hail, thawing and freezing, etc. Small ribs were gliding and swirling over the melting surface with a smooth, oily appearance, in channels of pure ice their quick, compliant movements contrasting most impressively with the rigid, invisible flow of the glacier itself, on whose back they all were riding.

Night drew near before I reached the eastern base of the mountain, and my camp lay many a rugged mile to the north; but ultimate success was assured. It was now only a matter of endurance and ordinary mountain-craft. The sunset was, if possible, yet more beautiful than that of the day before. The Mono landscape seemed to be fairly saturated with warm, purple light. The peaks marshaled along the summit were in shadow, but through every notch and pass streamed vivid sunfire, soothing and irradiating their rough, black

angles, while companies of small luminous clouds hovered above them like very angels of light. Darkness came on, but I found my way by the trends of the can~ons and the peaks projected against the sky. All excitement died with the light, and then I was weary. But the joyful sound of the waterfall across the lake was heard at last, and soon the stars were seen reflected in the lake itself, Taking my bearings from these, I discovered the little Pine thicket in which my nest was, and then I had a rest such as only a tired mountaineer may enjoy. After lying loose and lost for a while, I made a sunrise fire, went down to the lake, dashed water on my head, and dipped a cupful for tea. The revival brought about by bread and tea was as complete as the exhaustion from excessive enjoyment and toil. Then I crept beneath the pine-tassels to bed. The wind was frosty and the fire burned low, but my sleep was none the less sound, and the evening constellations had swept far to the west before I awoke.

After thawing and resting in the morning sunshine, I sauntered home— that is, back to the Tuolumne camp— bearing away toward a cluster of peaks that hold the fountain snows of one of the north tributaries of Rush Creek. Here I discovered a group of beautiful glacier lakes, nestled together in a grand amphitheater. Toward evening, I crossed the divide separating the Mono waters from those of the Tuolumne, and entered the glacier-basin that now holds the fountain-snows of the stream that forms the upper Tuolumne cascades. This stream I traced down through its many dells and gorges, meadows and bogs, reaching the brink of the main Tuolumne at dusk.

8

John Muir: The Mysteries of Mountains

Peter Wild

The final phase of America's westward expansion involved the exploration and settlement of the far western frontier. From the end of the Civil War through the early twentieth century, hundreds of thousands of native-born and immigrant Americans flooded into the region between the Rocky Mountains and the Pacific Coast to begin new lives as farmers and small-town businesspeople. But unlike America's earlier frontiers, the Far West brought more than farmers and shopkeepers. The region's dense forests and rich mineral deposits also attracted eastern lumber and mining companies intent on exploiting these lucrative natural resources. By the turn of the century, years of unrestricted logging, hydraulic mining, and careless dam-building threatened to destroy the natural beauty of America's last frontier.

This heedless exploitation of the wilderness of the Far West did not go unchallenged, however. Beginning in the 1880s, scientists and government officials joined together in a national conservation movement that sought to preserve the country's wilderness areas for the enjoyment and education of future generations of Americans. If any one man symbolized the conservationist impulse, it was the Scottish immigrant John Muir. Explorer, nature writer, and general spokesman for wilderness America, Muir played a pivotal role in popularizing the cause of conservation in America. In this biographical essay, Peter Wild traces Muir's love of nature to the restrictions of his early life and follows his efforts to preserve America's wilderness as a counterweight to modern industrial society.

*I must explain why it is that at night, in my own
    house,
Even when no one's asleep, I feel I must whisper.
Thoreau and Wordsworth would call it an act of
    devotion . . .*

                            —*Reed Whitemore*

At sunset in the Sierras some hikers chant John Muir's words: "I am always glad to touch the living rock again and dip my head in high mountain air." To them John Muir is a hero, the high priest of those who escape to the wilderness.

And well he might be. By tradition Americans long for the freedom of wilderness, a wilderness fast disappearing. Muir said that all he needed to flee was to "throw some tea and bread in an old sack and jump over the back fence." How can the schedule-bound and traffic-weary commuter not envy the man who, as Yosemite's cliffs collapsed around him, rushed into the night shouting, "A noble earthquake, a noble earthquake!" At times he seems one of the daring Americans who, we like to imagine, led us West through our short history. We prefer our heroes dressed in a simple guise, but with a vigor and joie de vivre just beyond our ken.

The danger is that Muir tends to become lost in his mythology, some of it his own making. A closer look shows him a complex man, like others capable of gloom and hesitation. After years of private struggle and doubt, he beat his conflicting practical and mystical bents into an unusually consistent and powerful personality. Yet the most dramatic events of his life are indeed telling, though often not fully appreciated.

One of the most famous of these, a catastrophe that ended in a spiritual change, occurred in 1867. While he adjusted a new belt in an Indianapolis carriage factory, a file flew from his hand, blinding his right eye. Soon after, the other eye went dark as though in sympathetic reaction. For weeks he lay in agony: "My days were terrible beyond what I can tell, and my nights were if possible more terrible. Frightful

dreams exhausted and terrified me." Muir was twenty-nine, an age of trial and decision for many prophets.

Up to this time, chances for a lucrative but unsatisfying career as an inventor contended with his love of extended wanderings through the woods. In his blindness he saw an answer: if his eyes healed he would give up tinkering with man's inventions and devote his life to "the study of the inventions of God." As he tossed in his room, slowly his sight returned. Significantly, he described his deliverance in religious terms: "Now had I arisen from the grave. The cup is removed, and I am alive!" From then on he would consistently equate God with light.

Likeable and talented, Muir was asked by his employers Osgood & Smith to stay on. However, a promotion to foreman, a raise, shorter hours, and a future partnership couldn't sway him. Lifting his pack containing a change of underwear and a few favorite books, he was off. His goal was to walk the thousand miles across the South—no mean feat in the bandit-ridden forests after the Civil War—to the tip of Florida, and from there to hitch a ride by boat to the Amazon. In the words of his biographer, Linnie Wolfe, he was resolved to become "one of God's fools." Yet as dramatic as the file incident might appear, the resulting conversion was neither simple nor complete. The five-month trip provided him with the time and space to mull over conflicts that had troubled him since childhood.

John Muir was born in Dunbar, Scotland, in 1838. Over the years his father's zealousness crossed the blurred line into a religious fanaticism the merchant brought with him when he settled his family in America. Daniel Muir sat in his homestead reading the Bible while his sons labored in the Wisconsin fields. When they returned weary at the end of the day, he beat them for sins they might have committed. To him books, paintings—even an adequate diet—smacked of the Devil. Precocious John, however, discovered that he could do with only a few hours sleep; in the darkness of early morning he'd secretly crawl down into the cellar to read and to whittle a variety of curious clocks.

Though Daniel scowled when he found out about the inventions, neighbors urged his son to exhibit them at the State Agricultural Fair. At the age of twenty-two, suffering his father's parting anger, John shouldered his pack stuffed with strange devices and headed for the state capital. There in the Temple of Art, Madison's citizens marveled at the youth from the backwoods, whose early-rising machine whirred and creaked to propel the reluctant sleeper out of bed.

But Muir found more than local fame in Madison. Like many an aspiring American youth, he strolled with opening eyes among the buildings of the nearby university, envious of the students who had stepped into a larger world of intellectual opportunity. Sometime later he enrolled with money earned from odd jobs, to spend two and a half pleasant years at the University of Wisconsin. There, after glimpsing the cosmos through his courses, he amused the other students with the devices that clicked and wheezed through their bizarre paces in his room at North Hall.

Restlessness overtook him in the spring of 1863, and he wandered through Canada, then back again into the Midwest. He was by now in his mid-twenties, a late bloomer tinged with guilt that he hadn't done more with his life. Far from being simply an enjoyable interim, however, the time spent in Madison would change and serve him more profoundly than he realized. In the frontier's atmosphere of intellectual democracy, Muir had made friends. His professors ignored the long hair and careless dress of the country boy and offered him confidence in his eccentric development. Dr. Ezra Carr and his wife Jeanne had graciously opened their Madison home and their private library to Muir. On the scientific side, Professor Carr instilled his students with Louis Agassiz's theory that a great Ice Age had carved out much of the northern hemisphere's topography. This grounding in science would result in Muir's first public controversy and his fame in California's Sierras. As for philosophy, both Carr and his wife were self-appointed missionaries of Ralph Waldo Emerson's transcendental ideas. They believed that through the oneness of nature a person could arrive intuitively at spiritual truth, if not ecstasy. It was just what young Muir needed to assuage his guilt and to justify wandering as a spiritual adventure.

And so with his boyhood and Madison as backgrounds, the dropout sat writing in his notebook among the palmettos and sand dunes of Florida's west coast, recording his thoughts and working his philosophical and personal conflicts into a unified view, the basis for future publications. He saw nature as a whole, a unity in flux. Man should stand in nature's temple, witnessing the eternal "morning of creation" occurring all about him. Emerson would have applauded the imagery, yet Muir went beyond the Concord philosopher. Unlike the flights of the cerebral Emerson, Muir's arose from perceptions grounded in science and elemental experiences in nature. Whether collecting specimens or hanging perilously by his fingertips from some yet unclimbed peak, he recognized that "a heart like our own must be beating in every crystal and cell" of the surrounding wilderness. Muir's ability to survive, botanize, and philosophize in the wilds was a rare power.

As his thinking developed, he realized—as Emerson did not—that if nature is a holy place, then civilization, with its sheep, axes, and dynamite, is the infidel, the wrecker in the temple. As Thomas Lyon has pointed out, the view represents a reversal of Muir's boyhood Calvinism. God, not the Devil, is to be found in the wilderness. Nature, not man, is the center of a timeless universe. With this in mind, Muir set his spiritual sights south on the Amazon basin; there he could glory in a nature steaming and writhing in the speeded-up processes of the jungle. But the semitropical winds already had blown him ill. Wracked by malaria, he turned back at Havana, Cuba, in hopes that the Sierra cold would purge his blood. The retreat made all the difference to a beginning conservation movement that as yet had no heroes.

In the early spring of 1868, the former inventor stepped off the boat in San Francisco. All around him that bustling city of commerce—a commerce based largely on resources hauled out of the interior—displayed "the gobble gobble school of economics." In a typical Muir scene, he told of stopping a carpenter to ask the fastest way out of town. Puzzled, the workman inquired where he wanted to go. Muir replied, "Anywhere that is wild." About the time that John Wesley Powell was bounding through the unknown Grand Canyon in his little boat, Muir was beginning a decade of Sierra exploration.

At first he supported himself by coming down out of the mountains to work on sheep ranches. The job disgusted him, and he branded the bleating, overgrazing creatures, degenerate cousins of the noble bighorns living high in his range of light, "hooved locusts." Eventually he chose Yosemite as a home base. Though accessible only by foot or horse, the striking canyon scenery attracted the more rugged variety of tourist. Muir took a job operating the sawmill for one of the two expanding hotels—with the stipulation that he would work only on wind-downed logs. On the sunny side of the valley, the sawyer built a little cabin for himself, complete with a wild fern growing inside and a brook running through it. Except for intermittent concessions to working for a few supplies, he was at peace, free to wander and enjoy the unexplored peaks.

Despite his pleasure in solitude, it should not be supposed that Muir was a cranky malcontent. Though he could chide people with his Scottish humor, he enjoyed company; if he had any social fault beyond his slipshod dress, it was his garrulousness. When in the mood around a camp fire, Muir could hold forth on the glories of the surroundings long after foot-weary companions wished they were in their sleeping bags. Even before he was stirring up the public in print, with the help of friends he

had become something of a celebrity, something of the "John of the Mountains" figure that persists to this day. Professor and Mrs. Carr of Madison days had moved to the University of California. They sent a stream of vacationing writers and scientists—many of them eminent personages from the East—knocking on the Hutchings Hotel door, asking to be shown Yosemite's wonders by the only authority on them, ragtag John Muir. He more than satisfied tourist expectations of a romantic character of the Wild West.

As he befriended these Eastern visitors, the amateur naturalist made connections that would serve him in future conservation battles. He guided scientific expeditions and showed off the valley to his aging Concord guru. Emerson added the young transcendentalist to his list of "My Men," but he seemed a little taken aback by all the wilderness, so much more wild than his modest Massachusetts woods. Whether intentionally or not, Muir charmed Viscountess Thérèse Yelverton, victim of a scandalous English divorce tangle, who viewed him as a transcendental noble savage. She wanted him to run away with her to Hong Kong, but to his credit he gently turned her aside. However, she continued the romance on a unilateral basis, writing the novel *Zanita*, which featured John Muir as its Pre-Raphaelite hero.

More importantly, in later years he camped out with President Theodore Roosevelt, who happened to be scanning the nation for places to preserve. In his boyish enthusiasm, TR declared that he had a "bully" time with Muir—a man who if pressed would admit that in attempting to scale Mount Whitney he had danced the Highland fling all night to keep from freezing in the −22° cold. Yet California, the bellwether of America, was fast filling with settlers and developers. John Muir's rugged peace could not last long. In one of several striking shifts in his life, he exchanged it for a public career as a writer and for a reputation that holds to this day as the nation's foremost protector of wilderness.

As a late bloomer, John Muir wrote his first article at the age of thirty-four, his first book at fifty-six. Drawing heavily from the journals kept throughout his adult life, he tended to poeticize the facts. Then, too, his mysticism slowed him down; he found his adventures so spiritually satisfying that writing about them gave only a secondary thrill. "Ink cannot tell the glow that lights me at this moment in turning to the mountains," he explained. On the other hand, his beliefs eventually compelled him to write in defense of nature; and, when the writing fire burned in him, he was far more than the reluctant author. A scientific wrangle provided the first spark.

California's State Geologist, Josiah D. Whitney, applied the popular cataclysmic theory of geology to Yosemite. Basically, Whitney maintained that in a dramatic shift of the earth's crust the floor had suddenly fallen out of the valley, creating the present gorge. Schooled in Agassiz's contrary glacial theory and believing in the slow processes of nature espoused by Emerson, Muir viewed Whitney's pronouncement as an affront. By the early 1870's proprietary feelings about the Sierras ran deep in Muir. He, after all, knew his "range of light" far better than any geologist, regardless of his lack of degrees and professional standing. Glaciers grinding over eons had carved out Yosemite, not a super earthquake. As it turned out, Muir happened to be right, though there was at least as much emotion as science on both sides of the debate.

Urged by visiting scientists supporting his minority opinion, he sent off "Yosemite Glaciers." When the New York *Tribune* not only published the article but paid him for the effort, it set the practical side of his Scottish mind to whirling. At the time, journalism offered far more lucrative returns than it does today; writing might be an alternative to his periodic bondage at the sawmill—as well as a vehicle for rebuffing exploiters. Boosted by influential contacts, his articles, both celebrating his country and warning the public of its imminent demise, won the praise and concern

of readers of the *Overland Monthly*, *Harper's*, and the *National Geographic*. Unlike many of the nature writers of the time, Muir grounded his rhapsody in the details of personal experience. He took readers with him from one detailed Sierra adventure to the next. Here he is edging along a cliff face to get a grand view of plunging Yosemite Creek:

> . . . the slope beside it looked dangerously smooth and steep, and the swift roaring flood beneath, overhead, and beside me was very nerve-trying. I therefore concluded not to venture farther, but did nevertheless. Tufts of artemisia were growing in clefts of the rock near by, and I filled my mouth with the bitter leaves, hoping they might help to prevent giddiness. Then, with a caution not known in ordinary circumstances, I crept down safely to the little edge, got my heels well planted on it, then shuffled in a horizontal direction twenty or thirty feet until close to the outplunging current, which, by the time it had descended thus far, was already white. Here I obtained a perfectly free view down into the heart of the snowy, chanting throng of comet-like streamers, into which the body of the fall soon separates.

It is perhaps a bit difficult for an age sated with television spectacles to appreciate the impact of his revelations, based on the union of the physical and spiritual. Upon considering a new Muir manuscript, one editor declared that he almost felt as if he had found religion. On the mystical side, the poetry of Muir's words had the ecstatic ring of a man who was "on the side of the angels and Thoreau," as Herbert Smith describes him. Muir was having the best of two worlds: new economic freedom allowed him to garner material for magazines while he enjoyed trips to Utah, Nevada, and Alaska.

Yet there was a hitch; at the age of forty, "John of the Mountains" longed for a home life. Again his friends came into play, this time in matchmaking. Jeanne Carr introduced Muir to Louie Wanda Strentzel, eligible daughter of a wealthy medical doctor exiled from Poland. The match was not as unlikely as it first sounds. Despite his wanderings, Muir could carry himself like a gentleman; by this time he was a writer of some note; he knew the value of money and had $1,000 in the bank. It took patience and subtle urgings on the part of Mrs. Carr, but in the middle of April, 1880, John Muir married Louie Strentzel. The groom's literary abilities lapsed into cliché, however, when he expressed his genuine domestic joy: "I am now the happiest man in the world!"

For a wedding present, Dr. Strentzel gave his new son-in-law an orchard and a house in Martinez, across the bay from San Francisco. Perhaps middle-aged Muir needed a rest from freezing on mountaintops and eating monk's fare from a bread bag. Whatever the case, his old farming instinct asserted itself. With the exception of significant trips to Alaska, in the next few years he stayed fairly close to home, laboring in the vineyards that provided the modest fortune that would support his final and most important years of activism. To his credit, though Muir showed astute business sense, he also was generous with his money, supporting relatives, giving heavily to charity. "We all loved him," said a friend, "for his thoughtfulness for others." And Muir loved the banter and refuge of a comfortable household, one much different from that of his severe childhood.

John Muir's grapevines prospered, but his health and writing, cut off from the strength of the Sierras, suffered. In a way that might not be fashionable today, his wife rearranged her life to deal with the problem. Louie insisted that he spend July through October, the slack season for orchardmen in Contra Costa County, trying to regain his vital contact with the mountains. Though she loved music, when he was laboring in his study, she kept her piano closed. Editors hadn't forgotten Muir; joined by his wife, they connived to get him out into the wilderness and his pen working again.

In time they succeeded in rebaptizing Muir with his old power—redoubled when Robert Underwood Johnson of *Century Magazine* took him on a camping trip to see what unre-

strained sheep and lumbermen had done to his beloved Yosemite. The plots of his friends worked just in time; the 1880's and 1890's marked the first cohesion and substantial victories of the early conservation movement. Pen in hand and backed by Johnson, the aging mountain man stood at its forefront. In 1890 the Eastern press reprinted his articles "Treasures of the Yosemite" and "Features of the Proposed Yosemite National Park." Telegrams and letters flooded Congressmen's offices. Saving Muir's old stamping grounds became a cause célèbre of national proportions. Congress reacted to the outcry for government preservation—a novel idea. Forced by popular pressure to ignore commercial interests opposing the plan, it created Yosemite National Park and provided a cavalry detachment to patrol the area. Muir and Johnson took advantage of the public's ire at its loss of scenic places and of its hope for saving what remained of them. Through writing and lobbying, in the same year they compelled a publicity-conscious Congress to add Sequoia and General Grant to the growing list of National Parks.

Things were going well for conservation. Supported by a core group of activists, including the young forester Gifford Pinchot in the East, the Enabling Act of 1891 allowed timberlands to be set aside by executive order. Before he left office, President Harrison created the forerunners of the National Forests by designating 13,000,000 acres of public land as Forest Reserves. Through these years, editor Johnson continued to be the man behind the somewhat shy John Muir. Individual concerns, however deep, could be effective in the political maelstrom only through united effort, Johnson urged. In 1892 Muir gathered a number of prominent Californians into a San Francisco law office to incorporate the Sierra Club, an organization Muir led until his death. One of the earliest citizen groups of its kind, the Club continues in the tradition of its founder to "explore, enjoy, and preserve" the country's resources. To support the movement, Muir was writing, writing—*The Mountains of California*

(1894), *Our National Parks* (1901), *My First Summer in the Sierra* (1911)—for a public that looked to the written word as a guide for its judgments.

Yet in the seesaw of politics, for a time it looked as if the new Forest Reserve system—if not the new National Parks—might be lost. Those whose livelihoods depended on exploiting the natural heritage were quick to call in political debts and mount an effective counterattack. By then, however, other magazines followed the example of *Century* with strong stands for conservation. And from John Muir's pen came prose with a stentorian thunder that echoed the fire and brimstone of his childhood. Readers opening the August, 1897, issue of the *Atlantic Monthly* found both their religion and patriotism at the stake:

> The forests of America, however slighted by man, must have been a great delight to God; for they were the best he ever planted. The whole continent was a garden, and from the beginning it seemed to be favored above all the other wild parks and gardens of the globe . . . Everywhere, everywhere over all the blessed continent, there were beauty, and melody, and kindly, wholesome, foodful abundance.

Muir knew his rhetoric. After presenting an historical survey of America's forests, comparing their abuse with the stewardship of Germany, France, and Switzerland, he concluded with a poetic appeal for firm government action:

> Any fool can destroy trees. They cannot run away; and if they could, they would still be destroyed,—chased and hunted down as long as fun or a dollar could be got out of their bark hides. . . . Through all the wonderful, eventful centuries since Christ's time—and long before that—God has cared for these trees, saved them from drought, disease, avalanches, and a thou-

sand straining, leveling tempests and floods; but he cannot save them from fools,—only Uncle Sam can do that.

Only ignorance and greed could challenge Muir's plea. There were successes—passage of the Lacey Antiquities Act of 1906, for example. Its provisions allowed creation of National Monuments by Presidential decree. Because of Muir's urging, Roosevelt set aside Petrified Forest and parts of the Grand Canyon. And Muir, at the age of seventy-four, would fulfill his youthful urge to explore the Amazon. But in the last years John Muir fought his most significant and agonizing battle—and lost.

In 1913, after years of bitter feuding, Congress voted to dam the Hetch Hetchy Valley, fifteen miles northwest of Yosemite, in order to provide water and power for San Francisco. Like so many plans touted by politicians as cure-alls, Hetch Hetchy proved a miserable, unnecessary boondoggle, a windfall for a few, with the public paying the bills. It hurt Muir that his friend and ally of the past, Forest Service Chief Gifford Pinchot—his eye always on use rather than preservation—joined its loudest promoters. Worse still, the Hetch Hetchy project violated the purpose of a National Park. Muir knew that it was a commercial wedge into an ideal, a wedge that has since been sunk into other parks. In Wolfe's words, Muir "was a prophet of the shape of things to come."

Yet to a reform-minded nation, the lost Hetch Hetchy Valley, whose beauty had once rivaled Yosemite's, became a symbol, part of John Muir's legacy. Stung by its mistake, Congress three years later passed a comprehensive National Parks bill. In 1914 "John of the Mountains" died, but he had shown the way to Aldo Leopold, Enos Mills, and Stephen Mather—and to thousands of others.

GLOSSARY

Ralph Waldo Emerson (1803–1882):   One of America's most renowned writers and a central figure of American transcendentalism. His poems, orations, and especially his essays are regarded as landmarks in the development of American thought and literary expression.

IMPLICATIONS

Muir's writings and the environmental movement he symbolized had wide resonance in American society. Why do you think so many Americans were concerned about the American environment? Which groups would you expect to be most receptive to Muir's ideas?

Past Traces

The arrival of several thousand Chinese immigrants in California during the 1849 Gold Rush was met by hostility, discrimination, and punitive legislation. Chinese workers were driven from the gold fields, their small holdings taxed at ruinous rates. When they left the gold fields, they were denied entry into better-paying jobs and were even denied the right to own property. Few Chinese women were allowed to enter the United States because white Americans feared that they would bear children who would be born American citizens. Fearing job competition, beginning in the 1870s, the California Workingmen's Movement sought to exclude further Chinese immigration. By the early 1880s, Chinese exclusion had become a popular political issue along the West Coast and in 1882, western politicians succeeded in forcing a national exclusion act through Congress. The major provisions of that act are reprinted in the document below.

The Chinese Exclusion Act (1882)

Whereas, in the opinion of the Government of the United States the coming of Chinese laborers to this country endangers the good order of certain localities within the territory thereof: Therefore,

Be it enacted by the Senate and House of Representatives of the United States of America in Congress assembled, That from and after the expiration of ninety days next after the passage of this act, and until the expiration of ten years next after the passage of this act, the coming of Chinese laborers to the United States be, and the same is hereby, suspended; and during such suspension it shall not be lawful for any Chinese laborer to come, or having so come after the expiration of said ninety days, to remain within the United States.

SEC. 2. That the master of any vessel who shall knowingly bring within the United States on such vessel, and land or permit to be landed, any Chinese laborer, from any foreign port or place, shall be deemed guilty of a misdemeanor, and on conviction thereof shall be punished by a fine of not more than $500 for each and every such Chinese laborer so brought, and may be also imprisoned for a term not exceeding one year.

SEC. 3. That the two foregoing sections shall not apply to Chinese laborers who were in the United States on the 17th day of November, 1880, or who shall have come into the same before the expiration of ninety days next after the passage of this act . . .

SEC. 4. That for the purpose of properly identifying Chinese laborers who were in the United States on the 17th day of November, 1880, or who shall have come into the same before the expiration of ninety days next after the passage of this act, and in order to furnish them with the proper evidence of their right to go from and come to the United States of their free will and accord, as provided by the treaty between the United States and China dated November 17, 1880, the collector of customs of the district from which any such Chinese laborer shall depart from the United States shall, in person or by deputy, go on board each vessel having on board any such Chinese laborer and cleared or about to sail from his district for a foreign port, and on such vessel make a list of all such Chinese laborers, which shall be entered in registry-books to be kept for that purpose, in which shall be stated the name, age, occupation, last place of residence, physical marks or peculiarities, and all facts necessary for the identification of each of such Chinese laborers, which books shall be safely kept in the custom-house; and every such Chinese laborer so departing from the United States shall be entitled to, and shall receive, free of any charge or cost upon application therefor, from the collector or his deputy, at the time such list is taken a certificate, signed by the collector or his deputy and attested by his seal of office, in such form as the Secretary of the Treasury shall prescribe, which certificate shall contain a statement of the name, age, occupation, last place of residence, personal description, and facts of identification of the Chinese laborer to whom the certificate is issued, corresponding with the said list and registry in all particulars . . .

SEC. 5. That any Chinese laborer mentioned in section four of this act being in the United States, and desiring to depart from the United States by land, shall have the right to demand and receive, free of charge or cost, a certificate of identification similar to that provided for in section four of this act to be issued to such Chinese laborers as may desire to leave the United States by water; and it is hereby made the duty of the collector of customs of the district next adjoining the foreign country to which said Chinese laborer desires to go to issue such certificate, free of charge or cost, upon application by such Chinese laborer, and to enter the same upon registry-books to be kept by him for the purpose, as provided for in section four of this act.

SEC. 6. That in order to the faithful execution of articles one and two of the treaty in this act before mentioned, every Chinese person other than a laborer who may be entitled by said treaty and this act to come within the United States, and who shall be about to come to the United States, shall be identified as so entitled by the Chinese Government in each case, such identity to be evidenced by a certificate issued under the authority of said government, which certificate shall be in the English language or (if not in the English language) accompanied by a translation into English, stating such right to come, and which certificate shall state the name, title, or official rank, if any, the age, height, and all physical peculiarities, former and present occupation or profession, and place of residence in China of the person to whom the certificate is issued and that such person is entitled conformably to the treaty in this act mentioned to come within the United States . . .

SEC. 7. That any person who shall knowingly and falsely alter or substitute any name for the name written in such certificate or forge any such certificate, or knowingly utter any forged or fraudulent certificate, or falsely personate any person named in any such certificate, shall be deemed guilty of a misdemeanor; and upon conviction thereof shall be fined in a sum not exceeding $1,000, and imprisoned in a penitentiary for a term of not more than five years.

SEC. 8. That the master of any vessel arriving in the United States from any foreign port or place shall, at the same time he delivers a manifest of the cargo, and if there be no cargo, then at the time of making a report, of the entry of the vessel pursuant to law, in addition to the other matter required to be reported, and before landing, or permitting to land, any Chinese passengers, deliver and report to the collector of customs of the district in which such vessels shall have arrived a separate list of all Chinese passengers taken on board his vessel at any foreign port or place, and all such passengers on board the vessel at that time . . .

SEC. 9. That before any Chinese passengers are landed from any such vessel, the collector, or his deputy, shall proceed to examine such passengers, comparing the certificates with the list and with the passengers; and no passenger shall be allowed to land in the United States from such vessel in violation of law . . .

SEC. 11. That any person who shall knowingly bring into or cause to be brought into the United States by land, or who shall knowingly aid or abet the same, or aid or abet the landing in the United States from any vessel of any Chinese person not lawfully entitled to enter the United states, shall be deemed guilty of a misdemeanor, and shall, on conviction thereof, be fined in a sum not exceeding $1,000, and imprisoned for a term not exceeding one year.

SEC. 12. That no Chinese person shall be permitted to enter the United States by land without producing to the proper officer of customs the certificate in this act required of Chinese persons seeking to land from a vessel . . .

SEC. 13. That this act shall not apply to diplomatic and other officers of the Chinese Government traveling upon the business of that government, whose credentials shall be taken as equivalent to the certificate in this act mentioned, and shall exempt them and their body and household servants from the provisions of this act as to other Chinese persons.

SEC. 14. That hereafter no State court or court of the United States shall admit Chinese to citizenship; and all laws in conflict with this act are hereby repealed.

SEC. 15. That the words "Chinese laborers," wherever used in this act, shall be construed to mean both skilled and unskilled laborers and Chinese employed in mining.

Approved, May 6, 1882.

9

Unbound Feet: Chinese Immigrant Women in Early Twentieth-Century San Francisco

Judy Yung

Chinese immigrants began coming to America soon after word of the California Gold Rush reached Asia in 1849. Nearly all were male sojourners, men who sought to build their modest fortunes on "Gold Mountain" (the Chinese name for the United States) and return home to purchase land and live out the remainder of their lives as prosperous peasant farmers. But while some succeeded in this quest, most remained in America, taking whatever jobs they could find. By the 1860s, growing numbers of Chinese immigrants gravitated to San Francisco's Chinatown, where they sought jobs, community, and protection from an increasingly hostile Anglo world. By the time white politicians passed the Chinese Exclusion Act of 1882, barring further immigration from China, Chinatown was fast becoming the center of Chinese life in America.

Mid-nineteenth-century Chinatown was mostly a male community, but slowly women came to Chinatown as husbands sent for their wives, and family life began to replace a bachelor's existence for a growing number of immigrant men. The 1882 Exclusion Act brought this trickle of Chinese women to an abrupt halt and the Chinese population of America actually began to decline. This all changed in the second and third decades of the twentieth century as social turmoil in China drove thousands of Chinese women to seek their fortunes on Gold Mountain. As the corrupt and ineffectual Qing Dynasty tottered and fell in 1911 and drought and crop failures brought widespread starvation to China, Chinese women looked for ways to circumvent the Exclusion Act.

In this essay, Judy Yung recounts the story of three of these women—Wang Ah So, Law Shee Low, and Jane Kwong Lee—all of whom came to America in the early 1920s. Hoping for jobs, marriage, and family life, they faced demeaning prejudice, job discrimination, and social segregation. These women nonetheless carved out successful lives for themselves in San Francisco's Chinese community. Like many other Asian immigrant women in twentieth-century America, the women portrayed here forged a unique synthesis of Chinese and American worlds.

....

From the beginning, social change for Chinese women in San Francisco was tied to the nationalist and women's movements in China. This became evident on the afternoon of November 2, 1902, when Sieh King King, an eighteen-year-old student from China and an ardent reformer, stood before a Chinatown theater full of men and women and "boldly condemned the slave girl system, raged at the horrors of foot-binding and, with all the vehemence of aroused youth, declared that men and women were equal and should enjoy the privileges of equals." Her talk and her views on women's rights were inextricably linked with Chinese nationalism and the 1898 Reform Movement, which advocated that China emulate the West and modernize in order to throw off the yoke of foreign domination. Beginning with the Opium War (1839–1842), China had suffered repeated defeats at the hands of Western imperialist powers and been forced to yield to their demands for indemnities and extraterritorial rights. Fearing the further partitioning of China and possibly national extinction, reformers and revolutionaries alike were advocating social, economic, and political changes for their country along the lines of the Western model. Elevating the status of women to the extent that they could become "new women"—educated mothers and productive citizens—was part of this nationalist effort to strengthen and defend China against further foreign encroachment.

What happened to women in China had a direct impact on Chinese women in the United States. Beginning in the early twentieth century, not only were new immigrants bringing a different set of cultural baggage with them in regard to women's roles, but political developments in China remained in general more meaningful to Chinese immigrants who had been barred from participation in mainstream American society. Aware that the racial oppression and humiliation they suffered in America was due in part to China's weak international status and inability to protect its citizens abroad, Chinese immigrants kept nationalist sentiment alive, focusing their attention and energies on helping China become a stronger and more modern country, even as they worked to change their unfavorable image and treatment in America. As reported in the local press, Chinese women were becoming "new women" in the homeland, and Chinese women in America were encouraged to do likewise. But aside from Chinese nationalism, the reform work of Protestant missionary women and the Chinese women's entry into the urban economy also helped to advance women's cause in San Francisco Chinatown.

JOURNEY TO GOLD MOUNTAIN

At the time of Sieh King King's speech, China was still suffering under the stranglehold of Western imperialism and the inept rule of the Manchus. China's defeat in the Sino-Japanese War (1894–95) and the Boxer Rebellion (1900) resulted in further concessions of extraterritorial rights and war indemnities to the imperialist powers, including Japan, Germany, Russia, France, England, and the United States. China's subjugation, by adding to the humiliation and economic burden of an overtaxed Chinese population, only strengthened the resolve of nationalists to modernize their country and rid China of both foreign domination and Manchu rule. But even after Sun Yat-sen's Tongmenghui (United Covenant League) succeeded in overthrowing the Qing dynasty in 1911, the problems of foreign control, internal dissension, and economic deterioration persisted. Political and social upheavals continued unabated as warlords, and then Nationalists, Communists, and Japanese, fought for control of China. Life for the ordinary Chinese remained disrupted; survival was precarious. Oppressed by the competition of imported foreign commodities, inflation, heavy taxes, increased rents, and rampant banditry, peasants could not hope to make enough money to meet their expenses. A common saying at the time was "The poor man who faces two swords—heavy farm rent and high interest—has three roads before him: to run away at night, hang himself, or go to jail." Consequently, many able-bodied peasants in Southeast China continued to emigrate overseas where kinfolk had already settled. Despite the Chinese Exclusion Acts and anti-Chinese hostilities, a good number went to America, the Gold Mountain, by posing as members of the exempt classes or by smuggling themselves across the borders.

Chinese immigration declined drastically during the Exclusion period (1883–1943). Since many Chinese in the United States were also returning to China (90,299 between 1908 and 1943), the Chinese population in the United States dropped significantly, from 105,465 in 1880 to 61,639 in 1920. By 1900 the industrial revolution was over, the American West had been conquered, and Chinese labor was no longer being recruited. Many Chinese continued to disperse eastward to cities, where they could find work and where their presence was better tolerated. By 1910, 40.5 percent of the Chinese in the United States were concentrated in cities

with populations above 25,000; by 1920, the percentage had increased to 66 percent. Most worked in ethnic enterprises in Chinatowns, as domestic servants for European American families, or opened small laundries, grocery stores, and restaurants in out-of-the-way places. Others found seasonal employment in agriculture or in canneries. Those who had the economic means got married and started families or sent for their wives and children from China.

Although there was a precipitous drop in the immigration of Chinese women to the United States following the passage of the Chinese Exclusion Act, their numbers began increasing steadily after 1900. A number of reasons explain this increase despite the effort to keep Chinese and their families out of the country. Conditions at home were worsening and becoming unsafe for family members left behind by overseas Chinese. These deteriorating conditions, combined with the lowering of cultural restrictions against women traveling abroad, encouraged increasing numbers of Chinese women to emigrate overseas to join their husbands or to pursue educational and employment opportunities on their own. Unlike in the nineteenth century, when there were no gainful jobs for them in America, they now had an economic role to play in the urban economy or in their husbands' small businesses. Only immigration legislation continued to limit the numbers of women (as well as dictate who could come at all).

Most Chinese women entered the country as merchant wives, the class most favored by immigration legislation throughout the Exclusion period. Until 1924, wives of U.S. citizens were also admissible. But the passage of the Immigration Act of 1924, which was aimed primarily at curbing immigration from eastern, southern, and central Europe, dealt Asian immigration a deadly blow when it included a clause that barred any "alien ineligible to citizenship" admittance. By law, this group included the Chinese, Japanese, Koreans, and Asian Indians. On May 25, 1925, the U.S. Supreme Court ruled that Chinese merchant wives were still admissible because of treaty obligations; the Chinese wives of U.S. citizens, however, being themselves ineligible for citizenship, were not. Alarmed by what this interpretation would mean for their future in America, American-born Chinese fought back through the organized efforts of the Chinese American Citizens Alliance. Arguing persuasively that every male American citizen had the right to have his wife with him, that it was inhumane to keep husbands and wives separated, and that aliens (merchants) should not be entitled to more rights under the immigration laws than U.S. citizens, they moved Congress to amend the 1924 act in 1930 to permit the entry of Chinese alien wives of U.S. citizens—but only those who were married prior to May 26, 1924. Another way for Chinese women to come to the United States was as daughters of U.S. citizens. In this case, however, they were allowed entry only if they claimed derivative citizenship through the father (not the mother), and they had to be unmarried. A few women also came as students, one of the classes exempted from exclusion. But Chinese female students amounted to only about thirty annually in the 1910s and several dozens annually in the 1920s.

Even those with the legal right to immigrate sometimes failed to pass the difficult interrogations and physical examinations required only of Chinese immigrants. Aware of the intimidating entry procedures, many were discouraged from even trying to immigrate. Many Chinese Americans shared the sentiments of Pany Lowe, an American-born Chinese man who was interviewed in 1924:

> Sure I go back to China two times. Stay ten or fifteen months each time. I do not want to bring my wife to this country. Very hard get her in. I know how immigration inspector treat me first time when I come back eighteen years old. . . . My father have to go to court. They keep me on boat for two or three days. Finally he got witness and affidavit prove me to be citizen. They let me go, so I think if they make trouble for me they make trouble for my wife. . . . I think most Chinese in this country like have their son go China get mar-

ried. Under this new law [Immigration Act of 1924], can't do this. No allowed marry white girl. Not enough American-born Chinese to go around. China only place to get wife. Not allowed to bring them back. For Chinaman, very unjust. Not human. Very uncivilized.

American immigration laws and the process of chain migration also determined that most Chinese women would continue to come from the rural villages of Guangdong Province, where traditional gender roles still prevailed. Wong Ah So and Law Shee Low, both of whom immigrated in 1922, serve as examples of Guangdong village women who came as obedient daughters or wives to escape poverty and for the sake of their families. Jane Kwong Lee, who also came to the United States in 1922, was among the small number of urbanized "new women" who emigrated on their own for improved opportunities and adventure. Together, these three women's stories provide insights into the gender roles and immigration experiences of Chinese women in the early twentieth century.

"I was born in Canton [Guangdong] Province," begins Wong Ah So's story, "my father was sometimes a sailor and sometimes he worked on the docks, for we were very poor." Patriarchal cultural values often put the daughter at risk when poverty strikes: from among the five children (two boys and three girls) in the family, her mother chose to betroth her, the eldest daughter, to a Gold Mountain man in exchange for a bride price of 450 Mexican dollars.

> I was 19 when this man came to my mother and said that in America there was a great deal of gold. Even if I just peeled potatoes there, he told my mother I would earn seven or eight dollars a day, and if I was willing to do any work at all I would earn lots of money. He was a laundryman, but said he earned plenty of money. He was very nice to me, and my mother liked him, so my mother was glad to have me go with him as his wife.

Out of filial duty and economic necessity, Ah So agreed to sail to the United States with this laundryman, Huey Yow, in 1922: "I was told by my mother that I was to come to the United States to earn money with which to support my parents and my family in Hongkong." Sharing the same happy thoughts about going to America as many other immigrants before her, she said, "I thought that I was his wife, and was very grateful that he was taking me to such a grand, free country, where everyone was rich and happy."

Huey Yow had a marriage certificate prepared and told her to claim him as her husband to the immigration officials in San Francisco, although there had been no marriage ceremony. "In accordance to my mother's demands I became a party to this arrangement," Ah So admitted later. "On my arrival at the port of San Francisco, I claimed to be the wife of Huey Yow, but in truth had not at any time lived with him as his wife."

Law Shee Low (Law Yuk Tao was her given name before marriage), who was a year younger than Wong Ah So, was born in the village of Kai Gok in Chungshan District, Guangdong Province. Economic and political turmoil in the country hit her family hard. Once well-to-do, they were reduced to poverty in repeated raids by roving bandits. As Law recalled, conditions became so bad that the family had to sell their land and give up their three servants; all four daughters had to quit school and help at home.

> My grandmother, mother, and an aunt all had bound feet, and it was so painful for them to get around. When they got up in the morning, I had to go fetch the water for them to wash up and carry the night soil buckets out. Every morning, we had to draw water from the well for cooking, for tea, and for washing. I would help grandmother with the cooking, and until I became older, I was the one who went to the village marketplace every day to shop.

Along with one other sister, Law was also responsible for sweeping the floor, washing dishes, chopping wood, tending the garden, and scrubbing the brick floor after each rainfall. In accordance with traditional gender roles, none of her brothers had to help. "They went to school. It was work for girls to do," she said matter-of-factly.

As in the case of Wong Ah So, cultural values and economic necessity led her parents to arrange a marriage for Law with a Gold Mountain man. Although aware of the sad plight of other women in her village who were married to Gold Mountain men—her own sister-in-law had gone insane when her husband in America did not return or send money home to support her—Law still felt fortunate: she would be going to America with her husband.

> I had no choice; we were so poor. If we had the money, I'm sure my mother would have kept me at home. . . . We had no food to go with rice, not even soy sauce or black bean paste. Some of our neighbors even had to go begging or sell their daughters, times were so bad. . . . So my parents thought I would have a better future in Gold Mountain.

Her fiancé said he was a clothing salesman in San Francisco and a Christian. He had a minister from Canton preside over the first "modern" wedding in his village. Law was eighteen and her husband, thirty-four. Nine months after the wedding, they sailed for America.

Jane Kwong Lee was born in the same region of China (Op Lee Jeu village, Toishan District, Guangdong Province) at about the same time (1902). But in contrast to Law Shee Low and Wong Ah So, she came from a higher-class background and emigrated under different circumstances. Her life story, as told in her unpublished autobiography, shows how social and political conditions in China made "new women" out of some like herself. Like Law and Ah So, Jane grew up subjected to the sexist practices of a patriarchal society. Although her family was not poor, her birth was not welcomed.

> I was the second daughter, and two girls in a row were one too many, according to my grandparents. Girls were not equal to boys, they maintained. Girls, after they married, belonged to other families; they could not inherit the family name; they could not help the family financially

no matter how good they were at housework. In this atmosphere of emotional depression I was an unwanted child, and to add to the family sadness the weather seemed to be against me too. There was a drought, the worst drought in many years, and all the wells dried up except one. Water had to be rationed. My long (youngest) uncle went out to get the family's share daily. The day after I was born, the man at the well gave him the usual allotment, but my uncle insisted on obtaining one more scoop. The man asked why and the answer was, "We have one more mouth." Then, and only then, the villagers became aware that there had been a baby born in their midst. My grandparents were ashamed of having two granddaughters consecutively and were reluctant to have their neighbors know they had one more person in their family. They wanted grandsons and hoped for grandsons in the future. That is why they named me "Lin Hi," meaning "Link Young Brother." They believed in good omens and I did not disappoint them. My brother was born a year and a half later.

Compared to Law's hard-working childhood, Jane lived a carefree life, playing hide-and-seek in the bamboo groves, catching sparrows and crabs, listening to ghost stories, and helping the family's *mui tsai* tend the vegetable garden. It was a life punctuated by holiday observances and celebrations of new births and marriages as well as the turmoil of family illnesses and deaths, droughts and floods, political uprisings and banditry.

Like Law, Jane came from a farming background. Her grandfather was successful in accumulating land, which he leased out to provide for the family. Her uncle and father were businessmen in Australia; their remittances made the difference in helping the family weather natural disasters and banditry and provided the means by which Jane was able to acquire an education at True Light Seminary in Canton. Social reforms and progressive views on women's equality at the time also helped to make her education possible:

Revolution was imminent. Progress was coming. Education for girls was widely advocated. Liberal parents began sending their daughters to school.

My long [youngest] aunt, sixth aunt-in-law, god-sister Jade and cousin Silver went to attend the True Light Seminary in Canton. Women's liberation had begun. It was the year 1911—the year the Ching [Qing] Dynasty was overthrown and the Republic of China was born.

Her parents were among the liberal ones who believed that daughters should be educated if family means allowed it. Her father had become a Christian during his long sojourn in Australia, and her mother was the first in their village to unbind her own feet. From the age of nine, Jane attended True Light, a boarding school for girls and women sponsored by the Presbyterian Missionary Board in the United States. She completed her last year of middle school at the coeducational Canton Christian College. It was during this time that she adopted the Western name Jane. By then, "the Western wind was slowly penetrating the East and old customs were changing," she wrote.

The curriculum stressed English and the three R's—reading, writing, and arithmetic—but also included classical Chinese literature. In addition, students had the opportunity to work on the school journal, learn Western music appreciation, and participate in sports—volleyball, baseball, and horseback riding. The faculty, all trained in the United States, exposed students to Western ideas of democracy and women's emancipation. During her last year in school, Jane, along with her classmates, was swept up by the May Fourth Movement, in which students agitated for political and cultural reforms in response to continuing foreign domination at the end of World War 1:

The 21 demands from Japan stirred up strong resentment from the students as well as the whole Chinese population. We boycotted Japanese goods and bought only native-manufactured fabrics. We participated in demonstration parades in the streets of Canton. Student delegates were elected to attend student association discussion meetings in Canton; once I was appointed as one of two delegates from our school. Our two-fold duty was to take part in the discussions and decisions and then to convince our schoolmates to take active parts in whatever action was decided. It was a year of turmoil for all the students and of exhaustion for me.

By the time she graduated from middle school, Jane had decided she wanted to become a medical doctor, believing "it would give me not only financial independence, but also social prestige." Her only other choices at the time were factory work or marriage. But further education seemed out of the question because her father's remittances from Australia could no longer support the education of both Jane and her younger brother. Arguing that graduates trained in American colleges and universities were drawing higher salaries in China than local graduates, Jane convinced her mother to sell some of their land in order to pay her passage to the United States. Her mother also had hopes that she would find work teaching at Chinese schools in America and be able to send some of her income home. In 1922, Jane obtained a student visa and sailed for the United States, planning to earn a doctorate and return home to a prestigious academic post. Her class background, education, and early exposure to Western ideas would lead her to a different life experience in America than Law Shee Low and Wong Ah So, who came as obedient wives from sheltered and impoverished families.

DETAINMENT AT ANGEL ISLAND

Like thousands of immigrants before them, Law Shee Low, Wong Ah So, and Jane Kwong Lee had to pass immigration inspection upon their arrival in America. In contrast to the frightening but relatively brief stay of European immigrants at Ellis Island in New York Harbor, most Chinese immigrant women experienced humiliation and despair during their extended detainment at the Port of San Francisco owing to the strict implementation of the Chinese Exclusion laws. Prior to the building of the Angel Island Immigration Station in 1910, Chinese immigrants were housed in a dilapidated wooden shed at the Pacific Mail

Steamship Company wharf. The testimony of Mai Zhouyi, a missionary from Canton and wife of a Chinese merchant, describes the ordeal of detainment suffered by Chinese immigrant women. Locked in the shed for over forty days pending investigation of her right to land, she spoke out against the inhumane treatment she received there at a public gathering in Chinatown following her release:

> All day long I faced the walls and did nothing except eat and sleep like a caged animal. Others— Europeans, Japanese, Koreans—were allowed to disembark almost immediately. Even blacks were greeted by relatives and allowed to go ashore. Only we Chinese were not allowed to see or talk to our loved ones and were escorted by armed guards to the wooden house. Frustrated, we could only sigh and groan. Even the cargo was picked up from the docks and delivered to its destination after custom duties were paid. Only we Chinese were denied that right. How can it be that they look upon us as animals? As less than cargo? Do they think we Chinese are not made of flesh and blood? That we don't have souls? Human beings are supposed to be the superior among all creatures. Should we allow ourselves to be treated like cargo and dumb animals?

Her sentiments echo those of European immigrants who experienced Ellis Island as the "Island of Tears," of bars, cages, and callous brutality on the part of immigration officials. As Fannie Kligerman, who had fled the pogroms in Russia, recalled:

> It was like a prison. They threw us around. You know that children don't know anything. They would say, "Stay here. Stay there." And you live through it, you just don't fight back. And when it came to food we never had fresh bread, the bread was always stale. Where they got it, we don't know. . . . Everybody was sad there. There was not a smile on anybody's face. Here they thought maybe they wouldn't go through. There they thought maybe my child won't go through. There was such a sadness, no smile any place. . . . Just so much sadness there that you have to cry.

Whereas most European immigrants remember the confusion of being quickly processed through the cursory physical, mental, and legal examinations, and the brief moment of fear at possibly being refused entry for reasons of health, morals, or finances, Chinese immigrants who passed through Angel Island have more haunting memories of being locked up in the "wooden building" for weeks and months, the fearful interrogation sessions where they were asked hundreds of questions regarding their past, and the frustration and humiliation of being treated as criminals for nothing more than the simple desire to enter the promised land. Ellis Island was an island not just of tears but also of hope for most European immigrants; for Chinese immigrants, however, Angel Island (nicknamed the "Ellis Island of the West" by immigration authorities) was a prison to men and women alike.

Jane Kwong Lee's status as a student spared her the agony of Angel Island. Along with other first-class passengers who were members of the exempt classes, she had her papers inspected aboard ship and was allowed to land immediately. In contrast, after their ship docked in San Francisco Bay, Law Shee Low and Wong Ah So were separated from their husbands and taken to Angel Island for physical examination and interrogation.

Like hundreds of other Chinese before her, Law had an unfavorable first impression of America via Angel Island. Unaccustomed to disrobing before male doctors and presenting stool samples in a test for parasitic diseases, Chinese women suffered personal humiliation during the physical examination. "Those with hookworms had to go to the hospital," said Law. "Liver fluke was incurable, but hookworm was. There was a new bride who had liver fluke and was deported." After the physical examination, Law remembers being locked up indefinitely in the women's barracks with a dozen other Chinese women to await interrogation.

It was like being in prison. They let us out for meals and then locked us up again when we came back. They brought us knitting things but we

didn't know how. They were willing to teach us but we weren't in the mood. We just sat there all day and looked out the windows. . . . We didn't even care to go out to eat, the food was so bad. . . . The bean sprouts was cooked so badly you wanted to throw up when you saw it. There was rice but it was cold. I just took a few spoonfuls and left. Same food all the time. We began craving for salted fish and chicken. We wanted preserved bean paste. Their food was steamed to death; smelled bad and tasted bad. The vegetables were old and the beef was of poor quality and fatty. They must have thought we were pigs.

Fortunately for Law, her husband sent her some *dim sum* (Chinese savory pastries), fresh fruit, and Chinese sausages, which she gladly shared with other women in the barracks. "The Western woman we called Ma [Deaconess Katharine Maurer, appointed by the Women's Home Missionary Society of the Methodist Episcopal Church to tend to the needs of Chinese women at Angel Island] delivered it. Called our names. Searched it first for fear of coaching notes [to help her during her interrogation]," Law explained.

Finally, after ten days of waiting, Law was called to appear before the Board of Special Inquiry. Following the advice of the other women, she drank a few mouthfuls of cold water to control the fear within her.

One woman who was in her fifties was questioned all day and then later deported, which scared all of us. She said they asked her about [life in China:] the chickens and the neighbors, and the direction the house faced. How would I know all that? I was scared. Fortunately, they didn't ask me all that. Just when I got married. When the interpreter asked me whether I visited my husband's ancestral home during the wedding, I said no because I was afraid he was going to ask me which direction the house faced like the woman told me and I wouldn't know. Evidently, their father [her husband] had said yes. So when they asked me again and I said no, their father, who was being interrogated at the same time the second time around, said, "*Choy!* You went back; why don't you say so?" The Westerner [immigration officer] hit the table with his hand [in objection] and scared me to death. So when he slapped the table, I quickly said, "Oh, I forgot. I did pass by [in the wedding sedan chair] but I didn't go in." So they let me land. But when they led me back to the barracks, I thought I would be deported so I cried. Later at 4 P.M., they called me to get on the boat to go to San Francisco and the others happily helped me gather my things together to leave.

Compared to others, Law's interrogation was unusual in that her husband was allowed to sit in and the process was concluded in one day. "It could have been because this church lady helped us," she suggested. It was generally known that a supporting letter from Donaldina Cameron of the Presbyterian Mission Home often helped get cases landed.

For many other Chinese immigrants, the ordeal at Angel Island was much more agonizing and prolonged. Because affidavits and records had to be reviewed and the testimonies given by immigrants and their witnesses corroborated, even the most expeditious case generally took at least a week. According to one study of procedures at Angel Island, "Each applicant is asked from two or three hundred questions to over a thousand. The records of the hearing generally runs in length from twenty to eighty typewritten pages, depending on the nature of the case." In contrast, European immigrants at Ellis Island were asked a total of twenty-nine questions. In all the Chinese cases, the burden of proof rested on the detainee to show that he or she was not an inadmissible alien. For those who failed the interrogation—usually because of discrepancies in their answers to detailed questions relating to their family history or village life in China— appeals to the Commissioner of Immigration in Washington, D.C., led to additional expenses and extended stays at Angel Island of another six months to a year. According to the testimony of an immigration inspector who was assigned to the Angel Island Immigration Station from 1929 to 1940, "More than

75 percent passed the interrogation at Angel Island. Of those that were denied here, there was always an appeal to Washington and probably only 5 percent of those denied were ever really deported." These statistics were similar in the experience of European immigrants at Ellis Island, where in general only 2 percent of them were deemed "undesirable aliens" and deported. But statistics do not reveal the different process that only Chinese immigrants were subjected to, a process different not only in degree but also in kind.

The disparate responses of Chinese men and women confronted by this harsh treatment reveal their respective gender roles as defined by their home culture and then adapted to their new environment at Angel Island. While the men passed the time actively—reading Chinese newspapers, playing sports outdoors in a fenced-in area, listening to Chinese phonograph records, and gambling or debating among themselves—the women sat around and waited quietly, some occupying their time with needlework. A few took advantage of the weekly walks outside under the watchful eyes of a guard. Whereas the men organized a Self-Governing Association for mutual assistance and to protest conditions at Angel Island, the women did not organize and seemed unable to voice objections to their harsh treatment. Their one defender and friend was Methodist Deaconess Katharine Maurer, known as the "Angel of Angel Island." Assigned to work among the Chinese detainees beginning in 1912, she shopped for the women, provided them with needlework materials, taught them the Bible and English, wrote letters, organized holiday programs for them, and administered to their various needs. Men were able to vent their anger and frustrations by carving poems into the barrack walls, many of which are still visible today. Women, deprived of education, were less literate, and although some remember seeing lines of poetry on the barrack walls, most could not express themselves in writing. One Chinese woman who was illiterate resorted to memorizing the coaching information on her family background by putting it into song.

As women waited for the ordeal to pass, many shared the sentiments of a Mrs. Jew, who was detained on Angel Island the same year as Law Shee Low and Wong Ah So:

> There wasn't anything special about it. Day in, day out, the same thing. Every person had to be patient and tell herself, "I'm just being delayed, it doesn't matter." I never even bathed. I kept thinking each day that I would be ready to leave and as each day went by, I just waited. I didn't eat much, nor move around much, so I never perspired. I had no clothes to wash. . . . I kept thinking, "Had I known it was like this, I never would have wanted to come!"

Confined in the barracks together for indefinite sentences, women maintained a pragmatic attitude and bonded in an effort to cope with the situation. They chatted with one another, shared whatever food they had, dressed one another's hair, consoled those who had failed the interrogation, and accompanied one another to the bathroom after hearing stories of women who had hung themselves there. When asked who comforted the women when they became depressed, Law replied:

> Who was depressed? There were two women who had been there for three months. They didn't cry; didn't seem to care. They even sang sometimes and joked with the man who came in to do the cleaning. Whenever this foreign woman offered to take us out for walks, usually on Fridays, just the two would go. They were two friends and very happy and carefree. They had little going for them, but they managed to struggle on.

Although sobbing was often heard in the women's barracks and there were known cases of suicide, this cultural attribute of "making do" helped many Chinese women through detainment at Angel Island. When finally granted permission to land, immigrant women like Law Shee Low and Wong Ah So tried to put Angel Island behind them as they began their new lives in America.

"NEW WOMEN" IN THE MODERN ERA OF CHINATOWN

The San Francisco Chinatown that Law Shee Low, Wong Ah So, and Jane Kwong Lee came to call home was different from the slum of "filth and depravity" of bygone days. After the 1906 earthquake and fire destroyed Chinatown, Chinese community leaders seized the opportunity to create a new "Oriental City" on the original site. The new Chinatown, in stark contrast to the old, was by appearance cleaner, healthier, and more modern with its wider paved streets, brick buildings, glass-plated storefronts, and pseudo-Chinese architecture. Dupont Street (now Grant Avenue), lined with bazaars, clothing stores, restaurants, newspaper establishments, grocery stores, drugstores, bookstores, and meat and fish markets, became the main business thoroughfare for local residents and a major tourist attraction by the time of the Panama-Pacific International Exposition in 1915. But behind the facade of the "Oriental City," hastily built with tourism and business in mind, was a ghetto plagued by overcrowding, substandard housing, and poor sanitation. Dwelling units for bachelors were constructed above, below, and behind shops in crowded quarters and often with poor lighting and ventilation. There were so few Chinese families then that little thought was given to their housing needs.

Aside from the change in physical appearance, Chinatown was also socially transformed by life under Exclusion. Internal economic and political strife mounted as the Chinese community—kept out of the professions and trades, and isolated within a fifteen-block area of the city—developed its own economic infrastructure, political parties, and social institutions. Merchant associations, trade guilds, and tongs fought over control of the distribution and commercial use of Chinatown's limited space and economic resources, often engaging in bloody warfare in the period from the 1880s to the 1920s. At the same time, strife developed among political factions that disagreed on the best strategy to save China. The Zhigongtang (the American counterpart of the Triad Society in China) favored restoring the Ming emperor; the Baohuanghui advocated a constitutional monarchy; and the Tongmenghui (forerunner of the Guomindang) saw a democratic republic as the answer to China's future. In an effort to establish order in the community, nurture business, and protect the growing numbers of families, the merchant elite and middle-class bourgeoisie established new institutions: Chinese schools, churches, a hospital, newspapers, and a flurry of organizations such as the Chinese Chamber of Commerce, Chinese American Citizens Alliance, Chinatown YMCA and YWCA, Christian Union, and Peace Society. Many of these new social groups also formed alliances with outside law enforcement agents and moral reformers to eliminate gambling, prostitution, and drugs in an effort to clean up Chinatown's image. Their work was met with strong resistance from the tongs that profited by these vice industries, but the progressive forces eventually won out. As reported in the community's leading newspaper, *Chung Sai Yat Po (CSYP),* soon after the 1911 Revolution in China, queues and footbinding were eliminated, tong wars and prostitution reduced, and more of Chinatown's residents were dressing in Western clothing and adopting democratic ideas. Arriving in San Francisco Chinatown at this juncture in time gave immigrant women such as Wong Ah So, Law Shee Low, and Jane Kwong Lee unprecedented opportunities to become "new women" in the modern era of Chinatown.

Decline In Prostitution

Fortunately for Wong Ah So, prostitution was already on the decline by the time she arrived in San Francisco, thanks to the efforts of Chinese nationalists, Protestant missionaries, and those who supported the social purity movement. As her case demonstrates, Chinese women brought to the United States as prostitutes at this time continued to suffer undue hardships but benefited from the socio-historical forces intent on eliminating prostitution in the city. Moreover, it reveals the inner workings of the Chinese prostitution trade, the complicit role of Chinese madams in the illegal business, and the coping mechanisms Chinese prostitutes devised to deal with their enslavement.

Upon landing, Ah So's dreams of wealth and happiness vanished when she found out that her husband, Huey Yow, had in fact been paid $500 by Sing Yow, a madam, to procure her as a slave.

> When we first landed in San Francisco we lived in a hotel in Chinatown, a nice place, but one day, after I had been there for about two weeks, a woman came to see me. She was young, very pretty, and all dressed in silk. She told me that I was not really Huey Yow's wife, but that she had asked him to buy her a slave, that I belonged to her, and must go with her, but she would treat me well, and I could buy back my freedom, if I was willing to please, and be agreeable, and she would let me off in two years, instead of four if I did not make a fuss.

For the next year, Ah So worked as a prostitute for Sing Yow in various small towns. She was also forced to borrow $1,000 to pay off Huey Yow, who was harassing her and threatening her life. Then, seeking higher profits, Sing Yow betrayed her promise and sold Ah So to another madam in Fresno for $2,500. "When I came to America," Ah So's story continues, "I did not know that I was going to live a life of slavery, but understood from women with whom I talked in Hongkong that I was to serve at Chinese banquets and serve as an entertainer for the guests. I was very miserable and unhappy. My owners knew this and kept very close watch over me, fearing that I might try to escape."

Meanwhile, her family in China continued to write her asking for money. Even as her debts piled up and she became ill, she fulfilled her filial obligation by sending $300 home to her mother, enclosed with a letter that read in part:

> Every day I have to be treated by the doctor. My private parts pain me so that I cannot have intercourse with men. It is very hard. . . . Next year I

certainly will be able to pay off all the debts. Your daughter is even more anxious than her mother to do this. As long as your daughter's life lasts she will pay up all the debts. Your daughter will do her part so that the world will not look down upon us.

In another letter to her mother, aside from reconfirming her commitment to fulfill the responsibilities of a filial daughter, Ah So also expressed the desire to "expiate my sin" by becoming a Buddhist nun—the correct move by traditional moral standards. She had indeed internalized the social expectations of virtuous Chinese women, putting these values to good use in helping herself cope with her present, desperate situation.

But before Ah So could realize her wish, help arrived. One evening at a tong banquet where she was working, she was recognized by a friend of her father's, who sought help from the Presbyterian Mission Home on her behalf. Ten days later, Ah So was rescued and placed in the care of Donaldina Cameron. As she wrote, "I don't know just how it happened because it was all very sudden. I just know that it happened. I am learning English and to weave, and I am going to send money to my mother when I can. I can't help but cry, but it is going to be better. I will do what Miss Cameron says." A year later, after learning how to read Chinese and speak English and after becoming a Christian, Ah So agreed to marry Louie Kwong, a merchant in Boise, Idaho.

Her connections to Cameron and the Presbyterian Mission Home did not end there, though. A few years later, Ah So wrote to complain about her husband and to ask Cameron for advice. Louie Kwong had joined the Hop Sing Tong, refused to educate his own daughters (by a previous marriage), had struck her and refused to pay her old boarding fees in the Mission Home, and, worst of all, threatened to send for a concubine from China because he had not borne him a son. This complaint to Cameron about her husband shows that she had evidently changed her attitude regarding traditional gender roles. In support, Cameron

promptly sent a Chinese missionary worker to investigate the matter. It must have helped because five years later, in another letter to Cameron dated December 28, 1933, Ah So wrote about being happily married and "busy, very busy" raising her husband's three daughters, their own two sons and a daughter, plus an adopted daughter and a brother-in-law's ten-year-old son. Ah So had made it back to China only to find that her mother had died and entrusted her with the lives of her two younger brothers and two younger sisters. "I am very grateful and thankful to God that my husband is willing to care for these smaller brothers and [unmarried] sister and help them," she wrote. With the closing assurance that "the girls and I are getting along fine," she enclosed a photograph of herself with her husband and enlarged family.

Immigrant Wives As Indispensable Partners

Immigrant wives like Law Shee Low also found life in America better than in China. They did not find streets paved with gold, but, practically speaking, they at least had food on the table and hope that through their hard work conditions might improve for themselves and their families. Although women were still confined to the domestic sphere within the borders of Chinatown, their contributions as homemakers, wage earners, and culture bearers made them indispensable partners to their husbands in their struggle for economic survival. Their indispensability, combined with changing social attitudes toward women in Chinatown, gave some women leverage to shape gender arrangements within their homes and in the community.

By the time Law arrived in 1922, women's roles and family life in San Francisco Chinatown had changed considerably related to the nineteenth century. U.S. census sources provide an important quantitative view of that change. After steadily decreasing in numbers since 1890, the Chinese female population in San Francisco increased 22 percent between

1910 and 1920, primarily because of the immigration of wives and the birth of daughters. At the same time, the Chinese sex ratio in San Francisco dropped from 553.3 males per 100 females in 1900 to 349.2 in 1920. Whereas most Chinese women in nineteenth-century San Francisco had been single, illiterate, and prostitutes, the 1920 manuscript census for the city indicates that 63 percent of Chinese women were married, only 28 percent were illiterate, and there were no prostitutes. These figures attest to a new pattern of life in Chinatown. More men were becoming settlers and establishing families; and the community was heeding the call among social reformers to educate the women and eradicate prostitution.

The manuscript censuses also indicate that fewer Chinese women were employed in 1920 (12 percent) as compared to 1910 (17 percent) and 1900 (31 percent) and that most of the employed women were seamstresses who worked at home. As was true in the previous two decades, in 1920 the majority of Chinese husbands worked as merchants, grocers, or business managers—occupations lucrative enough that these men could afford wives in America. Overall, however, more women probably worked for pay than were registered in the censuses. Indeed, except for wives of merchants and business managers, most women had to work for pay in order to supplement their husbands' low incomes. Like European immigrant women, some ran boarding houses. Others helped in family businesses or did handwork at home for pay. Because such work was not considered "gainful labor" by census takers, though, they were not accounted for in the censuses. Moreover, language and cultural barriers most likely contributed to the inaccurate recording of census information on the Chinese population.

In 1910, a total of 521 families (76 percent of all families) had a nuclear structure: a married couple and an average of 3.5 children (as compared to 1.5 children in 1880). Although there were no three-generation families living under one roof in 1880, there were thirty such

households in 1910. Thirty-seven households also included a mother-in-law. In 1880, 20 percent of the households had an average of two to three boarders. The 1910 census showed that 22 percent of the households with a female present had an average of 3.8 boarders, and 15 percent had an average of 2.5 relatives living in the household. These statistics show an increased tendency for families to take in boarders or relatives most likely out of economic necessity, for mutual kin support, or in compliance with work benefits accorded employees. In the absence of servants (only three households reported servants), it was most likely the wife who had to clean and cook for everyone else—no simple matter considering the living conditions then. For example, the Lee household, listed at 846 Clay Street in 1910, had a total of nineteen residents: a male head, who was listed as a grocer; his wife, who was listed as unemployed; their two children; two male relatives and one lodger, who apparently worked in the grocery store; and twelve other lodgers, who were listed variously as porters, laundrymen, janitors, farm workers, or fishermen. The wife, Lee Shee Jung, must have done all the housework for the entire household and the cooking for at least her immediate family and the three household members who worked for her husband—all without the assistance of any servants.

With the exception of twenty-one households (3 percent of the total), all of the families lived within the borders of Chinatown, which ran five blocks north and south between Sacramento and Broadway Streets and two blocks east and west between Stockton and Kearny Streets. Law Shee Low joined these families when she arrived in 1922. Her sheltered life in San Francisco Chinatown is typical of that of most immigrant wives, who by all appearances presented a submissive image in public but ruled at home. Their husbands continued to be the chief breadwinners, to control the purse strings, and to be the women's points of connection to the outside world. But, in the absence of the mother-in-law, immigrant wives held the reins in the household, maintaining the integrity of their families in an alien and often hostile land. With few exceptions, they were hard working, frugal, tolerant, faithful and respectful to their husbands, and self-sacrificing toward their children. As such, they were model wives in the traditional sense, but in America, they were also indispensable partners to their husbands in their efforts to establish and sustain family life.

Once released from Angel Island, Law moved into a one-room tenement apartment in Chinatown with her husband, where she lived, worked, and gave birth to eleven children, eight of whom survived. Owing to racial discrimination and economic constraints, they had little choice but to accept the poor, crowded housing conditions in Chinatown, which had been hurriedly built after the 1906 earthquake to accommodate bachelors, not families.

> We rented a room on Stockton Street for eleven dollars a month. We did everything in that one room: sleep, eat, and sit. We had a small three-burner for cooking. There was no ice box, and my husband had to shop for every meal. We did not use canned goods and things like that. We ate only Chinese food. There was no hot water, and we would all hand wash our clothes. We used to dry them on the roof or in the hallways. That's what happens when you are poor. It was the same for all my neighbors. We were all poor together.

Living in Chinatown encouraged the continuation of Chinese cultural practices and provided a sense of security and cultural sustenance for immigrants like Law. At the same time, however, it impeded their acculturation into American society. Compared to Chinese women who lived outside Chinese communities, women in San Francisco Chinatown continued to speak Chinese only, eat Chinese food, dress in Chinese clothing, and maintain Chinese customs much longer. Although by the 1920s most of them wore their hair in short, pageboy cuts or in marcelled waves and walked in Western shoes with low heels, many, like Law, still wore Chinese clothing—colorful shirts with high collars and flared

sleeves that stopped at the elbows, and lightly gathered skirts that fell below the knees.

Since their first responsibility was to their families, immigrant wives like Law found themselves housebound, with no time to take advantage of English classes offered by the churches or to engage in leisure activities outside the home. While her husband worked in a restaurant that catered to black customers on the outskirts of Chinatown, Law stayed home and took in sewing. The only other job opened to women like her was shrimp peeling, which earned them half as much as sewing. Like other immigrant women who followed traditional gender roles, Law believed that "nice Chinese ladies always stay home and take care of the house chores, children, and husband." This arrangement was also preferred by employers, who made larger profits when they could pass overhead costs such as space, lighting, equipment, electricity, and supplies on to employees working at home.

> At first someone from the Low family clan brought me things to sew by the dozens and taught me how to do the seams and how to gather. This one teacher I had specialized in baby clothes with beautiful decorations, embroidered pockets and all. He taught me well, and I made over two dozen pieces a day. The pay was over a dollar a dozen.

Even working twelve hours a day, her husband was bringing home only $60 a month, barely enough to cover rent and food. As she had one child after another, it was easier for her to stay home and sew, even though increasing numbers of women were working in Chinatown sewing factories that paid more than home work. When her husband didn't have time to do the shopping, she would pay to have groceries delivered. "That way with children at home, you didn't have to go out and waste time," she explained. "They would deliver pork and vegetables, and you could then cook it." When asked whether she felt imprisoned, she replied,

> There was no time to feel imprisoned; there was so much to do. We worked like crazy. We had to cook, wash the clothes and diapers by hand, the

floors, and sew whenever we had a chance to sit still. . . . Who had time to go out? It was the same for all my neighbors. We were all good, obedient, and diligent wives. All sewed; all had six or seven children.

Large families, which added to the burden of immigrant wives, were the norm in the 1920s. The Chinese birth rate in San Francisco was twice as high as the city-wide rate because of cultural values that favored large families and sons as well as the lack of knowledge of birth control among Chinese women. According to Law:

> Many had ten or more children. One had nine daughters and was still trying for a son. We didn't want that many, but we didn't know about birth control. Even if we didn't want it, we didn't have the money to go see the doctor. The midwife wanted us to have more babies. But even the midwife had a bad time because no one could afford to pay her. It was $25 a baby.

Law wasn't even aware that she was pregnant when she had the first of three miscarriages at home. The Chinese infant mortality rate was also high: 71 per 1,000 live births in 1929, compared to the city-wide rate of 49 per 1,000. As was common for poor families in those days, all of Law's children were born at home with the help of neighbors or the local midwife. "Who could afford to go to the hospital?" she said. Only when one of her children caught pneumonia did she and her husband make use of the hospital, but by then to no avail. Their son was only three years old when he died. "He was a good boy. . . . I cried for a few years; it was so tragic," she recalled sadly. "We didn't have any money, and we didn't know better."

Although they had more girls (seven) than boys (one survived), her husband was more than willing to provide for them all regardless of sex. "He liked children," Law observed.

> Other men would beat their children and kick them out of the house. He wasn't like that. Other men would scold their wives for having girls. One woman who had four children told me her husband would drag her out of bed and beat her because she didn't want to have any more chil-

dren. We heard all kinds of sad stories like that, but my husband never picked on me like that.

Fortunately for Law, her husband turned out to be cooperative, supportive, and devoted. Until he developed a heart condition in the 1950s, he remained the chief breadwinner, first cooking at a restaurant, then picking fruit in Suisun, sewing at home during the depression, and finally working in the shipyards during World War II. Although he refused to help with housecleaning or child care, he did all the shopping, cooked the rice, and hung out the wash. In Law's estimation of him as a husband,

> He wasn't bad. He did care about me. When he was afraid I wasn't eating, he would tell me to eat more. He was just a bit stubborn. . . . When he was first unemployed, he went and played Chinese dominoes one night. When he came back in the early morning, I said to him when he presented me with a chicken, "I don't want to eat your chicken; I don't like you to gamble." So he stopped going and went back to sewing. . . . I heard there was a building known as the Empress Building in Chinatown, where the wives beat the husbands if they were unemployed or did something wrong. But it wasn't so in our building.

He also asked a "Jesus woman" to come teach her English. But after her first baby, Law couldn't afford the time to study and told her not to come anymore.

It was not until her children were older that Law went out to work in the sewing factories and to the Chinese movies on Saturdays, but she still did not leave the confines of Chinatown. Prior to that, she went out so seldom that one pair of shoes lasted her ten years. Because they were poor, she was especially frugal. She gave most of her earnings to her husband (since he did the shopping), made her own clothes and those of her children, and managed to send periodic remittances home to her family. The neighbors in her building were all from the same area of Guangdong Province, and they became lifelong friends. They often chatted, and occasionally—three or four times a year—they would go out to visit friends in the evening or go shopping together. So insular was her life in Chinatown that to this day, Law still does not speak English or dare go outside Chinatown alone. And she still continues to wear Chinese clothing.

Marxist feminists like Heidi Hartmann would characterize Law Shee Low's life as oppressive. Because of the sexual division of labor at home and in the workplace, women like Law remained confined to the domestic sphere and in a subordinate position vis-à-vis men. But from Law's vantage point, although her life was hard, it was not "oppressive." She may have been restricted to the domestic sphere and stuck in low-wage work, but she was not subordinate or totally dependent on her husband. Because she also contributed to the family income, bore the responsibility of running the household, and provided cultural sustenance, their relationship was interdependent. As far as she was concerned, the family's well-being was of prime importance. Given the extra measure of racism that put Chinese at a disadvantage in the labor market, what counted between her and her husband was not economic equality, but the adequacy of overall family income.

Nor did she regard her housework and child care duties as a form of exploitation. Although doubly burdened by wage labor and household responsibilities, immigrant wives like Law were taught to regard the home as their domain and to rule it proudly with an iron fist. Most were strict with their children, demanding unquestioning obedience, adherence to traditional gender roles, and the continued observance of folk religion, Chinese language and food, and the celebration of annual festivals such as Chinese New Year, Ching Ming, Dragon Boat, Girls' Day, Mid-Autumn, and Winter Solstice. Preparations were time-consuming, but Chinese women took their role as culture bearer seriously and did not shirk their duties regardless of how hectic their lives were. Providing a cultural refuge became an important way for Chinese women to instill ethnic pride in their children and help their families resist the cultural assaults and racist denigra-

tion inflicted by the dominant society. Indeed, their daily struggle to improve the quality of life for themselves and their families was in itself an act of resistance. Although their family life exacted a heavy toll on their personal lives, it also served to sustain them. In this sense, family for them was a site of both oppression and resistance. Working hard had meaning for Chinese women because it enabled them to fulfill their filial obligations as well as provide a better future for their children. Many women shared Law's pragmatic views about life in America:

> It took a lot of hard work, sweat, and tears, but for the sake of the children, it was all worth it in the end. . . . My kids have been good to me. They always remember my birthday. They chip in for my rent, electricity, insurance, everything; and they give me spending money. Thank God and thank heaven!

Into the Public Sphere: Wage Work

Although housebound because of cultural constraints and child care responsibilities, immigrant women like Law Shee Low were still able to achieve a degree of socioeconomic mobility and to some extent reshape gender relations. But as the anthropologist Michelle Zimbaldist Rosaldo once argued, women remain oppressed, lacking value and status, as long as they are confined to the private sphere, cut off from other women and the social world of men. One way women could gain power and a sense of value was by transcending domestic limits and entering the men's world. In some ways, this framework is applicable to Chinese immigrant women like Jane Kwong Lee, who did indeed attain social mobility and status after she entered the public sphere as a wage earner and social activist. Nevertheless, as feminist critics of the public/private dichotomy have pointed out, female devaluation has no one cross-cultural cause. Other related factors, such as class, race, sexuality, institutional setting, place, and time, need to be acknowledged as well. In Jane's situation, her class and educational background facilitated her entry into the public sphere, but she still encountered difficulties owing to institutional racism and sexism.

Compared to Wong Ah So and Law Shee Low, Jane Kwong Lee had an easier time acclimating to life in America. Not only was she educated, Westernized, English-speaking, and unencumbered by family responsibilities, but she also had the help of affluent relatives who provided her with room and board, financial support, and important contacts that enabled her eventually to strike out on her own. B. S. Fong's family, with whom she stayed, lived in a three-bedroom unit over a Chinatown storefront. Jane had her own bedroom. During the first few weeks after her arrival she was taken shopping, to restaurants and church, to visit relatives, and introduced to a group of young women who took her hiking. Arriving in the middle of a school semester, she was unable to enroll in a college, so she decided to look for a job to support herself.

In spite of her educational background and qualifications, she found that only menial jobs and domestic service were open to her. "At heart I was sorry for myself; I wished I were a boy," she wrote in her autobiography. "If I were a boy, I could have gone out into the community, finding a job somewhere as many newcomers from China had done." But as a Chinese woman, she had to bide her time and look for work appropriate for her race and gender. Thus, until she could be admitted to college, and during the summers after she enrolled at Mills College, Jane took whatever jobs were open to Chinese women. She tried embroidery work at a Chinatown factory, sorting vegetables in the wholesale district, working as a live-in domestic for a European American family, peeling shrimp, sorting fruit at a local cannery, and sewing flannel nightgowns at home. Finding all of these jobs taxing and low-paying, she did not stay long at any of them; but she came away with a better appreciation of the diligence and hard work that immigrant women applied to the limited jobs open

to them. She described one job at a Chinese-owned cannery:

> We worked in rows alongside immigrant women from Italy and other European countries. First we sorted cherries. I liked cherries so much, I just ate, ate, and ate. Then we sorted apricots. That was easy. After apricots, we had to open peaches. I was so slow at it I hardly made any money. With cherries and apricots, I could make a dollar a day, but with peaches, I couldn't keep up with the women who worked very fast and made almost ten dollars a day because they were used to doing field work in China.

Here she acknowledged the class difference between herself and peasant women from China, knowing full well that while she could leave these jobs and move on to something better, they often did not have the same option.

As was true for European immigrant women, the patterns of work for Chinese women were shaped by the intersection of the local economy, ethnic traditions, their language and job skills, and family and child care needs, but in addition, race was an influential factor. At the time of Jane's arrival, San Francisco was experiencing a period of growth and prosperity. Ranked the eighth largest city in the country, it was the major port of trade for the Pacific Coast and touted as the financial and corporate capital of the West. Jobs were plentiful in the city's three largest economic sectors—domestic and personal service, trade and transportation, and manufacturing and mechanical industries—but they were filled according to a labor market stratified by race and gender. Native-born white men occupied the upper tier, consisting largely of white-collar professional and managerial positions; foreign-born white men dominated the middle tier, which included the metal and building trades and small merchants; and minority men were concentrated in the bottom tier as laborers, servants, waiters, teamsters, sailors, and longshoremen. In a similar racial scaling, native-born white women occupied the professional, manufacturing, trade, and transportation sectors; white immigrant women, the domestic and transportation sectors; and minority women, personal and domestic services. Within this occupational hierarchy, most Chinese could find work only in the bottom tier. Chinese men worked chiefly as laborers, servants, factory workers in cigar and garment shops, laundrymen, and small merchants, while Chinese women, handicapped further by gender, worked primarily in garment and food-processing factories for low piece-rate wages.

The majority of Chinese factory women were employed in the garment industry, which had been dominated by Chinese men since the 1870s. But as competition from Eastern seaboard manufacturers with superior equipment and labor resources cut into the margin of profit and lowered wages, the ranks of male operators shrank, and garment factories began looking to Chinese women as a source of cheap labor. As early as 1906, a Chinese sewing factory advertised jobs for thirty women workers in *CSYP*. Still, it wasn't until women's emancipation took hold in China that they began to leave the home to work in Chinatown factories. After World War I, Chinese immigrant women came to dominate the trade, working in Chinatown sweatshops that contracted work from white manufacturers. By 1930, there were over three hundred Chinese women employed in forty-six shops, sewing ladies' and male workers' garments for substandard wages and without the benefit of a labor organization.

According to an Industrial Welfare Commission investigation in 1922, Chinese women operated power machines and did handwork, pressing, and finishing for piece rates that fluctuated between factories and depended on the complexity of the task at hand. Aprons ranged from $0.60 to $1.75 a dozen, and nightgowns from $1.10 to $1.50 a dozen. Coveralls were $0.45 a dozen, while shirts and overalls were $1.00 a dozen. Those making buttonholes earned $0.30 a shirt, while those sewing on buttons made $0.18 a dozen. Based on the reported weekly earnings of women who did similar piece-rate work at home, we can calculate that the wages of gar-

ment workers averaged $31 a month. In contrast, Chinese houseboys averaged $80 a month, and Chinese cooks, $95 a month in 1926. As no time records were kept and there was no set pay period, and as women worked on an irregular schedule that revolved around family responsibilities, it was impossible for the Industrial Welfare Commission investigator to determine whether state minimum wages were being paid, though it was obvious that the eight-hour law was being violated. There was at least one indication of dual wages: one woman told the investigator that she earned 10 cents less per dozen sewing on fancy buttons than the men. With inadequate child care services in the community, most worked with their children close by or had their babies strapped to their backs. Women took breaks whenever family duties called. In the investigator's opinion, sanitary provisions were inadequate, particularly ventilation and lighting, but the toilet facilities were fairly clean.

Unlike the situation for Jewish women in the New York garment industry, Chinese women remained trapped in this seasonal, low-wage occupation with no opportunity for upward mobility. The garment industry in both New York and San Francisco operated under the same contracting system, in which manufacturing firms farmed out work orders to contractors who produced the clothing with the help of sweatshop labor paid on a piece-rate basis. Jewish and Chinese contractors who set up small sewing factories in their respective ethnic enclaves drew their cheap labor from a network of kin and *landsleit* (same geographic origins) connections. Whereas both Jewish men *and* women were recruited to the trade in New York, only Chinese women were available and willing to do garment work in San Francisco by the 1920s. Although Jewish women worked at a disadvantage because of the sexual division of labor (in which women are given the harder and less profitable tasks to perform) and dual wages (in which women are paid less than men for the same work), they had more options than Chinese women to change their circumstances. Jewish daughters could be promoted from low-paying, unskilled jobs to better-paying, skilled jobs within a factory, move on to work for larger factories outside the ghetto, and organize to improve conditions in the workplace. Chinese immigrant women, lacking the same language skills and political consciousness and further hindered by racism, often could not avail themselves of the same opportunities.

Immigrant women who worked outside Chinatown in the 1920s also experienced discrimination on the basis of race as well as gender and cultural differences. The records of the Chinese YWCA provide three concrete examples of the extent of this discrimination. In one large cigar factory that employed fifty to sixty Chinese to strip tobacco, one-third of whom were women, Chinese workers worked in a separate room from non-Chinese workers and were paid only half the minimum wage. According to the YWCA worker who investigated the situation, "This group of Chinese did not speak any English and had no knowledge of a minimum wage law, nor did they know of provisions for piece rate." In a similar case, a fruit preserve factory that employed a large number of non-English-speaking Chinese women continued to pay the women at the old rate, while English-speaking European workers who knew about the raise in the minimum wage and demanded such were paid at a higher rate. In the third case, Chinese immigrant women employed at a glacé fruit factory contracted sugar poisoning because the employer had not printed warnings in Chinese of job-related dangers.

Given these circumstances, for Jane Kwong Lee, being Chinese and a woman was a liability in the job market, but because she spoke English, was educated, and had good contacts among middle-class Chinese Christians, she was better off than most other immigrant women. She eventually got a scholarship at Mills College and part-time work teaching Chinese school and tutoring Chinese adults in English at the Chinese Episcopal Church in Oakland. After earning her bachelor's degree

in sociology, she married, had two children, and returned to Mills, where she received a master's degree in sociology and economics in 1933. She then dedicated herself to community service, working many years as coordinator of the Chinese YWCA and as a journalist and translator for a number of Chinatown newspapers.

Most immigrant women, however, because of their limited skills and economic needs, had no choice but to take menial jobs. Wong Shee Chew, whose husband was injured in a tong battle in 1918, supported her two sons single-handedly by laboring in a cannery from 6 A.M. to 8 P.M., six days a week. She also peeled shrimp and sewed garments on the side.

Margaret Leong Lowe, a widow with three children, embroidered flowers and sewed evening gowns to support her family. She said,

> I worked about six days a week. Sometimes I bring home work. I never go to somebody's house. I haven't got time. Sometimes the next door neighbor comes over to my house to talk a little bit. Sunday? Same work at home. Take three children to Sunday church. I be mother, I be father. I had to make money and take care of children. . . . I worked fifty-two years. Seventy-two years old stopped. I worked my whole life.

For women who worked outside the home, it was not an easy task juggling the double responsibilities of homemaker and wage earner. But as long as there were jobs for them and working outside paid more than home work, women were compelled to become factory laborers out of economic necessity. The piece-rate system and flexible schedule in some ways worked to the advantage of both employers and employees. The latter gained by being able to work whatever hours they could depending on family duties, while the former profited by paying women at piece rates they set. Against the backdrop of a cramped and unsanitary working environment, a grueling pace of work, and downward pressure on wages, this system also accounted for the unstructured work style, personal autonomy, and congenial atmosphere that made garment work more bearable to both Jewish and Chinese women. As the

Industrial Welfare Commission investigator observed in 1922:

> Most of the women drift into the factory from ten to eleven in the morning. They return home when the children are due, around luncheon and at three in the afternoon before they go to the Chinese school. They give them their bread and butter or whatever corresponds to it in Chinese. Children who were in the plant frequently needed the mothers' attention and there was cessation of work very often when we came into a workroom. Sometimes the power was shut off, so that no one missed anything of our business. There was stoppage too when a worker felt the need of a cup of tea, the tea caddy being a feature of several places.

Joining the labor market proved to be a double-edged sword for Chinese immigrant women: on the one hand, their earnings helped some to support their families and elevate their socioeconomic status; on the other hand, they became exploited laborers in the factory system, adding work and stress to their already burdensome family life. As immigrants and women of color, they were relegated to the lowest rungs of the labor market. On the positive side, however, working outside the home offered women social rewards—a new sense of freedom, accomplishment, and camaraderie. As was true for Jewish women who worked in the neighborhood garment shop, Chinese women developed long-lasting relationships with their employers and with fellow employees who shared a common past, culture, geographic origin, and concern for one another's well-being. The sewing factory was more than just a workplace. It was an arena for social interactions, where women could learn from one another, share problems, support one another, bicker and make up, and pass the time with storytelling and jokes, gossip and news, and singing while they worked. As one study pointed out, "It is apparent that some go to work in factories merely for a pastime so that they can mingle in groups and pass the time away quicker." Working outside the home also meant that Chinese women were no longer confined to the home; they were earning money for themselves or the family, and they were making new acquaintances and becoming exposed to new ideas. Some used their earnings to send remittances back to their families in China, while others invested in jewelry and property. As Jane Kwong Lee observed, having money to spend made the women feel more liberated in America than in China: "They can buy things for themselves, go out to department stores to choose their own clothes instead of sewing them." Once released from the confines of the home and exposed to the outside world, they also became more socially aware, and some were even drawn to community activism.

Immigration to the United States proved to be a double-edged sword for Chinese women in the early twentieth century. Saddled by cultural restrictions, racial and sex discrimination, and labor exploitation, many suffered undue hardships and led strenuous lives. Yet socioeconomic conditions and historical forces at the time afforded women like Wong Ah So, Law Shee Low, and Jane Kwong Lee opportunities to unbind their lives and reshape gender roles—in essence, to change their circumstances for the better. Their daughters, second-generation women born and raised in the United States, would benefit by their experiences. Without bound feet and bound lives but still fettered by race, gender, and class oppression, their challenge would be to break the double binds of cultural conflict at home and discrimination in the larger society, and take the first steps toward realizing their full potential as Chinese American women.

GLOSSARY

Sino-Japanese War: 1894–1895 war between China and Japan. The Japanese victory placed Formosa and Korea under its control.

Boxer Rebellion: The 1900 Boxer Uprising, led by Chinese nationalists, was a rebellion against foreigners, representatives of foreign powers, and Chinese Christians. The uprising resulted in part from resentment over economic and political exploitation of China by various Western powers and Japan.

Progressivism: A loose-knit group of reformers at the turn of the twentieth century who promoted progress toward better social conditions employing new policies, ideas, and methods.

Tong: An association or a secret society of Chinese in the United States, believed to be involved in organized crime.

Queue: A long braid of hair worn hanging down the back of the neck. All ethnic Chinese men were required to wear their hair in this fashion during the Manchu Dynasty (1644–1912) as a mark of their "inferior" ethnic status.

IMPLICATIONS

In this reading, Yung points out the ambiguity of Chinese women's lives in early twentieth-century San Francisco. Faced with traditional Chinese patriarchy and American sex and racial discrimination, first-generation Chinese women nonetheless forged an enlarged life for themselves. Do you think the advancement of Chinese women's position in America came from these women's reliance on traditional Chinese values (hard work, for example) or do you think that their "unbound" roles came mostly from their interaction with American culture and life?

Past Traces

When it was first introduced on a mass scale, radio was like no other previous media phenomenon. Treating radio personalities and announcers as guests in their homes, many Americans responded to radio broadcasts with the same sense of intimacy they normally reserved for family members and residents of their local towns. But the purpose behind radio broadcasts wasn't so much to entertain listeners as to sell products. This essay begins with two examples of contemporary radio advertising. Like radio itself, these advertisements appealed to people's deepest social and psychological needs.

Advertisements (1925, 1927)

Advertisement for Berkey & Gay Furniture Company (1925)

Do they know Your son at MALUCIO's?

There's a hole in the door at Malucio's. Ring the bell and a pair of eyes will look coldly out at you. If you are known you will get in. Malucio has to be careful.

There have been riotous nights at Malucio's. Tragic nights, too. But somehow the fat little man has managed to avoid the law.

Almost every town has its Malucio's. Some, brightly disguised as cabarets—others, mere back street filling stations for pocket flasks.

But every Malucio will tell you the same thing. His best customers are not the ne'er-do-wells of other years. They are the young people—frequently, the best young people of the town.

Malucio has put one over on the American home. Ultimately he will be driven out. Until then THE HOME MUST BID MORE INTELLIGENTLY FOR MALUCIO'S BUSINESS.

There are many reasons why it is profitable and wise to furnish the home attractively, but one of these, and not the least, is—Malucio's.

The younger generation is sensitive to beauty, princely proud, and will not entertain in homes of which it is secretly ashamed.

But make your rooms attractive, appeal to the vaulting pride of youth, and you may worry that much less about Malucio's—and the other modern frivolities that his name symbolizes.

A guest room smartly and tastefully furnished—a refined and attractive dining room—will more than hold their own against the tinsel cheapness of Malucio's.

Nor is good furniture any longer a luxury for the favored few. THE PRESCOTT suite shown above, for instance, is a moderately priced pattern, conforming in every detail to the finest Berkey & Gay standards.

In style, in the selection of rare and beautiful woods, and in the rich texture of the finish and hand decorating, it reveals the skill of craftsmen long expert in the art of quality furniture making.

The PRESCOTT is typical of values now on display at the store of your local Berkey & Gay dealer. Depend on his showing you furniture in which you may take deep pride—beautiful, well built, luxuriously finished, and moderately priced.

There is a Berkey & Gay pattern suited to every home—an infinite variety of styles at prices ranging all the way from $350 to $6,000.

Advertisement for Eveready Flashlight and Battery (1927)

The Song that STOPPED!

A child of five skipped down the garden path and laughed because the sky was blue. "Jane," called her mother from the kitchen window, "come here and help me bake your birthday cake." Little feet sped. "Don't fall," her mother warned.

Jane stood in the kitchen door and wrinkled her nose in joy. Her gingham dress was luminous against the sun. What a child! Dr. and Mrs. Wentworth cherished Jane.

"Go down to the cellar and get mother some preserver . . . the kind you like."

"The preserves are in the cellar," she chanted, making a progress twice around the kitchen. "Heigh-ho a-derry-o, the preserves are . . ." her voice grew fainter as she danced off. ". . . in the . . ."

The thread of song snapped. A soft *thud-thud*. Fear fluttered Mrs. Wentworth's heart. She rushed to the cellar door.

"Mother!" . . . a child screaming in pain. Mrs. Wentworth saw a little morsel of girlhood lying in a heap of gingham and yellow hair at the bottom of the dark stairs.

The sky is still blue. But there will be no birthday party tomorrow. An ambulance clanged up to Dr. Wentworth's house today. Jane's leg is broken.

If a flashlight had been hanging on a hook at the head of the cellar stairs, this little tragedy would have been averted. If Jane had been taught to use a flashlight as carefully as her father, Dr. Wentworth, had taught her to use a tooth-brush, a life need not have been endangered.

An Eveready Flashlight is always a convenience and often a life-saver. Keep one about the house, in the car; and take one with you wherever you go. Keep it supplied with fresh Eveready Batteries— the longest-lasting flashlight batteries made. Eveready Flashlights, $1.00 up.

NATIONAL CARBON CO., INC. EVEREADY FLASHLIGHTS & BATTERIES

A THOUSAND THINGS MAY HAPPEN IN THE DARK

10

Messenger of the New Age: Station KGIR in Butte

Mary Murphy

Before 1920, newspapers and magazines defined the limits of mass media in the United States. Until the end of World War I, Americans had learned about national and international events, sports contests, and the offerings of the new consumer culture by reading the columns of their local newspapers, by perusing the pages of such magazines as *Saturday Evening Post* and *Harper's Weekly*, or by browsing through nationally circulated catalogs such as those distributed by Sears, Roebuck, and Montgomery Ward. This all changed during the 1920s, however, as radio stations proliferated throughout the nation. First thought of as a public medium of education and moral uplift, by the end of the decade radio took on a new aspect as local stations and national networks began accepting commercial advertisements as a regular part of their programming. For the first time, Americans—even those living in the remotest parts of the country—could listen to "live" news coverage and participate in a national culture of consumption focused on the sale of an ever-increasing variety of goods.

In this essay, Mary Murphy uses the letters written by listeners to Station KGIR in Butte, Montana, to explore the impact that radio had on the lives of ordinary people. These letters, the equivalent to "letters to the editor" written to local newspapers, provide a rare opportunity to get inside the thoughts of people for whom sources are usually all but unobtainable.

As these letters reveal, KGIR listeners, like Americans everywhere, enthusiastically welcomed the new medium into their homes. On remote ranches and in small towns, families gathered around the radio to listen to news, sports, and especially the comedy and drama programs broadcast by the national networks. Even the Great Depression

"Messenger of the New Age: Station KGIR in Butte." *Montana: The Magazine of Western History*, 39 (Autumn, 1989), pp. 52–63. Reprinted by permission of the publisher.

failed to curtail the appeal of commercial radio in Butte, as radio helped to lift the spirits of local listeners and made people realize that they weren't alone in dealing with economic distress. During the 1930s, Murphy argues, radio became a companion for millions of Americans and created a national mass culture that altered the nation in fundamental ways.

···

Was dead from the waist both ways till I tuned in on KGIR but now hot dog I could climb a cactus bush sixty eight feet high with a panther under both arms trim my toe nails with a forty-five when I reached the summit slide back to earth without a scratch hot dawg whoopee cmon have one with us fellas wine for the ladies n everything.

With that classic western accolade greeting its inaugural program, radio station KGIR arrived in Butte, Montana, on February 1, 1929, just ahead of the Great Depression. It performed a dual, sometimes contradictory function during that economic crisis. In a time of almost universal belt-tightening, the allure of the radio impelled people to buy receivers on credit, and commercial programming bombarded listeners with advertisements designed to increase their desire for consumer goods. But the radio also provided a source of comfort, news, and entertainment for the unemployed and underemployed who could no longer afford movies, vacations, restaurant meals, and other pleasures of the consumer society. A radio was a substitute for many of the leisure activities that people gave up during those hard years, but it also prepared them to indulge freely in consumerism once good times returned. Through network programming, KGIR introduced Butte listeners to a developing national culture, while also giving considerable air time to local performers and shows. In this way, Butte's first commercial radio station created an amalgam of news and entertainment that celebrated local talent and served community groups, while exposing its audience to programs of national popularity and significance.

KGIR was Edmund B. Craney's brainchild. Until it began broadcasting, the only radio signals emanating from Butte were those of amateur operators. Arriving in Butte in 1927, Craney saw a potential market and applied for a commercial broadcast license. With wide-ranging and farsighted interests, Craney was the first station owner in Montana to affiliate with a national network, the National Broadcasting Company, in 1931. KGIR also became the flagship of a statewide network of radio stations known as the Z-Bar. In accordance with his own personal philosophy, Craney attempted through radio to instill in citizens of the Big Sky a sense of themselves as Montanans, rather than as isolated residents of an archipelago of small towns and cities.

Radio was the medium of communication of the 1920s and 1930s. The nation's first radio station, KDKA, Pittsburgh, broadcast the results of the Harding–Cox presidential election in 1920 and began regularly scheduled programs in 1921. Early radio fans were attracted not so much by regular transmissions or even the content of programs, but by the romance of distance. Radio telescoped the vast expanses of the West, bringing to rural dwellers the sounds of the city, facilitating communication between towns and outlying ranches, easing the loneliness of isolated lives. Edward P. Morgan, an Idahoan who became a broadcast commentator in Washington, D.C., dated the start of his love affair with radio to his father's purchase of a DeForest set in the mid-1920s. "My night sounds had been the sharp haunting bark of coyotes," Morgan remembered, "but now the boundaries of my world suddenly dilated far beyond the sagebrush hills of Idaho, and through the hissing swish of static, like a bell pealing in a snowstorm, came the sweet, wavering voices of KHJ, Los Angeles, KDKA, Pittsburgh, and, one enchanted evening, Havana, Cuba."

While entrancing, the signals from distant stations were irregular and spurred some Montanans to build local stations. Without the resources common in metropolitan areas, commercial radio in the state developed slowly and sporadically. Between 1922, when KDYS, Montana's first commercial station, debuted in Great Falls, and 1929, when KGIR went on the air in Butte, small stations opened in Havre, Missoula, Vida, Kalispell, and Billings. Programs depended on local talent and leaned heavily toward stock and grain market reports, coverage of school sports, updates on the weather, and direct messages to farm and ranch families.

Throughout the 1920s, commercial radio was distinctly non-commercial. Advertising agencies, sponsors, radio manufacturers, and broadcasters viewed the new medium as an educational tool, an avenue of cultural uplift. Sponsors limited their advertising to modest announcements of who was paying for the program at its beginning and end, or they attached brand names to orchestras and performers, such as the A & P Gypsies, the Lucky Strike Orchestra, and the Best Food Boys. Owen D. Young, chairman of General Electric and RCA, announced in 1926 that he considered the companies' new subsidiary, NBC, to be "semi-philanthropic."

By 1929, advertisers' insistence on sponsorship had faded. The advertising industry had mushroomed during the 1920s; its successful cultivation of a consumer society fed its continued growth. Agencies realized that the intimacy of radio offered an unprecedented opportunity to personalize advertising, and they discovered that listeners did not mind commercials. Listeners often heard the ads as part of the entertainment, and pollsters had found that what radio fans wanted was entertainment. Advertisers began to design commercials as part of the show and to listen to radio station managers who advised: "Ditch Dvorak. They want 'Turkey in the Straw.'"

Radio in Butte bypassed the semiphilanthropic days of the 1920s. When the Symons Company of Spokane announced its intention to start up KGIR, the *Montana Free Press* reported that the station would be "frankly a commercial proposition." Ed Craney, KGIR's manager, had been involved in the radio business for seven years when he came to Butte. Already an amateur operator when he graduated from high school in Spokane in 1922, Craney got a job running a radio parts store owned by lawyer Thomas W. Symons, Jr. As in many small metropolitan areas, the absence of good radio signals in Spokane made it difficult to sell receiving sets, so Craney and Symons started their own radio station to boost equipment sales. KFDC, Spokane went on the air in October 1922, one of the more than fourteen hundred stations that received licenses from the Department of Commerce in 1922–1923. Business picked up, and the two men expanded their sales to western Montana. It was during the course of his sales trips that Craney pinpointed Butte, "a real rip-roaring town," as a plum site for a new station.

Craney received a license for KGIR in 1928 and began construction on the station late that year. He built studios in the third floor of Shiner's furniture store in uptown Butte and, to make sure the transmitter's antenna was fully supported, rigged it from Shiner's roof across the street to the roof of the opposite building. Radio fans avidly followed Craney's progress and geared up for the initial broadcast, scheduled for January 31. Shiner's offered a special price on "Freshman" radios, and the *Butte Daily Post* promised a free crystal set to any boy or girl who enrolled three new subscribers to the paper. Craney later claimed that radio dealers told him they sold three thousand crystal sets during the first week of broadcasting.

On the night of January 31, Butte listeners tuned in to a recording of the "Star Spangled Banner" and the dedication of the station by the Catholic bishop, a Methodist minister, and a rabbi. Then followed twelve hours of musical selections and orations performed by men, women, and children from the Butte area, directed by three prominent Butte music teachers. Hundreds of letters and telegrams sent to the station the next day testified to listeners' delight.

About a month after KGIR's debut, Craney arranged to broadcast Herbert Hoover's inauguration. It was KGIR's first hookup with NBC and more than any other event illustrated the radio fever that gripped Butte. Days before the broadcast, a festive spirit infused the city, as radio owners planned "inauguration breakfasts" so that friends and relatives could gather to eat and drink and listen to Hoover's swearing-in. On inauguration day, crowds massed outside the stores of radio dealers who had hung loudspeakers on their buildings. The Butte Radio Club and the Montana Stock and Bond Company hosted open houses for listeners. Restaurants and department stores aired the broadcast for diners and shoppers. Public and Catholic high school students listened in their auditoriums. Two thousand seventh and eighth graders heard the program over a loudspeaker installed in the Broadway Theater and cheered as the bands passed the reviewing stand in Washington, D.C. The following day, the *Montana Standard*, which had absorbed most of the cost of the program, reported: "The inauguration was made actual, vital—something a great deal more than a remote happening . . . it was as if the listener here were standing among the throngs on the capital lawn. . . ."

The inauguration broadcast stimulated radio sales in Butte. Orton Brothers music store, which had lamented that "the only difficulty in recent months has been to obtain a sufficient number of sets to supply the demands of our customers," announced the imminent arrival of a major shipment of new radios. One trainload of four thousand Majestic receivers, the "biggest single shipment of radio receivers ever routed to the northwest," arrived at the Butte depot on March 23. Butte business directories had listed no radio dealers during the

1920s; by 1930 there were five, and by 1934 seven were serving the city's fans. People added radios to the list of durable goods, such as automobiles and furniture, that they purchased on installment plans. They accepted indebtedness for the delights provided by the radio and the ability of KGIR to link Butte to a larger world in ways more intimate and immediate than newspapers, traveling theater, or even the movies.

Between 1929 and 1931, before KGIR affiliated with NBC and began receiving nationally syndicated programs, the station explored the potential of broadcasting from Butte. Management created fanciful promotions to multiply advertising revenues, engaged local talent who performed in the station's studios, supplementing the phonograph records and occasional transcriptions that formed the bulk of programming, increased coverage of local events, and groped toward a determination of listeners' pleasures. Craney's unfamiliarity with Butte led to some gaffs that other staff members caught. A few months after its debut, for example, the station began a request hour. One night when Craney was running the program, his salesman Leo McMullen came in and asked what he was doing. Craney replied, "We're having request hour." "Request hour, hell," replied McMullen, "you're advertising every whore in Butte." "Gladys at 2 Upper Terrace" and "Dorothy at 8 Lower Terrace" had quickly discovered the commercial benefits of local broadcasting.

Most broadcasts, however, were aboveboard. Local celebrities like Howard Melaney, the "singing fireman" of the Northern Pacific Railway, joined a roster of performances by the Camp Fire Girls, the Rocky Mountain Garden Club, and other civic groups. In May 1929, KGIR observed National Music Week with a special choral broadcast of eighty-five Butte mothers and daughters. Craney solicited local groups to put on their own shows. The Marian White Arts and Crafts Club proudly noted that "our radio station" wanted programs from the club's various departments and promptly responded with short talks three times a week. In the fall of 1929, KGIR broadcast the Rotana Club's Montana Products Dinner from the Masonic Temple, a gala evening celebrating Montana-grown products, speeches, and music.

Beginning in 1929 Craney had appealed to NBC for "programs of national importance" and sought affiliate status with the network. He described the isolation of many Montana listeners who "can receive no other station than KGIR and many of them depend on our station for the newspaper can reach them only from 24 to 72 hours late." NBC was concentrated in the East. At the time of Craney's request it had extended its service to only a few cities west of the Mississippi and feared the unprofitability of a hook-up in a small market like Montana. Craney persuaded Senator Burton K. Wheeler to intercede; and NBC, hoping to please an increasingly powerful politician, partially accommodated Craney. On November 28, 1931, KGIR affiliated with NBC, although the network supplied only an incomplete roster of programs to the station.

Despite the new shows available through NBC, Craney continued to solicit local talent sponsored by local advertisers and to balance commercial broadcasting with community service. One of the most successful programs of the 1930s was the amateur hour sponsored by Symons Department Store. Ray Schilling, advertising manager for the store, decided to test the powers of radio, and Symons scheduled a sale and advertised only on KGIR; nothing appeared in the newspapers. The response was overwhelming, and Schilling was converted. He and his brother then developed Butte's own amateur hour—a fad that was sweeping the radio world during the mid-1930s. Art Chappelle played his accordion on the amateur hour; and shortly thereafter Craney approached Art's father, the owner of Chappelle's Cleaning Works, to sponsor a fifteen-minute program of Art's accordion music. Art, who during high school had a band called the Whirlwinds and still moonlighted as a musician in addition to driving his father's delivery truck, was happy to oblige. Three times a week he stopped his truck at the KGIR

studio, brought in his accordion, and played a selection of polkas and waltzes. Often he performed melodies popular with Butte's ethnic communities—an entire selection of Italian music, or Irish, Polish, or Finnish songs. Art played requests, signed an occasional autograph, and was delighted when he dropped off someone's dry cleaning and they said, "I just heard you on the radio!"

While hundreds of Butte residents performed on KGIR, thousands participated in station-sponsored contests or wrote unsolicited letters. In 1930, Craney began conducting listeners' surveys to determine the average number of hours each radio receiver was turned on each day (in 1930, ten hours; in 1937, nine and a half); how many hours it was tuned to KGIR (in 1930, seven hours; in 1937, eight and a half); what the favorite programs were and why; and what suggestions for new programs and new sponsors listeners might have. The responses that have been preserved reveal a wealth of detail about the likes and dislikes of Butte's radio audience and the role that radio played in the lives of KGIR listeners during the darkest days of the Great Depression. For instance, Craney determined that jazz and old-time string-band melodies were Butte's favorite kind of music and that comedy programs eased the worries of economic hard times.

Through the polls and the success of a few new programs, broadcasters and advertisers across the country discovered that during the Depression audiences wanted lighter fare than classical music and Department of Agriculture reports. The tremendous popularity of "Amos 'n' Andy" demonstrated the potential audience for comedy programs. Advertising agencies, who were producing most shows by the 1930s, experimented with transposing to radio many of the genres already present in popular literature—western, detective stories, serialized melodramas—as well as developing new formats like amateur hours and quiz shows.

Soap operas, churned out in assembly-line style, dominated air time between ten o'clock in the morning and five o'clock at night. Criticized by some for encouraging neuroses in housewives, "washboard weepers" also had their defenders in those who interpreted them as morality plays, easily digested lessons in good and evil. A national study discovered that despite the far-fetched story lines, women found the serials useful sources of information regarding interpersonal relationships. Listeners drew from the dramas some "dos and don'ts" of child-rearing, dating, and marriage. They saw in the characters reflections of people in their own families, or they put themselves in analogous situations and hoped to pattern their behavior to attain similarly successful outcomes. One young woman who followed a soap opera argument between a jealous boy and his girlfriend, observed: "that is just like my boyfriend . . . listening to the stories like that makes me know how other girls act and listening to the way the girl argued I know how to tell my boyfriend where he can get off at." A Butte woman wrote KGIR that her favorite program was the serial "One Man's Family," because "I have a younger brother like Jack and I have grown to understand his ways listening to Jack and Claudia talk." Another testified about the same program: "it is a thirty-minute picture of American life that might as well have been taken in Butte."

Historians of radio have noted how directly and personally Americans responded to the new medium. Listeners welcomed broadcasters into their family circle; and through their letters to stations, fans created a democratic dialogue of praise, criticism, and suggestion in which they conveyed a sense of themselves as direct participants in the broadcast experience. Stations and the networks encouraged fans to correspond with them. During the early 1930s, more than two-thirds of all NBC programs explicitly requested audiences to write in, and the volume of mail was phenomenal. In 1926, NBC received 383,000 communications; in 1929, one million; and in 1931, seven million. CBS claimed that it received over twelve million pieces of mail in 1931.

Much of the mail to stations during the 1930s was in response to free offers of prizes in exchange for a cereal box top or some other evidence of the purchase of a sponsor's product. Pictures of Little Orphan Annie, magnet rings, slide whistles, and Tom Mix decoder rings kept the mail bags of America full during the Depression. During the 1937 Christmas season, KGIR offered a free prize for every letter to Santa Claus it received. For a seasonal program, selected letters were read on the air, interspersed with chatter between Santa and his helpers. After two such shows, the station had received three thousand letters and exhausted its grab bag. Hoping to slow the flow of mail, it asked that future letters include a sales receipt from a station advertiser. Three thousand more letters poured in. Broadcasters' invitations to the radio audience encouraged a letter-writing habit that ranged from participating in contests to conveying intimate thoughts and opinions to the President of the United States. Ed Craney confirmed that at times the largest volume of mail received by KGIR was in response to a program sponsored by the Farmers' Union, which discussed New Deal legislation and urged people to write to President Roosevelt.

During the mid-1930s, KGIR kept a tally of the mail it received: 5,770 in 1934 and 23,065 in 1938. Butte women outnumbered men two to one as correspondents, paralleling national trends in which women outdistanced men who wrote radio fan mail. National studies also determined that lower income people and those with little education wrote the most letters to radio stations, radio stars, and advertisers. The small number of letters to KGIR that were saved, 165 of them from 1933 and 1935, tends to support that claim. Nevertheless, Butte was a working-class community, and it is natural that the majority of letters to KGIR would have come from working-class households. Of the 15,322 men employed in Butte in 1930, 62 percent of them were engaged either in mining or manufacturing, in contrast to the 10 percent employed as professionals or in clerical positions. Of those whose occupations could be determined, miners compromised 31 percent of the adult males who wrote letters preserved in KGIR's files. Of the remaining adult male writers, only one was a management position. A few women married to professionals, managers, and business owners also sent their opinions to the station. Eighty percent of the adult women writers, however, were wedded to working-class men or were themselves wage-earners.

National studies estimated that the majority of letter-writers wrote to stations in response to contests. But KGIR correspondents sent as many unsolicited letters and replies to surveys that did not promise any material reward as they did to prize offers. During nine months in 1934, the station received 2,121 survey responses, compared to 2,071 responses to offers. In 1935, the number of letters seeing prizes was only 76 more than the 6,253 other letters received. Clearly, KGIR listeners believed that it was not only appropriate, but perhaps also necessary, to share their opinions with station management.

Gratuitous advice, pungent criticism, and heartfelt best wishes accompanied both thoughtful and absurd suggestions. Some wrote to say that KGIR was the "only half-way decent program on the air," others to warn that it was playing too much jazz and should "crowd the trash off the air." George Hardesty, a carpenter, conveyed most eloquently the fondness that many listeners felt for their radios and for KGIR. Writing in 1933, Hardesty described his radio as a powerful spur to the imagination and spoke of the relief it delivered during the psychologically bleak days of the 1930s:

> There was a time when I saw a Movie twice a week, but not in these slim times. And with my radio, I really can't say that I mind so much. Any evening there are shows come to me over KGIR, but Wednesday evening when Sherlock Holmes unravels his mysteries, I am positive I don't miss my shows. I can see the two old gentlemen, as if they were in my room, poreing over their G. Washington Coffee [the show's sponsor]. Certainly I am entirely unaware of a depression

when one of these life and death mysteries is on, and honestly, anything that can make me do that is worth a lot. Thats one of the reasons I like it, perhaps the main one.

All over the country radio fans attested to the cheering effects of comedy and drama programs during the Depression, and the Butte audience was no exception. The character that elicited far and away the most responses from KGIR listeners was Ed Wynn's "Fire Chief," sponsored by Texaco. Fans wrote: "He will cure the worst case of the Blues and even make you forget the Depression"; "Ed sure keeps the radio audience in an uproar from start to finish, which is just what is needed by all of us during these trying times . . .", "It is humorous and produces a '*good laugh*' which I consider necessary to offset the serious problems of this strenuous life of ours." Wynn's show provoked some poignant compositions on the part of fans. Young Harry Lonner sent in this dispatch:

> A dance orchestra is on the air. Dad is reading the newspaper. Ma is busy with some sewing or other household task. Sis and I are doing schoolwork. Suddenly, comes the shrill scream of a siren! The clang of bells! Ed Wynn is on the air! Dad lets the newspaper drop in his lap, Ma comes into the parlor and sits close to the radio; and Sis and I stop our schoolwork. . . . Dad, Sis and I grin and chuckle after every joke, but Ma laughs till her sides ache. This is the one big reason why I like the Texaco Program. For fifteen minutes Dad forgets about his job, Ma quits worrying about how she is going to pay the bills, and I am happy to see them happy. Old Man Depression is forgotten and Happiness is King.

Time and again writers expressed gratitude that they had been able to buy their radios during good times, because now they were their only source of pleasure and news. Using empathy and imagination, radio listeners transported themselves, however briefly, from their surroundings. Listening to the travails of Little Orphan Annie made "our troubles so small compared to our more unfortunate fellow beings." The radio compensated those not able to travel during the vacation season—even though unemployment guaranteed "most of us are having quite a long vacation"—by taking them to the Mountains of the Moon, the jungles of Malaya and Africa. And the radio was democratic. As Ted Wilson, a clerk at Southside Hardware, remarked: "it is a A one entertainment equally alluring for the rich or poor."

By the 1930s, radio had become part of many people's daily lives, a companion that did more than lift the blues of the Depression. Mrs. George McCoy wrote KGIR that the comedy of an early morning show, "The Gazooks," along with three cups of coffee "make it possible to face the horrors of the new day with a smile." Mrs. Nellie Sacry chronicled a day "beginning with the Gazooks—who help us get up better natured for you can't be grumpy when someone makes you laugh." Her eight-year-old son waited at the door with his coat on to dash out to school as soon as "Cecil and Sally" was over, and the family's day continued through the "Music Box" at dinner time. Mrs. George Hardesty praised the sweet music that calmed her frayed nerves after a day of housework and made her "a better me, to meet my husband and family."

Radio fans took programs far more seriously and invested them with more importance than advertising men or writers ever imagined. They accepted radio almost uncritically, as a wise seer who provided advice, pleasure, and testimonials for reliable products. Listeners wrote amazingly innocent and intimate letters to fictional characters and national corporations. Mrs. J. W. Larson, a miner's wife, lauded a children's program sponsored by General Mills:

Personally, Skippy's program has helped me a great deal. My little girl is four years old, she can't tell time yet, but she never lets me forget Skippy. Skippy has taught her to brush her own hair and not to forget to clean her theeth [sic] and fingernails. Before Skippy was on the air I couldn't get her to eat any cereal, but now I have no trouble. She don't get Wheaties very often now, as her father isn't working. But she eats her oatmeal every morning. She had Wheaties every morning when her Dad was working.

Craney's calls during the 1930s for new programs and sponsors elicited a wide variety of suggestions and documented the energy and thought that many listeners put into "their station." More than one person thought a show relating tales of Butte and Montana history would be entertaining. Mrs. T. H. Wilkinson suggested having pioneers relate their experiences of settling the area or perhaps retelling some tales of hunting and fishing. "After all," she concluded, "Butte is a good old town and just full of good stories to tell." H. C. Howard proposed a different way of exploring Montana, a series of "short enthusiastic talks" recounting the "delights of motoring in Montana and describing each week some historical or scenic spot that is little known in the state and describing how it is reached, the condition of the roads to this spot and various points of interest along the route." The show would be accompanied by popular music and paid for by service stations, hotels, auto camps, or businesses patronized by tourists.

Housewives recommended programs that would interest them during the day: a morning exercise routine, advice to young housekeepers on arranging furniture, reports on new clothing styles, a menu contest of meals "that the average housewife could afford to serve." From Mrs. Adah Daugherty, wife of a salesman, came a letter that could have gotten her a job in any advertising agency:

There are things dear to the heart of every woman, and dearest of these things is her personal appearance. If she could go to the radio and tune in on a beauty talk that would deal with any phase of a woman's face, hair, figure, hands, and feet, I dare say that only the door bell could draw her away. These things she might be able to get in the advertisements in the current magazines, or an occasional article, but the busy woman has very little time for reading. There is a psychological difference between reading the printed word, and hearing the same spoken. The latter catches the instant attention and is retained longer. With this given by some firm or firms in Butte, and the talk read by a woman, it would prove most effective.

Mrs. Daugherty continued with a discussion of possible sponsors and a reflection on the future of advertising: "Radio is the new means of advertising, and is here to stay. More and more firms are going to adopt clever methods of advertising, and owing to the depression, more vigorous methods." She acknowledged that the intrinsic worth of the product was immaterial and that by appealing to women's vanity a manufacturer could successfully peddle anything. "Woman is eternally looking for the foundation of youth . . . she will be a susceptible listener to a program on beauty talks, and the firm to which she is listening will be the one to gain." And in words reminiscent of the personal testimony advertisements that were popular in magazines of the time, she concluded: "I am a woman. I know."

Mrs. Daugherty was unusual in analyzing the advertising industry's relationship to radio with such perspicacity. The overwhelming majority of listeners who wrote the station and mentioned sponsors conveyed a simple gratitude that corporations were providing them with so many hours of delight. Some avowed they enjoyed the advertising as much as the programming. Mrs. Henry Webking claimed that "the K.G.I.R. announcer tells us so much about the firm and its products during the course of the program, and in so few well chosen words, that we really enjoy the advertising and absorb it as much as we do the request numbers." Fans appeared to feel that the least they could do to demonstrate their appreciation was to buy the sponsor's product. Margaret Carolus, who enjoyed the Jack Benny program paid for by Jello, found the advertising so compelling "that it has encouraged me to eat and like Jello—though I had never cared for it before." Clarence Roper testified that smoking Edgeworth tobacco gave him as much of a thrill as the music on the Edgeworth program. Ruth O'Brien begged KGIR to "keep Orphan Annie on the radio for a little ten-year-old like me" and promised, "I'll drink lots and lots of Ovaltine."

Such promises and testimonials are weighty evidence of the power that advertisers exerted on the radio audience. Craney's device for generating new ideas may have provided the kernels for only a few marketable programs, but it reaped a harvest of radio fans participating actively in their own seduction by consumer culture. The lure of winning a prize coaxed them into experimenting with the language of sales, extolling the virtues of any and all products. The impetus of a contest may have led listeners to embellish their appreciation of certain products, but the internal structure of their letters, the way in which they linked product use to their daily lives, and the effort by which men, women, and children sat down to write lengthy missives—often much longer than that required or desired by contest rules—testify to the earnestness with which most correspondents wrote.

When Helen and Robert Lynd observed the popularity of radio in Middletown in the early 1920s, they also hypothesized that radio, along with national advertising and syndicated newspapers, would act to standardize much of Middletown's culture. Writer Dorothy Johnson certainly found that to be the case in Montana:

> Everybody, all over, could listen to the same demagogues, howl at the same comedians, make a fad of the new slang. Everybody with a radio . . . suddenly was sophisticated, part of the great outside world. . . . Listeners became addicts, so accustomed to having sounds of any old kind coming into the house that they were nervous when it was quiet. . . . For better or worse, the quiet, the isolation, the parochialism was gone.

KGIR brought those forces of homogenization to Butte. Yet, throughout the 1930s, the station continued to air programs that spotlighted local talent, that extolled the unique virtues of the Montana landscape, that caused listeners to feel an allegiance to their local station—not only gratitude to national sponsors. As much as fans appreciated syndicated shows, they loved listening to themselves and their neighbors more. Jim Harmon declared that "the very stuff of radio was imagination," and KGIR permitted citizens to let their imaginations run riot. Symons's amateur hour nourished the dreams of local performers.

Neighbors guessed at the hidden messages conveyed by songs on the request hour. Families gathered around the radio to listen to their sons and daughters sing, play in jazz bands, and recite poetry. Members of Butte's different ethnic communities waited for special holiday programs that featured their musical heritage. Private delights, broadcast over the air, assumed a cloak of public importance.

The effect that radio had on listeners is evident in the long and pleasurable memories that people associate with KGIR. Mona Daly "vividly" recalled in 1988 the afternoon in the 1930s on which her voice teacher at the Webster school chose her and a classmate to go to the KGIR studio and sing a duet of "Juanita"—"a definite thrill." Fifty years after he first heard the melodies, Jacob Jovick could name eighty-one songs that KGIR played on the request hour and thirty-one different programs that he listened to and apologize because "there were others I don't recall."

Ed Craney, his small staff, and the KGIR audience composed a score that harmonized strains of local, regional, and national culture. Craney had hoped that radio would make Montanans "realize that there was more in Montana than the little town that they lived in." To gain that end, he invited Montanans' participation in his enterprise. Miss May Gates of Opportunity was one of twenty-four would-be news editors who volunteered their services to pass on the tidings of their communities to the KGIR audience. KGIR's listeners thus had access not only to national news, New York opera, and southern string-band music, but also to "all the news and gossip that is told each evening at the Opportunity store"—and in stores in Butte, Melrose, Rocker, Deer Lodge, Twin Bridges, and a handful of other communities in KGIR's broadcast radius. KGIR introduced its audience to nationally standardized programs that some analysts feared would erase the cultural diversity of America. The station's commitment to airing the voices of its own region, however, guaranteed a medley of cultural expression. Listeners greeted radio's first decade in Butte with uncritical pleasure. KGIR became a source of delight, education, and emotional relief to thousands weathering the Great Depression, and May Gates spoke for many when she exclaimed, "What a wonderful invention the radio has been."

GLOSSARY

Antonin Dvőrák (1841–1904):   Czech composer best known for his Symphony in E Minor, from *The New World*, written while he was in the United States.

Little Orphan Annie: Popular comic strip character.

Tom Mix (1880–1940):   Film actor noted for his performances in silent Westerns.

Middletown: An early sociological study of an American community during the 1920s.

IMPLICATIONS

In this essay, Murphy reveals the multiple impacts that radio had on the lives of ordinary people in Butte, Montana. Why do you think ordinary Americans responded so personally to early radio broadcasts and advertising?

Past Traces

Since the Panic of 1819, Americans have learned to adjust to the upswings and downturns of the nation's economy. Enjoying the fruits of ample employment in good times and tightening their belts in bad, ordinary Americans have long drawn upon personal and family resources in weathering the cycles of American industrial life.

Yet nothing prepared the American people for the experience of the Great Depression of the 1930s. Beginning with the stock market crash of October 1929, Americans absorbed one economic blow after another until, by 1933, a quarter of the nation's workforce was unemployed. In the end, few families escaped the impact of the declining incomes and diminished expectations of the Depression era.

In this document, taken from the pages of the popular-radical magazine, *The Masses*, Meridel LeSueur takes us into the world of the unemployed. Focusing on people searching for work at a local employment bureau in Minneapolis, LeSueur documents the anxiety, frustration, and despair felt by millions of Americans in an era when there were few social programs—unemployment insurance, Medicare, or family income support—to aid those in need.

As you read this article, you may want to ask yourself to what degree the author's own views shaped the story she wrote. LeSueur's sympathies clearly lay with the plight of the unemployed; she went on to join the Communist party and to write about the labor movement and national politics for the remainder of her career. In what ways do you think LeSueur's personal history influenced the subjects she chose to write about and what she had to say? Could her account of the unemployed be objective despite her personal sympathies and point of view?

Meridel LeSueur, *Despair of Unemployed Women*

I am sitting in the city free employment bureau. It's the women's section. We have been sitting here now for four hours. We sit here every day, waiting for a job. There are no jobs. Most of us have had no breakfast. Some have had scant rations for over a year. Hunger makes a human being lapse into a state of lethargy, especially city hunger. Is there any place else in the world where a human being is supposed to go hungry amidst plenty without an outcry, without protest, where only the boldest steal or kill for bread, and the timid crawl the streets, hunger like the beak of a terrible bird at the vitals?

We sit looking at the floor. No one dares think of the coming winter. There are only a few more days of summer. Everyone is anxious to get work to lay up something for that long siege of bitter cold. But there is no work. Sitting in the room we all know it. That is why we don't talk much. We look at the floor dreading to see that knowledge in each other's eyes. There is a kind of humiliation in it. We look away from each other. We look at the floor. It's too terrible to see this animal terror in each other's eyes.

So we sit hour after hour, day after day, waiting for a job to come in. There are many women for a single job. A thin sharp woman sits inside a wire cage looking at a book. For four hours we have watched her looking at that book. She has a hard little eye. In the small bare room there are half a dozen women sitting on the benches waiting. Many come and go. Our faces are all familiar to each other, for we wait here every day.

This is a domestic employment bureau. Most of the women who come here are middle-aged, some have families, some have raised their families and are now alone, some have men who are out of work. Hard times and the man leaves to hunt for work. He doesn't find it. He drifts on. The woman probably doesn't hear from him for a long time. She expects it. She isn't surprised. She struggles alone to feed the many mouths. Sometimes she gets help from the charities. If she's clever she can get herself a good living from the charities, if she's naturally a lick spittle, naturally a little docile and cunning. If she's proud then she starves silently, leaving her children to find work, coming home after a day's searching to wrestle with her house, her children.

Some such story is written on the faces of all these women. There are young girls too, fresh from the country. Some are made brazen too soon by the city. There is a great exodus of girls from the farms into the city now. Thousands of farms have been vacated completely in Minnesota. The girls are trying to get work. The prettier ones can get jobs in the stores when there are any, or waiting on tables, but these jobs are only for the attractive and the adroit. The others, the real peasants, have a more difficult time.

Bernice sits next to me. She is a Polish woman of thirty-five. She has been working in people's kitchens for fifteen years or more. She is large, her great body in mounds, her face brightly scrubbed. She has a peasant mind and finds it hard even yet to understand the maze of the city where trickery is worth more than brawn. Her blue eyes are not clever but slow and trusting. She suffers from loneliness and lack of talk. When you speak to her, her face lifts and brightens as if you had spoken through a great darkness, and she talks magically of little things as if the weather were magic, or tells some crazy tale of her adventures on the city streets, embellishing them in bright colors until they hang heavy and thick like embroidery. She loves the city anyhow. It's exciting to her, like a bazaar. She loves to go shopping and get a bargain, hunting out the places where stale bread and cakes can be had for a few cents. She likes walking the streets looking for men to take her to a picture show. Sometimes she goes to five picture shows in one day, or she sits through one the entire day until she knows all the dialog by heart.

She came to the city a young girl from a Wisconsin farm. The first thing that happened to her, a charlatan dentist took out all her good shining teeth and the fifty dollars she had saved working in a canning factory. After that she met men in the park who told her how to look out for herself, corrupting her peasant mind, teaching her to mistrust everyone. Sometimes now she forgets to mistrust everyone and gets taken in. They taught her to get what she could for nothing, to count her change, to go back if she found herself cheated, to demand her rights.

She lives alone in little rooms. She bought seven dollars' worth of second-hand furniture eight years ago. She rents a room for perhaps three dollars a month in an attic, sometimes in a cold house. Once the house where she stayed was condemned and everyone else moved out and she lived there all winter alone on the top floor. She spent only twenty-five dollars all winter.

She wants to get married but she sees what happens to her married friends, left with children to support, worn out before their time. So she stays single. She is virtuous. She is slightly deaf from hanging out clothes in winter. She had done people's washings and cooking for fifteen years and in that time saved thirty dollars. Now she hasn't worked steady for a year and she has spent the thirty dollars. She had dreamed of having a little house or a houseboat perhaps with a spot of ground for a few chickens. This dream she will never realize.

She has lost all her furniture now along with the dream. A married friend whose husband is gone gives her a bed for which she pays by doing a great deal of work for the woman. She comes here every day now sitting bewildered, her pudgy hands folded in her lap. She is hungry. Her great flesh has begun to hang in folds. She has been living on crackers. Sometimes a box of crackers lasts a week. She has a friend who's a baker and he sometimes steals the stale loaves and brings them to her.

It's one of the great mysteries of the city where women go when they are out of work and hungry. There are not many women in the bread line. There are no flop houses for women as there are for men, where a bed can be had for a quarter or less. You don't see women lying on the floor at the mission in the free flops. They obviously don't sleep in the jungle or under newspapers in the park. There is no law I suppose against their being in these places but the fact is they rarely are.

Yet there must be as many women out of jobs in cities and suffering extreme poverty as there are men. What happens to them? Where do they go? Try to get into the Y.W. without any money or looking down at heel. Charities take care of very few and only those that are called "deserving." The lone girl is under suspicion by the virgin women who dispense charity.

I've lived in cities for many months broke, without help, too timid to get in bread lines. I've known many women to live like this until they simply faint on the street from privations, without saying a word to anyone. A woman will shut herself up in a room until it is taken away from her, and eat a cracker a day and be as quiet as a mouse so there are no social statistics concerning her.

I don't know why it is, but a woman will do this unless she has dependents, will go for weeks verging on starvation, crawling in some hole, going through the streets ashamed, sitting in libraries, parks, going for days without speaking to a living soul like some exiled beast, keeping the runs mended in her stockings, shut up in terror in her own misery, until she becomes too supersensitive and timid to even ask for a job.

Bernice says even strange men she has met in the park have sometimes, that is in better days, given her a loan to pay her room rent. She has always paid them back.

In the afternoon the young girls, to forget the hunger and the deathly torture and fear of being jobless, try to pick up a man to take them to a ten-cent show. They never go to more expensive ones, but they can always find a man willing to spend a dime to have the company of a girl for the afternoon.

Sometimes a girl facing the night without shelter will approach a man for lodging. A woman always asks a man for help. Rarely another woman. I have known girls to sleep in men's rooms for the night on a pallet without molestation and be given breakfast in the morning.

It's no wonder these young girls refuse to marry, refuse to rear children. They are like certain savage tribes, who, when they have been conquered, refuse to breed.

Not one of them but looks forward to starvation for the coming winter. We are in a jungle and know it. We are beaten, entrapped. There is no way out. Even if there were a job, even if that thin acrid woman came and gave everyone in the room a job for a few days, a few hours, at thirty cents an hour, this would all be repeated tomorrow, the next day and the next.

Not one of these women but knows that despite years of labor there is only starvation, humiliation in front of them.

Mrs. Grey, sitting across from me, is a living spokesman for the futility of labor. She is a warning. Her hands are scarred with labor. Her body is a great puckered scar. She has given birth to six children, buried three, supported them all alive and dead, bearing them, burying them, feeding them. Bred in hunger they have been spare, susceptible to disease. For seven years she tried to save her boy's arm from amputation, diseased from tuberculosis of the bone. It is almost too suffocating to think of that long close horror of years of childbearing, child-feeding, rearing, with the bare suffering of providing a meal and shelter.

Now she is fifty. Her children, economically insecure, are drifters. She never hears of them. She doesn't know if they are alive. She doesn't know if she is alive. Such subtleties of suffering are not for her. For her the brutality of hunger and cold. Not until these are done away with can those subtle feelings that make a human being be indulged.

She is lucky to have five dollars ahead of her. That is her security. She has a tumor that she will die of. She is thin as a worn dime with her tumor sticking out of her side. She is brittle and bitter. Her face is not the face of a human being. She has borne more than it is possible for a human being to bear. She is reduced to the least possible denominator of human feelings.

It is terrible to see her little bloodshot eyes like a beaten hound's, fearful in terror.

We cannot meet her eyes. When she looks at any of us we look away. She is like a woman drowning and we turn away. We must ignore those eyes that are surely the eyes of a person drowning, doomed. She doesn't cry out. She goes down decently. And we all look away.

The young ones know though. I don't want to marry. I don't want any children. So they all say. No children. No marriage. They arm themselves alone, keep up alone. The man is helpless now. He cannot provide. If he propagates he cannot take care of his young. The means are not in his hands. So they live alone. Get what fun they can. The life risk is too horrible now. Defeat is too clearly written on it.

So we sit in this room like cattle, waiting for a nonexistent job, willing to work to the farthest atom of energy, unable to work, unable to get food and lodging, unable to bear children— here we must sit in this shame looking at the floor, worse than beasts at a slaughter.

It is appalling to think that these women sitting so listless in the room may work as hard as it is possible for a human being to work, may labor night and day, like Mrs. Grey wash streetcars from midnight to dawn and offices in the early evening, scrub for fourteen and fifteen hours a day, sleep only five hours or so, do this their whole lives, and never earn one day of security, having always before them the pit of the future. The endless labor, the bending back, the water-soaked hands, earning never more than a week's wages, never having in their hands more life than that.

It's not the suffering of birth, death, love that the young reject, but the suffering of endless labor without dream, eating the spare bread in bitterness, being a slave without the security of a slave.

—*Source*: Meridel LeSueur, "Women on the Breadlines," *New Masses*, January 1932.

11

What the Depression Did to People

Edward R. Ellis

The American economy has a long history of cyclical recessions and depressions dating back to the eighteenth century. But none of the depressions could compare in severity or longevity to that which struck Americans between 1929 and 1941. Following a decade of unprecedented prosperity, which saw the rapid expansion of consumer goods production and the introduction of consumer credit to pay for these goods, the Great Depression took Americans by surprise. What had gone wrong?

Modern historians and economists now view the Depression as the consequence of underconsumption—that is, the overproduction of goods for sale and the lack of buyers with sufficient wages to purchase them. But to the unemployed workers, the dispossessed farmers, and their families, the Depression—whatever its cause—was the most disastrous event of their lives. By 1931, over eleven million workers, nearly a third of the labor force, were unemployed, and the average farm income had declined to 60 percent of 1929 levels. In this essay, Edward R. Ellis provides a wide panorama of life during the Depression, surveying its effects on the rich as well as the poor. He finds that the Great Depression scarred the lives of all people, regardless of social class, and shaped the outlook of everyone who lived through it.

The Depression smashed into the nation with such fury that men groped for superlatives to express its impact and meaning.

Edmund Wilson compared it to an earthquake. It was "like the explosion of a bomb dropped in the midst of society," according to the Social Science Research Council Committee on Studies in Social Aspects of the Depression.

Alfred E. Smith said the Depression was equivalent to war, while Supreme Court Justice Louis D. Brandeis and Bernard Baruch declared that it was worse than war. Philip La Follette, the governor of Wisconsin, said: "We are in the midst of the greatest domestic crisis since the Civil War." Governor Roosevelt agreed in these words: "Not since the dark days of the Sixties have the people of this state and nation faced problems as grave, situations as difficult, suffering as severe." A jobless textile worker told Louis Adamic: "I wish there would be war again." In a war against a foreign enemy all Americans might at least have felt united by a common purpose, and production would have boomed.

Poor and rich alike felt anxious and helpless.

Steel magnate Charles M. Schwab, despite his millions and the security of his Manhattan palace, freely confessed: "I'm afraid. Every man is afraid." J. David Stern, a wealthy newspaper publisher, became so terrified that he later wrote in his autobiography: "I sat in my back office, trying to figure out what to do. To be explicit, I sat in my private bathroom. My bowels were loose from fear." Calvin Coolidge dolorously told a friend: "I can see nothing to give ground for hope."

Herbert C. Pell, a rich man with a country estate near Governor Roosevelt's, said the country was doomed unless it could free itself from the rich, who have "shown no realization that what you call free enterprise means anything but greed." Marriner Eccles, a banker and economist who had *NOT* lost his fortune, wrote that "I awoke to find myself at the bottom of a pit without any known means of scaling its sheer sides." According to Dwight W. Morrow, a Morgan associate, diplomat and

Senator: "Most of my friends think the world is coming to an end—that is, the world as we know it." Reinhold Niebuhr, the learned and liberal clergyman, said that rich "men and women speculated in drawing-rooms on the best kind of poison as a means to oblivion from the horrors of revolution."

In Youngstown, Ohio, a friend of Mayor Joseph L. Heffernan stood beside the mayor's desk and said: "My wife is frantic. After working at the steel mill for twenty-five years I've lost my job and I'm too old to get other work. If you can't do something for me, I'm going to kill myself." Governor Gifford Pinchot of Pennsylvania got a letter from a jobless man who said: "I cannot stand it any longer." Gan Kolski, an unemployed Polish artist from Greenwich Village, leaped to his death from the George Washington Bridge, leaving this note: "To All: If you cannot hear the cry of starving millions, listen to the dead, brothers. Your economic system is dead."

An architect, Hugh Ferriss, stood on the parapet of a tall building in Manhattan and thought to himself that the nearby skyscrapers seemed like monuments to the rugged individualism of the past. Thomas Wolfe wrote: "I believe that we are lost here in America, but I believe we shall be found." Democratic Senator Thomas Gore of Oklahoma called the Depression an economic disease. Henry Ford, on the other hand, said the Depression was "a wholesome thing in general."

Obviously, the essence of a depression is widespread unemployment. In one of the most fatuous remarks on record, Calvin Coolidge said: "The final solution of unemployment is work." He might have added that water is wet. Senator Robert Wagner of New York called unemployment inexcusable.

A decade before the Crash the British statesman David Lloyd George had said: "Unemployment, with its injustice for the man who seeks and thirsts for employment, who begs for labour and cannot get it, and who is punished for failure he is not responsible for by the starvation of his children—that torture is something that private enterprise ought to remedy for its own sake." Winston Churchill now used the same key word, "torture," in a similar comment: "This problem of unemployment is the most torturing that can be presented to a civilized society."

Before Roosevelt became President and named Frances Perkins his secretary of labor, she was so pessimistic that she said publicly it might take a quarter century to solve the unemployment problem. A Pennsylvania commission studied 31,159 workless men and then reported that the typical unemployed man was thirty-six years old, native-born, physically fit and with a good previous work record. This finding contradicted Henry Ford's belief that the unemployed did not want to work.

However, the Pennsylvania study was *not* typical of the unemployed across the entire nation. Negroes and aliens were the last hired and the first fired. Young men and women were graduated from high schools and colleges into a world without jobs. Mississippi's demagogic governor and sometime Senator, Theodore G. Bilbo, vowed the unemployment problem could be solved by shipping 12,000,000 American blacks to Africa. The United Spanish War Veterans, for their part, urged the deportation of 10,000,000 aliens—or nearly 6,000,000 more than the actual number of aliens in the United States. Some noncitizens, unable to find work here, voluntarily returned to their homelands. With the deepening of the Depression, immigration dropped until something strange happened in the year 1932: More than three times as many persons left this country as entered it. No longer was America the Promised Land.

The Depression changed people's values and thus changed society.

The Chamber of Commerce syndrome of the Twenties became a mockery in the Thirties. Business leaders lost their prestige, for now it had become apparent to all Americans that these big shots did not know what they were talking about when they said again and again and again that everything would be all right if

it were just left to them. Worship of big business was succeeded by greater concern for human values. The optimism of the speculative decade was replaced by the pessimism of the hungry decade, by anguished interest in the problem of having enough food on the table.

People eager to make a big killing in the stock market had paid scant attention to politics, but now they wondered about their elected representatives and the kind of political system that could permit such a catastrophe to happen. Indifference gave way to political and social consciousness. Dorothy Parker, the sophisticate and wit, cried: "There is no longer I. There is WE. The day of the individual is dead." Quentin N. Burdick, who became a Senator from North Dakota, said long after the Depression: "I guess I acquired a social conscience during those bad days, and ever since I've had the desire to work toward bettering the living conditions of the people." Sylvia Porter, who developed into a financial columnist, said that while at Hunter College she switched from English to economics because of "an overwhelming curiosity to know why everything was crashing around me and why people were losing their jobs."

People lost their houses and apartments.

Franklin D. Roosevelt said: "One of the major disasters of the continued depression was the loss of hundreds of thousands of homes each year from foreclosure. The annual average loss of urban homes by foreclosure in the United States in normal times was 78,000. By 1932 this had increased to 273,000. By the middle of 1933, foreclosures had advanced to more than 1,000 a day."

In New York City, which had more apartments than private houses, there were almost 200,000 evictions in the year 1931. During the first three weeks of the following year there were more than 60,000 other evictions. One judge handled, or tried to handle, 425 eviction cases in a single day! On February 2, 1932, the *New York Times* described the eviction of three families in the Bronx:

Probably because of the cold, the crowd numbered only about 1,000, although in unruliness it equalled the throng of 4,000 that stormed the police in the first disorder of a similar nature on January 22. On Thursday a dozen more families are to be evicted unless they pay back rents.

Inspector Joseph Leonary deployed a force of fifty detectives and mounted and foot patrolmen through the street as Marshall Louis Novick led ten furniture movers in to the building. Their appearance was the signal for a great clamor. Women shrieked from the windows, the different sections of the crowd hissed and booed and shouted invectives. Fighting began simultaneously in the house and in the street. The marshal's men were rushed on the stairs and only got to work after the policemen had driven the tenants back into their apartments.

In that part of New York City known as Sunnyside, Queens, many homeowners were unable to meet mortgage payments and were soon ordered to vacate. Eviction notices were met with collective action, the residents barricading their doors with sandbags and barbed wire, flinging pepper and flour at sheriffs who tried to force their way inside. However, it was a losing battle; more than 60 percent of Sunnyside's householders lost their homes through foreclosure.

Harlem Negroes invented a new way to get enough money to pay their rent. This, as it came to be called, was the house-rent party. A family would announce that on Saturday night or Thursday night they would welcome anyone and everyone to their home for an evening of fun. Sometimes they would print and distribute cards such as this: "There'll be plenty of pig feet / And lots of gin; / Jus' ring the bell / An' come on in." Saturday night, of course, is the usual time for partying, while Thursday was chosen because this was the only free night for sleep-in black domestics who worked for white people. Admission to a house-rent party cost 15 cents, but more money could be spent inside. A festive mood was established by placing a red bulb in a light socket, by serving food consisting of chitterlings and pigs' feet and by setting out a jug of corn liquor. These parties

often went on until daybreak, and the next day the landlord got his rent. The innovation spread to black ghettos in other big cities across the land, and some white people began imitating the Negroes.

In Chicago a crowd of Negroes gathered in front of the door of a tenement house to prevent the landlord's agent from evicting a neighborhood family, and they continued to stand there hour after hour, singing hymns. A Chicago municipal employee named James D. O'Reilly saw his home auctioned off because he had failed to pay $34 in city taxes at the very time the city owed him $850 in unpaid salary.

A social worker described one pathetic event: "Mrs. Green left her five small children alone one morning while she went to have her grocery order filled. While she was away the constable arrived and padlocked her house with the children inside. When she came back she heard the six-weeks-old-baby crying. She did not dare to touch the padlock for fear of being arrested, but she found a window open and climbed in and nursed the baby and then climbed out and appealed to the police to let her children out."

In widespread areas of Philadelphia no rent was paid at all. In this City of Brotherly Love evictions were exceedingly common—as many as 1,300 a month. Children, who saw their parents' distress, made a game of evictions. In a day-care center they piled all the doll furniture in first one corner and then another. One tot explained to a teacher: "We ain't got no money for the rent, so we's moved into a new house. Then we got the constable on us, so we's moving again."

In millions of apartments, tension mounted and tempers flared toward the end of each month, when the rent was due. Robert Bendiner, in his book *Just Around the Corner*, wrote about conditions in New York City:

Evictions and frequent moves to take advantage of the apartment market were as common in middle-income Washington Heights as in the poor areas of town, and apartment hopping became rather a way of life. My own family moved six times in seven years. . . . Crises occurred monthly, and several times we were saved from eviction by pawning leftover valuables or by my mother's rich talent for cajoling landlords. On one more than routinely desperate occasion she resorted to the extreme device of having one of us enlarge a hole in the bathroom ceiling and then irately demanding repairs before another dollar of rent should be forthcoming.

In moving from one place to another, some families left their furniture behind because it had been bought on the installment plan and they were unable to meet further payments. Time-payment furniture firms owned warehouses that became crammed with tables and chairs and other items reclaimed from families without money. Whenever a marshal, sheriff or constable evicted a family from a house or apartment, the landlord would simply dump the furniture on the sidewalk. If the installment company failed to pick it up, each article would soon be carried away by needy neighbors.

What happened to people after they were dispossessed? Many doubled up with relatives—or even tripled up, until ten or twelve people were crammed into three or four rooms. Human beings are like porcupines: they like to huddle close enough to feel one another's warmth, but they dislike getting so close that the quills begin pricking. Now, in teeming proximity to one another, the quills pricked and relatives quarreled bitterly.

The Depression strained the family structure and sometimes shattered it. Well-integrated families closed ranks in the face of this common danger and became ever more monolithic. Loosely knit families, on the other hand, fell apart when the pressures on them became too great.

After a man lost his job, he would trudge from factory to factory, office to office, seeking other employment, but after weeks of repeated rejections he would lose heart, mutely denounce himself as a poor provider, shed his self-respect and stay at home. Here he found himself unwelcome and underfoot, the target of puzzled glances from his children and hostile looks from his wife. In the early part of the Depression some women simply could not understand that jobs were unavailable; instead, they felt there was something wrong with their men. In Philadelphia one unemployed man begged a social worker: "Have you anybody you can send around to tell my wife you have no job to give me? She thinks I don't want to work."

The idle man found himself a displaced person in the household, which is woman's domain, and in nameless guilt he crept about uneasily, always finding himself in the way. He got on his wife's nerves and she on his, until tension broke in endless wrangles. If the man tried to help by washing dishes and making beds, he lost status in the eyes of the rest of the family.

The Depression castrated some men by dethroning them from their position as the breadwinner and the head of the family. Ashamed, confused and resentful, they became sexually impotent. In Western culture a man tends to think of himself in terms of the work he does, this self-identity being what Jung calls his persona. Man does. Woman is. To rob a man of his work was to rob him of his idea of himself, leaving him empty and without much reason for living. The displacement of the man as the head of the family and the way some women moved in to fill this vacuum were described sensitively by John Steinbeck in his novel *The Grapes of Wrath*. This great book tells the story of the flight of the Joad family from the dust bowl of Oklahoma to the green valleys of California:

"We got nothin' now," Pa said. "Comin' a long time—no work, no crops. What we gonna do then? How we gonna git stuff to eat? . . . Git so I hate to think. Go diggin' back to a ol' time to keep from thinkin'. Seems like our life's over an' done."

"No, it ain't," Ma smiled. "It ain't, Pa. An' that's one more thing a woman knows. I noticed that. Man, he lives in jerks—baby born an' a man dies, an' that's a jerk—gets a farm an' loses his farm, an' that's a jerk. Woman, it's all one flow, like a stream, little eddies, little waterfalls, but the river, it goes right on. Woman looks at it like that. We ain't gonna die out. People is goin' on— changin' a little maybe, but goin' right on."

Some adolescent girls felt their fathers' agony and tried to comfort them with lavish expressions of love, much to the embarrassment of the man and the uneasiness of his wife. This did emotional damage to father, mother and the young girl, whose fixation on her father retarded her normal interest in boys her own age.

Strife between parents, together with the realization that it cost money to marry and have babies, resulted in a decision by many young people to postpone their weddings. One young man joined the Communist Party and swore he never would marry or have children under "the present system." Unable to repress their human needs, however, young men and women made love secretly and guiltily, regarding pregnancy as a disaster. Despite an increase in the sale of contraceptives, the abortion rate rose, and so did venereal disease. The birthrate dropped.

It has been estimated that the Depression postponed 800,000 marriages that would have occurred sooner if it had not been for hard times. Margaret Mead, the noted anthropologist, argued that there was nothing wrong about letting girls support their lovers so they could marry sooner. Surprisingly, there even was a decline in marriages among members of the *Social Register*. Liberals and feminists pointed out that half of all births were in families on relief or with incomes of less than $1,000 a year; they strongly advocated birth control. Who could afford babies when a sixty-one-piece layette cost all of $7.70? Gasps of horror arose when it was reported in Illinois that a sixteenth child had been born to a family on relief.

Housewives suffered as acutely as their husbands. Many had to send their kids to live with relatives or friends. Others took part-time jobs, while a few wives actually became temporary whores to earn enough money to keep the family going. Lacking money for streetcars and buses, without the means to buy clothes to keep them looking attractive, they remained cooped up in their homes until their nerves screamed and they had nervous breakdowns.

All too often their men simply deserted them. A California woman said: "My husband went north about three months ago to try his luck. The first month he wrote pretty regularly. . . . For five weeks we have had no word from him. . . . Don't know where he is or what he is up to."

A young man who lived in the French Quarter of New Orleans was solicited by five prostitutes during a ten-block stroll, each woman asking only 50 cents. In Houston a relief worker, curious about how the people were getting along, was approached by one girl after another. For the benefit of an insistent streetwalker, the man turned his pockets inside out to prove that he had no money. Looking at him ruefully, she said: "It doesn't cost much— only a dime!"

The close relationship between poverty and morals shocked Franklin D. Roosevelt, who told reporters about an investigator who went to southeastern Kentucky: "She got into one of those mining towns," Roosevelt said, "and started to walk up the alley. There was a group of miners sitting in front of the shacks, and they pulled down their caps over their faces. As soon as she caught sight of that she walked up and said, 'What are you pulling your caps down for?' They said, 'Oh, it is all right.' 'Why pull your caps down?' They said, 'It is sort of a custom because so many of the women have not got enough clothes to cover them.'"

The Depression made changes in the country's physical appearance.

Fewer pedestrians were to be seen on the streets since many men did not go to work and women shopped less frequently; for lack of warm clothing and fuel, many people stayed in bed most of the day during winter. The air became cleaner over industrial cities, for there was less smoke from factory chimneys. The downtown business districts of most cities had long rows of empty shops and offices. Trains were shorter, and only rarely did one see a Pullman car. However, gas stations multiplied because millions of Americans drove their battered family cars here and there in endless quest of work. In conflicting attempts to solve their problems, farmers moved into town while city folks moved into the country to build their own houses and grow their own food. More and more blacks were seen in northern cities as desperate Negroes fled from the hopeless South. Telephones were taken out of homes, and mail deliveries were lighter. Houses and stores, parks and fences sagged and lapsed into unpainted, flaked ugliness for want of money to make repairs.

In his novel called *You Can't Go Home Again*, Thomas Wolfe described a comfort station in front of New York City Hall:

> . . . One descended to this place down a steep flight of stairs from the street, and on bitter nights he would find the place crowded with homeless men who had sought refuge there. Some were those shambling hulks that one sees everywhere, in Paris as well as in New York. . . . But most of them were just flotsam of the general ruin of the time—honest, decent, middle-aged men with faces seamed by toil and want, and young men, many of them mere boys in their teens, with thick, unkempt hair. These were the wanderers from town to town, the riders of freight trains, the thumbers of rides on highways, the uprooted, unwanted male population of America. They drifted across the land and gathered in the big cities when winter came, hungry, defeated, empty, hopeless, restless, driven by they knew not what, always on the move, looking everywhere for work, for the bare crumbs to support their miserable lives, and finding neither work nor crumbs. Here in New York, to this obscene meeting place, these derelicts came, drawn into a common stew of rest and warmth and a little surcease from their desperation.

Heywood Broun devoted a column to a description of a slum in San Antonio, Texas:

> . . . The Church of Guadalupe stands upon the fringe of what had been described to me as the most fearsome slum in all America. It covers four square miles. At first I thought that the extreme description might have been dictated by local pride. It was my notion to protest and say, "Why, we in New York City know worse than that." But after we had gone up the third back alley I had to confess defeat gracefully.
>
> You can see shacks as bad as these in several States, but I do not know of any place where they have been so ingeniously huddled together. This is flat, sprawling country, and there is much of it, and so it seems devilish that one crazy combination of old lumber and stray tin should be set as a flap upon the side of another equally discreditable. I did not quite comprehend the character of the alley until I discovered that what I took to be a toolhouse was a residence for a family of eleven people.
>
> And these are not squatter dwellings. People pay rent for them, just as if a few rickety boards and a leaky roof constituted a house. They even have evictions and go through the solemn and obscene farce of removing a bed and a frying pan as indication that the landlord's two-dollars-and-a-half rent has not been forthcoming. . . .
>
> Back at the Church of Guadalupe, the priest said, "I have other letters from those who fight federal housing because they like their rents." He tossed over an anonymous message, which read, "I could start a story that there is a priest who writes love letters to young girls and gives jewels to women of his congregation."
>
> "Doesn't this worry you?" one of us asked.
>
> "No," said the priest. "Last month we buried thirty-nine persons, mostly children, from this little church alone.
>
> "I am worried," he said, "about people starving to death."

Louis Adamic and his wife were living with her mother in New York City in January, 1932. Born in Yugoslavia, now a naturalized American, he was a writer, a tall young man with a look of eager curiosity in his eyes. One cold morning at seven forty-five the doorbell rang, and Adamic, thinking it was the postman, opened the front door. In his book called *My America*, he told what happened next.

There stood a girl of ten and a boy of eight. They had schoolbooks in their arms, and their clothing was patched and clean, but hardly warm enough for winter weather. In a voice strangely old for her age, the girl said: "Excuse me, mister, but we have no eats in our house and my mother she said I should take my brother before we go to school and ring a door-bell in some house"—she swallowed heavily and took a deep breath—"and ask you to give us . . . something . . . to eat."

"Come in," Adamic said. A strange sensation swept over him. He had heard that kids were ringing doorbells and asking for food in the Bronx, in Harlem and in Brooklyn, but he had not really believed it.

His wife and her mother gave the children some food. The girl ate slowly. Her brother bolted his portion, quickly and greedily.

"He ate a banana yesterday afternoon," said his sister, "but it wasn't ripe enough or something, and it made him sick and he didn't eat anything since. He's always like this when he's hungry and we gotta ring doorbells."

"Do you often ring doorbells?"

"When we have no eats at home."

"What made you ring our bell?"

"I don't know," the girl answered. "I just did."

Her name was Mary, and her brother's name was Jimmie. They lived in a poor neighborhood five blocks away.

Mary said: "We used to live on the fourth floor upstairs and we had three rooms and a kitchen and bath, but now we have only one room downstairs. In back."

"Why did you move downstairs?"

The boy winced.

"My father," said the girl. "He lost his job when the panic came. That was two years ago. I was eight and Jimmie was six. My father he tried to get work, but he couldn't, the depression was so bad. But he called it the panic."

Adamic and the two women were astonished at her vocabulary: "panic" . . . "depression."

"What kind of work did your father do?"

"Painter and paperhanger. Before things got so bad, he always had jobs when his work was in season, and he was good to us—my mother says so, too. Then, after he couldn't get any more jobs, he got mean and he yelled at my mother. He couldn't sleep nights and he walked up and down and talked, and sometimes he hollered and we couldn't sleep, either."

"Was he a union man?"

"No, he didn't belong to no union."

"What did your father holler about?"

"He called my mother bad names."

At this point in the conversation, Adamic wrote, the little girl hesitated, and her brother winced again. Then she continued: "Uh . . . he was angry because my mother, before she married him, she was in love with another man and almost married him. But my mother says it wasn't my father's fault he acted mean like he did. He was mean because he had no job and we had no money."

"Where's your father now?"

"We don't know. He went away four months ago, right after Labor Day, and he never came back, so we had to move downstairs. The landlord didn't want to throw us out, so he told my mother to move in downstairs."

Between sips of milk the girl said her mother did household work whenever she could find a job, but earned very little money this way. A charity organization had been giving her $2.85 a week, but lately it had stopped. Mary did not know why. Her mother had applied for home relief, but had not yet received anything from that source.

The boy stopped eating, turned to his sister and muttered: "You talk too much! I told you not to talk!"

The girl fell silent.

Adamic said: "It's really our fault, Jimmie. We're asking too many questions."

The little boy glared and said: "Yeah!"

In Detroit someone gave another little girl a nickel, which seemed like such a fortune to her that she agonized three full days about how best to spend it.

In Erie, Pennsylvania, a seven-year-old boy named Tom received a tiny yellow chick as an Easter present. Using some old chicken wire, he built a coop for his pet beneath the back step to the house and fed and tended it carefully. His father was an unemployed molder, and the family often ate nothing but beans. Time passed. Now the little chick had grown into a full-sized chicken. One day Tom's father announced that the boy's pet would have to be killed and served for Sunday dinner, since everyone was hungry. Tom screamed in horrified protest but was unable to prevent his father from taking his chicken into the backyard and chopping off its head. Later that day the family sat around the table feasting on fowl, while the boy hunched in his chair, sobbing.

In 1933 the Children's Bureau reported that one out of every five children in the nation was not getting enough of the right things to eat. A teacher in a coal-mining town asked a little girl in her classroom whether she was ill. The child said: "No. I'm all right. I'm just hungry." The teacher urged her to go home and eat something. The girl said: "I can't. This is my sister's day to eat." In the House of Representatives, during a debate about appropriations for Indians living on reservations, a Congressman said that eleven cents a day was enough to feed an Indian child. A Senate subcommittee learned that the president of a textile firm had told his workers they should be able to live on six cents a day.

AFL President William Green said: "I warn the people who are exploiting the workers that they can only drive them so far before they will turn on them and destroy them. They are taking no account of the history of nations in which governments have been overturned. Revolutions grow out of the depths of hunger."

Sidney Hillman, president of the Amalgamated Clothing Workers of America, appeared at a Senate hearing in 1932 and was told that it was not yet time to give federal relief. Angrily, he cried: "I would ask by what standards are we to gauge that time! Must we have hundreds of thousands of people actually dead and dying from starvation? Must we have bread riots? What is necessary to convince them that there is a need for federal and speedy relief?"

The Communists took up the slogan: "Starve or fight!"

At the University of Pennsylvania a prim audience was shocked to hear Daniel Willard, president of the B & O Railroad, say: "While I do not like to say so, I would be less than candid if I did not say that in such circumstances I would steal before I would starve."

Obviously, less fortunate Americans agreed. Petty thievery soared. Children hung around grocery stores begging for food. Customers emerging from groceries had bundles snatched from their arms by hungry kids, who ran home with the food or ducked into alleys to gobble it as fast as they could. Small retail stores had their windows smashed and their display goods stolen. Grown men, in groups of two or three, walked into chain store markets, ordered all the food they could carry and then quietly walked out without paying for it. Chain store managers did not always report these incidents to the police for fear that publicity would encourage this sort of intimidation. For the same reason the newspapers engaged in a conspiracy of silence.

People of means thought up ways to protect themselves from panhandlers and from begging letters. Boston's mayor, James M. Curley, had a male secretary named Stan Wilcox, who was adept at brushing off approaches. Whenever a beggar asked if he had a quarter, Wilcox would reply: "Heavens, no! I wouldn't dream of taking a drink at this hour!" Alfred E. Smith received the following letter from Milwaukee: "This is unusual, but I am in need. Would you send me $2,500, as this is the amount I am in need of. I will give you as collateral my word of honor that I will repay you if possible. If not, let the good Lord repay you and he will also pay better interest."

Governor Gifford Pinchot of Pennsylvania flatly declared that starvation was widespread. Among the many pathetic letters he received was this one: "There are nine of us in the family. My father is out of work for a couple of months and we haven't got a thing eat [sic] in the house. Mother is getting $12 a month of the county. If mother don't get more help we will have to starve to death. I am a little girl 10 years old. I go to school every day. My other sister hain't got any shoes or clothes to wear to go to school. My mother goes in her bare feet and she crys every night that we don't have the help. I guess that is all, hoping to hear from you."

John Steinbeck has told how he survived the early part of the Depression before he became a famous author. "I had two assets," he wrote. "My father owned a tiny three-room cottage in Pacific Grove in California, and he let me live in it without rent. That was the first safety. Pacific Grove is on the ocean. That was the second. People in inland cities or in the closed and shuttered industrial cemeteries had greater problems than I. Given the sea, a man must be very stupid to starve. That great reservoir is always available. I took a large part of my protein food from the ocean.

"Firewood to keep warm floated on the beach daily, needing only handsaw and ax. A small garden of black soil came with the cottage. In northern California you can raise vegetables of some kind all year long. I never peeled a potato without planting the skins. Kale, lettuce, chard, turnips, carrots and onions rotated in the little garden. In the tide pools of the bay, mussels were available and crabs and abalones and that shiny kelp called sea lettuce. With a line and pole, blue cod, rock cod, perch, sea trout, sculpin could be caught."

The sale of flower seeds shot up as Americans, tired of the ugliness of their lives, turned to the beauty of homegrown flowers. As might have been expected, there was widespread cultivation of vegetable gardens. Many did this on their own, while others received official encouragement. Big railroads rented garden plots for their workers. The United States Steel Corporation used social workers and faculty members of Indiana University to develop an extensive garden project for its workers in Gary, Indiana. In New York State, in the summer of 1933, jobless men and women were tending 65,000 gardens. The city of Detroit provided tools and seed for "thrift gardens" on empty lots, an idea which Mayor Frank Murphy said he had borrowed from Hazen S. Pingree. During the Panic of 1893 Pingree had been the mayor of Detroit, and confronted with a city of jobless men, he provided them with gardens to cultivate— "Pingree's Potato Patches," receiving national attention.

Now, in the present emergency, Henry Ford ordered all his workmen to dig in vegetable gardens or be fired. Out of his imperious command there developed what the Scripps-Howard Washington *News* called 50,000 "shotgun gardens." Rough-grained Harry Bennett, chief of Ford's private police, supervised this vast project and kept a filing system on all Ford employees. If a man had no garden in his own backyard or on some neighborhood lot, he was assigned a patch of earth somewhere on Ford's 4,000 acres of farmland around Dearborn, Michigan. Each workman had to pay fifty cents to have his strip plowed.

More than one-third of the men employed in Ford's Dearborn plant lived 10 to 20 miles away, and some protested that since they did not own a car they would have to spend an extra two hours daily just traveling to and from their allotted patches. A Bennett henchman would snarl: "Why don't-cha buy a car? You're makin' 'em, ain't-cha?" Bone-weary workmen who simply couldn't muster the energy to toil on their garden plots soon were brought into line by Bennett's personal deputy, Norman Selby, the former boxer "Kid McCoy."

There was nothing surprising about the fact that men would risk injury or death by falling off a horse to earn an extra $3 a day. People felt that if they could just live through the Depression, they could *endure* anything else life had to offer. To *endure* was the main thing. Many took pay cuts without a murmur. A young man just out of college with a Bachelor of Journalism degree accepted a job on a newspaper at exactly *nothing* per week; a month later he was grateful to be put on the payroll at $15. Graduate engineers worked as office boys. College graduates of various kinds ran elevators in department stores. Unemployed architects turned out jigsaw puzzles. One jobless draftsman, Alfred Butts, used his spare time to invent the game of Scrabble.

Young men who might have grown into greatness chose, instead, to seek the security of civil service jobs, becoming policemen, firemen, garbage collectors. Fewer sailors deserted from the Navy. Enlistments rose in all branches of the nation's military establishment. When Congress voted a 10 percent pay cut for all federal employees, President Hoover secretly asked the Senate to make an exception for soldiers and sailors, because he did not wish to rely on disgruntled troops in case of internal trouble.

Women and children toiled for almost nothing in the sweatshops of New York City, welfare workers reporting these grim examples:

- A woman crocheted hats for 40 cents a dozen and was able to make only two dozen per week.
- An apron girl, paid $2\frac{1}{2}$ cents per apron, earned 20 cents a day.
- A slipper liner was paid 21 cents for every seventy-two pairs of slippers she lined, and if she turned out one slipper every forty-five seconds she could earn $1.05 in a nine-hour day.
- A girl got half a cent for each pair of pants she threaded and sponged, making $2.78 a week.

Connecticut's state commissioner of labor said that some sweatshops in that state paid girls between 60 cents and $1.10 for a fifty-five-hour week. In Pennsylvania men working in sawmills were paid 5 cents an hour, men in tile and brick manufacturing got 6 cents per hour, while construction workers earned $7\frac{1}{2}$ cents an hour. In Detroit the Briggs Manufacturing Company paid men 10 cents and women 4 cents an hour, causing auto workers to chant: "If poison doesn't work, try Briggs!" Also in Detroit, the Hudson Motor Car Company called back a small-parts assembler and then kept her waiting three days for a half hour of work, forcing her to spend 60 cents in carfare to earn 28 cents.

Two Marine fishermen put out to sea at four o'clock one morning and did not return to port until five o'clock that afternoon. During this long day of toil they caught 200 pounds of hake and 80 pounds of haddock. They burned up eight gallons of gas at 19 cents a gallon and used 100 pounds of bait costing two cents a pound. For their catch they were paid one cent a pound for the hake and four cents a pound for the haddock. Thus they earned less than two cents an hour for their day's work.

Meantime, Henry Ford was declaring: "Many families were not so badly off as they thought; they needed guidance in the management of their resources and opportunities." Ford needed no guidance. He managed to transfer $41\frac{1}{2}$ percent of stock in the Ford Motor Company to his son, Edsel, without paying a cent in inheritance or estate taxes.

Ford, who liked to boast that he always had to work, declared in 1930 that "the very poor are recruited almost solely from the people who refuse to think and therefore refuse to work diligently." Roger W. Babson, the statistician, pontificated two years later: "Better business will come when the unemployed change their attitude toward life." Most rich men were quick to moralize.

The concept of hard work was central to capitalism and the Protestant ethic. Americans had been raised on a diet of aphorisms praising work and self-reliance. Benjamin Franklin said: "God helps them that help themselves." The Bible insisted: "In the sweat of thy face shalt thou eat bread." Thomas Carlyle said: "All work, even cotton-spinning, is noble; work alone is noble." Elizabeth Barrett Browning wrote: "Whoever fears God, fears to sit at ease." It was either Bishop Richard Cumberland or George Whitefield (no one is sure) who first said: "Better to wear out than to rust out." Most Americans agreed, but now in these Depression times men did sit at home and rust, through no fault of their own, losing the fine edge of their skills.

Idle, dispirited, hungry, defeated, withdrawn, brooding—people began to feel that somehow they were to blame for everything, that somehow, somewhere, they had failed. Maybe the Depression was punishment for their sins. After all, Protestant Episcopal Bishop John P. Tyler attributed it to the lack of religion. Perhaps Christians, if they wished to be good Christians, should bow to fate by accepting Christ's words that "to everyone that hath shall be given; and from him that hath not, even that which he hath shall be taken from him." But some found it difficult to find comfort in a sermon preached by the Reverend William S. Blackshear, an Episcopalian clergyman, in the bleak year of 1932. Blackshear said in part: "Christ was happy to be at the banquets of the rich. It was at such a place that the woman broke the vial of costly ointment and anointed His feet. There were those who cried out for the improvident and rebuked the woman, saying that this should have been converted into cash and given to the poor. It was then that Christ spoke on the economic plan, 'The poor ye have always with you.'"

This kind of sermon, representing conservative Protestantism, offended liberal clergymen. Forced by the Depression to rethink their values, they began searching for a new theology. Some began with the premise that if the church were to serve any purpose or perform realistically, it had to divorce itself from economic and political values. This developing viewpoint was expressed with crystal clarity by H. Richard Niebuhr, a pastor and a brother of Reinhold Niebuhr. He wrote:

The church is in bondage to capitalism. Capitalism in its contemporary form is more than a system of ownership and distribution of economic goods. It is a faith and a way of life. It is faith in wealth as a source of all life's blessings and as the savior of man from his deepest misery. It is the doctrine that man's most important activity is the production of economic goods and that all other things are dependent upon this. On the basis of this initial idolatry it develops a morality in which economic worth becomes the standard by which to measure all other values and the economic virtues take precedence over courage, temperance, wisdom and justice, over charity, humility and fidelity. Hence nature, love, life, truth, beauty and justice are exploited or made the servants of the high economic good. Everything, including the lives of workers, is made a utility, is desecrated and ultimately destroyed. . . .

Other dissenters noted the supremacy of capitalism over every other value in the fact that church property was exempt from taxation. State constitutions and special statutes declared that no real estate taxes could be levied on church-owned properties, such as the church building itself, parochial schools, parsonages, the parish house and cemeteries. Why? A Missouri Supreme Court decision said that "no argument is necessary to show that church purposes are public purposes."

But was this really true? The United States of America was a Christian nation nominally, but not legally. No single religion, sect or church was recognized as the established church. Although the phrase "separation of church and state" does not appear in the Constitution of the United States or in that of any state but Utah, the idea for which it stands is found in the constitutional provisions against religious tests and in the words of the First Amendment: "Congress shall make no law respecting an establishment of religion. . . ."

During the Depression some liberal Christians, agnostics, atheists and others fretted about the special status given churches and church property. A few scholars recalled that President Ulysses S. Grant had said: "I would suggest the taxation of all property equally, whether church or corporation, exempting only the last resting place of the dead, and possibly, with proper restrictions, church edifices." Dissenters objected on principle to the exemption of church property, regarded this as an indirect subsidy by the state to religion and pointed out that personal taxes might be less if churches bore their share of the tax burden.

They got nowhere. At the core of capitalism was the belief that God looked with favor on the rich. This idea had been expressed as long ago as 1732 by one of J. P. Morgan's ancestors, the Reverend Joseph Morgan, who sermonized: "Each man coveting to make himself rich, carries on the Publick Good: Thus God in His Wisdom and Mercy turns our wickedness to Publick Benefit. . . . A rich Man is a great friend of the Publick, while he aims at nothing but serving himself. God will have us live by helping one another; and since Love will not do it, Covetousness shall."

J. P. Morgan himself flatly told a Senate committee: "If you destroy the leisure class you destroy civilization." When reporters pressed for a definition of the leisure class, Morgan said it included all who could afford a maid. In 1931, according to *Fortune* magazine, there still were 1,000,000 families with servants. One wealthy family announced that it had solved its Depression problem by discharging fifteen of its twenty servants—although the family members showed no curiosity or concern about the fate of the unemployed fifteen.

John Jacob Astor came of age in 1933 and thereupon inherited about $4 million. Nonetheless, he dabbled at a job in a downtown Manhattan brokerage house. Before long he quit with the explanation: "I didn't finish until five o'clock and by the time I got uptown it was six. And then I had to get up early the next morning." At a later date Astor was employed briefly by a shipping firm, and when he quit this second job, he commented: "I have discovered that work interferes with leisure."

He was a representative of that leisure class which Morgan felt must be maintained to save civilization.

When Dwight Morrow was running for governor of New Jersey, he said: "There is something about too much prosperity that ruins the fiber of the people. The men and women that built this country, that founded it, were people that were reared in adversity." Morrow made this statement and died before Adolf Hitler declared: "It was poverty that made me strong." Joseph P. Kennedy, a busy member of the leisure class, felt that the rich had to make some sacrifices. Writing about the Depression, Kennedy said: "I am not ashamed to record that in those days I felt and said I would be willing to part with half of what I had if I could be sure of keeping, under law and order, the other half."

One member of the enormously wealthy Du Pont family seems to have been out of touch with reality. An advertising agency wanted his company to sponsor a Sunday afternoon radio program, but this Du Pont rejected the idea, saying: "At three o'clock on Sunday afternoons everybody is playing polo."

Everybody except the millions of Americans gobbling the last morsel of food from their plates in the fear that it might be their last meal—a habit that persisted in some people down through the next three decades. As Sinclair Lewis commented in his novel *It Can't Happen Here*, people were so confused, insecure and frustrated that they hardly could do anything more permanent than shaving or eating breakfast. They were tortured with feelings of inadequacy and guilt.

A young Alabama schoolteacher with eight years of tenure was fired after the Wall Street Crash. Eager to work, willing to take any job however low in the social scale, she became a maid in a private home. However, upon learning that she would be expected to work seven days a week, getting room and board but no wages, she quit. Then she took a job in a convalescent home which paid her room and board and $3 a week, but soon the home closed for lack of funds. The gentle school-teacher completely lost faith in herself, confessing to a caseworker: "If, with all the advantages I've had, I can't make a living, then I'm just no good, I guess!"

Forty experienced secretaries found work after being unemployed a year, but the first few days on the job they were unable to take dictation from their bosses without weeping from sheer nervousness. After seeking employment for a long time, a man finally landed a job and became so overwrought with joy that he died of excitement. A corporation executive was given the nasty chore of firing several hundred men. A kind and compassionate person, he insisted on talking to each of them personally and asking what plans each had for the future. In a few months the executive's hair had turned gray.

The Depression began to erode freedom.

Some Americans, a little more secure than others, asked harsh questions. How about fingerprinting everyone on relief? Was it proper for a man on relief to own a car—even if he needed it to try to find work? Wasn't it wrong to sell liquor to the head of a family on relief? Did anyone owning a life insurance policy deserve relief? Should reliefers be allowed to vote? Did they deserve citizenship?

In New Orleans a federal judge denied citizenship to four qualified persons because they were on relief and therefore, in the judge's words, "unable financially to contribute to the support of the government." In California another judge withheld citizenship from Jacob Hullen; in response to the judge's questions Hullen had said he believed in municipal or federal ownership of public utilities.

In New York City, one cold and rainy day, the police arrested 38 men who had taken shelter in the Pennsylvania Railroad's ferry terminal on Cortlandt Street. All were marched to the nearest police station. Fifteen of them, able to prove that they had a few nickels and dimes in their pockets, were released. The other 23 men, who did not have a cent on them, were led before a magistrate, who sentenced them to jail for vagrancy. Newspaper stories about this obvious injustice raised such a hullabaloo, however, that the 23 prisoners soon were freed.

Robert Morss Lovett, a professor of English literature at the University of Chicago, wrote in his autobiography:

> An example of the injustice meted out to foreign-born workers involved a Yugoslav named Perkovitch. When conditions were at their worst in 1932–33 the unemployed on the West Side [of Chicago] were in the habit of crossing the city to the South Side where food was sometimes available from bakeries, disposing of yesterday's bake, and where, at least, the garbage was more lavish.
>
> One morning these itinerants were picked up by the police and held at the station house on the absurd pretext that a revolution was planned. Perkovitch told me that he and about one hundred others were kept in the basement all day without food. Once a lieutenant with a bodyguard of patrolmen raged through the room, striking and kicking the men in an ecstasy of sadism. At six the prisoners were released with no charges.

Paul D. Peacher, the town marshal of Jonesboro, Arkansas, arrested a group of Negro men without cause and forced them to work on his farm. A federal grand jury indicted him under Title 18 of the Anti-Slavery Act of 1866 for "causing Negroes to be held as slaves" on a cotton plantation. This was the first case ever tried under the slavery statute. A county grand jury absolved Peacher, but the federal Department of Justice would not drop the case. Now the marshal was forced to stand trial—this time before a *federal* jury. Taking the witness chair in his own behalf, he denied that he had done anything wrong. However, the jury disagreed with him and found him guilty. Peacher was sentenced to two years in prison and fined $3,500. He appealed, lost his appeal, paid the fine and accepted a two-year probationary sentence.

Someone asked Eugene Talmadge, the governor of Georgia, what he would do about the millions of unemployed Americans. Talmadge snarled: "Let'em starve!" It made him happy when the city fathers of Atlanta put unwanted nonresidents in chain gangs. When some textile workers went on strike in Georgia the governor had barbed-wire concentration camps built and threw pickets into them. Frank Hague, the mayor and ruthless boss of Jersey City, called for the erection in Alaska of a concentration camp for native "Reds."

Wise and temperate men worried about the growing loss of liberty in America, the land of the free and the home of the brave. George Boas, a professor of philosophy, sadly said: "It is taken for granted that democracy is bad and that it is dying." Will Durant, busy writing his many-volumed *Story of Civilization*, asked rhetorically: "Why is it that Democracy has fallen so rapidly from the high prestige which it had at the Armistice?"

GLOSSARY

Social Register: A directory listing persons of social prominence in a community.

Pullman Car: A railroad sleeping car.

Children's Bureau: An agency of the Labor Department that dealt with issues involving children, especially early nurture, poverty, and child labor.

American Federation of Labor: The nation's central trade union organization from the 1890s to the present.

John Steinbeck (1902–1968): Writer whose works are marked by a compassionate understanding of the world's disinherited. His best-known novel, *The Grapes of Wrath*, treats the plight of 1930s Dust Bowl farmers turned migrant laborers.

Reinhold Niebuhr (1892–1971): Theologian who wrote primarily about morality and Christianity's refusal to confront social problems.

IMPLICATIONS

The Depression disrupted the personal and public fabric of American life in a variety of ways. What do you see as the most important changes that the Depression brought to American life? What creative adaptations did Americans make to the new circumstances of their lives?

Past Traces

While most people think of the 1930s as a painful time of economic depression, unemployment, and widespread poverty, the decade also witnessed the rise of new modes of popular entertainment. Radio flourished in this era, as did the new motion picture and recording industries. Reaching huge national audiences, these media had a profound impact on popular culture. One of the most far-reaching of these influences was the rise of "Big Band" music and dances, such as the Jitterbug, that accompanied them. Building on American Jazz music of the 1920s, swing became an enormously popular form of entertainment during the middle and late 1930s, especially among men and women in their teens and twenties. Like many new cultural phenomena, however, swing was often misunderstood by parents and community leaders, who saw in the youthful exuberance of the new music and dance forms a potential for national moral degeneration. In this essay, Benny Goodman, one of the inventors of swing, sets out to explain this musical form to a broad American audience. Rather than degenerate, he commends his youthful audiences for understanding the sophistication of swing.

Benny Goodman Explains Swing (1939)

The emergence of swing as a national enthusiasm at the particular time it occurred may be attributed to any one of several factors—the persistence of a small group of enthusiasts; the concentration of enough fine jazz musicians in a single white band to direct attention to it that no colored band, however good, could hope to attract; astute promotion; the repeal of prohibition, which opened more opportunities for dance bands (in hotels and night clubs) than had existed in years.

But the resurgence of this music at some time (whether in 1934, 1935 or 1936) was inevitable as a reaction from the prettified jazz which had become the white man's fashion in the twenties. The innovations of Art Hickman and Paul Whiteman—the use of arrangements and the employment, as jazz musicians, of men who could read, whose abilities were trained and cultivated—necessarily were revolutionary in a field previously occupied by players whose principal resource was instinct.

As the distinction between the two kinds of jazz playing became more pronounced—the aspiration on the one hand, of some bands to a style that refined away the crudities of early jazz, and the concentration, by others, on combining improvisation and arrangement in a single structure—it became apparent that there was an element in the playing of the best Negro bands (such as Fletcher Henderson's, Louis Armstrong's and Duke Ellington's) that could not be identified as an expression of anything in the written parts they were using. It was a style of performance, an interrelation of rhythms, *a product of a mere enthusiasm for the act of playing, a freshness and spontaneity that could not be indicated by accents, note-values or other written symbols.*

It is this quality, originally peculiar to the performance of Negro bands playing freely, without arrangements of any sort (and still to be encountered in its most pronounced form in such playing), that was characteristically described as swing.

For almost a decade the excitement in this kind of playing was realized only by a small group of musicians (either of Chicago or New Orleans origin), by a few enthusiasts, and, of course, by the Negroes themselves. It was only when an attempt was made to transfer this atmosphere and enthusiasm to a large white band that a large public became aware of the particular stimulation and interest that authentic jazz, in its straightforward, undiluted form possesses.

It is thus apparent that swing has this elementary distinction from ordinary ballroom jazz—it can be listened to as well as heard. That is to say, there is some element of fresh and changing interest *which challenges the attention* of the listener, whereas the unchanging formulae of ordinary stereotyped jazz are designed merely as a *soporific to his senses.* If this merely applied to the rhythmic pattern, it would be a factor of unceasing interest. But the combination of this with the improvisational element, multiplies its possibilities by as many good soloists as a band possesses, and extends its interests indefinitely.

This element of individual expression, in combination with the all-important stimulation of a rhythmic, impelling background, has given this type of performance an interest and variety not contained in any previous manifestation of the jazz spirit. "Fats" Waller's "Honeysuckle Rose," in its actual notated form, is a pleasant enough tune. But "Fats" himself would never play it on two successive nights in the same way. And "Fats" Waller's "Honeysuckle Rose" embellished by a Goodman, a Teagarden, a Bud Freeman, a Johnny Hodges, a Count Basie or Louis Armstrong becomes something else again—an expression of Goodman, Teagarden, Freeman or Armstrong even more than of Waller.

All this implies the possession by these and a hundred other jazz personalities of some definite element of style—which is as true as the fact that there can be no swing save in four-four metre. Moreover, the style consists not only of what is said, but of how it is said. A Teagarden phrase played on Goodman's clarinet would no longer have the connotations it originally did, no more than an Armstrong figure played on the alto saxophone would. It would assume a new coloration when played on an instrument other than the original one, with different inflections, accents, intonation and phrasing.

The citation of such terms (usually considered suitable only for the playing of a Szigeti or the singing of a Marian Anderson) suggests that some subtle system of evaluation has grown up in relation to such playing unknown in jazz of the earlier type. But how, one can hear the outraged voices asking, can there be such appraisal of performers who play with raw and raucous tone quality, with an abandoned use of glissando, of half-sharp, half-flat equivocations of perfect pitch such as no respectable musician would tolerate?

The error lies in the assumption that such departures from a round and exactly centered tone (to consider merely one aspect of the matter) are involuntary, a result of an *inability* to produce a more conventional quality of tone. Nothing could be more remote from the facts. There is no member of a prominent swing band who could not if he were asked, or felt the inclination, "play pretty." What musicians accustomed to traditional roundness and conventional purity of tone consider raucous and strident is precisely the element in the playing of a Harry James, a Louis Armstrong, a Lester Young, a Peewee Russell, which the player, other jazz musicians and the initiate value as the symbol of his individual style, the measure of the intensity he imparts to his playing on any particular occasion.

Thus there are any one of a hundred outstanding jazz musicians who may be recognized by an experienced listener merely through the particular type of vibrato they use, in combination with a characteristic rise and fall of line, a typical distribution of rhythmic accents. Combine this with the fertility in melodic invention, in endless capacity for variation on a few simple chords, in the subtlety of emphasis that many of them possess (such a saxophonist as Lester Young or a trumpet player such as Louis Armstrong can build thirty or forty choruses on a standard tune without repeating himself, with the sequence rising to an inevitable climax) and you have the elements of a musical system as

complex, and in its own terms, as valid as anything the concert hall can offer.

When a half dozen such players working freely and under favorable circumstances (meaning that there is no exhibitionism either among the players or the listeners) are gathered into a jam session, or when enough such men are present in a band to color its personality, the music that results is unlike anything otherwise expressed in tone. It has a variety and a homogeneity, a diffusion and concentration that is both moving and exhilirating.

For the best jazz players are possessed of musical impulses unequalled, for originality and emotional fervor, elsewhere in American music. Who is to say what accomplishments a Beiderbecke, an Armstrong or a Teagarden might not have achieved had his talent been directed along more conventional lines? Their backgrounds in Iowa, Louisiana and Texas inclined them to the most convenient outlets that came to hand— bringing them eventually to a jazz band rather than a Philharmonic, to Fifty-second Street (in New York) rather than Fifty-seventh Street.

The common belief that only music that is fast and loud may be said to possess swing is a misconception that may eventually be banished, though the prospects do not look too bright. Probably this is a consequence of the fact that the public has been led to confuse sensationalism with primitive abandon. But such a record as Louis Armstrong's "I Can't Give You Anything But Love" (the early OKEH version) has tremendous swing, though it is neither fast nor loud; there are numerous records by the Goodman trio which exemplify the same fact; and Mildred

Bailey, who is neither loud-voiced nor raucous, and who frequently sings in a leisurely tempo, is unquestionably one of the foremost swing singers of the day. In addition, there is a vast literature of authentic blues (the actual source of this whole style of performance) which only conveys its true effect when played or sung in a moderate tempo.

Despite the presence in swing playing of these numerous and ponderable qualities, it is apparent that there has been no time in the history of popular music when any one type of performance has been as popular with the youth of the country as this music is today. Moreover, it is for the most part an extremely aware and critical public, eager with its enthusiasms, uncompromising in its demands and expectations. It has a background of taste that would astound those unacquainted with its predilections, a discrimination that is sometimes amazing.

Mixed with this, of course, is a considerable amount of mere exhibitionism, which has won the epithet of "jitterbug" as descriptive of the purely physical response that accompanies the worst phases of sensationalism by certain players. But this is no more an indictment of swing than children who hitch rides on the back of street-cars are an indictment of rapid transit. It is a normal property of adolescence, a letting-off of steam, the expression of a desire for calling attention to itself. That they lack manners in interfering with the enjoyment of others is unquestionable—but that is a penalty that the more sensitive souls must pay for the enjoyment this music provides them.

It is a certainty however that the youngsters who share this enthusiasm with several million other Americans comprise a generation more sensitive to musical values—if only of this order—than any that have gone before them. In contrast to their elders, who valued dance music only as an undertone to conversation, the youngsters of today have a respect for the men who play it, an appreciation of their status as individuals, and, in many cases, a critical valuation of their performance on any given occasion.

12

The Crowd Goes Wild: The Youth Culture of Swing

Lewis A. Erenberg

Between the late 1920s and the early 1940s, young Americans created a cultural revolution. Drawing on African American music and bands that were little known outside black communities, white teenagers and young adults listened and then danced to a new fusion of jazz and syncopated rhythms that came to be called swing. Swing built on the public dance crazes of the 1920s—the Lindy and Charleston—and created a place where young men and women could create their own worlds, independent of their families and the constraints of contemporary social norms. Cutting across ethnic lines, swing also allowed young people to forget the immigrant roots from which most had come.

In this essay, Lewis A. Erenberg explores the contours of this mid-twentieth-century youth culture. Searching beneath the outward energy and flamboyant style of the swing era, he finds that young listeners actively participated in the creation of a distinctive style, a style formed in contrast to the homogeneous nature of the emerging national radio and motion picture markets. Swing, Erenberg shows, was at once a democratic and a utopian phenomenon that rejected conformity and focused instead on personal liberation. In this, and many other respects, swing set the stage for the development of popular music and dance that would bear full fruit in the post-World War II phenomenon of Rock and Roll. At the same time, swing created an attitude of personal liberation that led directly to the youth culture of the 1960s.

"The Politics of Sacrifice on the American Home Front in World War II." *Journal of American History*, 77 (1991), pp. 1296–1318. Copyright © 1991 by the Organization of American Historians. Reprinted by permission of the *Journal of American History*.

The melting pot boils over, and now we have the hoarse and jitterbuggy days. No longer prim, we've all gone primitive.
—Chicago Daily Tribune, 26 August 1938

Swing is the voice of youth striving to be heard in this fast-moving world of ours. Swing is the tempo of our time. Swing is real. Swing is alive.
—New York Times, 26 February 1939

Intent on giving the city's young people a rare opportunity to hear their music live, the New Century Committee of Chicago staged a free Swing Jamboree at Soldier Field on the evening of 24 August 1938. Drawing a racially mixed audience, the concert presented twenty white and black big-name orchestras, amateur band and dance contests; and "free public truckin'" on three dance stages. Before the gates closed, 100,000 fans streamed into the cavernous football stadium; outside almost as many gathered. Then, "with a deafening groan, the gates caved in, and the boys and girls poured in." The result "was a barrelhouse, boogie-woogie, bacchanal worthy of 18-year-old ecstasy, as it seemed the whole younger generation of the city—a generation born since the World War and scarred by the depression—let down its hair, lost its hat and danced wherever there was room to dance to the hot lick rhythms of gutbucket gorillas."

Despite the crush, the Jamboree proved "the most hysterical orgy of joyous emotions by multitudes ever witnessed on the American continent." As Jimmy Dorsey's band went into "Flat Foot Floogie," one of the major anthems of the swing era, "men climbed over each other, girls perched on their partners' shoulders, babies were held aloft, the younger generation scrambled up on the stands, car tops and construction work at the north end . . . and swing really broke loose." Surging through police lines, the crowd overran the three dance platforms, "drove the white-coated dance bands to cover," and knocked out the microphones. When Jamboree officials finally managed to restore order, no time remained for the amateur contests. Before the professional bands resumed, however, young black men and women, stimulated by the Earl "Fatha" Hines Band, snake-danced through the crowd while other impatient fans played their own instruments, beat time on their bodies, and went wild over two seventeen-year-old amateur dancers who trucked, shagged, and pecked to "the off beat and wild rhythm of swing. The crowd loved 'em."

Shocked reactions greeted this outpouring of "jitterbug ecstasy." Struck by such an unfettered emotional display, observers pondered the unprecedented crowd behavior. The *Daily News,* noting "the world's largest crowd . . . for a musical event," called the concert "the strangest manifestation of youthful exuberance perhaps ever witnessed since the Middle Ages' ill-fated Children's Crusade." Some psychologists warned of "mass hysteria" linked to "unrest, insecurity, repression . . . and . . . sex," but others dismissed the behavior as merely "simple, uncomplicated childishness." Instead of coupling, young people "came out in the circle . . . and danced in a mass."

Whatever their views, all agreed with *Metronome* that "this is a perfect example of the powerful hold that swing has on its followers." For observer after observer who followed in the wake of Benny Goodman's surprising breakthrough in 1935, jazz had reached a mass audience by becoming the favorite music of American youth. Most historians, however, have tended to treat the swing audience as passive receivers of musical products rather than as active participants in creating a music vital to their own lives. In fact, black and white jitterbugs, like those at the Swing Jamboree, crashed the gates to express themselves through music despite parental objections and the restrictions on youthful lives and dreams created by the depression. More than ever before, the difficulties of earning a living and gaining independence through social mobility or marriage reduced the differences among young people. Increasingly part of the crowd, young people helped transform the whole concept of mass culture. When new voices of youth appeared in the 1930s, they forced dramatic changes in musical performance, democratized the consumption of music, and helped create what jazz critic Ralph Gleason calls a "whole way of life" around swing.

VOICES OF YOUTH

Audience behavior sparked widespread debate over the nature of the most intense swing fan, the "jitterbug," and the dangers of mass musical culture. Worried about the nation's youth, critics attacked swing as a contagion spread by insidious rhythms that undermined self-control. One scientist maintained that the music caused sexual boldness, while classical violinist Fritz Kreisler claimed that jazz was "the expression of primeval instincts." Fears that black rhythms led to sexual barbarism underlay these concerns. James Moynahan traced swing's roots to "the rhythmic jungle chants of the descendants of Africans" and their "jungle discords." In the most extreme attack, Francis J. L. Beckman, the Catholic archbishop of Dubuque, denounced swing as "evil" and "communistic": "We permit jam sessions, jitterbug and cannibalistic rhythmic orgies," he declared, "to occupy a place in our social scheme of things, wooing our youth along the primrose path to hell."

Even more prominent was the fear of a crowd psychology bordering on mass hysteria. Large public events, critics worried, would lead to youth riots and violence. Observers of the Swing Jamboree, for example, feared that the crowd's emotional intensity and interracial composition might have led to "real trouble." Some outbursts did occur, such as that at a Jimmie Lunceford concert at Los Angeles's Shrine Auditorium in March 1940, where white, black, Mexican, and Filipino jitterbugs rioted. The rise of fascism led to anxiety that jitterbugs represented the decline of rationality and the rise of a mass psychology that could produce what a Barnard College social scientist called "Musical Hitlerism."

While many critics viewed the jitterbug as symbolic of mass culture's flaws, others defended swing as a positive expression of modern youth. Indeed, the negative reactions seem tame compared to those heard in the 1920s, when jazz was attacked in the name of defending white Protestant small-town values or the hierarchy of genteel American culture. In the 1930s, attacks rarely rose above the level of personal morality to that of national xenophobia. It became increasingly apparent that the country had indeed survived the jazz age. Even William Allan White, who considered swing "merely syncopated raw emotion," acknowledged that each generation created "its own rowdy modern music." Many parents shared this attitude. Some were hostile to what they considered "wild and strange" music and behavior, but this was tempered by the recollection of their own youthful musical foibles. Cultural relativism thus undercut the fears of critics and parents and permitted a modern youth culture to flower.

Meanwhile, cultural commentators defended swing as a positive expression of modern youth. Irving Kolodin, for example, pointed out that "youngsters who have reached adolescence during its vogue recognize it as something of their own, an exciting and stimulating sound to which they react spontaneously." Similarly, a self-described jitterbug argued that one could not expect "a modern girl who drives a car, knows about planes and fast ships to monkey around with minuets. . . . Those dances go with horses and buggies." Music critic Cecelia Ager said that swing expressed "the immortal right of adolescence to assert itself" after the "darkest despair" of the depression. As a letter to the *New York Times* declared, "Swing is the voice of youth striving to be heard in this fast-moving world of ours."

Defenders of swing further argued that it represented a democratic form of artistic expression. While deploring jitterbug excesses, Kolodin declared that swing contained "elements of a new art, the symbols of a significant musical renaissance." Gama Gilbert found it "the most widespread artistic medium of popular emotional expression." Another advocate noted that popular music "is the music of the cities" and "has a definite place in our musical expression." Agreeing, violinist Mischa Elman saw jitterbug dancing as "merely the social outlet for our city just as folk-dancing goes on in the country." Many music critics, writing in new jazz magazines, praised swing as a national art form created by blacks and adopted by a pluralistic society; jitterbugs, they said, only detracted from a true appreciation of the music's artistic potential. Avid defenses of swing and fervent attacks on fan behavior often issued from the same pens.

Together, attackers and defenders viewed swing as the center of a national youth culture that transcended class, ethnicity, and race. Bandleader Larry Clinton called it "the most popular diversion in colleges," the "favorite sport of youngsters." In 1934 small groups of collegians kept jazz's flame alive by collecting records and forming "Hot Clubs" to sponsor jazz events, lobby for jazz recordings, and serve as listening groups. Many Ivy League newspapers, like Columbia University's *Spectator,* started swing record columns, which served as outlets for informed student opinion on popular music. Close to New York and Harlem and an early stop on the swing band circuit, New England colleges and cities strongly supported swing tours.

Mass interest and a growing music industry quickly extended this musical youth culture beyond elite colleges. As bandleader Joe Reichman noted in 1942, everyone danced to the same numbers. With regional variations, "kids in Tennessee shag to the same music as the 'sharpies' in the Bronx." From the start, urban campuses and dancers asked for more jump tunes, while the more culturally conservative Midwest preferred ballads and novelties. Surveys in *Variety* and *Billboard* found that Midwestern colleges lagged in swing interest, and then, as the editor of the University of

Missouri's paper argued, "'It's gotta be smooth.'" The racially conservative South especially lagged behind other regions in appreciation for swing, but even there young people danced to black and white swing bands at proms and hops. Once Glenn Miller, the most popular dance band leader after 1939, moderated dance tempos, small-town youth across the nation also caught the bug. The eastern seaboard, the West Coast, and big midwestern cities, with numerous colleges and many blacks, Jews, and Italians, continued to lead the way.

But it was high school students who composed the largest following for swing bands. Middle-class light schools had been important centers of youth culture in the 1920s, but in the 1930s lack of jobs forced even more working-class teens to stay in school. (From 1930 to 1940, high school enrollment rose from half to three-quarters of all fourteen- to eighteen-year-olds.) Often the attraction began in junior high, just as youth began to assert autonomy. Jack McNulty, the son of Irish working-class parents in Lawrence, Massachusetts, entered swing's subculture in 1937 at junior high hops. "Every aspect of my life and that of my friends, revolved around big bands, jazz, dancing, jitterbugging, in my formative teens." At that age "our heroes, our dress, look, styles, morals, sex lives" were based on immersion in bands and "the lives they showed us." The same year, fourteen-year-old Orin Stambaugh of York, Pennsylvania, was hooked by Harry James. "The freewheeling playing, the ad lib solos, the driving rhythms, all struck a very responsive chord. Although we did not articulate it then, we had found the music of our time."

The utopian possibilities of swing attracted young people aspiring to establish their independence from their families and to affirm a more vigorous personal experience that cut across ethnic, class, and, at times, racial lines. More than ever before, popular music meant a new life for an expanding youth audience. Fans included prep school student Sidney Curran, whose father "detested [swing] so much so that

I never played any in his hearing"; it was "an unconscious form of generation gap." In his quest for autonomy, McNulty found his parents less hostile, but his father despaired of his clothes and "ducktail haircut." For many, swing defined an American world of personal freedom different from their immigrant roots. Ted Karamanski came from a Polish working-class family in Chicago; his father worked half-time in the stockyards, his mother was a janitor. Going to high school gave Ted the chance to "do things like ordinary American children." His social club, the Jolly Jives—young men of Bohemian, Polish, and Irish descent—danced avidly but had little interest in their parents' polkas. In jitterbug dances, "for the first time [we] expressed [our] own ways," and created a new American identity built on personal experimentation, dating, and self-discovery. Small-town youth also sought new ways. Jean Lukhard's family left sharecropping to return to Marshall, Texas, in 1940 when her father got a part-time job. The Lukhards now had indoor plumbing, electricity, "and best of all: a RADIO!!" Her family loved Grand Ole Opry, but she chose "Glenn Miller and the others," who better expressed her "awakening hormones." In York, Pennsylvania, Louise Strayer's friends also saw Opry as "the worst kind of music," and she didn't want her friends to know that her parents listened to it.

As they made this music their own, white youth from varied class and ethnic backgrounds identified less with traditional icons of wealth and more with a musical expression created by those who had been left out of the American success story. In fact, it was youth from racial groups outside white society who invested swing with an intense search for liberation from the racial and class restrictions of their lives. Black youth invented most of the new dances that accompanied the music, created swing's slang and clothing, and idolized black musicians as heroes. Urban black youth faced more unemployment than their white peers and had fewer leisure outlets. Living in rooming houses apart from families more than

other groups did, young black men and women could more readily frequent dance halls and clubs. Sixteen-year-old Malcolm Little, for instance, a recent migrant to Boston from East Lansing, Michigan, was free to absorb the "neon lights, night clubs, poolhalls, bars" where juke boxes blared the music of "Erskine Hawkins, Duke Ellington, Cootie Williams, dozens of others." Mexican Americans also followed the music intensely. Together with her friends, Gloria Vargas, a poor girl in the Lincoln Heights section of Los Angeles, won playground dance contests and frequented ballrooms and theaters whenever her favorite bands played. She loved the challenge and recognition of the dance contests and "the high that I would get hearing the band playing." For a time she styled herself a Zoot Suit girl, and the music became more important to her than school.

Youth of all races thus followed black and white bands as extensions of their own hopes and dreams. As they criss-crossed the nation, performing endless one-nighters for young people in small towns and cities, bands were as powerful as the railroad trains that chugged across the prairies, and the musicians seemed as glamorous as movie stars. "You must never forget that you're making rhythms for the kids," noted one bandleader. "You're . . . the only flesh-and-blood entertainment thousands of rural communities experience since minstrel shows and vaudeville disappeared." Dressed in sleek uniforms, playing behind streamlined music stands shimmering with the excitement of modern urban life, they heralded dynamic movement over fixity, inclusiveness over exclusivity. When bands swung the classics or folk tunes, as in Maxine Sullivan's treatment of "Loch Lomond," or created flagwavers like "In the Mood" or novelties like Ella Fitzgerald and Chick Webb's "A Tisket a Tasket," they challenged the authority of the past and provided a picture of a future open to new experience. That potential also gave boys and girls the chance to experiment with the opposite sex on their own terms. In a world of music, the swing bands and their young fans articulated a desire "to live 'in marble halls'—even though the plumbing be bad."

MAKE BELIEVE BALLROOM

In creating a swing subculture, young people transformed the consumption of jazz. While movies and radio shows courted general audiences, young people forced music institutions to cater to their desires to form a world of their own in more inclusive spaces. By creating a national network of musical outlets, for instance, band agencies, radio stations, and jukeboxes brought urban culture to smaller towns, made musicians household names, and gave youth easy access to music of their choice. Without cost on radio or for the price of a nickel in a jukebox or twenty-five cents at a movie theater, young people could hear their favorite bands at will. A combination of ready access and the mechanical reproduction of music removed some of the sacredness surrounding works of art, enabling young fans to treat swing as particularly theirs. When they screamed at a concert or danced in the aisles to an exciting band, they were exercising their right to respond to music in their own ways—not as parents, bandleaders, or swing critics told them they must behave. At the same time, swing musicians operated nationally, in more open, democratic spaces. Those spaces now included greater interaction between whites and blacks than ever before. As aural media, radio and records removed some of the visual definitions of race, allowing music played by blacks or whites to reach the senses in direct, unrestricted ways. The swing era thus witnessed the possibility for mass personal liberation and the democratization of cultural connoisseurship.

During the depression, radio "was our main source for big band music," recalls Elliot White of Graham, North Carolina. As the cheapest form of commercial amusement, radio grew steadily in popularity. "Few of us," noted Sidney Curtan of New Britain, Connecticut,

"could afford records, let alone record players." For firms hit hard by the economic crisis, radio offered direct access to mass audiences of youthful consumers. Eager to tap this economic potential, advertisers featured in prime time the type of music they thought would attract a large following. Yet sponsors could not always predict the type of music that would grab listeners. In 1935, for example, National Biscuit's *Let's Dance* program on NBC presented three types of music—melodic, Latin, and Benny Goodman's jazz, with the latter on from 12:30 to 1 A.M. After a single season sponsors dropped Goodman, but West Coast fans, who had heard him from 9:30 to 10 P.M., knew about the band and turned out to hear it several months later in Los Angeles. Because of his new popularity with youth, Camel Cigarettes and CBS decided to sign Goodman on to a nationally broadcast *Camel Caravan* show, and Camel sponsored Bob Crosby as well. Other cigarette and personal care firms dependent on a youth market soon joined them: Chesterfield sponsored Hal Kemp, Glenn Miller, and Harry James; Philip Morris backed Horace Heidt; and Raleigh offered Tommy Dorsey. Over the years, Old Golds sponsored Whiteman and Woody Herman, Coca-Cola had a *Spotlite* on various bands, and Wildroot Cream Oil presented Woody Herman.

Late-night remote broadcasts, meanwhile, transported youth to nightclubs, ballrooms, and theaters where bands played live. After the New York and Chicago stations signed off, Milwaukeean Carl Smaida noted, West Coast programs were broadcast "until the wee hours of the morning. This was the usual fare for radio stations after the news ended at 10:30 P.M. until their sign-off time." As Chicagoan Howard Becker recalled, "I used to listen to earshots from night clubs and ballrooms . . . I would hear everything in the distance . . . from everywhere: Wichita, Pittsburgh, and Denver." In sum, "I had a whole geography in my head, of places where big bands played." For young people, according to critic John Wilson, radio created a mixture of places, names, and events that "were immediately and exhilaratingly real, but at the same time were part of the fabric of dream-world fantasy." Announcers fed the fantasy, describing the crowd at the dreary Essex House Hotel, for instance, as "a sea of happy faces dining and dancing here in this beautiful dining room overlooking lovely Central Park in New York." Hokum or not, fans at home could construct a world of excitement outside the everyday humdrum.

While most sponsored radio was racially segregated, there were opportunities for youth of all races to hear black bands. On *Camel Caravan,* for example, Goodman regularly presented his integrated trio and quartets featuring "professors" Gene Krupa, Teddy Wilson, and Lionel Hampton as well as regular guests such as Ella Fitzgerald, Count Basie, and Billie Holiday. But Goodman was an exception; as the King of Swing, he had the leverage to get his way with reluctant sponsors and music business executives. As a consequence, it was the sustaining programs (known as "sustainers"), either remote broadcasts ("remotes") from various locations or local late-night programming, that offered greater chances to hear black bands than nationwide shows whose sponsors worried about losing the southern white market. Roy Porter, a poor black youth in Colorado, for example, had few luxuries other than his radio. During prime time he heard white bands, and afterward, "once in a while you could hear Jimmie Lunceford, Count Basie, and Erskine Hawkins' bands from the Savoy Ballroom in Harlem or Duke Ellington and Earl Hines from the Grand Terrace Ballroom in Chicago." At the same time, Count Basie rose to national fame through remotes from the Famous Door on Fifty-second Street in 1938. Late-night broadcasts not only added to a black band's allure, they also attracted white fans.

In addition to remotes from Harlem's Cotton Club, Savoy Ballroom, and Apollo Theater, black bands received some exposure on local radio shows that featured the first disc jockeys spinning records and on unsponsored programs. Independent (local) radio stations around the country saw an opportunity to compete with the powerful networks by playing "an inexhaustible supply of recorded jazz" that included work by Louis Armstrong, Duke Ellington, and Benny Goodman. The more commercially valuable the airtime became, of course, the less attention was given to the music. Such was the case with WNEW's (New York) *Make Believe Ballroom,* which had a national audience. For years the show was, according to one listener, "a letter from home for jazzophiles," as disc jockey Martin Block played "the best new records." The highlight of the week was *Saturday Night in Harlem,* a two-hour version of the program featuring the finest black bands in New York. As the show attracted a larger following, however, it became commercially valuable, and an increasing number of ballads replaced jazz. Other network shows, responding to youth demand, presented a mix of black and white swing to the public. The fledgling CBS network, competing hard with the more established NBC, relied on popular music shows to attract young audiences. WABC in New York broadcast swing shows on morning and afternoon sustainers, reserving the Saturday slot for "Saturday Night Swing," the "hottest show ever put on." The Raymond Scott Quintet, an innovative and wacky swing unit, did the house band chores, with guest appearances by the top jazzmen in New York, including Benny Carter, Roy Eldridge, Fats Waller, and Jack Teagarden. The least "commercial" programs were usually the most innovative—both musically and racially.

Teenage listeners recognized the link between music and personal identity, and their first declaration of independence was often an argument with parents over control of the radio. At fourteen, Leonard Pratt of Des Moines argued "with my dad, who wanted to hear *Amos 'n' Andy,* while I wanted to listen to the *Hit Parade.*" To avoid such battles, many teens simply went out and purchased their own radios. Jean Lukhard noted that "most of us had our own little radios at bedside (mine was a little white Philco named Oscar)." So popular were band shows that parents of high schoolers often prohibited radios in their childrens' rooms. As one parent put it, "It's not that I object to swing. But I don't think they should study to it or go to sleep to it." Yet many did. Every night, Elliot White fell asleep with "the radio tuned to late-night band broadcasts." If they could afford it, teens used car radios to define their world. Pratt saved his paper-route money to put a radio "in the family car as soon as I was allowed to drive it." Music "on the car radio while joy riding or parked in lovers lane" led to intimacy with the opposite sex. "Many times, the car battery was drained . . . while listening and necking in a secluded parking space." South Carolinian Sara Vann said, "If someone we dated had a car with a radio . . . we would park somewhere, maybe at the end of a dead-end street, and dance on the pavement."

The young used radio in their dating culture in other ways. Teens had inexpensive dates at home, in which they danced to the radio, drank beverages, necked, and used the lyrics to communicate their feelings to the opposite sex. At another level, certain programs were generational rituals, with young fans as devoted listeners. "One of our almost religiously observed" activities at Prep School, notes Curran, was listening to *Make Believe Ballroom.* At Davidson College, White reports, "every radio on campus would be turned to the same station. No one cracked a book" until Miller's closing theme "faded from the airways." *Your Hit Parade* on Saturday nights was another icon, according to June Canter. She and her friends were glued to the radio "waiting to hear if [their] favorite song was number one." They rooted for their favorites as the songs climbed the charts and debated the worth of each tune. (And for ten cents, one could buy various *Hit Parade* books of popular song lyrics.) Others rooted for different reasons. During a parlor date, Lukhard's boyfriend asked, "If Amapola is number one, may I kiss you?" When it hit the top spot, "I got my first kiss."

While radio linked the private home to the public world, the jukebox transformed public spaces into inexpensive arenas for youth dancing and dating removed from the parental eye. Young people could select their music for a nickel in soda fountains, candy shops, restaurants, and pool rooms. As a result, jukeboxes exploded in popularity, accounting for 44 percent of all popular records sold, or 30 million a year at swing's height. To attract patrons, for example, Orin Stambaugh reports that Sadie Stover installed a jukebox in her restaurant in Spring Grove, Pennsylvania, in 1939, "cleared the center area for dancing and invited the young adults to eat, dance, and enjoy the music." Seeking people her own age with her own tastes, Louise Strayer frequented a soda fountain "where in the middle of everything was that beautiful Juke Box with bright lights and for only a nickel we could listen to that great sound and forget all the troubles." Since no alcohol was served, parents were more willing to let their young go to dance and mix with members of the opposite sex. At the same time, jukeboxes let whites hear the music of black bands and singers. Given exposure on remotes from the Savoy Ballroom, Levaggi's in Boston, and Moe Gale's "Goodtime Society," Ella Fitzgerald and Chick Webb, for example, had several major jukebox hits. They started with "A Tisket a Tasket," followed by "Undecided," both on Decca, which specialized in records for jukeboxes. Similarly, while selections by black performers were often limited, Jack McNulty recalls frequenting a pool hall run by a Syrian American whose jukebox played only tunes by Count Basie and Jimmie Lunceford. He had thought that black bands were only "natural" swingers, incapable of fine ensemble work. But "I learned to be tolerant in that pool room." McNulty soon joined Al Kattar's "motor caravans, to see these black bands, whenever they played within 150 miles of Boston."

Similarly, movie theaters featured swing bands at cut rates to draw youth. When the depression made it impossible for New York's Paramount Theater to fill its 3,664 seats, manager Bob Weitman turned to big-name bands, realizing that "at least half the public who patronized a boisterous young band in the fall of 1936 were as happy listening as they were dancing to it." *Metronome* found attendance up 100 percent at matinees, with teens the "foundation of box office receipts" during the day. Theaters across the country followed suit. "Early shows were the norm everywhere, because our music was the entertainment of youth," noted Woody Herman. "Kids would skip school to hear us before the prices changed [at] noon." Sitting through B movies was a small price to pay as the fans waited for the band to rise from the pit, creating magic with "their gleaming golden instruments flashing in the spotlights that bathed the whole scene." Unlike the 1920s, when bands were part of a longer program, now they were "a show in itself, as the current fashion has it." By putting bands on stages with special lighting and sets— and, at the Paramount, on stages that elevated the band over the pit—film houses promoted the concert status of swing bands, showcasing their artistry and power. Of Count Basie at Omaha's Orpheum in 1941, for instance, a listener noted, "the acoustics in the old, traditional movie houses captured the sounds of the great swing bands in a unique way. The cathedral-like height of the stage and back stage and the width and breadth of the seating auditorium gave the music a special resonance." "There was hardly time to catch your breath," another fan noted; "the band was already pulsating with life, the front sax section filling the hall with sweet notes, the brass setting your ears afire."

In staging swing bands, movie houses became unexpected arenas of youthful audience participation, as formerly staid movie palaces featured Jitterbug Nights and dance contests. Radio City Music Hall presented amateur lindy hoppers from Harlem's Savoy Ballroom, where they competed for cash prizes. In fact, several Savoy groups traveled a circuit of theaters and clubs putting on shows and competing for prize money in front of audiences large and small, with audience applause determining the winners. In Philadelphia, one maestro drew his best house the night "bugs were turned loose on the stage." Jitterbug contests became a major attraction at Harlem's Apollo Theater, and on Wednesday night (amateur night) youngsters could display their talents backed by a top swing unit.

Meanwhile, the young fans in the audience let go their emotions, challenging the rules of theater decorum and setting themselves on an equal footing with the band. Whenever a band would take off and play a killer-diller, as particularly loud and fast numbers such as Goodman's "Sing, Sing, Sing" or Basie's "One o'Clock Jump," were called, young people would go wild. Although Goodman was often annoyed by such behavior, he was forced to recognize something unique about swing fans: "We looked at them, I guess, [as if] they were the show and we were the audience." They clapped time, bounced in their seats, and screamed. They also danced in the aisles and onstage, a practice that began with Goodman's first Paramount stint in March 1937. Unlike the sedentary audience that most sweet bands observed, noted the *Los Angeles Times* about that climactic engagement, a polyglot group of kids would "jump out of their seats and actually hold a Carnival in the aisles." When "the band played a hot, fast one a . . . youth grabbed his best girl and proceeded to shag in the main aisle." Ushers rushed to stop them, according to the *San Francisco Chronicle*, but "theater history was made when . . . a few more of the enthusiastic swingdings tried to climb onto the stage, lured irresistibly forward by the Pied Piper of the clarinet," and took "to shagging *on the stage* with the audience beating out a vast rhythm with their palms." Dozens more jammed the pit, content to stand there and "soak in the throbbing rhythms." Ultimately the manager was forced to throw a cordon of ushers around "the plague spots."

After this, audience response often bordered on the riotous. At the Stanley Theater in Pittsburgh in 1941, the management was forced to call the police to quell a commotion of young fans. Trombonist Lou McGarrity, who was in charge of the band while Benny Goodman was undergoing his army physical, said, "Go away man. We've got this place jumping." When Duke Ellington played the Palace in Fort Wayne, Indiana, noted Charles Travelbee, "there was pure pandemonium, dancing in the aisles, in the orchestra pit . . . we all went nuts." In Des Moines, Leonard Pratt said, "more than once we impulsively got out of our seats to swing in the aisles to the faster numbers, not hearing the ushers screaming 'Please sit down.'" It was the same at a Glenn Miller Bond Rally in St. Louis in 1944, according to Leonard Meenach. "The young people were dancing in the aisles and the lobby. This was a very exciting reminder of present day rock concerts and just as loud and wild. It took several policemen to control the crowd." Indeed, the Brandt Theatres in New York had house police patrol the aisles to "curb effervescent jitterbugs." Other forms of behavior reached extremes too. When Tommy Dorsey played the Paramount, Travelers' Aid agents grabbed a girl in the first row who had followed Dorsey to New York from Pittsburgh via Washington, D.C. Each day she entered the theater as it opened and stayed seated until the last performance of the night. She lasted through fifty-four successive shows before they sent her home.

This carnival helped young people transcend the depressing outside world and the restraints of adult prescription. In reviewing Glenn Miller at a Cleveland theater, a critic showed how out of place adults felt when the young let go. The more rhythmic the music, "the louder the cheers and applause from the audience, and when the brasses and the drummer began to work on the emotion of the crowd, I began to question both its sanity and mine." Another wrote, "The frenzy and the ecstasy" Miller created "are as far beyond me as they always are when the boys and girls get into the groove." Swing's elemental nature, he added, was both "impolite and inconsiderate. It seems to be a case of every emotion for itself . . . it stirs other emotions as well as other individuals to be up and doing—and shouting." This expressiveness also transformed genteel concert halls. When Goodman's sextet played Rochester's Eastman Theater, for example, "one could almost feel the temperature of the audience rise as the session progressed, with the floor vibrating to the 'jitterbugging' of the enraptured audience, over whom an hypnotic rhythmic spell was so astonishingly exerted."

DANCE OF THE JITTERBUGS

If the desire for release transformed theaters into impromptu ballrooms, dance halls assumed new importance as settings for mass self-expression in an era of scarcity. "It was not that places did not exist in the Twenties," a fan said, "but then there were more things to do and see, and there was more money for traveling." In fact, ballrooms replaced nightclubs as key jazz institutions because the former appealed to a mass rather than a class clientele. Ballrooms competed with clubs by adding a "nitery atmosphere with tables, liquors and foods." *Variety* noted that the "idea that dancing was dancing and clubbing was clubbing and the two could never meet has been dissipated." As a result, bands played music for dancing and put on shows with singers, small combos, and special arrangements.

By adapting the cabaret to more modest circumstances, and by mixing dancing with performing, the ballroom of the 1930s helped democratize the nightclub. With its new aura of sophistication, the dance hall allowed young people to experiment with adulthood. To aid those on limited budgets, many halls abolished the "taxi dance" custom—charging men to dance with hostesses. Ballrooms also stopped charging a couple for each dance. Instead, halls now established a fixed entrance fee to encourage couple dancing. "The fact that they can dance whenever they want to without thinking of the money involved each time, encourages them," noted the manager of Broadway's

Arcadia Ballroom. As part of the democratization process, halls also offered a variety of contests and special events to attract a diverse patronage. Harlem's Savoy Ballroom, for example, instituted Thursday Kitchen Mechanics Nights, bathing beauty contests, and Sunday Opportunity Days when dancers competed for cash prizes. Exciting and more inclusive than in the past, modern ballrooms took jazz outside the swanky club or low-class dive and made it accessible to ordinary young people.

Like jukeboxes, ballrooms also made black bands more accessible to white audiences. While hotels, theaters, and sponsored radio programs rarely presented black bands, dance halls booked them for one-nighters. In general, the swing era witnessed an increase in dancing by whites to black bands and in listening and dancing by black audiences to white or mixed units. The Savoy attracted a sizable white patronage, and white units like those of Charlie Barnet, Goodman, and Miller played there or at the Apollo. A surprised *Metronome* noted "the great reception accorded white bands in Harlem recently" and the "near riot that broke out when Charlie Barnet shattered all precedent and opening day records as he brought the first white band into the Apollo Theatre." When Goodman and his integrated quartet played the Paramount, black patronage jumped from 3 to 15 percent of the house.

Black dancers may not have been welcome at white dance halls, but black bands regularly crossed racial lines to play white dances. As R. L. Larkin noted, "The swarms of jitterbugs of the 1937–39 period . . . knew no color lines, and to them Chick Webb and Count Basie were as fine to jig to as Goodman and Shaw." Fan accounts support this observation. Down South, black bands played for whites or for whites and blacks divided by a rope across the dance floor in elegant ballrooms or in huge cotton or tobacco warehouses. Despite segregation, white fans patronized black bands. Ruth Shapiro, a young white woman from Dallas, found herself uncomfortable listening to Count Basie in Harlem, but she eagerly went to hear black bands in whiter settings in Texas. Elliot White on several occasions drove or hitchhiked across North Carolina to attend dances played by Chick Webb and Basie. Once, he and several friends sat outside a tobacco warehouse for hours listening to Erskine Hawkins. "It was a black dance. So we couldn't go in. So much for segregation!"

Whatever the setting, white jitterbugs crossed racial barriers by doing black dances. Not only did whites and blacks perform similar dances, whites acknowledged that the steps originated in black culture and that the best dancers were black. As the *New York Times* put it, "The white jitterbug is oftener than not uncouth to look at, but his Negro original is quite another matter. His movements are never so exaggerated that they lack control, and there is an unmistakable dignity about his most violent figures." A fan who was a junior high school girl in the Bronx notes wistfully that "we all wished we were old enough to go to the Savoy Ballroom, as that was where the really hip jitterbugs showed their stuff." Even in Bangor, Maine, and Holdenville, Oklahoma, it was clear that Harlem created the new dances. Newspaper headlines in both towns read, "Mad 'Suzy-Q' Is Harlem's New Gift to Swing." Uncouth or not, whites adopted black moves in their quest for greater personal freedom.

The inventive new dance styles were sparked by black jitterbugs at Harlem's Savoy Ballroom. A "folk avant garde" created the lindy hop in 1927 while improvising variations on the Charleston. The lindy's simple open hold and the relaxed 4/4 beat of swing allowed dancers to invent the lindy's most unusual feature, the "breakaway." Encouraged by the underlying security of the beat, dancers engaged in flights of improvisational fancy. At the climactic moment partners let go of each other's hands, and then, noted the dancer Shorty Snowden, "anything you could dream up was okay for the breakaway, you tried all kinds of things." In 1936, a group of younger dancers added air steps. In moves such as the back flip, the over-the-head, and the snatch, men threw their partners in the air, between their legs, and over their backs and caught them on the beat as they came down. In swing, one could fly.

As the new forms swept the swing subculture from the bottom up, according to Marshall and Jean Stearns, they caused "a general revolution in the popular dance in the United States." White youth took up the black vernacular variations on the lindy and delivered the death blow to the ballroom gentility that had linked dance to social manners and courtship rather than to individual freedom. The Charleston had opened up the traditional couple embrace in the 1920s, to be sure, but its movements usually were a momentary, jerky, and vertical diversion in the fox-trot. Even then most dancers had a standard step, "always dancing close to our partners," in the basic waltz and fox-trot. By grounding the movements of the dancers in a steady, 4/4 horizontal beat, however, swing let one "get with it and be carried away." And, when partners became separated, they would truck or strut "or maybe improvise something on their own." At first middle-class whites were shocked by the pelvic rotation necessary to keep one moving with the flow of swing rhythms. Pittsburgh dancer Ernie Smith turned to the working-class girls in nearby mill towns for with-it partners. Moving in authentic flowing style, they were the first white girls who "could really dance." With Glenn Miller's more relaxed tempos, introduced in 1939, the lindy achieved mass success. Still, Smith noted, it remained "a black dance even when whites were doing it" and became "the bread-and-butter style" of subsequent generations as it consolidated steps from the turkey trot to the Charleston into a full-fledged American form that *Life* called "a true national folk dance." Since "the Lindy revolution," notes dancer George Wendler, no "conservative style of dancing" has succeeded.

With these decidedly improvisational steps, black and white dancers discarded "the sophisticated mask" of the ballroom. As Cecelia Ayer put it, "After years of dancing in darkest despair, of straying about the dance floor as if they didn't care if they lived or died," young people now came "into their birthright" to enjoy themselves again. Earlier steps had been "very smooth, very uniform, very easy, very lifeless and very unrhythmic." Now kids "could try improvising with their feet and bodies, instead of just listening to somebody else do it with a horn." The new steps gave the young a great amount of personal freedom. "You don't see a whole ballroom moving sedately around in the same direction with the same steps—ice-skating style." Instead, noted music critic Mike Levin, "you see some very good and very bad stabs at really original styles."

An important part of interaction between the sexes, these steps featured honest emotional expression more than overt sexuality or obsessive and sentimental love. Levin reported that "the way most of these kids dance, they are seldom less than four feet apart—which permits of far less jive than I remember in the dreamy Lombardo days." There was sexual suggestion, to be sure, as girls twirled with enough force to show legs and panties, but it was playful absorption in the moment. Rooted in the dance's earthy horizontal movements and the steady beat, both partners could be themselves rather than play the usual social and gender roles. According to Ager, both sexes "care less than nothing about how they look. They are dancing entirely for themselves, animated by high and supremely honest emotion." Letting "oneself go naturally," there was little room for social niceties: "People can't talk in a trance." Free improvisation let girls and boys break through sentimental facades and fixed roles to more independent selves.

The lindy held out a model for the sexes. The dance depended on coordination between partners, which took practice. "Young people in those days took their dancing very seriously," says dancer Dean Collins. "They spent a lot of time with their partner." The Bronx fan notes that partners practiced all week to big band arrangements for the Friday afternoon school dances. Moreover, the dance's hand clasp engaged boys and girls in intimate communication, ensuring that the couple could survive the centrifugal force and the obstacles of the dance. At the same time, the rooted quality of the beat balanced flight. To let go, both sexes had to be down to earth. It was not that slow dancing and romance were not important, but rather that the lindy created a sense of liberating camaraderie and interplay. The males still led, but toward the freedom of both genders in an erotic relationship removed from the world. "He may improvise all sorts of fantastic figures and even try a touch of acrobatics, to all of which his partner will respond with calm and cooperative agility," noted the *New York Times*. Couples aimed for a spontaneous union. "During the faster numbers," notes Leonard Pratt, "there was the simultaneous sharing of the quicker steps, the twirls and turns which gave us a feeling inside of togetherness not achieved in any other activity."

At any ballroom where a swing band played, the message was as clear as Harry James's or Roy Eldridge's trumpet: on the dance floor, amid a crowd of other people, ecstasy and personal freedom could be asserted against the depersonalized and restrictive modern world. In these dances both sexes expressed their individuality. In their improvisations, young men and women confidently carved out the space around them with their horizontal thrusts and recreated themselves through their unique movements. Without the aid of teachers, new popular dances spread quickly from black culture into the white working and middle classes. Joyful yet serious, swing dancing, as expressed by Jimmie Lunceford and Trummy Young's "'Taint What You Do (But the Way That Ya Do It)," elevated stylistic, relaxed movement as a form of grace under pressure and a way to withstand the chaos and uncertainty of the modern world.

Swing bands played more than fast lindys. When a good swing band focused its hot sound on love songs, it intensified the personal meanings of ballads. "We had fun dancing to swing," notes Kentuckian Susie Tucker. "We knew about romance from the love songs." Chummy MacGregor, Glenn Miller's pianist, writes that during the last hour of a dance, "we made a lot of friends with those long dreary dance sessions with the lights low, the tempo relaxed, those nice saxophones, and Ray Eberle stirring the imagination of all the 'jail bait' sub-debs in the hall." As he asserts, "more engagement rings" were "contracted for (on the installment plan)" at school dances or lakeside pavilions than anywhere else. Often, notes Leonard Pratt, "the initial romantic relationship began on the dance floor." As he and a girl danced, their cheeks touched and they drifted along to the "dreamy melody," and "whispers of the romantic lyrics in her ear soon followed."

Unlike sweet music, however, swing fused love songs to a jazz style that gave ballads a lift and heightened their emotional power. Each band's use of individualized arrangements and versatile instrumentation helped make love songs seem more personal. Band singers performed a chorus of a song much as an instrumental soloist would, while the full band teased out the emotional nuances. At the end, no matter the sentiment, the band picked up the tempo as if to affirm that life goes on despite obstacles and that dreams come true. In "These Foolish Things," "It's All Yours," "I'll Never Smile Again," "Stardust," "Memories of you," "Green Eyes," "Dam That Dream," "Begin the Beguine," and "I Let a Song Go out of My Heart"—to cite only a few—love was an agent that would transport one from the everyday to the exalted. Yet these romantic songs lacked the self-pity, insecurity, and obsessive sentimentality of early '30s torch songs. Instead, they promised possibility, even in a depression. In "It's All Yours," Helen Forrest, who sang with Artie Shaw, Benny Goodman, and Harry James, offers "everything you see" to encourage her love to come out of his "cloister" and enjoy life. When singing "Imagination," Frank Sinatra mused that dreaming of his girl made "a cloudy day sunny." With her swing sensibility and her spectacular improvisational skills, Billie Holiday transformed even the most maudlin tune into a testament to the power of the human spirit.

Many songs emphasized dreams of love that all listeners could share, rather than hopes of success or status, which the depression rendered much more difficult to achieve. In fact, the songs asserted the importance of dreams, as against the obstacles placed in the way of their realization, and still chose love over money. In Jimmie Lunceford rendition of "Slumming on Park Avenue," the singer juxtaposes her modest social position to that of the "rich," while "Position's Everything in Life" holds up a basic truth. In "I Can't Afford to Dream," Tony Pastor, the singer for Artie Shaw, announces, "I dream but I shouldn't," because he lacks money to make the dreams come true. Martha Tilton, a vocalist with Benny Goodman, sang the depression standard "I Can't Give You Anything But Love," observing that "diamond bracelets Woolworth's doesn't sell." Although lack of money was a problem, the rich were too concerned with money to have any fun. In "The Honorable So and So," Helen Forrest portrays a woman kept by a socialite more interested in social position than in love. In the bitterest song of the era, "God Bless the Child," Billie Holiday notes that rich relations might give handouts, but it was better to be "the child that's got his own."

Despite obstacles of class and circumstance, the young followed Forrest in yearning, "I Want My Share of Love." They might be "rented dreams," but "rented or not, they help a lot." Comparing Wall Street to empty pockets, "I've Got a Pocketful of Dreams" held up the superior worth of ideals and hopes for the future. "I Can't Get Started," another standard of the era, moreover, has the singer traveling around the world in a plane, settling revolutions in Spain, but all his wealth and power do not satisfy him. While some songs were undeniably escapist, an indomitable spirit emerges in tunes such as "I've Got a Right to Dream." Despite the depression, these songs seemed to say, one had a right to feet good, find love, and

enjoy life. Irene Daye, who sang with Gene Krupa's band, for instance, claimed that she "Never Had Less, Never Felt Better." As in the fast dances, moreover, the search was less for frivolity than for a mate who could love you for yourself. In "You're a Lucky Guy," the singer notes that "you've got a honey who wants no money / who'll take you just as you are." Similarly, Frank Sinatra and Tommy Dorsey essayed a better world where "There Are Such Things" as someone "not caring what you own / but just what you are." In a parallel, Ella Fitzgerald sang "I've Got a Guy" who "don't dress me in sable / He looks nothing like Gable / But he's mine." Although he is tough, "He's just a gem, in the rough."

TO HELL WITH THE JITTERBUGS

For many jitterbugs, the emotional experience of swing transcended romance. Eager fans transformed dance hall culture by crowding around bandstands to watch and listen; some listeners exhibited wild bodily exertions even without partners. Goodman described the first jitterbug he ever saw. At a Kansas City ballroom in 1934, a male dancer began to go "off his conk. His eyes rolled, his limbs began to spin like a windmill in a hurricane—his attention, riveted to the rhythm, transformed him into a whirling dervish." Releasing his partner, he "went into a little neo-African footwork." Members of the band thought he was drunk, but "it was just that the music did things to him." When not dancing he stood in front of Ziggy Elman's horn and "put on an emotional display of adoration that would have shamed a Father Divine fish fry." The next night "the worshipper" stood before the stand "growing more and more plastered by the music as the evening wore on." Male jitterbugs were soon joined by their female counterparts. Some observers described impresario John Hammond as a jitterbug. In response to the music, "he begins to move his head, his feet, and sometimes his whole body," said the *New Yorker*. "His eyebrows go up, his mouth opens wide and reveals a set of even, gleaming teeth, and a long-drawn-out 'Yeah' slides out of his throat." But he does not "shag. He never dances at all."

Described as "dervishes"—"violent," "nervous," and "plastered"—jitterbugs changed dance floor behavior. In the past, noted a band booker, "it was only a dozen or two hep musicians that crowded the floor space around a band shell." Now, of a thousand crowded into a ballroom, "only 100 or so are actually dancing, while the others jam the floor and render themselves hysterical by the gymnastics of the hot horns getting in a groove." To get in free and be first in front of the bandstand, Jack McNulty and his friends went to the ballrooms two hours early, waited for the band bus, and helped carry the equipment backstage. They would stay there all night "unless our girls dragged us away to dance, but we left them, and went back up front." Unexpected interactions with musicians often resulted. One night at a hall in Lynnfield, Massachusetts, bandleader Tony Pastor leaned over and asked Charles Hayden to dance with his vocalist to keep her warm. "There I was with that little darling in my arms and doing my best Fred Astaire."

The close proximity of artistic idols in ballrooms and theaters and the important role that they played in expressing the yearnings of young men and women rendered musicians and singers accessible gods—often under the control of audiences who easily crossed stage barriers to interject themselves into the performance. Unlike rock stars, who often perform in huge stadiums, Helen Forrest noted, "when we were in a theater or at a ballroom we were really in reach and we loved it, we loved the adulation." Fans reached across footlights and bandstands or waited outside for autographs. At a Waltham, Massachusetts, hall, for example, "autograph hounds [were] pleading for something to show their grandchildren. Everything was used for signatures, from the back of a card advertising" to "huge placards." On another occasion, hundreds of black fans tore off Ella Fitzgerald's clothes in a scramble for her autograph as she left the bandstand at New Orleans's New Rhythm Club. Many kids collected autographs, and they often judged musicians by their willingness to meet their demands. A letter to *Down Beat,* for instance, complained that Charlie Barnet was not a "solid guy" because he "refused to sign autographs" or shake hands at a ballroom. Another letter writer praised Gene Krupa as "the finest guy there is," because he took him behind the stand and gave him five autographed pictures.

Excited fans often became pests. Much to the dismay of musicians, they shouted for "killer-dillers" and disturbed performances by clapping and yelling during quiet passages, dancing in theater aisles, and climbing onto the stage. While singing with the Chico Marx Orchestra at Denver's Lakeside Ballroom in 1942, for example, Mel Torme felt a pain in his leg. Looking down, he found a young tough yelling "Sing 'Sweet Eloise.'" As he tried to go on, the boy "pinch[ed his] right calf so hard that [he saw] stars." When Torme kicked him in the mouth, two of the boy's pals tried "to climb onto the stage to kill [him]." Excited fans sometimes grabbed instruments too, or tried to beat Hampton's vibes or Krupa's drums at intermission, or, worse, tried to blow Goodman's clarinet. Others took instruments, "for what truer expression of worship could a jitterbug display than to take it home and worship it as a fetish?"

These constant annoyances raised the ire of fans, critics, and bandleaders. *Down Beat* critic George Frazier charged that audience reaction to Goodman's Boston Symphony Hall concert "was damned distracting." The three thousand fans "behaved so bastardly that some magnificent jazz was completely drowned out." The crowd yelled for the killer-dillers, and "there was so much deafening noise from the audience that one had to strain to hear the subtle passages." Critic Dick Jacobs complained that the jitterbug "knows how to shag," and "he can whistle and hog call louder than three ordinary human beings," but "his clamor makes it impossible for a real fan to enjoy a band's playing" and retards "the appreciation of swing as a fine American art." Bandleaders agreed. Goodman yelled at "ickies"—the most exhibitionistic of the jitterbugs—to shut up. Artie Shaw found that kids demanded "hot licks" so that they could go "dance crazy," but their demands undermined his wish to evoke varied moods. "They won't even let me play without interrupting me. They scream when I play, they don't listen." Once he was so enraged that he called the fans "morons." In 1939, at the height of his fame, he quit to get away from the "hundreds and thousands of crazy people pushing and shoving and crowding and milling around in mobs, shrieking for your autograph, or your picture or something—or just plain shrieking for no reason."

VOTE FOR MR. RHYTHM

While critics and bandleaders decried the jitterbugs as symbols of mass culture excess, many fans claimed that real jitterbugs did not go "crazy every time they hear a lot of drums or trumpets and shout out loud at every climax whether it's good or bad." As one self-proclaimed "bug" argued, real jitterbugs distinguished good from bad swing, collected record's according to their own taste, and listened seriously. In essence, many fans appreciated the artistic power of the music, producing in a variety of ways the democratization of artistic connoisseurship. According to historian Alice Goldfarb Marquis, the mass arts of the 1930s saw the last aristocracy, "the peerage of art, music, literature," give way "to the democratic impulse" as ordinary fans treated popular music with the devotion usually accorded to high culture. William Glackin, for example, notes that swing stimulated him "intellectually" as well as physically. Many fans sat entranced or crowded around bandstands to better hear the music. Jazz critic Nat Hentoff, for example, idolized the Duke Ellington Orchestra. At dances "[I] stood as close as I could to the band to gape as these necromancers conjured up mobile mosaics of sound . . . I was in awe." Ellington noted in 1937 that audiences "invariably crowd around the bandstand eager to grasp every solo note and orchestral trick, and certain to 'shush' down any rowdiness that may hamper the enjoyment of the music." Swing thus enlarged "the public's knowledge of music, mainly in the world of modern American jazz." Goodman agreed. "Jitterbugs helped us drag jazz out of the old saloon mechanical piano, and give it new life and dignity." Even at the Savoy Ballroom, known for its ecstatic dancing, listening often took precedence too. When Teddy Hill's men swung the last choruses of "Christopher Columbus," for example, "dancers forg[o]t about dancing and flock[ed] around the stand ten deep, to register the time merely with their bones and muscles, standing there in one place with their heads back and letting it flow over them like water."

In fact, as discerning listeners, swing fans were called on to play active roles as critics and connoisseurs in popular plebiscites to decide the winners of the many battles of the bands held in the nation's ballrooms. As a regular part of the entertainment, for instance, Chick Webb battled Benny Goodman in June 1937 at the Savoy, Charlie Barnet fought Louis Armstrong in Washington D.C., Count Basie and Jimmie Lunceford sparred at the Larchmont Casino, and at the Savoy, Basie and Webb competed in a much-publicized event. Such bouts encouraged intense audience involvement. They were advertised for weeks and discussed in the press, and they drew huge audiences eager to cheer on their favorites. Often fans were asked to fill out ballots. At other times they chose their champions through applause or dancing fervor. However decided, the plebiscite lay with the fans. In one battle, Ella Fitzgerald, Chick Webb's singer, urged listeners in song "to vote for Mr. Rhythm," in this case Webb, because he was "the people's choice."

Music publications and fans treated the battles as championship fights or other heroic male contests. Such was the case when Benny Goodman journeyed to the Savoy to battle Chick Webb, giving the contest an interracial dimension frequently seen during the swing era. As *Metronome* described it, "On the left platform was Benny Goodman, White King of Swing. On the right was Chick Webb, idol of Harlem." Police kept the crowd at bay as "Benny's boys fired the first shot. The crowd went wild. Its white idol was really shelling out." After the first barrage, Chick opened up on drums, and "from then on Chick fought Benny every inch of the way, and Benny fought Chick every inch of the same way." In sum, "it was really a torrid battle." The crowd of jitterbugs, black and white, proclaimed Webb the winner with its applause. In this plebiscite talent rather than color prevailed. On another occasion, in Madison Square Garden, Count Basie, the "Kansas City Killer," was voted the winner over "Barrelhouse Benny" by a largely white crowd.

Hepcats took pride in their musical sophistication. To help them, specialized magazines emerged in the mid-1930s. *Down Beat,* the first American periodical devoted exclusively to jazz, debuted in 1934 as swing took off and grew to a circulation of more than 50,000. The tabloid featured sexy heartthrobs, record reviews, combative music critics, and coverage of black and white bands. Its lively slang, outrageous articles, screaming headlines, biting criticism, and screwball mix of serious commentary and offbeat humor gave the magazine, according to swing critic Dave Dexter, Jr., "the wild approach and the unsophisticated and rowdy touch which made it so popular with musicians as a form of free expression comparable to saving itself." In 1935, *Metronome* turned its attention from standard dance orchestras to swing bands, while a host of other swing periodicals emerged to give fans direct and inside access to the band world. Howard Becker, an amateur musician and fan, read *Down Beat* for its updates on band personnel every two weeks; "we kept track of that the way people keep track of football or baseball." In North Carolina, Elliot White and his friends passed copies of *Metronome* around to find out "how each band was doing and what

sideman was leaving one band to join another. It listed the latest releases on records, with a critical review." Indeed, critics were as outspoken and direct as swing solos. "George T. Simon's comments were read with anticipation. He spared no one!"

Moreover, the magazines invited active critical participation through lively letters columns. In the contested terrain between critics and fans, critics often acted as glorified fans and fans as incisive critics. The combative style of critics such as George Frazier and John Hammond stimulated outspoken fan response. *Metronome,* for example, carried a constant stream of arguments over particular bands and performers. Simon graded bands on a scale of A to D in his "Simon Says" column and did the same for records in "DISCussions." The responses were heated as well as knowledgeable. Fans defended favorites or attacked other fans. In April 1943, for instance, Barbara Wright angrily wrote, "I, like many others who read this issue, am inclined to disagree" with a review of a hotel appearance by Johnny Long. Some issues caused hotter reactions than others, as in the responses to sweet music fans who wrote to protest that the critics were biased against sweet bands like Kay Kyser's and Harry James's. An outraged P. Biagini declared that "Kay couldn't even be a 'can pusher' for the Duke, and James wouldn't even be able to shine Cootie [William]'s shoes." Another angry fan wondered "how you gentlemen can rave about a lot of meaningless and out of tune tenors" like Bud Freeman, "just about the world's worst tenor man." In a combative era, swing fans pulled few punches.

Readers' polls offered a more structured form of registering opinion. *Metronome* and *Downbeat* ran yearly polls in which musicians and fans voted for their favorite bandleaders, instrumentalists, and vocalists in a variety of categories. As an example of their democratic nature, the magazines advertised the polls well in advance, carried running accounts of the balloting, and gave full totals at the end. Winners were then assembled for special "All-

Star" concerts and recording sessions that constituted meetings of the swing gods. Moreover, radio shows, college and high-school newspapers, general magazines, and other periodicals conducted fan polls. In Los Angeles, for example, Don Otis of KFAC's *Dance Time* polled listeners on whether they preferred Goodman to Guy Lombardo. In a 59–16 decision, the *Times* announced, "right prevailed." Martin Block's *Make Believe Ballroom* poll on WNEW New York also gave fans the opportunity to vote for their favorites. In 1936 and 1937 the poll ran for six weeks, with over 90,000 votes cast. Not to be outdone, *Radio Guide* exhorted its readers to vote for their favorites. "It's up to you to do your part!" they shouted, "Vote! and vote now!"

Until the 1940s, poll winners were generally white, as black bands had fewer chances to be heard on a regular basis by white audiences. Black newspapers took up the slack, however, by giving black audiences an opportunity to be heard. In 1939 the *Pittsburgh Courier* began an "All-American Band Poll," followed by similar polls in the *Amsterdam News* and the *Chicago Defender*. As *Courier* columnist Frank E. Bolden declared, "A musician is a musician— so sez us, the people—regardless of the color of skin." A promo for the 1941 poll stressed the populist ethos of such polls. "YOUR VOTES DECIDE THE WINNER. No stuffed shirt, long haired judges will decide what band, YOU THE PUBLIC SHOULD HAVE AS KING OF SWING. . . . That makes the decision more democratic and void of partiality." The public should vote because "you spend your money to dance to your favorite band, buy your favorite wax recordings, play every juke box within nickel range and listen to them over the radio." Fans agreed. More than 100,000 readers took part in the *Defender*'s first poll, and the winners played special dances in important swing cities.

While battles of the bands, polls, and letters measured the bands' popularity, they also expanded the musical knowledge of a good portion of the swing audience. As Harry James put it, "Swing created a following of music-conscious kids such as jazz was never able to do." Radio and the jukebox, often viewed as encouraging passivity, actually helped expand musical sophistication to a mass audience. Albert Murray suggests that radio acted as a "concert hall without walls" as listeners "huddled around radios all over the nation." An integral part of youth culture, radio also fostered serious and active listening to and debate about swing. Leonard Pratt and his friends often discussed the music on the radio. "We had some knowledge of the members of various bands and we debated about who was the best trumpet player, drummer, pianist." Moreover, one had to be an expert. Elliot White and his friends spent a lot of time debating the worth of various bands. "Was Shaw better than Goodman on clarinet? . . . Could the Basie band outswing Lunceford's? . . . Each person had his own opinions and stoutly defended them." In Charles Hayden's Haverhill, Massachusetts, home the radio was always on, prompting the query, "what's the tune?" One had to know or "you were a dope and you only got a few seconds to answer." Miller Tucker and a friend at the University of Tennessee played a similar game. "We would twist the dial until we heard a song, then we would guess whose band it was. We prided ourselves that we could name the band after no more than eight bars." The jukebox expanded listening too. As Orin Stambaugh notes, he and his musician friends "would drop a nickel in the slot, stand in front of the juke box, and listen to our favorite tunes paying particular attention to any good solo work or comment on the fine arrangements. We were so enthralled by the music that we seldom danced."

Radio also fostered musical knowledge by encouraging fans to play instruments. Amateur band contests abounded. Frank Mathias, a high school saxist in Carlisle, Kentucky, for instance, followed bands on radio, but, he says, "I yearned to play that music myself, to share the work of a sax section as it swung the lovely ballads and exciting jump tunes of the day." At state amateur contests he was criticized for "going astray," which he could not help, "for limited every great sax man I heard on the radio," from Coleman Hawkins to Jimmy Dorsey. After Leonard Pratt heard Goodman on the radio, moreover, he took up the clarinet, which he learned to play by ear. After school band practice, he and several bandmates "had jam sessions until the school janitor forced us [to] leave." Together, he and his friends formed a five-piece band to play lodges and taverns. "We listened closely to the big band programs on radio and desperately attempted to follow the various styles and arrangements of the day." The movies helped too. After Mel Torme saw Goodman and Krupa in *Hollywood Hotel*— "no less than five times"—he drove his parents crazy practicing to killer-dillers on the radio. So many amateur bands formed during the era that Goodman called them "the nicest compliment paid to Swing."

Youth audiences were part of the process by which jazz crossed the barrier from dance music to the concert hall and the public festival. The mass culture of the 1930s did not destroy rational controls and cheapen art; rather, radio, jukeboxes, movie theaters, and dance halls included the mass audience in the artistic process. The jitterbug represented both the emotional loosening of American musical culture and its democratization. Emotional spontaneity and personal freedom on the part of the young were linked not to fascism, as some critics feared, but to a revitalization of mass democratic culture in which the boundaries—around the self, between various ethnic and racial groups, and around the concept of art—faded. The spread of popular musical appreciation and the rise in listening—as well as dancing—gave to swing the designation of art, but art rooted in popular knowledge and the desires of young men and women. It is no accident that, in this cultural environment, the concert hall and the public festival took on the flavor of the crowd, while the movie theater and the dance hall became "concert halls without walls." Listeners did not replace exhibitionist jitterbugs. Rather, they inhabited the same spaces and together made possible a popular art that crossed the boundary between the highbrow and the lowbrow. The growth of this mass youth audience made possible the many concerts, jam sessions, festivals, and swing jamborees that marked the era by merging listening and dancing. In swing, personal liberation and the revitalization of democratic culture went together.

Big bands lay at the heart of this new youth culture. They expressed the hopes and feelings of young people, put them in touch with modern culture, and produced a new generation of popular heroes and heroines. No band embodied this revitalized democratic culture better than Benny Goodman's.

GLOSSARY

Earl "Fatha" Hines (1905–1983):   African American jazz pianist and composer. In the 1920s, while working for Louis Armstrong, Hines transformed the role of the piano in jazz by making it a solo instrument. His nickname came from a radio announcer's acknowledgment of his role as "the father of modern jazz piano."

Benny Goodman (1909–1986):   American clarinetist and bandleader. In 1934, he formed a big band and went on to become the "King of Swing," performing for radio, motion pictures, and records.

Jitterbug: A strenuous dance performed to quick-tempo swing or jazz music and consisting of various two-step patterns embellished with twirls and sometimes acrobatic maneuvers.

William Allen White (1868–1944):

American newspaper editor and writer noted for his politically influential editorials and for his 1946 autobiography.

Zoot Suit:

A man's suit popular during the early 1940s, characterized by full-legged, tight-cuffed trousers and a long coat with wide lapels and heavily padded, wide shoulders.

Juke Box:

A coin-operated phonograph, equipped with push buttons for the selection of records. The first all-electric jukeboxes are introduced by the Automatic Musical Instrument Co. of Grand Rapids, Michigan, and Seeburg Co. of Chicago. Large-scale mass production began in 1934 and by 1939 there were 350,000 jukeboxes in U.S. bars, restaurants, and other establishments.

Harlem:

A section of New York City in northern Manhattan bordering on the Harlem and East rivers. A rapid influx of African Americans beginning in the 1910s made it one of the largest Black communities in the United States.

Fred Astaire (1899–1987):

American dancer and actor noted for his elegant style and his partnership with Ginger Rogers in several motion pictures, including *Top Hat* (1935).

IMPLICATIONS

Although many parents and social observers condemned swing and the jitterbug as leading to immorality and social breakdown, Erenberg claims that the new youth culture of the 1930s in fact democratized American cultural life. Do you think that the youth culture of swing was simply a generational revolt against the older parental culture? Or was it a measure of democratization at work? Could it have served both functions?

PART THREE

A Resilient People

The post–World War II generation lived through a unique era in the nation's history. Driven by the world's strongest economy, protected by the world's preeminent military establishment, and enjoying unprecedented personal prosperity at home, ordinary people and national leaders alike looked forward to living in what one observer dubbed the "American Century." In the end, however, that century would last a mere 20 years. By 1967, the costs of the Vietnam War pushed the nation's economy into an inflationary spiral; during the 1970s, foreign products made serious inroads into American markets; and in 1974, the Vietnam War ended in American withdrawal and defeat. Pressed economically, national pride diminished by failure in Vietnam, the United States witnessed a resurgence of conservatism that threatened the existence of the liberal welfare state.

The 1960s was a remarkable decade of tumult and affluence that produced a profound shift in American popular culture. The Civil Rights Movement, protests against the Vietnam War, the introduction of the birth control pill and consequent "sexual revolution," and an exuberant youth culture of rock music and recreational drug use profoundly challenged traditional American values. In "The Making of the 1960s Youth Culture," Maurice Isserman and Michael Kazin examine the myths and realities of the bedrock of 1960s culture: sex, drugs, and rock-n-roll. In doing so, they suggest that the cultural changes, both good and bad, inaugurated by the youth culture of the 1960s are still with us.

One of the most significant consequences of the 1960s was the rise of ethnic identity and sustained collective action among minority groups. Building on foundations established in the early twentieth century, American Indians, African Americans, Asian Americans, and Hispanic Americans built organizations and social movements that demanded full inclusion in mainstream America. Although not technically a minority, women also drew upon the changing culture of the 1960s to demand full equality in American life. In "Claiming Public Space," Vicki Ruiz recounts the struggles of Mexican American women who worked to organize themselves in the workplace and in society at large. As she reveals, Mexican American women drew on a long tradition of mutual assistance and collective action to gain control over their own lives.

The unprecedented prosperity of the immediate postwar decades created a virtual revolution in consumer goods and in the consumption patterns of ordinary Americans. One result was the creation of what Kenneth T. Jackson calls a "Drive-In Culture," based on a precipitous rise in automobile ownership during the postwar years. By the 1960s, motels and drive-in restaurants, movies, banks, and even churches were a regular part of everyday life in the United States.

The collapse of postwar prosperity beginning in the late 1960s and early 1970s cast a lengthening shadow over the lives of ordinary Americans. As wages failed to keep pace with inflation, growing numbers of married women with preschool-aged children were forced into the labor market simply to maintain the postwar standard of living. The political fallout of economic decline was immediate and long-lived. In "The Overthrow of LBJ," Allen J. Matusow argues that the combination of a faltering economy and the failure of the United States to achieve a decisive victory in Vietnam brought down one of the most powerful political leaders of the postwar era.

One of the truly momentous developments of the postwar era occurred in the realm of race relations. As record numbers of African Americans moved from the South during World War II and gained better-paying jobs in defense industries and greater power and acceptance in northern and western cities, they began to demand an end to discrimination and segregation throughout the nation. The Civil Rights and Voting Rights acts of 1964 and 1965 capped a decades-long struggle by African Americans to end discrimination and achieve equal opportunity in American society. In "After Civil Rights: The African American Working and Middle Classes," Robin D.G. Kelley explores the impact of the civil rights revolution on African Americans in the decade following the passage of the civil right acts. He finds that a nationwide economic downturn during the 1970s crippled attempts by the black working class to achieve equality in the workplace while, at the same time, some black professionals and entrepreneurs prospered because of the removal of formal racial barriers. This divergence, he notes, would continue to shape African American life through the twentieth and into the twenty-first century.

As the economy began to recover in the late 1980s and boomed during the 1990s, Americans went on a national spending spree. Moving from modest homes to "McMansions," leasing expensive and prestigious cars and SUVs, investing in the stock market via the Internet, millions of Americans redefined the middle-class standard of living. In "The Insidious Cycle of Work and Spend," Juliet B. Schor evaluates the consequences of this new lifestyle. She finds that the middle-class emulation of wealthy lifestyles has come at the price of unremitting work, little leisure, and a frantic pace of life.

Past Traces

The 1950s is usually thought of as a decade of gray conformity, personal repression, and political conservatism. Yet from this seemingly uncreative period emerged a number of powerful reform movements among America's youth. This essay begins with an early document of the student movement, the Port Huron Statement of the Students for a Democratic Society. In it, the SDS articulates a view of American life very different from their own experiences growing up during the 1950s.

Students for a Democratic Society, *The Port Huron Statement (1962)*

We are the people of this generation, bred in at least modest comfort, housed now in the universities, looking uncomfortably to the world we inherit.

When we were kids the United States was the wealthiest and strongest country in the world; the only one with the atom bomb, the least scarred by modern war, an initiator of the United Nations that we thought would distribute Western influence throughout the world. Freedom and equality for each individual, government of, by, and for the people—these American values we found good, principles by which we could live as men. Many of us began maturing in complacency.

As we grew, however, our comfort was penetrated by events too troubling to dismiss. First, the permeating and victimizing fact of human degradation, symbolized by the Southern struggle against racial bigotry, compelled most of us from silence to activism. Second, the enclosing fact of the Cold War, symbolized by the presence of the Bomb, brought awareness that we ourselves, and our friends, and millions of abstract "others" we knew more directly because of our common peril, might die at any time. We might deliberately ignore, or avoid or fail to feel all other human problems, but not these two, for these were too immediate and crushing in their impact, too challenging in the demand that we as individuals take the responsibility for encounter and resolution.

13

The Making of the 1960s Youth Culture

Maurice Isserman and Michael Kazin

The 1960s was a watershed in American life. Not only did the Civil Rights and Voting Rights acts of 1964 and 1965 begin the process of serious integration of African Americans and other minorities into the mainstream of American society, but the women's rights movement that grew directly out of the civil rights struggles promised to negate centuries of subordinate status for American women. The 1960s was, by all accounts, a decade of revolutionary change.

But the inclusion of hitherto excluded people and their full participation in American life was only one part of the social and cultural revolution of the 1960s. Equally significant was the growth of a youth culture that sought to transform America from a nation of cultural and sexual repression to one that embraced freedom in all aspects of personal life. Based on the remarkable economic prosperity of the post-World War II era and coupled with a rejection of the hypocritical lifestyles of their parents' generation, this youth culture sought a complete overturning of American cultural life. Central to this new culture was the widespread availability of reliable birth control, the explosive growth of rock music, and experimentation with drugs. Whatever its ultimate aims, the youth culture embraced in singer Janis Joplin's phrase, "sex, drugs, and rock-and-roll."

In this essay, Maurice Isserman and Michael Kazin explore the roots of this cultural triad, tracing the attitudes of the 1960s youth culture to its roots in the "Beat" culture of the 1950s. Though oppositional and iconoclastic in nature, Isserman and Kazin argue that the 1960s youth culture ultimately sought to create a true sense of integration and community for all Americans.

In October 1955, an announcement of a poetry reading circulated around the North Beach neighborhood of San Francisco. "Remarkable collection of angels all gathered at once in the same spot," it promised. "Wine, music, dancing girls, serious poetry, free satori. Small collection for wine and postcards, Charming event." The venue was the Six Gallery, a converted auto-repair shop.

Both the reading and the whimsical notice were the creation of 29-year-old writer Allen Ginsberg. During the previous decade, Ginsberg's life had wildly diverged from values most Americans held dear. A Jew and a homosexual, he entered Columbia University in 1944 on scholarship. Within months, he was suspended for writing an obscenity on his dirty dormitory window to irk a careless cleaning lady. Then he got arrested for letting a poetic drifter named Herbert Huncke hide stolen goods in his apartment. To avoid jail, Ginsberg agreed to spend several months in a psychiatric hospital. There, he and a fellow patient feigned insanity by smashing down on the keys of a piano while screaming at the top of their lungs.

Ginsberg was an exceedingly generous soul. He delighted in sharing his poetic visions, his semen, and a variety of mind-altering drugs with an ever expanding number of male writers—including erstwhile college football player Jack Kerouac, who later published the autobiographical novel *On the Road*. Ginsberg also read deeply in the sacred texts of Zen Buddhism and became a lifelong devotee (which explains his reference to satori—Japanese for "a state of enlightenment").

With little money, the young poet worked at odd jobs and slept on borrowed beds in various Manhattan apartments belonging to his friends. Ginsberg also found time to travel around North America. In Mexico, he marveled at intricate temple ruins, took long hikes wearing nothing but shoes, built a set of wooden drums that he played at all hours, and harvested cocoa beans alongside Mayan Indians. He hitchhiked to Florida, flew to Cuba in expectation of orgies that did not occur, and then returned to Greenwich Village.

By the time he arrived in the San Francisco Bay Area in the mid-'50s, Ginsberg was at the center of a small but growing band of young artists and erotic adventurers one of them dubbed the Beat Generation. "Beat" was Jack Kerouac's term; in half-serious tribute to his Catholic upbringing, he claimed it was short for "beatitude." By 1955 a few articles about the group had appeared in newspapers and small magazines. But most Americans were quite unaware of their outrageous escapades and unorthodox spiritual quests. That would change after Ginsberg's performance at the Six Gallery.

Ginsberg was nervous as he stepped to the front of the small stage to recite a long poem entitled, simply, "Howl." He had never read poetry in public before and had bolstered himself with many glasses of cheap wine. But almost immediately, his exuberance began to flow:

> I saw the best minds of my generation destroyed by madness, starving hysterical naked,
> dragging themselves through negro streets at dawn looking for an angry fix,
> angelheaded hipsters burning for the ancient heavenly connection to the starry dynamo in the machinery of light . . .

From that opening to the poem's last lines—"in my dreams you walk, dripping from a sea-journey on the highway across America in tears to the door of my cottage in the Western night"—Ginsberg swirled together candid glimpses of his own life with laments about the damage American culture had done to maverick souls. Ginsberg's name for that culture was "Moloch," a Semitic deity who gobbled up children. As the crowd whooped and Kerouac yelled "Go" from a corner of the stage, Ginsberg chanted a series of rapid portraits of the (mostly unnamed) "best minds" on their wild ride of the past decade: "who got busted in their public beards returning through Laredo with a belt of marijuana for New York . . . or purgatoried their torsos night after night with dreams, with drugs, with waking nightmares, alcohol and cock and endless balls." In the face of sexual repression and Cold War hysteria, he and his friends had emerged, strangely triumphant.

That evening at the Six Gallery was a declaration of independence from the rigid, authoritarian order the Beats believed was throttling the nation. It enabled the Beats to create themselves as an icon-smashing legend. Rebel dramatist Michael McClure later wrote, "In all our memories no one had been so outspoken in poetry before—we had gone beyond a point of no return—and we were ready for it. . . . None of us wanted to go back to the gray, chill, militaristic silence . . . to the spiritual drabness." "Howl" was indeed a protest against social evils. But Ginsberg drew no distinction between those who resisted Moloch by letting "themselves be fucked in the ass by saintly motorcyclists" and other sorts of heretics who handed out "Supercommunist pamphlets in Union Square," mecca of a once-influential American left. Surviving on one's own terms was rebellion enough.

Some powerful San Franciscans clearly agreed. In May 1957, vice-seeking local police arrested Lawrence Ferlinghetti, the publisher of *Howl and Other Poems,* at his North Beach bookstore where the book was sold. The trial was reported around the world; it ended in aquittal. In his decision, the presiding judge hewed to the standard for obscenity recently laid down by the Supreme Court; "Howl," ruled the judge, was *not* entirely lacking in social importance."

Sexual controversy proved a splendid form of advertising. Ginsberg's brief volume sold well over 100,000 copies during the next few years. And, in 1966, the Supreme Court, in the case of *Redrup v. New York,* essentially abandoned its role as a moral guardian of the arts. Liberal intellectuals argued that censorship could backfire, encouraging the victims of repression to seek "unhealthy" sexual outlets.

The Beats helped to plant seeds that would sprout, quite luxuriantly, during the 1960s and after—particularly among white people in their teens and twenties. One was a desire for sexual adventure, untethered to the values of monogamy and heterosexuality that had reigned

supreme in the Western world since the dawn of Christianity. Another was glorification of the outlaw spirit, as embodied in men and women who viewed conventional jobs and sanitized entertainment as akin to a living death. Millions of young people would act out such beliefs with the aid of illegal drugs like marijuana, peyote, and especially LSD. The Beats also generated a romantic yearning for "authentic" experiences, which they associated with poor and working-class people, black and white and Latino. The cultural downscaling of middle-class white youths would take place most energetically through the mushrooming medium of rock 'n' roll. In 1960 an obscure English band paid tribute to Ginsberg and friends by changing their name to the Beatles.

The congregation of Beats also helped generate a new burst of spirituality—at once more personal, eclectic, and fervent than the kind found in most established churches and synagogues. Seeking alternative routes to the transcendent, many Americans explored aspects of the Buddhist and Hindu traditions, and invented their own recombinant faiths. Finally, "Howl" proclaimed the perilous beauty of small, beloved communities composed of rebels loyal to no one but each other and bound by a common vision of hedonistic liberation. To belong to such a fellowship was to believe that one grasped the cause of all contemporary miseries and, perhaps, possessed the key to healing them.

Such notions flowered among members of a generation whose dreams seemed unlimited. Familiar with a world of mass consumption, many middle-class white baby boomers believed that an era of perpetual affluence and total freedom of choice was at hand. They were eager, at least for a few years, to forego the quest for economic security and its material tokens that had driven their elders. By the early '60s, youth communities had sprung up on the outskirts of college campuses, often in cheap housing available near black or Latino ghettos. South Campus in Berkeley, Mifflin Street in Madison, Wisconsin, and the neighborhood behind the Drag in Austin, Texas, were among the more famous of such venues. Surrounded by one's peers and largely free from the responsibilities of career, family, and mortgage, young people could experiment with their bodies and minds in ways that usually shocked and enraged older people raised amid the constricted horizons of the Great Depression and World War II.

At the same time, the "generation gap" was often a matter of differences more stylistic than ideological. Cultural rebels were acting out a vision of individual fulfillment as old as the free market and the Protestant Reformation. "To dance beneath the diamond sky with one hand waving free," sang Bob Dylan who, as a teenager, read Ginsberg's poetry and later became his friend. Young people who consumed psychedelic ("mind-revealing") drugs and attended rock concerts grumbled about big corporations and the warfare/welfare state, but had little notion of what might replace them.

Meanwhile, some of the nation's biggest corporations quickly learned to tap the generation gap with slogans like Pepsi's ("For those who think young") and low-slung, fast cars like the Ford Mustang. "To be young is to be with it," remarked a business journalist in 1968. "Youth is getting the hard sell." Advertising agencies, filled with people who considered themselves hip and creative, churned out commercials that made fun of conformity, snobs, and the very products they were selling. "Moloch" proved to be a most accommodating fellow.

Still, there was a rebellious edge to the youth culture of the 1960s that retains its capacity to fascinate some Americans and to repel others. What was fresh and daring about the phenomenon always intermingled with its tendency to equate freedom with bigger and better thrills. Many young people combined the breaking of taboos with an effortless shift in consumer habits. Others followed the Beats in exalting the former and scorning the latter. Inevitably, the persistent hierarchy of wealth, race, and status framed one's opinions and cultural options. The lifestyle of a white suburbanite who attended Harvard or MIT mixed uneasily with that of a black youth from across the river in Roxbury who, after a few years of high school and a few weeks of boot camp, was likely to end up in Vietnam.

One way to understand this complex, but seldom boring, phenomenon is to focus on sex, drugs, and rock 'n' roll—the triad that became a clichéd marker for the entire popular culture of the young. That daring experiences could so rapidly turn into commonplace ones helps reveal how much changed during those years—and why many Americans feared and resisted the cultural transformation.

What *was* the "sexual revolution" of the 1960s? Most significantly, it was an insurgency rooted in the conviction that the erotic should be celebrated as an utterly normal part of life. Thus, Hugh Hefner's *Playboy* magazine helped legitimate the mass marketing of female nudity—by coupling abundant photos of young women (accompanying text stressed their wholesome values and career ambitions) to a "philosophy," that equated multiple sex partners with the drinking of good liquor and the wearing of sleek clothes. Thus, popular comedian Lenny Bruce mocked censors who had no problem with violence in films but forbid any depiction of sexual intercourse (which Bruce, a Jew, called *schtupping*—Yiddish slang—to avoid trouble with the police): "Well for kids to watch killing—Yes; but *schtupping*—No! Cause if they watch *schtup* pictures, they may do it some day." Thus, high school girls screamed orgasmically at the very sight of Elvis Presley and the Beatles. Some ran *en masse* after their idols and tore away bits of their clothing. Thus, Helen Gurley Brown's 1962 best-seller *Sex and the Single Girl* encouraged her typical reader to have sex whenever "her body wants to" and gave birth to *Cosmopolitan* magazine. Thus, many gay men and lesbians rejected their burdens of self-hatred and "came out" to friends, families, and coworkers.

The most avid participants in all this were in their teens and twenties, the age of sexual awakening. Millions of the young abandoned old strictures against premarital intercourse, oral sex, and candid public discussion of all aspects of lovemaking. In the "underground" newspapers that proliferated in youth communities, one could find guilt-free narratives of erotic experiences and personal ads that either offered or requested partners of every conceivable persuasion. Sweeping changes in technology and the law lessened the fear of pregnancy. The birth control pill, first available in 1960, and the spread of legal abortions in a number of states, gave young women, for the first time, options they themselves could control.

Higher education was in the front line of the sexual "revolution." Gradually over the course of the '60s, students pressured college authorities, who had traditionally acted as surrogate parents, to stop policing their carnal lives. Attacked first and most successfully were "parietal" rules that strictly limited the hours when men could visit women in their dormitory rooms and vice versa. Administrators were more reluctant to acquiesce to off-campus cohabitation. In 1968 Barnard College disciplined a student named Linda LeClair for lying about the fact that she was living with her boyfriend. Hundreds of her fellow students, as well as many faculty members, protested the decision. In the end, college officials meted out a rather strange "punishment": LeClair was barred from the Barnard cafeteria.

Those who argued the cause of sexual liberty in the '60s could cite some well-known studies in their defense. The most prominent of these was the Kinsey Report, two thick volumes of interviews with some 18,000 white adults about their sexual practices. The report—a volume on men published in 1948 and one on women in 1953—exploded the myth of a puritanical America. Over a third of the men told the biologist Alfred Kinsey and his team of researchers that they had achieved orgasm via a homosexual act, while a large majority admitted to premarital intercourse, often with a prostitute. Over half the women confessed to sexual activity before marriage; most, like the men, said they masturbated regu-

larly when no partner was available. The gulf between the public morality of Americans and their private pleasures was hard to ignore. In a golden age of social science, the Kinsey Report set a new standard for sexual realism.

But critics quickly pointed out that Kinsey and his associates were trafficking in secondhand knowledge. The researchers made no attempt to judge whether people had told them the truth. That was not a problem for Dr. William Masters and his coworker (and future wife) Virginia Johnson. In a laboratory on the campus of Washington University in St. Louis, the couple observed hundreds of men and women having orgasms, some with a partner and others through masturbation.

Masters and Johnson shared a mission—to help every adult achieve maximum sexual pleasure. In 1966 huge sales of their first book, *Human Sexual Response,* seemed to further that goal. Readers who managed to slog through the couple's often obscure prose (and millions of others who read or heard their findings distilled in the media) learned one critical fact: the clitoris, not the vagina, was the site of female orgasm. Masters and Johnson also discovered that women could have multiple orgasms in rapid order; thus, the female of the species was sexually superior to the male. The couple also recommended various methods, based on their research, for curing impotence and premature ejaculation. Despite or perhaps because of their assumption that good sex was merely a matter of correct technique, Masters and Johnson seemed to many Americans like liberators. One newspaper headlined a glowing review of their work, "A Short Course in How to Be Happy."

Homosexuals probably benefited most from the new tolerance toward sexual matters. Until the 1960s, with few exceptions, their intimate lives had to be kept hidden. Exposure stripped uncounted numbers of men and women of their children, jobs, military careers, and reputations. Every authority—from churches to the federal government to the American Psychiatric Association—agreed that homosexuality was a form of "perversion" whose victims had to be cured, lest their depravity spread to others. Metropolises harbored a homosexual underground of bars, restaurants, and pornographic movie theaters. But such institutions were always fair game for police raids. In the early 1950s, police in the District of Columbia arrested over a thousand adults a year for homosexual activity, and comparable totals were registered in other big cities. Guilt and self-hatred drove many homosexuals to alcoholism and others to suicide.

In the '50s, the Kinsey Report and the ribald candor of the Beats cracked open the wall of fear and loathing. In the '60s, the youth culture's embrace of open and promiscuous sexuality dismantled it. By the end of the decade, a growing number of homosexuals were proudly calling themselves "gay" and celebrating behavior they had once felt forced to conceal. Some gay activists even advised "straights" to learn from their example. The essayist Paul Goodman wrote in 1969:

> queer life . . . can be profoundly democratizing, throwing together every class and group more than heterosexuality does. . . . I myself have cruised rich, poor, middle class, and petit bourgeois; black, white, yellow and brown; scholars, jocks and dropouts; farmers, seamen, railroad men, heavy industry, light manufacturing, communications, business and finance, civilians, soldiers and sailors, and once or twice cops. There is a kind of political meaning, I guess, in the fact that there are so many types of attractive human beings.

Nearly all the ardent champions of the new sexuality, whether straight or gay, were male. Young women could applaud the "discovery" of clitoral orgasms and the loosening of restrictions on where they could live and with whom. But it was men who produced the words and pictures that challenged obscenity statutes. And only men equated personal liberation with the desire, even the right to have sex with a diversity of partners, regardless of emotional commitment. This conviction united Hugh Hefner, a mansion-dwelling millionaire, with the working-class revolutionary John Sinclair, flamboyant leader of a popular Detroit rock band, the MC-5, and of the White Panther Party, a radical youth group briefly active in the Midwest. "We have found," asserted Sinclair, "that there are three essential human activities of the greatest importance to all persons, and that people are . . . healthy in proportion to their involvement in these activities: rock and roll, dope, and fucking in the streets. . . . We suggest the three in combination, all the time."

For biological and cultural reasons, few women had ever embraced such a raging vision. The male libido, when unrestrained by custom or law, often led to rape, unwanted pregnancy, and/or abandonment. In 1968 the White Panthers slipped into their manifesto the line, "Fuck your woman so hard . . . she can't stand up." Some men reading that cringed, but, for women, it confirmed the link between sex and subordination that all the glee about "liberation" had somehow neglected. This became a major theme of the thousands of "consciousness-raising" groups that sprang up by the end of the decade—free spaces where women spoke honestly about the pain that inequality and a lack of both respect and self-respect had caused.

Budding feminists angrily rejected the countercultural image of the braless madonna, content merely to bake bread and have sex with her "old man." The male hippie became a figure to condemn. "Here they come," mocked writer Leni Wildflower at the end of the '60s, "Those strutting roosters, those pathetic male chauvinists. . . . Here come the freaks in those tight bell-bottoms, tie-dyed T-shirts which their 'old lady' . . . made for them. . . . Male liberators, you are stepping on my neck." The flowering of a new "sisterhood" that fused intimacy with a wariness toward men, nudged some heterosexual women into experimenting with lesbian relationships, and encouraged life-long lesbians to speak their minds. Could any man, trained as he was to dominate the other gender, really make a woman happy? In the erotic realm, at a time when porno theater marquees were pitching "THE INCREDIBLE SEX REV-OLUTION," feminists may have been asking the most radical question of all.

Were any revelations to be found in drugs? Since the '60s, it has been risky to offer even the most qualified assent. Parents and teachers, government officials and journalists condemn the chemicals most identified with the bygone youth culture—marijuana, LSD, peyote, and psilocybin—as nothing but instruments of self-destruction, for both individuals and society. Slogans like "Just say no" substitute for rea-soned debate about the motivations of drug users and the effect of the chemicals on mind and body. Members of new generations con-sume the substances anyway, although few expect more than a short-lived thrill. It is diffi-cult to capture a time when many young people, and not a few of their elders, believed the ingestion of certain substances was the pivot of a cultural renaissance. "Drugs were the fundamental text," remembered critic Geoffrey O'Brien, "If you had not read the book, you couldn't participate in the discussion that followed." Or as rock icon Jimi Hendrix sang, "Scuse me, while I kiss the sky."

The most common drug in the '60s was marijuana, nearly as ubiquitous in youth com-munities as was bottled beer everywhere else in America. The potency of the "grass" smoked or swallowed varied widely—from the hallu-cinogenic to the mildly intoxicating. As with any consumer product, so did the price. That marijuana had been illegal since 1937 (simple possession was a felony in many states) did little to slow the commerce. It may even have increased it, as young people bonded against what seemed an irrational, vindictive prohibi-tion. Few restrictions were placed on sales of alcohol and tobacco products, despite the obvi-ous risks to public health. So why were America's rulers and many conservative citi-zens so frightened by the dreamy, often erotic qualities of marijuana? The answers only heightened the cultural conflict that Allen Ginsberg and his friends had declared in the mid-'50s.

But it was LSD, the acronym for lysergic acid diethlyamide #25, that occasioned the greatest claims and the greatest censure. Ginsberg journeyed to Auschwitz in 1967 and, standing before the entrance to the camp where Nazis had slaughtered millions of Jews and other victims, glibly recommended "that every-body who hears my voice, directly or indirectly, try the chemical LSD at least once, every man and woman and child in good health over the age of 14." Fellow poet Gary Snyder com-mented, more prosaically, "Acid just happened to turn up as the product of this particular soci-ety, to correct its own excesses."

Such statements appalled Theodore Roszak, a professor at San Francisco State, who popu-larized the term "counter-culture." "The gadget-happy American has always been a figure of fun," wrote Roszak in 1969, "because of his facile assumption that there exists a tech-nological solution to every human problem. It only took the great psychedelic crusade to per-fect the absurdity by proclaiming that personal salvation and the social revolution can be packed in a capsule."

Ironically, the object of so much promise and dread was discovered by accident. One April day in 1943, Swiss chemist Albert Hofmann was at work near Geneva at the sprawling complex of Sandoz Laboratories. Hofmann decided to synthesize a fresh batch of a compound made from rye fungi that he had created five years earlier and put away. In the process of mixing the chemicals, Hofmann spilled a small amount on his fingertips. Quite soon his diary notes, the scientist was over-come by "a remarkable but not unpleasant state of intoxication, characterized by an intense stimulation of the imagination and an altered state of awareness of the world." He closed his eyes and "there surged before me a succession of fantastic, rapidly changing image[s] of a striking reality and depth, alter-nating with a vivid, kaleidoscopic play of colors." This continued for almost three hours. Albert Hofmann had taken the world's first acid trip.

After World War II, Sandoz quietly began marketing LSD to psychiatrists and other scientific researchers in Europe and North America. But, in the United States, two quite different sorts of client latched onto the amazing compound. One, predictably, was the bohemian artist who sought to test and broaden the imagination. Early trippers included jazz musicians Thelonious Monk and Dizzy Gillespie, as well as British novelist Aldous Huxley, then a resident of southern California. But an equally keen customer was the Central Intelligence Agency.

Hofmann's invention seemed, at first, to be a spymaster's dream come true. Under its influence, an enemy agent might divulge secrets lodged deep in his or her unconscious. LSD had neither odor, color, nor taste. Small quantities sprayed into a room or diluted in a water supply could, it was hoped, defeat one's foes humanely. Disoriented and frightened, they would simply surrender.

During the 1950s, the agency spent millions of dollars to test the miracle drug. One group, working out of CIA headquarters in Langley, Virginia, did some self-experimentation. A staff member would dose his morning coffee with LSD and then become subject for a day. One man wept after tripping and refused "to go back to a place where I wouldn't be able to hold on to this kind of beauty." Another ran across a bridge over the Potomac River and went temporarily mad before his colleagues rescued him. Every automobile, he swore, looked like a bloodthirsty monster.

The CIA and the Army's Chemical Corps also tested LSD on hundreds of unwitting subjects, despite a provision of the Nuremberg Code, signed in the wake of the Holocaust, that forbade such experiments. Some of the victims were government scientists, others were prisoners, mental patients, and clients of prostitutes— all coerced into doing their bit for national security. A handful of suicides resulted, and a larger number of severe psychoses. And the CIA gained nothing. By the end of the '50s, those in charge abandoned research on the "magic" drug. Under its influence, subjects had failed to give accurate information and often failed to concentrate on the interrogation process itself.

In the meantime, however, word of the drug's existence had reached the Ivy League. At Harvard's Department of Psychology, junior professors Timothy Leary and Richard Alpert began in 1960, giving psilocybin mushrooms to selected students and other curious guests— including Allen Ginsberg. Within two years, the pair had graduated, enthusiastically, to LSD. They dutifully published scientific papers on their research in respected academic journals. But fellow professors criticized them for indulging freely in the drugs under study, and parents complained when, according to Leary, "bright youths phoned home to announce that they'd found God and discovered the secret of the universe." In 1963 Leary left Harvard and became a relentless promoter of LSD consciousness. After Congress outlawed the drug in 1960, a series of arrests only added to his fame. Alpert began a personal voyage that soon resulted in his conversion to Hinduism and a change of name to Baba Ram Dass.

Among the young, the ban on LSD only enhanced its luster. By the late '60s, one could buy the drug in most college towns and big cities. The greatest supplies, and lowest prices, could be found on either coast. In Berkeley, a young chemist known as Owsley (short for Augustus Owsley Stanley III) got rich producing some 12 million high-quality doses from his own underground laboratory and distributing them throughout northern California.

A certain lore grew up around the potent liquid. Which form of it was purest and strongest—on a square of blotter paper, on a slab of clear gelatin, or on multicolored tablets? The drug's allure was enhanced by learning that many of the world's most prominent rock musicians were using and writing songs about it—the Beatles, Bob Dylan, the Rolling Stones, Jimi Hendrix, the Grateful Dead, and Jefferson Airplane. LSD never achieved the popularity— or cultural acceptance—of marijuana which became ubiquitous in mass gatherings of the college-aged young by the late 1960s. But "tripping" had become an indispensable rite of initiation; one emerged from the experience with matchless stories to tell.

One set of these tales brimmed with oracular glory, while another set warned against the equation of self-knowledge with getting high. It was safest to take LSD with a band of friends, at least one of whom had tripped before. Such an environment could help create an experience of intense pleasure and emotional catharsis. A group of trippers might begin by talking quietly and listening to music; then one person would notice an object in the room, on the grass, or just focus on a stray remark and mention it to the others—and the whole gathering would break into wild laughter.

Many spoke of feeling saner and more aware of their thoughts while "on acid" than during normal life. The chemical laid bare one's obsessions and focused the mind on what seemed the greater spiritual unity present in the natural world—a common theme of mystics in a variety of cultures. As Aldous Huxley wrote about a trip on mescaline, whose effects mirrored those of LSD: "what Adam had seen on the morning of creation—the miracle, moment by moment, of naked existence . . . flowers shining within their own inner light and all but quivering under the pressure of the significance with which they were charged." In mundane terms, LSD made it possible to have a decent conversation with a tree.

But if LSD opened a portal to the extraordinary, it also screened out the rational. Trippers mistook the obvious for great insight; acid wisdom often reduced itself to disjointed rambling about the wonders of a drink of water or the setting sun. The day after he first took LSD, the writer Arthur Koestler told Timothy Leary, "This is wonderful no doubt. But it is fake. . . . I solved the secret of the universe last night, but this morning I forgot what it was."

The belief that acid was a magic potion that would change one's life—or the arrangements of society—was a terrible delusion. Serious depression struck many a persistent tripper,

and some turned to drugs like heroin to soothe a mind jarred and jazzed instead of opened. To parry "straight" critics, acid devotees routinely cited all the legal chemicals—caffeine, nicotine, tranquilizers, barbiturates—that Americans consumed in huge quantities. By what right, they asked, do you condemn *our* choice of drugs? But the question negated the claim that psychedelics were a force for liberation. In the '60s, the Du Pont company began to advertise itself as providing "Better Living through Chemistry." Hippie street merchants sold buttons and multicolored posters emblazoned with the same words.

And the bond of drugs produced some horrific consequences. Thousands of young people moved to San Francisco's Haight–Ashbury neighborhood ("the Haight") in the mid-'60s seeking, as had the Beats a decade earlier, both sensual thrills and spiritual enlightenment. Such brilliant local bands as the Grateful Dead and Jefferson Airplane catered to the new bohemians. Soon the lush green hills of Golden Gate Park, adjacent to the Haight, were packed with barefooted adolescents and young adults getting high on marijuana and LSD. Many of these people had little or no money and no plans to get a job. So they lived off the generosity of relatives, local businesses and, for several months, a group of anarchists called the Diggers who distributed free food and used clothing.

The Haight was an instant village with no moral center, where drugged-out vapidity passed for self-knowledge. Writer Joan Didion spent several weeks there in the spring of 1967 and sent back numbing reports from the new cultural front: young people shifting to hard drugs like heroin and amphetamine after a spate of "bad" acid trips, adopting new lovers and new "organic" diets with the same mercurial bemusement. Didion met one 5-year old girl who remarked, quite matter-of-factly, that she was "in High Kindergarten"; her mother routinely dosed her with LSD and peyote. What she had witnessed, remarked Didion, was "the desperate attempt of a handful of pathetically unequipped children to create a community in a social vacuum." The Haight was clearly a village without a future.

In contrast, rock and roll was definitely here to stay. The music rapidly conquered the tastes and swayed the emotions of people whom other aspects of the youth culture had only grazed. LSD and sexual liberty were repellent to most churchgoing whites and blacks in the South. But they generally adored both Chuck Berry and Elvis Presley; soul singers like Aretha Franklin and Otis Redding also claimed fervent fans on both sides of the color line. By the mid-'70s, Americans were spending more on rock tapes and records than on movies and sports events—and four-fifths of all recordings were rock. All over the globe, young people who could buy or borrow a guitar were trying to emulate the musical avatars whose sounds filled the air and their imaginations.

The diffusion of rock and roll was one of the wonders of the postwar world. Emerging in the early '50s from the urban black music called rhythm and blues, rock quickly revealed its protean nature, altering every species of popular music—folk, country and western, jazz, romantic pop, Mexican ballads, even Christian hymns. Cheap, portable devices—the transistor radio and the 45 rpm recording—as well as high-quality car radios helped weld rock fans to their music in a way no earlier style had matched. The pioneers of rock seldom paused to reflect upon the cultural sea change they had initiated; they were content to reap the rewards of fame, monetary and otherwise. Still, as critic Greil Marcus wrote, "they delivered a new version of America with their music, and more people than anyone can count are still trying to figure out how to live in it."

The newness began with a critical truth: the roots of rock and roll were mainly black. The term itself derives from services held in rural Holiness churches in the Deep South during the '20s and '30s. There, congregations of African American laborers and domestics "rocked and reeled" to fast, bluesy rhythms played on guitars, horns, and drums. Since the days of slavery, the black church had been developing a style of singing—the call-and-response pattern

and percussive accents that artists like Ray Charles and James Brown adapted to secular purposes in the 1950s. At the same time, the creators of rock freely borrowed whatever they needed—melodies, chord progressions, lyrics—from other musical traditions; particularly significant were the ballads and twangy guitar sounds of Scotch-Irish Protestants whose ancestors had settled in the foothills and mountains of the South. But rock and roll always remained a hybrid grafted from robust black stock.

Ironically, that helps to explain why rock had such enormous appeal to young Americans who knew nothing of gospel music and didn't suffer from Jim Crow. Like the Beats, many whites in high school and college viewed black popular culture as a vibrant, emotionally honest alternative to a dominant culture they experienced as safe, boring, and hypocritical. In his 1957 essay "The White Negro," Norman Mailer had made clear that "in this wedding of the white and the black it was the Negro who brought the cultural dowry."

Mailer's own examples were jazz and marijuana, but rock music provided more salient and infinitely more profitable ones. Elvis Presley modeled himself on black bluesmen like Arthur Crudup, and one of his first hits was a cover of Crudup's "That's All Right." In 1956 Elvis said of his music, "The colored folks been singing it and playing it . . . for more years than I know. . . . I used to hear old Arthur Crudup bang his box the way I do now, and I said if I ever got to the place where I could feel all old Arthur felt, I'd be a music man like nobody ever saw." Across the Atlantic, white British groups like the Beatles and the Rolling Stones started out playing blues for youths like themselves who longed for the raw authenticity symbolized by such black artists as Muddy Waters and Howlin' Wolf.

The emerging demigods and demigoddesses of rock and roll were hardly the first young whites to adopt black styles. In the nineteenth century, minstrel shows featuring white actors pretending to be slaves were the nation's most popular form of entertainment. In the 1920s, white performers imbibed from the rich Creole musical traditions of New Orleans to create jazz bands that, along with the black combos of Duke Ellington and Count Basie, dominated the airwaves and record charts through the 1940s.

Rock, however, carried a generational charge whose power transcended the sphere of racial borrowing. Spurred by wartime migrations and the end of child labor, teenagers from diverse class backgrounds began flooding into high schools that once had been the nearly exclusive province of affluent whites. Old barriers between musical traditions fell quickly too, as young bands scavenged through a cornucopia of ethnic styles.

Social mingling spawned a taste for rebellion. During the mid-'50s, George "Hound Dog" Lorenz, a white disk jockey broadcasting from Buffalo, gained a huge following among young people of all races. Lorenz sported a goatee and purple trousers, used the "jive" lingo then associated with black musicians, and was a hero to working-class kids who chafed at the self-disciplined lives their parents had led. Meanwhile, in East Los Angeles, Mexican American teenagers like Ritchie Valens were writing and playing rhythm and blues songs with bilingual lyrics.

But rock was not a political insurgency. Cultural leftists like John Sinclair and Abbie Hoffman, a former civil rights organizer, certainly tried to harness the music to their ideological purposes. The White Panthers were an outgrowth of Sinclair's rock band, and Hoffman hailed the birth of a quasi-revolutionary "Woodstock Nation" after the music festival held in a pasture north of New York City in the late summer of 1969 that attracted half a million people who got stoned and frolicked in the mud.

Such efforts to hitch the culture of rock and roll to political rebellion invariably flopped. The crowd at Woodstock booed the flamboyant Hoffman, when, high on LSD, he began denouncing the arrest of Sinclair for possession of marijuana. Peter Townshend, leader of the Who, promptly whacked Hoffman off the stage with his guitar. Rock musicians, even more than most artists, mistrusted political figures who wanted them to articulate a certain message they themselves had not conceived. "Won't get fooled again," chanted the Who in one of their more memorable songs. For reasons of ego or creativity, few rock and rollers joined any contingent of the radical movement. "My music isn't supposed to make you riot," explained Janis Joplin, "It's supposed to make you fuck."

Joplin's own life demonstrated rock's power to reinvent the individual—and its limits as liberation. Growing up with bad skin and a weight problem in the working-class town of Port Arthur, Texas, Joplin had few friends and little prospect of a brighter future. She spent a good deal of time in her room—listening to and writing music, making her own clothes, and taking drugs. A few years after high school, Joplin moved to San Francisco when the Haight–Ashbury scene was in full flower. There, backed by the exuberant band Big Brother and the Holding Company, she began to sing the blues in a most arresting fashion.

To hear Joplin's renditions of such blues standards as "Ball and Chain" and "Piece of My Heart" (originally recorded by black artists) was to glimpse a woman in the throes of shredding her inhibitions by displaying her pain. Joplin alternately moaned, screeched, and purred the lyrics—evoking agony and ecstasy in equal measure. She lured hordes of both male and female fans; the latter copied her wardrobe (feather boas, flowered shifts, and strand upon strand of costume jewelry) and a bit of her bawdy toughness. "It was seeing Janis Joplin that made me resolve, once and for all, not to get my hair straightened," recalled critic Ellen Willis.

But adulation did not make Joplin happy. "Onstage I make love to 25,000 people," she told a reporter, "then I go home alone." After a half-decade of performing, her voice was reduced to a rasp, and she was punctuating road trips with frequent shots of heroin and hard liquor. Once famous for a manner both brash and gentle, Joplin had turned into a bitter and desperate woman. In 1970, she died from an overdose of heroin. Like other rock stars who killed themselves in similar accidents (Elvis Presley and Jimi Hendrix, most prominently), she could not bear the thought of living in the twilight after her surge into the spotlight was done.

Yet millions of young rock fans experienced rock and roll not as romantic tragedy but as a series of tiny discoveries. They quoted and sang scraps of lyrics at school, work, and in bed; melodies, rhythms, and chord changes became elements of a secret language that lost everything in the translation.

Consider the tangled history of "Louie Louie," a song written and first recorded in 1956 by Richard Berry, a black musician from Los Angeles, with his band, the Pharoahs. At home in LA's multiracial potpourri, Berry heard a local Filipino group that sang mostly in Spanish play a version of the tune. He reworked the melody into a mixture of calypso (a popular craze at the time) and a cha-cha, then added new lyrics. A Jamaican sailor tells a sympathetic bartender named Louie about the love who waits for him at home: "There nights and days we sailed the sea. Me think of girl constantly. On the ship, I dream she there. I smell the rose in her hair. Louie, Louie, me gotta go."

The song had a catchy Caribbean beat, the meld of Latin and African styles. But it was heard mainly on the West Coast and sold a decidedly modest 40,000 copies. Berry, who received just two cents per record, moved on to other projects. But, near Seattle, a young white singer named Rockin' Robin Roberts found a copy of "Louie, Louie" in a remainder bin and decided to make the tune his own. Roberts wailed the lyrics instead of crooning them and added the phrase, "Let's give it to 'em, right now!" which turned the song into a sexual anthem of sorts. In the Pacific Northwest, his version became a regional hit.

One spring morning in 1963, the Kingsmen cut another recording of "Louie, Louie" in their hometown of Portland, Oregon, and unintentionally created a rock legend. While rehearsing the tune, Jack Ely, the band's lead singer, had to strain to reach the microphone above him; fatigue and the braces on his teeth caused him to slur the lyrics even more. The drummer and lead guitarist were nervous and so performed more crudely than in their many live gigs. Having finished the unpolished runthough, the Kingsmen were amazed to hear their manager rave, "That was *great,* man, you never did that song better." Disk jockeys were soon playing the song as a novelty.

Through a manic whim of fortune, the Kingsmen's version of "Louie Louie" rapidly shed its status as a joke recording and became the second-best-selling single in the country. The rough instrumental was, no doubt, part of the reason; it made the Kingsmen sound like a bar band at the climax of a long night—careening somewhere between ecstasy and exhaustion. But what made the song unforgettable was Ely's incomprehensible vocal. What *was* that guy singing? Mythical lyrics proliferated. Most were pornographic, transforming the lovesick sailor into an emblem of every teenaged boy's lust-filled fantasies. Parents and ministers protested, and J. Edgar Hoover's FBI soon took up the case. Following more than two years of an investigation that employed the latest in audio technology, the bureau concluded that the lyrics were "unintelligible at any speed." Remarkably, no agent ever questioned Jack Ely.

Such stupidity helped ensure "Louie Louie" a long and prosperous life. If the raunchy-sounding song was officially deemed a cultural menace, then it *had* to be good. In decades to come, over 200 different versions were recorded—by punk bands, surf bands, swing bands, Latin bands, Russian bands, French bands, two college marching bands, and the comedian John Belushi for the soundtrack of the movie *Animal House*. When Richard Berry died in 1997, the *New York Times* graced him with a lengthy obituary, solely because of his creation of a sea chantey then more than four decades old. Berry had lived to see "Louie

Louie" enshrined in the cultural pantheon of he '60s—a mediocre song that became an underground phenomenon and grew over time into a quirky kind of generational statement. Therein lay the beauty of rock and roll; anyone of a certain age could appreciate the joke.

* * *

In a society that now takes flamboyant self-expression for granted, the youth culture of the 1960s may seem no more than a grand hedonistic fling. How could millions of American kids have equated smoking dope, having sex, and listening to rock 'n' roll with the making of radical change? Granted, the pursuit of individual happiness, enhanced by new consumer products, was not an innovation on the American scene. And many young people only dabbled with new sounds and substances or strained to act hip—often injuring themselves and others in the process.

But thoroughgoing cultural rebels—following the Beats—were seeking to build self-regulating *communities* that would heal and transcend the multiple ruptures—of race, class, religion, and political ideology—that embattled their elders. "Freedom"—sexual and chemical—was supposed to be only a means to that end. In its utopian moments, the youth culture groped towards becoming what German emigré philosopher Herbert Marcuse (a popular writer and teacher in the '60s) called, "the Great Refusal—the protest against that which is." Radicals believed that the path to defeating repression, both societal and personal, lay in the rapid spread of a sensual, creative lifestyle. In an economy whose abundance would be equally shared, millions would cooperate to build a more pleasurable world. In 1968 the young French radical Daniel Cohn-Bendit put it well, "I am a revolutionary because it is the best way of living."

GLOSSARY

Baby Boomers: The generation born as part of a sudden, steep increase in the American birthrate in the decade and a half following World War II.

Generation Gap: A broad difference in values and attitudes between young people and their parents during the 1960s.

Vietnam: Reference to the Vietnam War (1959–1974) and the drafting of young men to serve in the U.S. armed forces there.

Woodstock: A rock festival that took place near Woodstock, New York, on August 15, 16, and 17, 1969, and that became a symbol of the 1960s American counterculture and a milestone in the history of rock music.

IMPLICATIONS

With its emphasis on "sex, drugs, and rock-and-roll," the youth culture of the 1960s sought to transform American and world culture. Do you think that the 1960s youth culture achieved its goals of transforming American society? In what ways was its influence positive? In what ways negative?

The growing prominence and effectiveness of the Black Civil Rights Movement during the mid-1960s brought other minority groups to form local coalitions and national organizations to advance the position of their own groups in the public arena. One of the earliest of these groups was the National Chicano Youth Liberation Front, an organization of Hispanic youth led by activist, Rudolfo "Corky" Gonzales. The first convention of this early Chicano movement met in Denver, Colorado, in March 1969 and brought forth a variety of responses. One of the most critical of these responses came from Enriqueta Longeaux y Vásquez, an early Chicana feminist. Reprinted here are her observations about the fledging movement and its first convention. Much like African American feminists, Longeaux y Vásquez was as critical of the male-dominated leadership of the movement as of white society itself.

Enriqueta Longeaux y Vásquez, *A Chicana Critique of the Chicano Movement (1969)*

While attending a Raza conference in Colorado this year, I went to one of the workshops that were held to discuss the role of the Chicana woman. When the time came for the women to make their presentation to the full conference, the only thing that the workshop representative said was this: "It was the consensus of the group that the Chicana woman does not want to be liberated."

As a woman who has been faced with having to live as a member of the "Mexican American" minority as a breadwinner and a mother raising children, living in housing projects and having much concern for other humans leading to much community involvement, this was quite a blow. I could have cried. Surely we could have at least come up with something to add to that statement. I sat back and thought, why? Why? I understood why the statement had been made, and I realized that going along with the feelings of the men at the convention was perhaps the best thing to do at the time.

Looking at our history, I can see why this would be true. The role of the Chicana woman has been a very strong one, although a silent one. When the woman has seen the suffering of her peoples, she has always responded bravely and as a totally committed and equal human. My mother told me of how, during the time of Pancho Villa and the revolution in Mexico, she saw the men march through the village continually for three days and then she saw the battalion of women marching for a whole day. The women carried food and supplies; also, they were fully armed and wearing loaded "carrilleras." In battle they fought alongside the men. Out of the Mexican Revolution came the revolutionary personage "Adelita," who wore her *rebozo* crossed at the bosom as a symbol of a revolutionary woman in Mexico.

Then we have our heroine Juana Gallo, a brave woman who led her men to battle against the government after having seen her father and other villagers hung for defending the land of the people. She and many more women fought bravely with other people. And if called upon again, they would be there alongside the men to fight to the bitter end.

And now, today, as we hear the call of the Raza and as the dormant, "docile" Mexican American comes to life, we see the stirring of the people. With that call, the Chicana woman also stirs, and I am sure that she will leave her mark upon the Mexican American movement in the Southwest.

How the Chicana woman reacts depends totally on how the "Macho" Chicano is treated when he goes out into the so-called "Mainstream of Society." If the husband is so-called successful, the woman seems to become very domineering and demands more and more in material goods I ask myself at times. "Why are the women so demanding?" But then I realize: This is the place of owning a slave.

A woman who has no way of expressing herself and realizing herself as a full human has nothing else to turn to but the owning of material things. She builds her entire life around these and finds security in this way. All she has to live for is her house and family, and she becomes very possessive of both. This makes her a totally dependent human, dependent on her husband and family. Most of the Chicana women in this comfortable situation are not particularly involved in the movement. Many times it is because of the fear of censorship in general—censorship from the husband, the family, friends, and society in general. For these reasons she is completely inactive.

Then you will find the Chicana with a husband who was not able to fare so very well in the "Society" and perhaps has had to face defeat. She is the woman that really suffers. Quite often the man will not fight the real source of his problems, be it discrimination or whatever, but will instead come home and take it out on his family. As this continues, his Chicana becomes the victim of his machismo, and woeful are the trials and tribulations of that household.

Much of this is seen particularly in the city. The man, being head of the household and unable to fight the system he lives in, will very likely lose face, and for this reason there will often be a separation or divorce in the family. It is at this time that the Chicana faces the real test of having to confront society as one of its total victims.

14

Claiming Public Space: Mexican Women in Twentieth-Century America

Vicki Ruiz

The largest group of Latino immigrants have come to the United States from Mexico. Until fairly recently, however, the story of these Mexican immigrants has centered around men, their work, and organizations. Yet Mexican women played a prominent and essential role in creating Mexican American life in the twentieth century, although often in ways different from those of men. Taking low-paying jobs as cooks and maids, Mexicanas began to carve a place for themselves in an American society that constantly attempted to marginalize them. In claiming personal, cultural, and public space for themselves throughout the twentieth century, Mexican and Mexican American women have consistently turned to mutual assistance and collective action as a means to gain control over their lives.

In this essay, Vicki L. Ruiz, discusses a crucial aspect of this dual approach to women's independence: collective involvement in community-based organizations. Whether working through labor unions or community action groups and organizations, family and friendship networks formed the hub and a secure base from which Mexican and Mexican American women moved decisively into the public sphere in the late twentieth century.

During the second week of May 1972, Elsa Chávez, a twenty-six-year-old El Paso garment worker, left her post at the Paisano plant of Farah Manufacturing. Joining 4,000 Farah employees in El Paso, San Antonio, Victoria, Texas, and Las Cruces, New Mexico, Chávez became part of a twenty-two month strike for seniority rights, higher wages, pension issues, and union recognition. Management's manipulation of production quotas sparked the most indignation among Mexican women who formed the backbone of Farah's line personnel. Chávez's anger is easy to understand. Imagine that you have been hired to sew belts onto slacks. To get a raise, you must meet a quota of 3,000 belts per day, which translates into sewing six belts per minute. Forget your lunch hour, for if you fall too far behind in fulfilling your quota, you will be fired. As a "checker" of freshly sewn garments, Chávez felt fortunate in that she did not have to meet a quota; yet she understood the situation of the seamstresses with whom she worked. "Some of my fellow workers . . . were very nervous because they were always told, 'Hurry up' . . . 'You're going to be fired.' There was so much pressure that they started fighting for the bundles." Although Chávez perceived herself as earning good money and facing little personal harassment, she too walked out.

Successful union organization depends, in large measure, on a sense of solidarity and community among workers. Effective political and community action requires the intertwining of individual subjectivities within collective goals. Claiming public space can involve fragile alliances and enduring symbols, rooted in material realities and ethereal visions. On a situational, grass-roots level, informal and formal voluntary organizations do serve as conduits for women's collective identity and empowerment. For the Mexican women whose voices foreground this study, the individual bonds formed at work, at church, or in the neighborhood reflect a mosaic of subjectivities, strategies, and goals but remain rooted in collective struggles for recognition and respect.

Gender and social justice—doesn't that equal feminist consciousness? As contemporary Mexican women know all too well, it depends on whose feminism and whose context. As one Farah striker bluntly stated, "I don't believe in burning your bra, but I do believe in having our rights." Mediated by gender, race, culture, and class, activism transforms individual conceptions of self, changes that alter people's lives with subtlety or drama. Labor disputes raise the stakes in the precarious politics of work and family. [An] examination of the Farah strike provides a powerful case of community building through union organization.

When she joined her striking co-workers, Elsa Chávez had little inkling of the struggles that lay ahead. Farah Manufacturing was the largest private employer in El Paso; its chief executive officer Willie Farah had a reputation as a patriotic, civic-minded business leader; and labor activism found few friends in a conservative border city notorious as a "minimum wage town." Indeed, the May 1972 walkout was not the culmination of an overnight organizing drive by representatives of the Amalgamated Clothing Workers (ACW), but the result of a protracted campaign begun in 1969. Events on the picket lines outside the El Paso plants quickly convinced the ACW that the strike could not be won within the city limits. Willie Farah responded with armed security guards walking with unmuzzled police dogs and he obtained a court order upholding an 1880 law stipulating that pickets must stand at least fifty feet apart. From 800 to 1,000 people, many of them women, were arrested, some during midnight raids at their residences. Instead of the usual $25 bail set for misdemeanor offenses, those arrested during the Farah strike were required to post a $400 bond.

Within a few months, the 1880 picketing law was declared unconstitutional and Farah was ordered to "call off" the dogs and desist from interfering with peaceful picketing. Farah decided to take his case to the U.S. Supreme Court, but in August Justice Lewis Powell ruled against him by affirming the decisions of the lower court. At the same time the National Labor Relations Board charged Farah with unfair practices with regard to intimidation and harassment.

But if Willie Farah found little solace outside his native El Paso, he found plenty of local support. Both El Paso dailies offered him a friendly hearing. And when El Paso's Catholic bishop Sidney Metzger openly supported the strikers, an area Protestant minister Paul Poling wrote a highly charged anti-union pamphlet endorsed by thirteen other clergy. Yet, despite being insulted at street corners where they picketed department stores, in their neighborhoods, and in letters to the editor, the Farah strikers continued their vigil.

As one El Paso activist reflected, "We thought when we went out on strike that our only enemy was Farah . . . but we found out it was also the press, the police, the businessmen. . . . This strike was not just for union recognition." The Farah strike distilled the racial and class cleavages within El Paso, cleavages evident in both the daily lives of the strikers and the opinion sections of local newspapers. Letters to the editor typically chastised the Farah strikers for their ingratitude, ignorance, and gullibility to outside agitators. Or as one retired El Paso retail saleswoman wrote,

> Mr. Farah did not invite one of the people who are working for him to come and work for him. They all asked for a job and should thank God that they got one. If they think they are such hot stuff and qualified for a better job then why don't they quietly fold their tents and leave? . . . The Farah family has worked hard for what they have and no-one has the moral right to harm them. I would like to give my boot—and you know where—to those picking [sic] in front of The Popular.

Although their letters appeared less frequently than those of their opponents, strikers and their supporters responded in kind, and the editorial pages impart a sense of the polarity of opinions surrounding the "morality" of the Farah dispute. In a spirited letter critical of media coverage, Irma Camacho wrote, "The Farah struggle,

since its conception was a moral fight for human dignity, since then through the use of your newspaper, the controlling 'powers that be' have stolen what objectivity there could exist and have subjectively used the facts to place economic value over human rights."

Realizing that "the strike won't be won in El Paso," the Amalgamated Clothing Workers called for a national boycott of Farah suits and slacks. Supported by AFL-CIO unions, campus activists, celebrities, and liberal politicians, Citizens Committees for Justice for Farah Workers sprung up in cities from the Pacific Coast to the Atlantic seaboard. In addition to holding fundraisers, these groups organized picket lines in front of department stores that carried Farah products and during "Don't Buy Farah Day" on December 11, 1972, an estimated 175,000 people, predominately AFL-CIO members, held rallies and parades across the country. United Farm Workers President Cesar Chávez visited the workers as did Sergeant Shriver, the Democratic vice-presidential nominee of 1972. The Farah strikers also listened as U.S. Representative Edward Roybal from California spoke of his youth as a garment presser and ACW member. Support even crossed party lines with Nelson Rockefeller's public endorsement.

The national boycott slowly began to have its desired effect. Sales declined from $150 million in 1972 to $126 million in 1974. As an article in *Texas Monthly* revealed, some retailers gladly took Farah slacks off their racks not in response to pickets but in retaliation for Willie Farah's "high-handed methods of doing business." While the boycott undoubtedly contributed to bringing Farah to the bargaining table in March 1974, the dedication of the Mexicanas holding the line cannot be underestimated.

As weeks turned into months, the Farah picketers turned to one another for support, friendship, advice, and action. Critical of ACW support in El Paso, one group of women formed a rank-and-file committee within the union. According to historians Coyle, Hershatter, and

Honig, the "members . . . shared a strong sense of themselves as workers and a desire to build a strong and democratic trade union." The women "put out their own leaflets, participated in marches and rallies, helped to found the Farah Distress Fund, and talked to other strikers about the need for a strong union." This caucus continued its work after the strike's successful settlement under the name *Unidad Para Siempre*.

The strike, however, divided friends and families since a little less than one-half of the original workforce had walked out. Elsa Chávez recalled how this schism affected her personally.

> I had a fiancé there—we were going to get married, but he was from the inside, I was from the outside. So we broke up because he didn't want anything to do with the strikers. After the strike, he came back and (then) I told him "good-bye."

Chávez continued, "But you wouldn't believe the number of divorces caused by the strike. A lot of couples broke up either the wife was inside and the husband was outside or the other way around."

As amply documented in "Women at Farah," tensions among kin and friends took its toll and, as the strike wore on, financial pressures mounted. Many families lost their homes, automobiles, and other possessions. Although the union had an emergency strike fund and distributed groceries and clothing, many Farah activists found themselves in severe economic straits. One woman explained, "A lot of people lost their homes, cars—you name it, they lost it." Such circumstances fueled marital tensions, but 85 percent of the strikers were women and they sought ways to balance picket and family duties.

Children taking their place on the picket line occurred throughout modern Chicano labor history, as early as the 1930s. While perhaps mothers initially brought their children to the line because they had little choice, the youngsters began to prove themselves useful in distributing leaflets outside stores. Adults were less likely to make abusive comments toward a child. In the words of Farah activist Julia Aguilar, "Now, we just bring our children to our meetings, and we bring them to the picket lines. Sometimes they ask. 'Are we going to the picket line today, mommy?'" Aguilar continued. "It's kind of hard with kids. But I'm willing to sacrifice myself and I think my husband is beginning to understand."

The settlement of the Farah Strike in March 1974 had, for many women, come at great personal cost. Few activists would enjoy the benefits since many of the most vocal were fired after a few months, ostensibly for failing to meet inflated production quotas; union representatives blithely refused to generate any grievance procedures to protect and retain these women. Mexican women have not fared well in their affiliation with mainstream labor unions even though they have contributed much of the people power, perseverance, and activism necessary for successful organization. As in the case of Farah, they typically have been denied any meaningful voice in the affairs of the local they had labored so valiantly to build.

Yet the Farah strikers had created community with one another and asserted their claims for social justice. As Coyle, Hershatter, and Honig wrote, "The Chicanas who comprise the majority of the strikers learned that they could speak and act on their own behalf as women and as workers, lessons they will not forget." Elsa Chávez represents one of the women activists who have sought to merge personal and community empowerment. After she was fired, Chávez began to work at another clothing factory, but came to the realization that she wanted—and could achieve—a college education. I first met Ms. Chávez when she was a student in my Chicano history class at U.T. El Paso: two former strikers had enrolled in the class, a fact I discovered as I lectured on the Farah strike and noticed the two reentry women, both bilingual education majors, sitting in the front row winking and giggling to each other. "Oh, we're sorry, Dr. Ruiz, but we were *there.*" A bit nonplussed, I turned the class over to them. Elsa Chávez dreamed of opening up "a school for slow learners" and had begun to organize a group of Mexican American women in her education classes for this school.

Labor struggles can also be centered around the involvement of the entire family. The United Farm Workers provides the most well-known example. Drawing on his experience with the Community Service Organization (CSO), Cesar Chávez in 1962 began to organize farm workers in the San Joaquin Valley. During the grape boycotts of the late 1960s and 1970s, Chávez and his United Farm Workers Organizing Committee (later the UFW) utilized tactics, such as the secondary boycott, national support committees, and identification with the Catholic Church. A charismatic leader preaching social justice and nonviolence, Chávez became the most prominent advocate for the rights of Mexicans in the United States. By 1973, the UFW "had contracts with 80% of the grape growers in the San Joaquin Valley" and "at its height the union had 100,000 members."

UFW organizers, many of whom grew up as farm workers themselves, recognized that the family formed the unit of production in agriculture and consequently focused on the involvement of every family member. Referring to campesinas, Chávez related, "We can't be free ourselves if we can't free our women." Signing union membership cards has always been a monumental decision for most farm workers because they risk not one job, but the livelihood of the entire family. While the husband might be the first to sign the card, he often does so at the insistence of his wife. Former UFW legal department volunteer Graciela Martínez Moreno explained:

> At the beginning, women were more afraid of the union. But once they got the information about the benefits their children would receive, the women became good supporters. The biggest problem was getting through the initial fear, but if you got to the wife, the husband was sure to follow. The quiet, subtle pressure of the wife was very effective.

But there is more to the story than this, for Mexican women have been well represented at the leadership and service levels of the United Farm Workers. Women, to a large extent, operate the service centers, health clinics, day nurseries, and legal departments. Founding the first UFW Service Center in the Midwest in concert with her husband, María Elena Lucas offered a realistic portrayal of exhaustion. "And I worked such long hours, during the nights and on the weekends . . . but I just didn't know how to say no to people. I got very skinny. Sometimes I'd have thirteen or fourteen people waiting for me to do different things for them. It was just impossible." She continued, "Cesar had told me, 'It's not good to play Santa Claus to the people. It'll be neverending,' and I started getting to the point where I understood . . . I was burning out."

Frustrated by the UFW's reluctance to organize migrant laborers in Illinois and exhausted from her job as a union social worker, Lucas became an organizer in 1985 with the Farm Labor Organizing Committee (FLOC) led by Baldemar Velásquez. Joined by four of her compañeras, including her own daughter, and their children (Gloria Chiquita had six kids), Lucas helped organize over 5,000 Midwestern farm workers and orchestrated a successful union election and contract. María Elena Lucas and her friend Gloria Chiquita both became vice-presidents in the FLOC, although Lucas expressed a feeling of powerlessness with regard to decision-making within the union board. She also recognized the difference in support systems between men and women organizers. Referring to men, she remarked, "They have the support of their wives and families, but most of us women have to work against our husbands and all of the services they expect."

Fran Leeper Buss's oral history of María Elena Lucas, *Forged Under the Sun/Forjada bajo el sol* provides the most nuanced portrait of a woman rank-and-file organizer. What emerges most vividly from Buss's skillful editing of Lucas's life story is the strength and comfort migrant women find in their friendships with one another. Lucas gives unvarnished testimony to the oppression and abuse women face in the fields and at times in the home and the union hall.

In her pathbreaking dissertation, "Women in the United Farm Workers," Margaret Rose documents women's networks in the *campesino* centers, ranch committees, and boycott campaigns. Rose divides UFW women into two typologies—"nontraditional" (UFW vice-president Dolores Huerta) and "traditional" (Helen Chávez, Cesar's widow). Although Rose portrays Huerta as someone fitting her union nickname of "Adelita" (the symbolic *soldadera* of the Mexican Revolution), she notes how even the "nontraditional" Huerta relied on extended kin and women friends in the union (the "union family") to care for her eleven children during her frequent absences. Although criticized for putting la causa first, Dolores Huerta has had few regrets. As she informed Rose, "But now that I've seen how good they [my children] turned out, I don't feel so guilty."

Dolores Huerta is a fearless fighter for social justice. In 1962, she taught school in Stockton, California while being a political activist with the CSO and a mother of six with a seventh on the way. "When I left my teaching job to go start organizing farm workers, a lot of people thought I had just gone completely bananas." A tough, savvy negotiator, Huerta skillfully manipulated her positionality as a mother at the bargaining table.

> When I had my younger children and I was still negotiating, I would take nursing breaks . . . everybody would have to wait while the baby ate. Then I would come back to the table and start negotiating again . . .
>
> I think it made employers sensitive to the fact that when we're talking about benefits and the terms of a contract, we're talking about families and we're talking about children.

Although they contributed in different ways, Dolores Huerta, more public, and Helen Chávez, more private, there was no separation of home and union. For Helen Chávez, the UFW became an extension of her familial responsibilities. She worked in the fields while her husband organized, took care of the children and household, and participated in the social service end of the union. In a rare interview, Helen Chávez offered a glimpse of daily family life: "I hadn't worked for a while, because at the time of the year you could only pick up a day's or a week's worth of work. . . . You just made a few hampers [of peas] and that was it." She further recalled winning a supermarket contest:

> Everytime you went to Safeway, they would give you a little coupon. . . . Everytime we went to the store we saved these. . . . So when we got one of those little tags, I told the checker, "This is going to be my winner," and he laughed. I was just joking with him. I gave the tag to the kids . . . I think it was one of the girls who put saliva on it, and came in yelling, "Mom, Mom, you got the flag! You won!" . . . I rushed back to Safeway. I was really excited. I had won $100 and, oh boy, what a lot of food for the kids! After I got my check, I told Cesar, "Look, we can get some things." And he said, "I'm sorry, but this going to our gas bill." He said he was about to lose his gasoline credit card because he owed $180. I was so disappointed, I sat and cried. I made so many plans for that $100!

As the union grew, Helen Chávez left the fields and became the manager of the credit union. Her integration of family, work, and activism exemplifies the "political familialism" described by sociologist Maxine Baca Zinn. Many women, like Helen Chávez, preferred to work behind the scenes and, as Margaret Bose remarked, "Their contribution remains vital, but largely unrecognized."

Wages, benefits, safer working conditions, seniority, and union recognition are not the only reasons women will go out on strike. Regarding women's labor activism, modes of consumption can be as important as modes of production. In 1973, Tejana pecan shellers employed by McCrea and Son in Yancy, Texas, went out on strike for equal pay for equal work and for more sanitary conditions, but also because they resented "being coerced into buying 'Avon' products from the employer's wife." Activism among Mexican women workers takes many forms, and the contours of their individual and collective agency shift in response to work environment, familial roles, and personal subjectivities.

As a labor historian, I will try to resist the temptation of privileging the workplace as *the* locus for claiming public space. Mexican women have relied on others as well, including, historically, the Roman Catholic Church. In *Hoyt Street,* her autobiography of growing up in Pacoima, Mary Helen Ponce portrays the local parish as the heart of her neighborhood in which time is recorded according to holidays and sacraments. In the barrios of the Southwest, Mexican women have been the stalwart volunteers for church fundraisers. At *jamaicas,* they sell tamales and *cascarones,* operate the cake walk, serve punch, organize the raffle, and help aspiring young anglers at the "go fish" booth. As feminist theologian Yolanda Tarango has argued, church activities were for many Latinas "the *only* arena in which they could legitimately, if indirectly, engage in developing themselves."

Over the last twenty-five years, the Catholic Church, as both an institutional funding source (e.g., the Campaign for Human Development) and as community centers, began to support grassroots organizing campaigns among Mexican Americans. The most well known is the Alinsky-based Communities Organized for Public Service (COPS) in San Antonio, Texas. In 1973, with the support of local parishes, especially parish women, Ernie Cortés, Jr., began to organize neighbor by neighbor in San Antonio's Westside. He asked residents about their needs and concerns. This grassroots approach has permeated the infrastructure of COPS, with leadership emerging from local networks. Women's voluntary parish labor now became channeled for civic improvement and, indeed, several Tejanas have been elected president of the organization.

Drainage problems and unpaved streets became their first order of business. Heavy rains made "peanut butter" of Westside roads; along with mud gushing into area homes and businesses, at times children died in "flash floods on their way to and from school." Calling a public meeting with the city manager at the local high school in August 1974, COPS representatives caught him off guard with their numbers (over 500 people attended), their research, and their polite, yet firm queries. As former COPS president Beatrice Gallegos stated, "I sir'ed him to death." Through the use of demonstrations, political mobilization, research, and negotiation, COPS has significantly improved the material conditions of Westside and Southside neighborhoods. Focusing on municipal issues and boards, members of the twenty-five chapters of COPS ensure that developers, planners, school administrators, city officials, and Northside politicians do not ride roughshod over their communities. COPS has decisively influenced the distribution of Community Development Block Grants (CDBG) with "56 percent of the CDBG money allotted to San Antonio has gone to COPS-endorsed projects." They have also been active in local utility and environmental issues and opposed the funneling of over one million dollars of federal urban renewal funds into a suburban country club. COPS also engaged in voter registration drives and, while not endorsing candidates, its members closely monitored the positions taken by local politicians.

Along with issues of family and neighborhood, COPS has cultivated the leadership of women. In the words of former COPS president Beatrice Cortez, "Women have community ties. We knew that to make things happen in the community, you have to talk to people. It was a matter of tapping our networks." Unfortunately, Peter Skerry fails to appreciate the importance of women's civic labor as he impugns weakness in leadership to the organization's reliance on "housewives." Referring to what he considers "the authoritative role of organizers," he writes:

Because organizers expend considerable time . . . working with them, leaders tend to find their involvement . . . quite stimulating. Unaccustomed to the sort of attention they receive, leaders typically experience marked personal growth. . . . But at the same time, these leaders . . . must be willing to put up with the organizers' demanding, sometimes harsh treatment. . . . For those who have a lot to learn, the bargain may seem a reasonable one. But for those with broader horizons and opportunities, it may not. As a result, the leaders . . . have been, with few exceptions, working-and lower-middle-class Mexican American housewives with limited career prospects. These organizations have a much tougher time attracting college-educated Mexican Americans, especially well-educated men.

Such condescension hardly merits elaboration. Skerry misses the significance of Mexican women's histories of community responsibility, education, and action. Or as Ernie Cortés simply stated, "COPS is like a university where people come to learn about public policy, public discourse, and public life."

With COPS as the model, similar organizations have emerged throughout the Southwest. Although beyond the scope of this study, Los Angeles alone has at least three recognized and vital Alinsky-style community confederations: United Neighborhood Organization (UNO), South Central Organizing Committee (SCOC), and East Valleys Organization (EVO). Recently, members of SCOC tried to get Food 4 Less to build on a neighborhood lot owned by the discount grocery firm and the Community Redevelopment Agency. In the words of activist Orinio Ospinaldo,

But having seen no progress at the Vermont site for many years, we were forced to take a dramatic step. . . . SCOC launched an "action" against Food 4 Less. We 65 adults and children went by bus to the Claremont [an upscale college community] office of Food 4 Less' chairman, Ron Berkel. His office was closed, so we distributed flyers outside. The leaflets compared the price of his home to the price of opening a new grocery store.

Such direct action brought Berkel to meetings with the SCOC and Los Angeles Mayor Richard Riordan and, according to Ospinaldo, "Suddenly, things look promising." A single parent of three, Ospinaldo linked both family and community in the following remarks. "No matter where you live, that's your community and you have to fight to claim it. . . . But don't do it alone. You need the strength of people . . . [united] for a common good." He continued, "Second, try to involve your children. I've found an activity that is fulfilling and that acts as an example for my children." Despite these articulated goals, the regional Catholic hierarchy has not always supported Latino and Latino/African American community endeavors even when initiated by members of its own religious orders. *Calpulli* in San Bernardino provides such an example.

For over twenty years, Sister Rosa Marta Zarate and Father Patricio Guillen have pursued a vision of a dynamic *mesitizaje* of Latin American theology, Mesoamerican traditions, and community development projects. Forming Comunidades Ecclesiales de Base (CEBs) in San Bernardino, Ontario, Riverside, San Diego, and the Imperial Valley, *calpulli* (the Aztec equivalent of neighborhood) fosters self-sufficient economic cooperatives. Unlike COPS, which works within the system, CEBs seek to build financially sustainable communities outside the arena of municipal politics. In some respects, *calpulli* represents an indigenous settlement house, offering classes in English, vocational education, and other commonly defined immigrant services. In addition, it closely resembles economic cooperatives found in Nicaragua, El Salvador, and other parts of Latin America. For example, *calpulli*'s projects "include a travel agency, tax and legal counseling, book store, gardening and landscaping service, clothing manufacturing, and food service." Scholars Gilbert Cadena and Lara Medina summarize Zarate and Guillen's efforts as follows:

Today, they and a team of lay people successfully apply the tenets of liberation theology by creating a system of profit and nonprofit cooperatives employing residents from the local community. Their goal is to create economically self-sufficient organizations that operate based on the principles of shared profit, shared responsibility, and shared power.

Calpulli's successes have not gone unnoticed by church officials in Los Angeles. Several have looked askance at what they perceive as unorthodox community organizing. Indeed, Sister Rosa Marta Zarate received an ultimatum—return to Mexico or leave her order. She chose *calpulli* over the convent.

Zarate and Guillen also seek to make connections with southern California Native Americans and to educate project members in Mesoamerican history. Sister Rosa Marta Zarate reinterprets Aztec society from popular conceptions of feathered warriors and flamboyant sacrifices to understanding the economic cooperation that girded Aztec neighborhoods as well as an appreciation for their gendered spiritual values (e.g., recognizing Tonantzín, the earth mother). Preserving a historical memory also applies to contemporary activism. *Calpulli* has inaugurated an oral history project among its members. El Plan de Acción de Calpulli encapsulates its mission as "an organization inspired by the cultures of our people, our history, our projects, and our destiny." Or as Lara Medina relates, "The underlying theme is living out their faith in a God who wants justice and humanity." She continues, "This faith motivates them to develop projects that will empower the personal and communal lives of la gente."

Contemporary women's activism, however, does not necessarily revolve around the church. The work of sociologist Mary Pardo, for example, clearly delineates the networks of neighborhood organization among Mexican women in East Los Angeles. Founded in 1984, the Mothers of East Los Angeles (MELA) arose out of Resurrection Parish [no pun intended] to halt the construction of a prison in their community. This group of concerned women attracted 3,000 supporters as it staged demonstrations and rallies and engaged in political lobbying.

Juana Gutiérrez summed up her involvement as follows, "I don't consider myself political. I'm just someone looking out for the community, for the youth . . . on the side of justice."

State Assemblywoman Gloria Molina fervently supported their cause. She pointed out that the new prison would be built "within a four mile radius" of four correctional facilities and "within two miles" of twenty-six schools. Believing that enough is enough, Molina asked the rhetorical question:

> Do you think this could happen to Woodland Hills or Torrance? LA is supposed to have a prison, consequently, our community must bear the burden because we don't have the political strength to oppose it.

However, the Mothers of East Los Angeles would forge that political strength.

While Peter Skerry characterized the women as housewives "led by a parish priest," Mary Pardo delineates Mexican women's organizing strategies that evolved independently of the Catholic Church. In her dissertation "Identity and Resistance: Mexican American Women and Grassroots Activism in Two Los Angeles Communities," Pardo offers compelling portraits of women as neighborhood activists, women who contextualize their civic labor as an extension of familial responsibilities. Although considered as "political novices," the Mothers of East Los Angeles took on Governor George Deukmejian and the Department of Corrections and won. The prison was never built.

From almost its inception, the Mothers of East LA have dedicated themselves to environmental issues. Their activities have ranged from leading the fight against a proposed incinerator to distributing free toilets to neighborhood residents. MELA has also raised money for scholarships and organized graffiti clean-up teams. The fusion of family and community resonates in the voices of these women. "The mother is the soul of the family; but the child is the heartbeat," Aurora Castillo, one of MELA's founders, explained. "We must fight to keep the heart of our community beating. Not just

for our children, but for everyone's children."
Like Dolores Huerta and the women of the
United Farm Workers, the Mothers of East LA
have drawn on familial motifs for community
and personal empowerment.

Mexican women's community activism is
not limited to city streets. In his photojournal,
*Organizing for Our Lives: New Voices from
Rural Communities,* Richard Street poignantly
documents the struggles of Mexican and Southeast Asian farm workers against toxic waste,
pesticides, labor abuses, and discrimination in
housing and education. Highlighting the
activism among women, Street profiles several
grass-roots associations represented by California Rural Legal Assistance. In chronicling
organized protests against the building of an
incinerator by Chem Waste in Kettleman City,
Street photographs a young Mexican girl
dressed in her frilly Sunday best. The Mex-
icanita is holding a large sign featuring Bart
Simpson with the balloon caption, "DON'T
HAVE AN INCINERATOR, MAN!" This appropria-
tion of an icon of U.S. popular culture represents a bifurcation of consciousness where the
boundaries blur to the point that cultural codes
converge in this subversion of the image.

In 1988, Mujeres Mexicanas, a campesina
organization, was formed in the Coachella
Valley. This group has participated in voter registration drives and electoral politics. Richard
Street credits its members for the election of
three Chicano city council candidates as well as
the initiation of AIDS education in the valley.
"They provided pamphlets, condoms, and
bleach to disinfect needles. No local government or health agency in Coachella Valley was
attempting anything like it."

Many of the *mujeres* also belong to the
United Farm Workers, in which Millie Treviño-
Sauceda has been a rank-and-file organizer. In
explaining the mission of Mujeres Mexicanas,
Treviño-Sauceda revealed:

> Since the beginning we all agreed that our role
> was to promote the socio-political and psycho-
> logical empowerment of *campesinas*. We also
> agreed that professional women—the ones with

college educations—could only be advisors, not
active members, because professionals tend to
take over the leadership of the group. We wanted
campesinas to be in control.

The testimonies of the campesinas give witness
to the power of women's collective action. In
the words of María "Cuca" Carmona, "We
have found our place within our community
and even within our homes."

Sustaining community space can be as
important as finding it. For some areas, economic survival is resistance. In northern New
Mexico, former SNCC volunteer and Chicano
Movement activist María Varela has helped
create and foster viable economic cooperatives
among impoverished Hispano farmers, shep-
herds, and weavers. Los Ganados del Valle,
which was founded in 1983, "operates on
$150,000 annual budget and has 50 families as
members." The cooperatives market yarns,
quilts, clothing, and rugs; in 1990 its Tierra
Wools subsidiary reached an annual sales of
$250,000. Los Ganados del Valle has also
organized around local environmental issues
with regard to grazing rights. A recipient of a
MacArthur Genius Award, Varela astutely contends, "I learned . . . that it is not enough to
pray over an injustice or protest it or research it
to death, but that you have to take concrete
action to solve it."

"Concrete action" resonates in the voices
presented throughout this book. In examining
women's activism, I am struck by the threads of
continuity, the intertwining of community,
family, and self. For some women, their
involvement remains couched in familial ideology while others articulate feelings of personal
empowerment *or* contexualize their actions
within a framework of community-based feminism. Whether or not they proclaim feminist
identities, their actions privilege collective politics over personal politics. Claiming public
space, furthermore, can sustain, not subordinate, women's personal needs. Struggles for
social justice cannot be boiled down to a
dialectic of accommodation and resistance, but
should be placed within the centrifuge of

negotiation, subversion, and consciousness. Building community is both a legacy and a responsibility. As a storyteller, listener, recorder, and amateur theorist, I am reminded of a passage in Eudora Welty's *Becoming a Writer*:

> Each of us is moving, changing, and with respect to others. As we discover, we remember; remembering, we discover; and most intensely do we experience this when our separate journeys converge.

Feminist theorist Chela Sandoval has adroitly distilled "the differential mode of oppositional consciousness" that underlies "concrete action." In her words: "The differential mode of oppositional consciousness depends upon the ability to read the current situation of power and of self-consciously choosing and adopting the ideological form best suited to push against its configurations." In reflecting on her positionality in the hegemonic racial and economic structures of El Paso, Farah striker Estela Gómez addressed her grievances in a courageous letter to the editor:

> A lot of people in the El Paso community ask quite often, with all of these good benefits Willie Farah provides at his factory, why did these people walk on strike? . . . These benefits were only there for the good of the company, not for the worker. . . . All these benefits put together could never make up for the only thing we are now struggling for and that is human dignity.
>
> What good was the vaccuum [sic] cleaner he gave us for Christmas, when a lot of us didn't even earn enough to afford a carpet. . . . And the turkey for Thanksgiving—was it to make up for the time your supervisor made you cry because he wanted more production from you, as if you were a machine and not a human being? . . .
>
> Be grateful to Farah they say, for all this man has done for you. I say Farah should be grateful to us, the Mexican American, who from our sweat have [sic] worked hard to make the pants that have built his empire.

Mexicana/Mexican American/Chicana activists, with determination, creativity, acumen, and dignity, have strived to exercise some control over their lives in relation to material realities and individual subjectivities as forged within both the spatial and affinitive bonds of community. Their courage comes forth out of the shadows.

GLOSSARY

Amalgamated Clothing Workers: An AFL-CIO union representing clothing workers.

Secondary boycott: A sympathetic strike by union members not directly involved in an industrial dispute.

Compañeras: Literally, companions. Refers to close supporters in a public action.

Campesina: Women farm workers of Mexican descent.

Soldadera: Women soldiers in the Mexican Revolution.

Mesitizque: The Spanish American system of racial classification derived from the multiethnic experience in colonial America. A mestizo/mestiza is a person of European and Indian ethnic ancestry.

Saul Alinsky: (1909–1972), A U.S. radical activist best known for his book, *Rules for Radicals* (1971).

IMPLICATIONS

One of the most important consequences of the Civil Rights Movement of the 1950s and 1960s was the rise of collective organization and collective action on the part of people previously excluded from the public realm. This was especially true of women, who had faced discrimi-

nation both in the workplace and at home. Do you think the impetus for Mexican and Mexican American women to enter the public realm came from the examples of public organizations, such as unions, or from their family experiences?

One of the most significant pieces of legislation of the postwar era was the passage of the G. I. Bill. Providing subsidized education and guaranteed mortgages to returning soldiers and their families, the G. I. Bill contributed greatly to the postwar economic boom that made the United States the envy of the world. One of the results of government-guaranteed mortgages was the development of large-scale housing tracts, such as that in Levittown, Pennsylvania. This essay is introduced by the Levittown covenants—the rules homeowners agreed to follow. Drawing from a wide range of classes, the covenants enforce a firmly middle-class standard of community life in Levittown.

Restrictions of Levittown (late 1940s)

Every good community has restrictions that will insure its continued maintenance. As a result property values increase and greater enjoyment results to all homeowners. Here is a summary of those at Levittown. If you read them carefully you will see that they have but one purpose in mind: that you and your neighbors benefit from them.

1. You can add another carport or garage or room—IF it is similar in architecture, color and material to the dwelling—IF it doesn't project in front of the original house at all, or *more than 15 feet* in back of it—and IF at all times there still remain at least 20 feet of open yard in the rear and 7 feet on each side. (On corner lots, *each* side of the house facing a street is considered a front. If your house fronts on 2 streets you must leave at least 6 feet of open yard at one interior side and 15 feet at the other; if you bought one of the rare corners fronting on 3 streets, you must leave at least 6 feet of open yard at the remaining interior side).

2. You may display a residence sign but don't make it more than one square foot in size.

3. You may keep a couple of household pets (dogs or cats, etc.) but no commercial breeding or maintaining is allowed.

4. If you are a physician or a dentist or other similar professional person, you may have your office in your home *BUT no business of any kind is permitted*—the *residential* sections of Levittown must remain residential.

5. When you put your garbage out for collection make sure it is in a *tightly closed* metal container. Don't strew rubbish or garbage around your property.

6. You may plant a shrub or other *growing* fence *BUT* keep it no

higher than 3 feet. If you have a young child or a pet and want to pen them in, try a good thorny barberry or similar hedge fence of that height—it should do the job perfectly. NO FABRICATED FENCES (wood, metal, etc.) WILL BE PERMITTED. In laying out the plots at Levittown we have achieved a maximum of openness and parkline appearance. Fences will cut this up into small parcels and spoil the whole effect no matter how good-looking the fence material itself might be—and some of it is pretty terrible! This item is of prime importance.

7. Laundry can be hung in the rear but please use one of the revolving portable dryers. Old-fashioned clotheslines strung across a lawn look messy. And please don't leave laundry hanging out on Sundays or holidays when you and your neighbors are most likely to be relaxing on your rear lawn.

8. If your property backs on a road, the lot has been made 20 feet deeper than usual. This is so the rear 20 feet can be landscaped and screened, thereby protecting your privacy from passing automobiles and pedestrians. You must—and we're sure you'll want to—take care of this landscaping. With reasonable attention it will soon grow thick and high enough to give you complete privacy. This is the one and only place where shrub fencing is permitted to grow *higher* than 3 feet (see item 6 above). If you live on a corner plot, the same is true as regards the diagonal corner line connecting the sidewalks.

9. Mow your lawn and remove weeds at least *once a week* between April 15th and November 15th. Nothing makes a lawn—and a neighborhood—and a community—look shabbier than uncut grass and unsightly weeds. A lot of thought, work and money has gone into the preparation of your lawn. It will flourish if you take care of it—but it will quickly grow wild and unkempt if you don't.

10. If you live on a corner you cannot remove or add anything to the planting at the corner. If anything dies you may re-plant the same items if we don't. We go to special pains on corners and that's why we don't want them changed.

15

The Drive-In Culture of Contemporary America

Kenneth T. Jackson

Nothing has so transformed the landscape and architecture of America as the automobile. At the beginning of the twentieth century the automobile was a plaything of the rich, but by the end of World War II a majority of Americans owned automobiles, and the proportion has grown ever since. As more and more Americans purchased cars in the postwar decades, and as an increasing proportion of the nation's manufactured goods was transported by highway instead of rail, entirely new kinds of industries emerged to service an increasingly motorized society.

In this essay, Kenneth T. Jackson documents the tremendous impact of the automobile and truck on contemporary America. From the interstate highway system inaugurated during the Eisenhower administration to such innovations as shopping centers, motels, and service stations, "automobility" has done much to turn America into a service society. But, Jackson suggests, this thirty-year trend may be coming to an end. A countertrend has recently emerged, he tells us, in which central cities are increasingly being revitalized as living and shopping spaces, while the corporate consolidation of the gasoline, motel, and retail sales industries has led to the closing of independent service stations and many other artifacts of the early automobile age. If he is correct, the next decades may usher in yet another phase in America's constantly changing architectural landscape.

The postwar years brought unprecedented prosperity to the United States, as color televisions, stereo systems, frost-free freezers, electric blenders, and automatic garbage disposals became basic equipment in the middle-class American home. But the best symbol of individual success and identity was a sleek, air-conditioned, high-powered, personal statement on wheels. Between 1950 and 1980, when the American population increased by 50 percent, the number of their automobiles increased by 200 percent. In high school the most important rite of passage came to be the earning of a driver's license and the freedom to press an accelerator to the floor. Educational administrators across the country had to make parking space for hundreds of student vehicles. A car became one's identity, and the important question was: "What does he drive?" Not only teenagers, but also millions of older persons, literally defined themselves in terms of the number, cost, style, and horsepower of their vehicles. "Escape," thinks a character in a novel by Joyce Carol Oates. "As long as he had his own car he was an American and could not die."

Unfortunately, Americans did die, often behind the wheel. On September 9, 1899, as he was stepping off a streetcar at 74th Street and Central Park West in New York, Henry H. Bliss was struck and killed by a motor vehicle, thus becoming the first fatality in the long war between flesh and steel. Thereafter, the carnage increased almost annually until Americans were sustaining about 50,000 traffic deaths and about 2 million nonfatal injuries per year. Automobility proved to be far more deadly than war for the United States. It was as if a Pearl Harbor attack took place on the highways every two weeks, with crashes becoming so commonplace that an entire industry sprang up to provide medical, legal, and insurance services for the victims.

The environmental cost was almost as high as the human toll. In 1984 the 159 million cars, trucks, and buses on the nation's roads were guzzling millions of barrels of oil every day, causing traffic jams that shattered nerves and clogged the cities they were supposed to open up, and turning much of the countryside to pavement. Not surprisingly, when gasoline shortages created long lines at the pumps in 1974 and 1979, behavioral scientists noted that many people experienced anger, depression, frustration, and insecurity, as well as a formidable sense of loss.

Such reactions were possible because the automobile and the suburb have combined to create a drive-in culture that is part of the daily experience of most Americans. Because of unemployment and war, per capita motor-vehicle ownership was stable (at about 30 million vehicles) between 1930 and 1948, and as late as 1950 (when registrations had jumped to 49 million) an astonishing 41 percent of all American families and a majority of working-class families still did not own a car. Postwar prosperity and rising real wages, however, made possible vastly higher market penetration, and by 1984 there were about seventy motor vehicles for every one hundred citizens, and more cars than either households or workers. Schaeffer and Sclar have argued that high auto ownership is the result of real economic needs rather than some "love affair" with private transportation. Moreover, the American people have proven to be no more prone to motor vehicle purchases than the citizens of other lands. After World War II, the Europeans and the Japanese began to catch up, and by 1980 both had achieved the same level of automobile ownership that the United States had reached in 1950. In automotive technology, American dominance slipped away in the postwar years as German, Swedish, and Japanese engineers pioneered the development of diesel engines, front-wheel drives, disc brakes, fuel-injection, and rotary engines.

Although it is not accurate to speak of a uniquely American love affair with the automobile, and although John B. Rae claimed too much when he wrote in 1971 that "modern suburbia is a creature of the automobile and could not exist without it," the motor vehicle has fundamentally restructured the pattern of everyday life in the United States. As a young man, Lewis Mumford advised his countrymen to "forget the damned motor car and build cities for lovers and friends." As it was, of course, the nation followed a different pattern. Writing in the *American Builder* in 1929, the critic Willard Morgan noted that the building of drive-in structures to serve a motor-driven population had ushered in "a completely new architectural form."

THE INTERSTATE HIGHWAY

The most popular exhibit at the New York World's Fair in 1939 was General Motors' "Futurama." Looking twenty-five years ahead, it offered a "magic Aladdin-like flight through time and space." Fair-goers stood in hour-long lines, waiting to travel on a moving sidewalk above a huge model created by designer Norman Bel Geddes. Miniature superhighways with 50,000 automated cars wove past model farms en route to model cities. Five million persons peered eventually at such novelties as elevated freeways, expressway traffic moving at 100 miles per hour, and "modern and efficient city planning—breathtaking architecture—each city block a complete unit in itself (with) broad, one-way thoroughfares—space, sunshine, light, and air." The message of "Futurama" was as impressive as its millions of model parts: "The job of building the future is one which will demand our best energies, our most fruitful imagination; and that with it will come greater opportunities for all."

The promise of a national system of impressive roadways attracted a diverse group of lobbyists, including the Automobile Manufacturers Association, state-highway administrators, motor-bus operators, the American Trucking Association, and even the American Parking Association—for the more cars on the road, the more cars would be parked at the end of the journey. Truck companies, for example, promoted legislation to spend state gasoline taxes on highways, rather than on schools, hospitals, welfare, or public transit. In 1943 these groups came together as the American Road Builders Association, with General Motors as the largest contributor, to form a lobbying enterprise second only to that of the munitions industry. By the mid-1950s, it had become one of the most broad-based of all pressure groups, consisting of the oil, rubber, asphalt, and construction industries; the car dealers and renters; the trucking and bus concerns; the banks and advertising agencies that depended upon the companies involved; and the labor unions. On the local level, professional real-estate groups and home builders associations joined the movement in the hope that highways would cause a spurt in housing turnover and a jump in prices. They envisaged no mere widening of existing roads; but the creation of an entirely new superhighway system and the initiation of the largest peacetime construction project in history.

The highway lobby inaugurated a comprehensive public relations program in 1953 by sponsoring a national essay contest on the need for better roads. The winner of the $25,000 grand prize was Robert Moses, the greatest builder the world has yet known and a passionate advocate of the urban expressway. The title of his work was "How to Plan and Pay for Better Highways." As his biographer Robert A. Caro has noted, Moses was "the world's most vocal, effective and prestigious apologist for the automobile," and he did more than any other single urban official to encourage more hesitant officials to launch major road-building efforts in their cities.

The Cold War provided an additional stimulus to the campaign for more elaborate expressways. In 1951 the *Bulletin of the Atomic Scientists* devoted an entire issue to "Defense through Decentralization." Their argument was simple. To avoid national destruction in a nuclear attack, the United States should disperse existing large cities into smaller settlements. The ideal model was a depopulated urban core surrounded by satellite cities and low-density suburbs.

Sensitive to mounting political pressure, President Dwight Eisenhower appointed a committee in 1954 to "study" the nation's highway requirements. Its conclusions were foregone, in part because the chairman was Lucius D. Clay, a member of the board of directors of General Motors. The committee considered no alternative to a massive highway system, and it suggested a major redirection of national policy to benefit the car and the truck. The Interstate Highway Act became law in 1956, when Congress provided for a 41,000-mile (eventually expanded to a 42,500-mile) system, with the federal government paying 90 percent of the cost. President Eisenhower gave four reasons for signing the measure: current highways were unsafe; cars too often became snarled in traffic jams; poor roads saddled business with high costs for transportation; and modern highways were needed because "in case of atomic attack on our key cities, the road net must permit quick evacuation of target areas." Not a single word was said about the impact of highways on cities and suburbs, although the concrete thoroughfares and the thirty-five-ton tractor-trailers which used them encouraged the continued outward movement of industries toward the beltways and interchanges. Moreover, the interstate system helped continue the downward spiral of public transportation and virtually guaranteed that future urban growth would perpetuate a centerless sprawl. Soon after the bill was passed by the Senate, Lewis Mumford wrote sadly: "When the American people, through their Congress, voted a little while ago for a $26 billion highway program, the most charitable thing to assume is that they hadn't the faintest notion of what they were doing."

Once begun, the Interstate Highway System of the United States became a concrete colossus that grew bigger with every passing year. The secret of its success lay in the principle of nondivertibility of highway revenues collected from gasoline taxes. The Highway Trust Fund, as it was called, was to be held separately from general taxes. Although no less a person-

age than Winston Churchill called the idea of a nondivertible road fund "nonsense," "absurd," and "an outrage upon . . . common sense," the trust fund had powerful friends in the United States, and it easily swept all opposition before it. Unlike European governments, Washington used taxes to support the highway infrastructure while refusing assistance to railroads. According to Senator Gaylord Nelson of Wisconsin, 75 percent of government expenditures for transportation in the United States in the postwar generation went for highways as opposed to 1 percent for urban mass transit.

The inevitable result of the bias in American transport funding, a bias that existed for a generation before the Interstate Highway program was initiated, is that the United States now has the world's best road system and very nearly its worst public-transit offerings. Los Angeles, in particular, provides the nation's most dramatic example of urban sprawl tailored to the mobility of the automobile. Its vast, amorphous conglomeration of housing tracts, shopping centers, industrial parks, freeways, and independent towns blend into each other in a seamless fabric of concrete and asphalt, and nothing over the years has succeeded in gluing this automobile-oriented civilization into any kind of cohesion—save that of individual routine. Los Angeles's basic shape comes from three factors, all of which long preceded the freeway system. The first was cheap land (in the 1920s rather than 1970s) and the desire for single-family houses. In 1950, for example, nearly two-thirds of all the dwelling units in the Los Angeles area were fully detached, a much higher percentage than in Chicago (28 percent), New York City (20 percent), or Philadelphia (15 percent), and its residential density was the lowest of major cities. The second was the dispersed location of its oil fields and refineries, which led to the creation of industrial suburbs like Whittier and Fullerton and of residential suburbs like La Habra, which housed oil workers and their families. The third was its once excellent mass-transit system, which at its peak included more than 1,100 miles of track and constituted the largest electric inter-urban railway in the world.

The Pacific Electric Company collapsed in the 1920s, however, and since that time Los Angeles has been more dependent upon the private automobile than other large American cities. Beginning in 1942, the Los Angeles Chamber of Commerce, the automobile club, and elected officials met regularly to plan for a region-wide expressway network. They succeeded, and southern California's fabled 715 miles of freeways now constitute a grid that channels virtually all traffic and sets many communal boundaries. They are the primary form of transportation for most residents, who seem to regard time spent in their cars as more pleasurable than time walking to, waiting for, or riding on the bus. More than a third of the Los Angeles area is consumed by highways, parking lots, and interchanges, and in the downtown section this proportion rises to two-thirds. Not surprisingly, efforts to restore the region's public transportation to excellence have thus far failed. In 1976, for example, the state of California attempted to discourage single-passenger automobiles by reserving one lane in each direction on the Santa Monica Freeway for express buses and car pools. An emotional explosion ensued that dominated radio talk shows and television news, and Los Angeles's so-called "diamond lanes" were soon abolished.

More recently, southern California has followed the growing national enthusiasm for rail transit, and Los Angeles broke ground in 1984 for an 18-mile, $3.3 billion subway that will cut underneath the densely built, heavily trafficked Wilshire Boulevard corridor, cut through Hollywood, and end up in the residential San Fernando Valley. The underground will hopefully be the centerpiece of an eventual 160-mile network, second in size in the United States only to New York City's.

THE GARAGE

The drive-in structure that is closest to the hearts, bodies, and cars of the American family is the garage. It is the link between the home and the outside world. The word is French, meaning storage space, but its transformation into a multipurpose enclosure internally integrated with the dwelling is distinctively American.

In the streetcar era, curbs had been unbroken and driveways were almost unknown. A family wealthy enough to have a horse and carriage would have stored such possessions either in a public livery stable or in a private structure at the rear of the property. The owners of the first automobiles were usually sufficiently affluent to maintain a private stable. The first cars, therefore, which were open to the elements, often found lodging in a corner of the stable, side by side with the carriages they were soon to replace. These early accommodations for the automobile were often provided with gasoline tanks, for filling stations at the time were few and far between. This and the fact that cars often caught fire were good and sufficient reasons to keep the motor vehicles away from the family.

After World War I, house plans of the expensive variety began to include garages, and by the mid-1920s driveways were commonplace and garages had become important selling points. The popular 1928 *Home Builders* pattern book offered designs for fifty garages in wood, Tudor, and brick varieties. In affluent sections, such large and efficiently planned structures included housing above for the family chauffeur. In less pretentious neighborhoods, the small, single-purpose garages were scarcely larger than the vehicles themselves, and they were simply portable and prefabricated structures, similar to those in Quebec today, that were camouflaged with greenery and trellises. As one architect complained in 1924: "The majority of owners are really ashamed of their garages and really endeavor to keep them from view," and he implored his readers to build a garage "that may be worthy of standing alongside your house." Although there was a tendency to move garages closer to the house, they typically remained at the rear of the property before 1925, often with access via an alley which ran parallel to the street. The car was still thought of as something similar to a horse—dependable and important, but not something that one needed to be close to in the evening.

By 1935, however, the garage was beginning to merge into the house itself, and in 1937 the *Architectural Record* noted that "the garage has become a very essential part of the residence." The tendency accelerated after World War II, as alleys went the way of the horse-drawn wagon, as property widths more often exceeded fifty feet, and as the car became not only a status symbol, but almost a member of the family, to be cared for and sheltered. The introduction of a canopied and unenclosed structure called a "car port" represented an inexpensive solution to the problem, particularly in mild climates, but in the 1950s the enclosed garage was back in favor and a necessity even in a tract house. Easy access to the automobile became a key aspect of residential design, and not only for the well-to-do. By the 1960s garages often occupied about 400 square feet (about one-third that of the house itself) and usually contained space for two automobiles and a variety of lawn and wood-working tools. Offering direct access to the house (a conveniently placed door usually led directly into the kitchen), the garage had become an integrated part of the dwelling, and it dominated the front facades of new houses. In California garages and driveways were often so prominent that the house could almost be described as accessory to the garage. Few people, however, went to the extremes common in England, where the automobile was often so precious that living rooms were often converted to garages.

THE MOTEL

As the United States became a rubber-tire civilization, a new kind of roadside architecture was created to convey an instantly recognizable image to the fast-moving traveler. Criticized as tasteless, cheap, forgettable, and flimsy by most commentators, drive-in structures did attract the attention of some talented architects, most notably Los Angeles's Richard Neutra. For him, the automobile symbolized modernity, and its design paralleled his own ideals of precision and efficiency. This correlation between the structure and the car began to be celebrated in the late 1960s and 1970s when architects Robert Venturi, Denise Scott Brown, and Steven Izenour developed such concepts as "architecture as symbol" and the "architecture of communication." Their book, *Learning from Las Vegas*, was instrumental in encouraging a shift in taste from general condemnation to appreciation of the commercial strip and especially of the huge and garish signs which were easily recognized by passing motorists.

A ubiquitous example of the drive-in culture is the motel. In the middle of the nineteenth century, every city, every county seat, every aspiring mining town, every wide place in the road with aspirations to larger size, had to have a hotel. Whether such structures were grand palaces on the order of Boston's Tremont House or New York's Fifth Avenue Hotel, or whether they were jerry-built shacks, they were typically located at the center of the business district, at the focal point of community activities. To a considerable extent, the hotel was the place for informal social interaction and business, and the very heart and soul of the city.

Between 1910 and 1920, however, increasing numbers of traveling motorists created a market for overnight accommodation along the highways. The first tourists simply camped wherever they chose along the road. By 1924, several thousand municipal campgrounds were opened which offered cold water spigots and outdoor privies. Next came the "cabin camps," which consisted of tiny, white clapboard cottages arranged in a semicircle and often set in a grove of trees. Initially called "tourist courts," these establishments were cheap, convenient, and informal, and by 1926 there were an estimated two thousand of them, mostly in the West and in Florida.

Soon after clean linens and comfortable rooms became available along the nation's highways, it became apparent that overnight travelers were not the only, or even the largest, pool of customers. Convenience and privacy were especially appealing to couples seeking a romantic retreat. A well-publicized Southern Methodist University study in 1935 reported that 75 percent of Dallas area motel business consisted of one man and one woman remaining for only a short stay. Whatever the motivation of patrons, the success of the new-style hotels prompted Sinclair Lewis to predict in 1920:

> Somewhere in these states there is a young man who is going to become rich. He is going to start a chain of small, clean, pleasant hotels, standardized and nationally advertised, along every important motor route in the country. He is not going to waste money on glit and onyx, but he is going to have agreeable clerks, good coffee, endurable mattresses and good lighting.

It was not until 1952 that Kemmons Wilson and Wallace E. Johnson opened their first "Holiday Inn" on Summer Avenue in Memphis. But long before that, in 1926, a San Luis Obispo, California, proprietor had coined a new word, "motel," to describe an establishment that allowed a guest to park his car just outside his room. New terminology did not immediately erase the unsavory image of the roadside establishments, however. In 1940 FBI Director J. Edgar Hoover declared that most motels were assignation camps and hideouts for criminals. Perhaps he was thinking of Bonnie and Clyde, who had a brief encounter with the law at the Red Crown Cabin Camp near Platte City, Missouri, one evening in July of 1933. Many of Hoover's "dens of vice" were once decent places that, unable to keep up, turned to the "hot pillow trade." Some Texas cabins, said the FBI director, were rented as many as sixteen times a night, while establishments elsewhere did business by the hour, with "a knock on the door when the hour was up."

Motels began to thrive after World War II, when the typical establishment was larger and more expensive than the earlier cabins. Major chains set standards for prices, services, and respectability that the traveling public could depend on. As early as 1948, there were 26,000 self-styled motels in the United States. Hard-won respectability attracted more middle-class families, and by 1960 there were 60,000 such places, a figure that doubled again by 1972. By that time an old hotel was closing somewhere in downtown America every thirty hours. And somewhere in suburban America, a plastic and glass Shangri La was rising to take its place.

Typical of the inner-city hotels was the Heritage in Detroit. The big bands once played on its roof, and aspiring socialites enjoyed crepethin pancakes. In 1975 a disillusioned former employee gestured futilely, "It's dying; the whole place is dying," as the famed hotel closed its doors. By 1984 about fifty historic establishments in downtown areas, such as the Peabody in Memphis, the Mayflower in Washington, the Galvez in Houston, the Menger in San Antonio, and the Biltmore in Providence, were reopening with antique-filled rooms and oak-paneled bars. But the trend remained with the standard, two-story motel.

THE DRIVE-IN THEATER

The downtown movie theaters and old vaudeville houses faced a similar challenge from the automobile. In 1933 Richard M. Hollinshead set up a 16-mm projector in front of his garage in Riverton, New Jersey, and then settled down to watch a movie. Recognizing a nation addicted to the motorcar when he saw one, Hollinshead and Willis Smith opened the world's first drive-in movie in a forty-car parking lot in Camden on June 6, 1933. Hollinshead profited only slightly from his brainchild, however, because in 1938 the United States Supreme Court refused to hear his appeal against Loew's Theaters, thus accepting the argument that the drive-in movie was not a patentable item. The idea never caught on in Europe, but by 1958 more than four thousand outdoor screens dotted the American landscape. Because drive-ins offered bargain-basement prices and double or triple bills, the theaters tended to favor movies that were either second-run or second-rate. Horror films and teenage romance were the order of the night, as *Beach Blanket Bingo* or *Invasion of the Body Snatchers* typified the offerings. Pundits often commented that there was a better show in the cars than on the screen.

In the 1960s and 1970s the drive-in movie began to slip in popularity. Rising fuel costs and a season that lasted only six months contributed to the problem, but skyrocketing land values were the main factor. When drive-ins were originally opened, they were typically out in the hinterlands. When subdivisions and shopping malls came closer, the drive-ins could not match the potential returns from other forms of investments. According to the National Association of Theater Owners, only 2,935 open-air theaters still operated in the United States in 1983, even though the total number of commercial movie screens in the nation, 18,772, was at a 35-year high. The increase was picked up not by the downtown and the neighborhood theaters, but by new multi-screen cinemas in shopping centers. Realizing that the large parking lots of indoor malls were relatively empty in the evening, shopping center moguls came to regard theaters as an important part of a successful retailing mix.

THE GASOLINE SERVICE STATION

The purchase of gasoline in the United States has thus far passed through five distinct epochs. The first stage was clearly the worst for the motorist, who had to buy fuel by the bucketful at a livery stable, repair shop, or dry goods store. Occasionally, vendors sold gasoline from small tank cars which they pushed up and down the streets. In any event, the automobile owner had to pour gasoline from a bucket through a funnel into his tank. The entire procedure was inefficient, smelly, wasteful, and occasionally dangerous.

The second stage began about 1905, when C. H. Laessig of St. Louis equipped a hot-water heater with a glass gauge and a garden hose and turned the whole thing on its end. With this simple maneuver, he invented an easy way to transfer gasoline from a storage tank to an automobile without using a bucket. Later in the same year, Sylvanus F. Bowser invented a gasoline pump which automatically measured the outflow. The entire assembly was labeled a "filling station." At this stage, which lasted until about 1920, such an apparatus consisted of a single pump outside a retail store which was primarily engaged in other businesses and which provided precious few services for the motorist. Many were located on the edge of town for safety and to be near the bulk stations; those few stations in the heart of the city did not even afford the luxury of off-street parking.

Between 1920 and 1950, service stations entered into a third phase and became, as a group, one of the most widespread kinds of commercial buildings in the United States. Providing under one roof all the functions of gasoline distribution and normal automotive maintenance, these full-service structures were often built in the form of little colonial houses, Greek Temples, Chinese pagodas, and Art Deco palaces. Many were local landmarks and a source of community pride. One cartoonist in the 1920s mocked such structures with a drawing in which a newcomer to town confused the gas station with the state capitol. Grandiose at the time, many of them molder today—deserted, forlorn structures with weeds growing in the concrete where gasoline pumps once stood. Their bays stand empty and silent, rendered that way by changing economics, changing styles, and changing consumer preferences.

After 1935 the gasoline station evolved again, this time into a more homogeneous entity that was standardized across the entire country and that reflected the mass-marketing techniques of billion-dollar oil companies. Some of the more familiar designs were innovative or memorable, such as the drumlike Mobil station by New York architect Frederick Frost, which featured a dramatically curving facade while conveying the corporate identity. Another popular service station style was the Texaco design of Walter Dorwin Teague—a smooth white exterior with elegant trim and the familiar red star and bold red lettering. Whatever the product or design, the stations tended to be operated by a single entrepreneur and represented an important part of small business in American life.

The fifth stage of gasoline-station development began in the 1970s, with the slow demise of the traditional service-station businessman. New gasoline outlets were of two types. The first was the super station, often owned and operated by the oil companies themselves. Most featured a combination of self-service and full-service pumping consoles, as well as fully equipped "car care centers." Service areas were separated from the pumping sections so that the two functions would not interfere with each other. Mechanics never broke off work to sell gas.

The more pervasive second type might be termed the "mini-mart station." The operators of such establishments have now gone full circle since the early twentieth century. Typically, they know nothing about automobiles and expect the customers themselves to pump the gasoline. Thus, "the man who wears the star" has given way to the teenager who sells six-packs, bags of ice, and pre-prepared sandwiches.

THE SHOPPING CENTER

Large-scale retailing, long associated with central business districts, began moving away from the urban cores between the world wars. The first experiments to capture the growing suburban retail markets were made by major department stores in New York and Chicago in the 1920s, with Robert E. Wood, Sears's vice president in charge of factories and retail stores, as the leader of the movement. A student of population trends, Wood decided in 1925 that motor-vehicle registrations had outstripped the parking space available in metropolitan cores, and he insisted that Sears's new "A" stores (their other retail outlets were much smaller) be located in low-density areas which would offer the advantages of lower rentals and yet, because of the automobile, be within reach of potential customers. With the exception of Sears's flagship store on State Street in Chicago (which was itself closed in 1983), Woods's dictum of ample free parking was rigorously followed throughout the United States. Early examples of the formula were the Pico Boulevard store in Los Angeles and the Crosstown store in Memphis. A revolution in retailing followed. Writing in the *American Builder* in 1929, the critic Willard Morgan found it natural that traffic congestion at the center would drive thousands of prospective customers to turn instead to suburban marketing centers.

Another threat to the primacy of the central business district was the "string street" or "shopping strip," which emerged in the 1920s and which were designed to serve vehicular rather than pedestrian traffic. These bypass roads encouraged city dwellers with cars to patronize businesses on the outskirts of town. Short parades of shops could already have been found near the streetcar and rapid transit stops, but, as has been noted, these new retailing thoroughfares generally radiated out from the city business district toward low-density, residential areas, functionally dominating the urban street system. They were the prototypes for the familiar highway strips of the 1980s which stretch far into the countryside.

Sears's big stores were initially isolated from other stores, while the retail establishments of highway strips were rarely unified into a coordinated whole. The multiple-store shopping center with free, off-street parking represented the ultimate retail adaptation to the requirements of automobility. Although the

Guinness Book of World Records lists the Roland Park Shopping Center (1896) as the world's first shopping center, the first of the modern variety was Country Club Plaza in Kansas City. It was the effort of a single entrepreneur, Jesse Clyde Nichols, who put together a concentration of retail stores and used leasing policy to determine the composition of stores in the concentration. By doing that, Nichols created the idea of the planned regional shopping center.

Begun in 1923 in a Spanish-Moorish style with red tile roofs and little towers—its Giralda Tower is actually a replica of the original in Seville—Country Club Plaza featured waterfalls, fountains, flowers, tree-lined walks, and expensive landscaping. As the first automobile-oriented shopping center, it offered extensive parking lots behind ornamented brick walls. Most buildings were two stories high, with the second-floor offices typically occupied by physicians, dentists, and attorneys, whose presence would help stimulate a constant flow of well-heeled visitors. An enormous commercial success, Country Club Plaza stood in organic harmony with the prairie surroundings, and it soon became the hub of Kansas City's business and cultural activities.

Nichols's Country Club Plaza generated considerable favorable publicity after it became fully operational in 1925, and by the mid-1930s the concept of the planned shopping center, as a concentration of a number of businesses under one management and with convenient parking facilities, was well known and was recognized as the best method of serving the growing market of drive-in customers. But the Great Depression and World War II had a chilling effect on private construction, and as late as 1946 there were only eight shopping centers in the entire United States. They included Upper Darby Center in West Philadelphia (1927); Suburban Square in Ardmore, Pennsylvania (1928); Highland Park Shopping Village outside Dallas (1931); River Oaks in Houston (1937); Hampton Village in St. Louis (1941); Colony in Toledo (1944);

Shirlington in Arlington, Virginia (1944); and Belleview Square in Seattle (1946). Importantly, however, they provided many of the amenities that shoppers would take for granted half a century later. In 1931, for example, Highland Park Village outside Dallas offered department, drug, and food stores, as well as banks, a theater, beauty and barber shops, offices, studios, and parking for seven hundred cars. The Spanish architecture was uniform throughout, and the rental charge included a maintenance fee to insure that the property was adequately cared for during the term of the lease.

The first major planned retail shopping center in the world went up in Raleigh, North Carolina, in 1949, the brainchild of Homer Hoyt, a well-known author and demographer best known for his sector model of urban growth. Thereafter, the shopping-center idea caught on rapidly in the United States and less rapidly in Canada, where the first shopping center—Dixie Plaza near Toronto—did not open until 1954. The most successful early examples, such as Poplar Plaza in Memphis, offered at least thirty small retailers, one large department store, and parking for five hundred or more cars. By 1984 the nation's 20,000 large shopping centers accounted for almost two-thirds of all retail trade, and even in relatively centralized cities like New York, Boston, and San Francisco downtown merchants adapted to the suburban shift. Easy facilities for parking gave such collections of stores decisive advantages over central city establishments.

The concept of the enclosed, climate-controlled mall, first introduced at the Southdale Shopping Center near Minneapolis in 1956, added to the suburban advantage. A few of the indoor malls, such as the mammoth Midtown Plaza in Rochester, New York, were located downtown, but more typical were Paramus Park and Bergen Mall in New Jersey; Woodfield Mall in Schaumburg outside Chicago; King's Plaza and Cross County outside Gotham; and Raleigh Mall in Memphis—all of which were located on outlying highways and all of which attracted shoppers from trading areas of a hundred square miles and more: Edward J. Bartolo, Sr., a self-made millionaire and workaholic, operated from a base in Youngstown, Ohio, to become the most prominent mall developer in the United States, but large insurance companies, especially the Equitable Life Assurance Society, increasingly sought high yields as shopping-center landlords.

During the 1970s, a new phenomenon—the super regional mall—added a more elaborate twist to suburban shopping. Prototypical of the new breed was Tyson's Corner, on the Washington Beltway in Fairfax County, Virginia. Anchored by Bloomingdale's, it did over $165 million in business in 1983 and provided employment to more than 14,000 persons. Even larger was Long Island's Roosevelt Field, a 180-store, 2.2 million square foot mega-mall that attracted 275,000 visitors a week and did $230 million in business in 1980. Most elaborate of all was Houston's Galleria, a world-famed setting for 240 prestigious boutiques, a quartet of cinemas, 26 restaurants, an olympic-sized ice-skating pavilion, and two luxury hotels. There were few windows in these mausoleums of merchandising, and clocks were rarely seen—just as in gambling casinos.

Boosters of such mega-malls argue that they are taking the place of the old central business districts and becoming the identifiable collecting points for the rootless families of the newer areas. As weekend and afternoon attractions, they have a special lure for teenagers, who often go there on shopping dates or to see the opposite sex. As one official noted in 1971: "These malls are now their street corners. The new shopping centers have killed the little merchant, closed most movies, and are now supplanting the older shopping centers in the suburbs." They are also especially attractive to mothers with young children and to the elderly, many of whom visit regularly to get out of the house without having to worry about crime or inclement weather.

In reality, even the largest malls are almost the opposite of downtown areas because they are self-contained and because they impose a uniformity of tastes and interests. They cater exclusively to middle-class tastes and contain no unsavory bars or pornography shops, no threatening-looking characters, no litter, no rain, and no excessive heat or cold. As Anthony Zube-Jackson has noted, their emphasis on cleanliness and safety is symptomatic of a very lopsided view of urban culture.

Despite their blandness, the shopping malls and the drive-in culture of which they are a part have clearly eclipsed the traditional central business districts, and in many medium-sized cities the last of the downtown department stores has already closed. The drive-in blight that killed them, like the Dutch Elm disease that ravaged Eastern towns in years past, has played hopscotch from one town to another, bringing down institutions that had once appeared invincible. The targets of this scourge, however, were not trees, but businesses, specifically the once-mighty department stores that anchored many a Main Street.

The most famous retailing victim of the drive-in culture thus far has been the stately J. L. Hudson Company of Detroit. It was a simple fact that all roads in the Motor City led to Hudson's. Featuring tall chandeliers, wood-paneled corridors, and brass-buttoned doormen, the 25-story full-square-block emporium at its height ranked with Macy's in New York and Marshall Field in Chicago as one of the country's three larges stores. After 1950, however, the once-proud store was choked by its own branches, all of them in outlying shopping centers. As soon as Hudson's opened Northland, its biggest suburban outlet and one of the earliest in the nation, sales downtown began to fall. They declined from a peak in 1953 of $153 million to $45 million in 1981. Finally, in 1981, the downtown landmark closed its doors for good. Hudson's was a victim of the product that made Detroit: the car.

In a Christmastime obituary for Detroit's most famous retailer, a WWJ radio commentator maintained that white flight to the suburbs, hastened by the Motor City's 1967 race riot, helped deal Hudson's a mortal blow. Actually, the 91-year-old store was killed by the free parking, easy accessibility, and controlled environment of the mega-malls.

By the 1960s, the primary rival to the shopping center as the locus of brief, informal communication and interaction had become the highway strip, with its flashing neon signs and tacky automobile showrooms. Especially in medium-sized cities, the vitality after dark is concentrated in the shopping malls or along the highway, not along Main Street.

A DRIVE-IN SOCIETY

Drive-in motels, drive-in movies, and drive-in shopping facilities were only a few of the many new institutions that followed in the exhaust of the internal-combustion engine. By 1984 mom-and-pop grocery stores had given way almost everywhere to supermarkets, most banks had drive-in windows, and a few funeral homes were making it possible for mourners to view the deceased, sign the register, and pay their respects without emerging from their cars. Odessa Community College in Texas even opened a drive-through registration window.

Particularly pervasive were fast-food franchises, which not only decimated the family-style restaurants but cut deeply into grocery store sales. In 1915 James G. Huneker, a raconteur whose tales of early-twentieth-century American life were compiled as *New Cosmopolis*, complained of the infusion of cheap, quick-fire "food hells," and of the replacement of relaxed dining with "canned music and automatic lunch taverns." With the automobile came the notion of "grabbing" something to eat. The first drive-in restaurant, Royce Hailey's Pig Stand, opened in Dallas in 1921, and later in the decade, the first fast-food franchise, "White Tower," decided that families touring in motorcars needed convenient meals

along the way. The places had to look clean, so they were painted white. They had to be familiar, so a minimal menu was standardized at every outlet. To catch the eye, they were built like little castles, replete with fake ramparts and turrets. And to forestall any problem with a land lease, the little white castles were built to be moveable.

The biggest restaurant operation of all began in 1954, when Ray A. Kroc, a Chicago area milkshake-machine salesman, joined forces with Richard and Maurice McDonald, the owners of a fast-food emporium in San Bernardino, California. In 1955 the first of Mr. Kroc's "McDonald's" outlets was opened in Des Plaines, a Chicago suburb long famous as the site of an annual Methodist encampment. The second and third, both in California, opened later in 1955. Within five years, there were 228 golden arches drive-ins selling hamburgers for 15 cents, french fries for 10 cents, and milkshakes for 20 cents. In 1961 Kroc bought out the McDonald brothers, and in the next twenty years this son of an unsuccessful realtor whose family came from Bohemia built an empire of 7,500 outlets and amassed a family fortune in excess of $500 million. Appropriately headquartered in suburban Oak Brook, Illinois, the McDonald's enterprise is based on free parking and drive-in access, and its methods have been copied by dozens of imitators. Late in 1984, on an interstate highway north of Minneapolis, McDonald's began construction of the most complete drive-in complex in the world. To be called McStop, it will feature a motel, gas station, convenience store, and, of course, a McDonald's restaurant.

Even church pews occasionally were replaced by the automobile. In early 1955, in suburban Garden Grove, California, the Reverend Robert Schuller, a member of the Reformed Church in America, began his ministry on a shoestring. With no sanctuary and virtually no money, he rented the Orange Drive-In movie theater on Sunday mornings and delivered his sermons while standing on top of the concession stand. The parishioners listened through speakers available at each parking space. What began as a necessity became a virtue when Schuller began attracting communicants who were more comfortable and receptive in their vehicles than in a pew. Word of the experiment—"Worship as you are . . . In the family car"—spread, the congregation grew, and in 1956 Schuller constructed a modest edifice for indoor services and administrative needs. But the Drive-in Church, as it was then called, continued to offer religious inspiration for automobile-bound parishioners, and in succeeding sanctuaries facilities were always included for those who did not want a "walk-in" church. By 1969 he had six thousand members in his church, and architect Richard Neutra had designed a huge, star-shaped "Tower of Power," situated appropriately on twenty-two acres just past Disneyland on the Santa Ana Freeway. It looked like and was called "a shopping center for Jesus Christ."

In 1980 a "Crystal Cathedral" was dedicated on the grounds. Designed by Philip Johnson, the $26 million structure is one of the most impressive and gargantuan religious buildings on earth. More than 125 feet high and 415 feet wide, its interior is a stunning cavern without columns, clad in over 10,000 panes of transparent glass. Yet the drive-in feature remains. Instead of separate services for his indoor and outdoor followers, Schuller broadcasts his message over the radio from an indoor/outdoor pulpit. At the beginning of each session, two 90-foot glass walls swing open so that the minister can be seen by drive-in worshippers. Traditionalists come inside the 3,000-seat "Crystal Cathedral," while those who remain in the "pews from Detroit" are directed to the announcement: "If you have a car radio, please turn to 540 on your dial for this service. If you do not have a radio, please park by the amplifiers in the back row." The appeal has been enormously successful. By 1984 Schuller's Garden Grove Community Church claimed to be the largest walk-in,

drive-in church in the world. Its Sunday broadcasts were viewed by an estimated one million Californians and commanded the nation's highest ratings for religious programming.

THE CENTERLESS CITY

More than anyplace else, California became the symbol of the postwar suburban culture. It pioneered the booms in sports cars, foreign cars, vans, and motor homes, and by 1984 its 26 million citizens owned almost 19 million motor vehicles and had access to the world's most extensive freeway system. The result has been a new type of centerless city, best exemplified by once sleepy and out-of-the-way Orange County, just south and east of Los Angeles. After Walt Disney came down from Hollywood, bought out the ranchers, and opened Disneyland in 1955, Orange County began to evolve from a rural backwater into a suburb and then into a collection of medium and small towns. It had never had a true urban focus, in large part because its oil-producing sections each spawned independent suburban centers, none of which was particularly dominant over the others. The tradition continued when the area became a subdivider's dream in the 1960s and 1970s. By 1980 there were 26 Orange County cities, none with more than 225,000 residents. Like the begats of the Book of Genesis, they merged and multiplied into a huge agglomeration of two million people with its own Census Bureau metropolitan area designation—Anaheim, Santa Ana, Garden Grove. Unlike the traditional American metropolitan region, however, Orange County lacked a commutation focus, a place that could obviously be accepted as the center of local life. Instead, the experience of a local resident was typical: "I live in Garden Grove, work in Irvine, shop in Santa Ana, go to the dentist in Anaheim, my husband works in Long Beach, and I used to be the president of the League of Women Voters in Fullerton."

A centerless city also developed in Santa Clara County, which lies forty-five miles south of San Francisco and which is best known as the home of "Silicon Valley." Stretching from Palo Alto on the north to the garlic and lettuce fields of Gilroy to the south, Santa Clara County has the world's most extensive concentration of electronics concerns. In 1940, however, it was best known for prunes and apricots, and it was not until after World War II that its largest city, San Jose, also became the nation's largest suburb. With fewer than 70,000 residents in 1940, San Jose exploded to 636,000 by 1980, superseding San Francisco as the region's largest municipality. As the automobile-based circulation system matured, the county's spacious orchards were easily developed, and bulldozers uprooted fruit trees for shopping centers and streets. Home builders, encouraged by a San Jose city government that annexed new territory at a rapid pace and borrowed heavily to build new utilities and schools on the fringes of town, moved farther and farther into the rural outskirts. Dozens of semiconductor and aerospace companies expanded and built plants there. In time, this brought twice-daily ordeals of bumper-to-bumper traffic on congested freeways. The driving time of some six-mile commutes lengthened to forty-five minutes, and the hills grew hazy behind the smog. As Santa Clara County became a national symbol of the excesses of uncontrolled growth, its residents began to fear that the high-technology superstars were generating jobs and taxes, but that the jobs attracted more people, and the taxes failed to cover the costs of new roads, schools, sewers, and expanded police and fire departments.

The numbers were larger in California, but the pattern was the same on the edges of every American city, from Buffalo Grove and Schaumburg near Chicago, to Germantown and Collierville near Memphis, to Creve Couer and Ladue near St. Louis. And perhaps more important than the growing number of people living outside of city boundaries was the sheer physical sprawl of metropolitan areas. Between 1950 and 1970, the urbanized area of Washington, D.C., grew from 181 to 523

square miles, of Miami from 116 to 429, while in the larger megalopolises of New York, Chicago, and Los Angeles, the region of settlement was measured in the thousands of square miles.

Since World War II, the American people have experienced a transformation of the man-made environment around them. Commercial, residential, and industrial structures have been redesigned to fit the needs of the motorist rather than the pedestrian. Garish signs, large parking lots, one-way streets, drive-in windows, and throw-away fast-food buildings—all associated with the world of suburbia—have replaced the slower-paced, neighborhood-oriented institutions of an earlier generation. Some observers of the automobile revolution have argued that the car has created a new and better urban environment and that the change in spatial scale, based upon swift transportation, has formed a new kind of organic entity, speeding up personal communication and rendering obsolete the older urban settings. Lewis Mumford, writing from his small-town retreat in Amenia, New York, has emphatically disagreed. His prize-winning book, *The City in History*, was a celebration of the medieval community and an excoriation of "the formless urban exudation" that he saw American cities becoming. He noted that the automobile megalopolis was not a final stage in city development but an anticity which "annihilates the city whenever it collides with it."

There are some signs that the halcyon days of the drive-in culture and automobile are behind us. More than one hundred thousand gasoline stations, or about one-third of the American total, have been eliminated in the last decade. Empty tourist courts and boarded-up motels are reminders that the fast pace of change can make commercial structures obsolete within a quarter-century of their erection. Even that suburban bellwether, the shopping center, which revolutionized merchandising after World War II, has come to seem small and out-of-date as newer covered malls attract both the trendy and the family trade. Some older centers have been recycled as bowling alleys or industrial buildings, and some have been remodeled to appeal to larger tenants and better-heeled customers. But others stand forlorn and boarded up. Similarly, the characteristic fast-food emporiums of the 1950s, with uniformed "car hops" who took orders at the automobile window, are now relics of the past. One of the survivors, Delores Drive-In, which opened in Beverly Hills in 1946, was recently proposed as an historic landmark, a sure sign that the species is in danger.

GLOSSARY

Lewis Mumford (1895–1990): Social critic and writer whose works, such as *The Culture of Cities*, decry dehumanizing technology and call for a return to humanitarian and moral values.

Winston Churchill (1874–1965): British statesman, soldier, and author; Prime Minister during World War II.

Art Deco: A decorative and architectural style of the period 1925–1940, characterized by geometric designs, bold colors, and the use of plastic and glass.

Tract house: One of the numerous houses of similar design constructed on a tract of land.

IMPLICATIONS

Although we take automobiles, trucks, and SUVs for granted today, automobile ownership became commonplace only during the 1950s. Why do you think automobiles were so attractive to Americans in postwar America? Why do you think automobiles had such a dramatic impact on the American way of life?

Lyndon Johnson is remembered as a consummate power broker, but he was also a powerful liberal reformer whose guiding philosophy was the provision of equal opportunity for all Americans. This essay begins with excerpts from Johnson's commencement address at Howard University, the nation's most prestigious predominantly African American college. In it, Johnson clearly articulates his guiding philosophy.

Lyndon B. Johnson, *Commencement Address at Howard University (1965)*

Our earth is the home of revolution.

In every corner of every continent men charged with hope contend with ancient ways in pursuit of justice. They reach for the newest of weapons to realize the oldest of dreams: that each may walk in freedom and pride, stretching his talents, enjoying the fruits of the earth.

Our enemies may occasionally seize the day of change. But it is the banner of our revolution they take. And our own future is linked to this process of swift and turbulent change in many lands. But nothing, in any country, touches us more profoundly, nothing is more freighted with meaning for our own destiny, than the revolution of the Negro American.

In far too many ways American Negroes have been another nation: deprived of freedom, crippled by hatred, the doors of opportunity closed to hope.

In our time change has come to this nation too. Heroically, the American Negro—acting with impressive restraints—has peacefully protested and marched, entered the courtrooms and the seats of government, demanding a justice long denied. The voice of the Negro was the call to action. But it is a tribute to America that, once aroused, the courts and the Congress, the President and most of the people, have been the allies of progress.

Thus we have seen the high court of the country declare that discrimination based on race was repugnant to the Constitution, and therefore void. We have seen—in 1957, 1960, and again in 1964—the first civil rights legislation in almost a century. . . .

The voting rights bill will be the latest, and among the most important, in a long series of victories. But this victory—as Winston Churchill said of another triumph for freedom—"is not the end. It is not even the beginning of the end. But it is, perhaps, the end of the beginning."

That beginning is freedom; and the barriers to that freedom are tumbling. Freedom is the right to share, fully and equally, in American society—to vote, to hold a job, to enter a public place, to go to school. It is the right to be treated, in every part of our national life, as a man equal in dignity and promise to all others.

But freedom is not enough. You do not wipe away the scars of centuries by saying: Now, you are free to go where you want, do as you desire, and choose the leaders you please.

You do not take a man who, for years, has been hobbled by chains, liberate him, bring him to the starting line of a race, saying "you are free to compete with all the others," and still justly believe you have been completely fair.

Thus it is not enough to open the gates of opportunity. All our citizens must have the ability to walk through those gates.

This is the next and the more profound stage of the battle for civil rights. We seek not just freedom but opportunity—not just legal equity but human ability—not just equality as a right and a theory, but equality as a fact and a result.

For the task is to give twenty million Negroes the same chance as every other American to learn and grow—to work and share in society—to develop their abilities—physical, mental, and spiritual, and to pursue their individual happiness.

To this end equal opportunity is essential, but not enough. Men and women of all races are born with the same range of abilities. But ability is not just the product of birth. It is stretched or stunted by the family you live with, and the neighborhood you live in—by the school you go to, and the poverty or richness of your surroundings. It is the product of a hundred unseen forces playing upon the infant, the child, and the man.

This graduating class at Howard University is witness to the indomitable determination of the Negro American to win his way in American life.

The number of Negroes in schools of high learning has almost doubled in fifteen years. The number of nonwhite professional workers has more than doubled in ten years. The median income of Negro college women now exceeds that of white college women. And these are the enormous accomplishments of distinguished individual Negroes—many of them graduates of this institution.

These are proud and impressive achievements. But they only tell the story of a growing middle class minority, steadily narrowing the gap between them and their white counterparts.

But for the great majority of Negro Americans—the poor, the unemployed, the uprooted and dispossessed—there is a grimmer story. They still are another nation. Despite the court orders and the laws, the victories and speeches, for them the walls are rising and the gulf is widening. . . .

We are not completely sure why this is. The causes are complex and subtle. But we do know the two broad basic reasons. And we know we have to act.

First, Negroes are trapped—as many whites are trapped—in inherited, gateless poverty. They lack training and skills. They are shut in slums, without decent medical care. Private and public poverty combine to cripple their capacities.

We are attacking these evils through our poverty program, our education program, our health program and a dozen more—aimed at the root causes of poverty.

We will increase, and accelerate, and broaden this attack in years to come, until this most enduring of foes yields to our unyielding will.

But there is a *second* cause—more difficult to explain, more deeply grounded, more desperate in its force. It is the devastating heritage of long years of slavery; and a century of oppression, hatred and injustice.

For Negro poverty is not white poverty. Many of its causes and many of its cures are the same. But there are differences—deep, corrosive, obstinate differences—radiating painful roots into the community, the family, and the nature of the individual.

These differences are not racial differences. They are solely and simply the consequence of ancient brutality, past injustice, and present prejudice. They are anguishing to observe. For the Negro they are a reminder of oppression. For the white they are a reminder of guilt. But they must be faced, and dealt with, and overcome; if we are to reach the time when the only difference between Negroes and whites is the color of their skin.

Nor can we find a complete answer in the experience of other American minorities. They made a valiant, and largely successful effort to emerge from poverty and prejudice. The Negro, like these others, will have to rely mostly on his own efforts. But he cannot do it alone. For they did not have the heritage of centuries to overcome. They did not have a cultural tradition which had been twisted and battered by endless years of hatred and hopelessness. Nor were they excluded because of race or color—a feeling whose dark intensity is matched by no other prejudice in our society.

Nor can these differences be understood as isolated infirmities. They are a seamless web. They cause each other. They result from each other. They reinforce each other. Much of the Negro community is buried under a blanket of history and circumstance. It is not a lasting solution to lift just one corner. We must stand on all sides and raise the entire cover if we are to liberate our fellow citizens.

One of the differences is the increased concentration of Negroes in our cities. More than 73 per cent of all Negroes live in urban areas compared with less than 70 per cent of whites. Most of them live in slums. And most of them live together; a separated people. Men are shaped by their world. When it is a world of decay ringed by an invisible wall—when escape is arduous and uncertain, and the saving pressures of a more hopeful society are unknown—it can cripple the youth and desolate the man.

There is also the burden a dark skin can add to the search for a productive place in society. Unemployment strikes most swiftly and broadly at the Negro. This burden erodes hope. Blighted hope breeds despair. Despair brings indifference to the learning which offers a way out. And despair coupled with indifference is often the source of destructive rebellion against the fabric of society. . . .

Perhaps most important—its influence radiating to every part of life—is the breakdown of the Negro family structure. For this, most of all, white America must accept responsibility. It flows from centuries of oppression and persecution of the Negro man. It flows from the long years of degradation and discrimination which have attacked his dignity and assaulted his ability to provide for his family. . . .

Unless we work to strengthen the family—to create conditions under which most parents will stay together—all the rest: schools and playgrounds, public assistance and private concern—will not be enough to cut completely the circle of despair and deprivation.

There is no single easy answer to all these problems.

Jobs are part of the answer. They bring the income which permits a man to provide for his family.

Decent homes in decent surroundings and a chance to learn are part of the answer.

Welfare and social programs better designed to hold families together are part of the answer.

Care for the sick is part of the answer.

An understanding heart by all Americans is also part of the answer.

To all these fronts—and a dozen more—I will dedicate the expanding efforts of my administration. . . .

It is the glorious opportunity of this generation to end the one huge wrong of the American nation—and in so doing to find America for ourselves, with the same immense thrill of discovery which gripped those who first began to realize that here, at last, was a home for freedom.

All it will take is for all of us to understand what this country is and what it must become.

The Scripture promises: "I shall light a candle of understanding in thine heart, which shall not be put out."

Together, and with millions more, we can light that candle of understanding in the heart of America.

And, once lit, it will never go out.

16

The Vietnam War, the Liberals, and the Overthrow of LBJ

Allen J. Matusow

The Vietnam War dominated much of American life in the decade between 1964 and 1974. With an active draft supplying the bulk of the quarter of a million American troops and advisers fighting in Vietnam, three presidents—Kennedy, Johnson, and Nixon—sought to project American military power into southeast Asia in an effort to "contain communism."

Between 1954—when the United States assumed the role of supporter of the corrupt but anti-Communist South Vietnamese regime—and the early 1960s, American involvement in Vietnam was limited to small numbers of military and civilian advisers. But beginning in 1962, when President John F. Kennedy created the Green Berets, a special counterinsurgency force, American involvement in the region took the path of escalation. Slowly at first, but with increasing speed after the mid-1960s, the American military presence grew until daily reports from the war zone dominated the nightly television news.

As the war continued, with little evidence of success or purpose, growing numbers of Americans began to question the propriety of the war. At the same time, students and other Americans, including many church leaders, organized the most effective antiwar movement in American history. By the late 1960s, antiwar protest took on epic proportions as tens of thousands of Americans—men and women, young and old alike—demonstrated across the country to end the war and bring American troops home.

One of the Vietnam War's more famous casualties was President Lyndon Johnson. In the arrogance of his belief that he could convert the peasants of Vietnam into his image of upwardly mobile American farmers, Johnson escalated U.S. involvement on an unprecedented scale. Mindless of local conditions and the history of the

From *The Unraveling of America* by Allen J. Matusow (New York: Harper & Row, 1984), pp. 376–394.

Vietnamese people, Johnson and his advisers committed billions of dollars to a war that many military analysts agreed could not be won. As Allen J. Matusow shows in this essay, Johnson's arrogance cost him the support of American liberals and ultimately the presidency itself.

··

In April 1965, three months after Lyndon Johnson made his decision to bomb North Vietnam, Democratic Senator Wayne Morse of Oregon predicted that Johnson's war policy would send him "out of office the most discredited President in the history of the nation." Given the popularity of both the war and the president at the time, Morse's prophecy seemed absurd on its face. But, as Vietnam dragged on month after month, it did indeed become an acid eroding Johnson's political base, until in the end it destroyed his presidency. The first constituency to be alienated by Vietnam—and the most dangerous opponent of Johnson's war policy—proved to be the liberal intellectuals.

At first glance the split between the president and the intellectuals seemed surprising. He was, after all, attempting to govern in the liberal tradition not only in his conduct of domestic policy but in foreign affairs as well. They must hate him, he came to believe, not really for anything he did but because of who he was—a crude Texas cowboy without a Harvard degree. What he failed to understand was that his liberalism and theirs—apparently so similar in 1964—thereafter rapidly diverged, his remaining rooted in the ideas of the 1950s, theirs moving far beyond.

The root of the difficulty was the breakup of the Cold War consensus. In the 1950s, of course, liberal intellectuals typically had embraced the Cold War as a holy crusade, becoming in the process staunch defenders of the American way of life. Even after Sputnik in 1957, when the intellectuals began denouncing the nation for its materialism and complacency, they did so primarily to goad the people into greater sacrifice for the struggle against world Communism. The first sign of restlessness began to appear around 1960. That was the year, for example, when Norman Podhoretz, a New York intellectual who had been a dutiful Cold War liberal but now felt the old ideas going stale, "going dead," became editor of the influential magazine *Commentary*. Daring to open his early issues to dissident voices, he discovered among the intellectuals who wrote for his magazine and read it "a hunger for something new and something radical." Radicalism was hardly the term to describe the outlook of the intellectuals in the Kennedy era, but they were more open to novelty, more willing to acknowledge the flaws in American society, than they had been for years. In 1963, when Kennedy and Kruschchev moved toward détente following the Cuban missile crisis, the international tension that for so long had sustained the Cold War mentality began to dissipate, the old obsession to bore. Liberal intellectuals supported Johnson's 1964 presidential campaign because they believed he shared not only their renewed commitment to social justice but their growing willingness to reach an accommodation with the Russians.

Strains in Johnson's relations with the liberals first appeared in February 1965 when Johnson launched his air war over North Vietnam. Immediately the *New Republic*, a leading journal of liberal opinion, and the Americans for Democratic Action (ADA), the leading liberal organization, condemned the bombing and called for a negotiated settlement. Johnson was perplexed by the criticism since he correctly believed that he was merely applying in Vietnam the doctrine of containment so recently espoused by the liberals themselves. He did not grasp that that doctrine had suddenly fallen from fashion. Among the prominent liberal intellectuals who attempted to account for the shifting views of their community were Hans Morgenthau, an academic specialist in foreign affairs, member of the ADA board, and an early and formidable war critic; Reinhold Niebuhr, the renowned theologian and a founder of ADA, ailing but still influential; Arthur Schlesinger, Jr., a historian, former White House aide of Kennedy and Johnson, half-hearted defender of the war in 1965, but a leading foe by 1966; John Kenneth Galbraith, the Harvard economist, Kennedy's ambassador to India, and in 1967 the ADA chairman; Richard Goodwin, a precocious speech writer for Johnson till September 1965, and a war critic by the following spring; and Richard Rovere, the prestigious political correspondent of *The New Yorker*, a late but important convert to the dove side of the war argument.

The liberal intellectuals did not apologize for their past support of the Cold War. So long as Communist parties everywhere had subordinated themselves to the malign purposes of the Soviet Union, every Communist gain threatened American security. But times had changed, the liberals said. The Communist world was now "polycentric" (many-centered), a situation resulting from the Sino-Soviet split and the emergence of conflicting national aspirations among Communist states. Wrote Schlesinger, "Communism is no longer a unified, coordinated, centralized conspiracy." According to Rovere, since Tito's break with Stalin in 1948, the U.S. should have known that "international Communism" was a myth, "that national interest was more powerful than ideology, and that while we might on occasion find it advisable to resist the outward thrust of certain Communist nations, it made absolutely no sense to have a foreign policy directed against an alliance that did not exist." In short, it was no longer necessary to oppose every Communist initiative on every part of the globe.

With the exception of Morgenthau, who favored recognizing spheres of influence, these intellectuals continued to advocate containing China. But they denied that the war in Vietnam followed logically from this policy. Secretary of State Dean Rusk's opinion to the contrary, China was not the enemy here. The war in South Vietnam, they argued, was primarily a civil war, pitting indigenous revolutionaries against the corrupt and repressive regime in Saigon. If the Communists won, Vietnam might well become a bulwark against the spread of Chinese influence in the region. As a practical matter, the U.S. could not win. Escalation on the ground in the South could easily be offset by the enemy and would do nothing to remedy the defects of the Saigon government. Bombing the North would merely strengthen the enemy's will to fight. If Johnson proceeded on the course of escalation, he would destroy the country he was trying to save or else provoke war with China.

The war, the liberals said, was not a result of American imperialism but a mistake of policy deriving from obsolete assumptions about international Communism. Unfortunately, it was a mistake not easily remedied. Liberals rejected unilateral withdrawal on the grounds that it would mean abandonment of America's friends in the South, a blow to U.S. prestige, and maybe even the rise at home of a new Joe McCarthy to exploit the frustrations attending defeat. The liberal solution was a negotiated settlement—the middle course, they called it. Stop the foolish bombing in the North, since Hanoi demanded it as a precondition for negotiations. Convince Ho Chi Minh that the U.S. could not be dislodged by force. Offer the Vietcong a seat at the conference table and a role in the postwar political life of South Vietnam. It was possible, of course, that negotiations would fail. In that event, said Galbraith, "We must be prepared to defend for the time being the limited areas that are now secure." Indeed, on close inspection, it turned out that the liberals were waist deep in the Big Muddy along with LBJ and were no more certain than he of getting back to shore. The difference was that they thought the war was all a big mistake, and he was there on principle.

As opposition to the war among the intellectuals mounted, so did their impatience with the administration's response to the great racial and urban crisis that was tearing the country apart. As they never would have done during the American celebration that had characterized the heydey of the Cold War, liberals were now earnestly discussing the menace of corporate monopoly, redistribution of income, and a Marshall Plan for the cities. In its January 1967 issue *Commentary* ran both a long article by Theodore Draper attacking Johnson's foreign policy for its "willingness to use and abuse naked military power" and an essay by the Keynesian economist Robert Lekachman summarizing the case of many liberal intellectuals against the president's domestic policies. Lekachman wrote:

> Possibly Mr. Johnson went just about as far as a conservative politician in a conservative, racist country could have gone. The Great Society has distributed the nation's income even less equally than it was distributed before 1960. It has enlarged the prestige and influence of the business community. It has lost its token bouts with racism and poverty. The Great Society, never a giant step beyond the New Deal which was President Johnson's youthful inspiration, has ground to a halt far short of a massive attack on urban blight, far short of the full integration of Negroes into American society, and far short of a genuine assault upon poverty and deprivation.

Where liberal intellectuals led, liberal politicians usually followed. But politicians skeptical of the war in Vietnam initially hesitated to tangle with a president to whom most were bound by ties of party loyalty and whose vindictive character was legend. In 1965 even senators held their tongues, excepting of course Oregon's Wayne Morse and Alaska's Ernest Gruening, the lone opponents of the 1964 Gulf of Tonkin Resolution. Among those who privately worried but publicly acquiesced in Johnson's war policy were Senators Mike Mansfield, George McGovern, Frank Church,

Joseph Clark, Eugene McCarthy, and J. William Fulbright. Fulbright was the pivotal figure. If he moved into the open against Johnson, the rest would follow.

A senator from the ex-Confederate state of Arkansas, Fulbright was a gentleman of inherited wealth, excellent education, and illiberal record on matters of race and social reform. But for more than twenty years, on matters of foreign policy, Fulbright had been the leading spokesman in Congress for the views of the liberal community. Though he had had his share of arguments with presidents, he was by nature a contemplative rather than a combative man, a Senate club member who played by the rules. Fulbright's early opinions on Vietnam were hardly heretical. In March 1964, in a wide-ranging speech attacking Cold War mythology, he paused over Vietnam long enough to make a few hawkish observations. The allies were too weak militarily to obtain "the independence of a non-Communist South Vietnam" through negotiations, he said. The only "realistic options" were to hasten the buildup of the regime in the South or to expand the war, "either by the direct commitment of large numbers of American troops or by equipping the South Vietnamese Army to attack North Vietnamese territory." In August 1964 Fulbright sponsored the Gulf of Tonkin Resolution, which gave Johnson authority to expand the war.

For reasons unknown, Fulbright had second thoughts about escalation once it actually began. Publicly in the spring of 1965 he backed Johnson's policy, though he called for a temporary bombing halt to induce Hanoi to negotiate. Privately, he warned his old friend in the White House against waging war on North Vietnam and tempted him with the vision of a Communist Vietnam hostile to China. Johnson seemed bored by Fulbright's conversation. Fulbright gave a Senate speech in June that both criticized the bombing and praised Johnson's statesmanship. In July Johnson began the massive infusion of ground troops into South Vietnam.

Fulbright's first real attack on the Johnson administration was occasioned not by Vietnam but by policy in the Dominican Republic. In April 1965 Johnson sent U.S. troops into the midst of a developing civil war, ostensibly to protect Americans but really to prevent a possible Communist takeover. Fulbright brooded over this intervention, held secret hearings on it, and finally in September delivered a powerful Senate speech attacking the administration's conduct as ruthless and lacking in candor. The president promptly ended all pretense of consulting the chairman of the Foreign Relations Committee and cut him socially.

As Fulbright edged toward open rebellion on the issue of the war, so did the other Senate doves, almost all of whom were liberal Democrats. This was probably one reason why Johnson halted the bombing of North Vietnam on Christmas Eve, 1965, and launched a well-advertised peace offensive allegedly to persuade Hanoi to negotiate. The State Department moved closer to Hanoi's conditions for negotiations in early January, and both sides scaled down ground action in South Vietnam. Diplomats in several capitals worked to bring the wary antagonists together. But on January 24, 1966, Johnson hinted to a group of congressional leaders that he might soon resume the bombing. Two days later fifteen senators, all of them liberal Democrats, sent a letter to Johnson urging him to continue the pause. Fulbright and Mansfield did not sign but were on record with similar views. On January 29, Johnson ordered the air attack to recommence. The episode convinced many liberals that Johnson's talk about peace masked his private determination to win total military victory.

In February 1966 Fulbright held televised hearings on the war. The scholar-diplomat George Kennan and the retired general James Gavin argued the case against it on grounds of American self-interest. Dean Rusk and General Maxwell Taylor parried the thrusts of liberal committee members now openly critical of Johnson's policy. Neither side drew blood in debate, but by helping legitimize dissent, the Fulbright hearings were a net loss for Johnson. Fulbright, meantime, was reading, talking to experts, and rethinking first principles. In the spring of 1966 he took to the lecture platform to hurl thunderbolts at orthodoxy. Revised and published as a book later in the year, Fulbright's lectures were a critique of American foreign policy far more advanced than any yet produced by the liberal academicians.

"Gradually but unmistakably America is showing signs of that arrogance of power which has afflicted, weakened, and in some cases destroyed great nations in the past," Fulbright said. Harnessing her might to a crusading ideology, America had overextended herself abroad and was neglecting vital tasks at home. Americans meant well overseas, Fulbright conceded, but they often did more harm than good, especially in the Third World. A conservative people, Americans supported necessary social revolutions in traditional societies only if they were peaceful, that is, in "our own shining image." To violent revolutions, which "seem to promise greater and faster results," Americans reacted with automatic hostility or panic. Fulbright was hardly an apologist for revolutions, but neither would he oppose them, even if they were led by Communists. Fulbright dared to find much that was praiseworthy in Castro's Cuba and even extended sympathy to the aims of the Chinese revolutionaries, whose regime he would recognize de facto. In Vietnam, he said, the U.S. had blundered into a war against Communism in the only country in the world "which won freedom from colonial rule under communist leadership." Fulbright favored a negotiated settlement that would provide self-determination for South Vietnam through the mechanism of a referendum.

President Johnson had expected his main trouble to come from hawks who wanted to escalate faster than he did. Stung by the sweeping attacks of Fulbright and other doves, he resorted to a scoundrel's last refuge. Before a friendly audience of Democratic politicians in

Chicago mid-May 1966, Johnson defended the war as a patriotic effort to secure lasting peace by punishing aggression and then said, "There will be some 'Nervous Nellies' and some who will become frustrated and bothered and break ranks under the strain, and some will turn on their leaders, and on their country, and on our own fighting men. . . . But I have not the slightest doubt that the courage and the dedication and the good sense of the wise American people will ultimately prevail." The attack failed to silence the critics. The majority of the people still backed the war, but not with the passion aroused by wars of the past. Fulbright continued to assault the premises of American foreign policy and, indirectly, the president who was acting on them. Confronted with irreconcilable views of world politics, members of the liberal public in ever-increasing numbers deserted the president and sided with the senator.

To make matters worse for Johnson, he faced a personal as well as an intellectual challenge to his party leadership. When Robert Kennedy emerged from mourning in early 1964, he discovered a remarkable fact. Despite his squeaky voice, diffident public manner, private shyness, and reputation as a ruthless backroom operator, he was the sole beneficiary of his brother's political estate. In him resided the hopes of millions who believed the myth of Camelot and longed for a Kennedy restoration. Robert Kennedy believed the myth himself and shared the longing. Lyndon Johnson, however, despised Kennedy personally and made himself the great obstacle to the younger man's ambitions. After Johnson denied him the vice-presidential nomination in 1964, Kennedy repaired to New York, where he successfully ran for the Senate. Soon there grew up around him what the political columnists called the Kennedy party—Kennedy loyalists still in the bureaucracy, some senators, New Frontiersman out of favor, and lesser politicians, lawyers, and professors scattered around the country. Most of the Kennedy loyalists were liberals, but by no means all liberals were Kennedy loyalists.

Robert Kennedy, after all, had been an ally of Joe McCarthy, an advocate of wiretapping, too zealous a pursuer of the Teamster chief Jimmy Hoffa, and a frequent offender of liberal sensibilities. But liberals unhappy with Johnson needed a popular leader, and Kennedy needed to broaden his party base. The one issue guaranteed to bring them together was Vietnam.

The issue posed problems for Kennedy. As a Cabinet officer, he had been an enthusiastic student of guerrilla warfare and a strong supporter of his brother's counterinsurgency program in South Vietnam. When Johnson escalated in 1965, Kennedy questioned less the attempt to rescue South Vietnam by force of arms than the tendency to subordinate political to military considerations in fighting the war. Speaking at the graduation ceremony of the International Police Academy in July, he said, "I think the history of the last 20 years demonstrates beyond doubt that our approach to revolutionary war must be political—political first, political last, political always." To avoid offending Johnson, he excised from his prepared text the view that "victory in a revolutionary war is won not by escalation but by de-escalation." Kennedy waited one whole year after escalation before putting real distance between his position and Johnson's. It bothered Kennedy that, when Fulbright asked Rusk during the television hearings of February 1966 to state the options other than "surrender or annihilation" that he was offering the Vietcong, Rusk had replied, "They do have an alternative of quitting, of stopping being an agent of Hanoi and receiving men and arms from the North." The war could go on forever if this was the American requirement for peace. So Kennedy decided to propose another option. On February 19, 1966, he became the first senator to suggest a negotiated settlement that would give the Vietcong "a share of power and responsibility"—in what he did not say. Assuming he meant the government of Vietnam, the administration dismissed the idea contemptuously. Kennedy's proposal, said Vice

President Humphrey, would be like putting "a fox in the chicken coop" or "an arsonist in a fire department." Kennedy spent the next week clarifying and qualifying, and though he retreated some, he was clearly moving toward the peace wing of his party.

Strange things were happening to Bobby Kennedy. Perhaps prolonged grief deepened his social sympathies, perhaps he was trying in his own life to vindicate his brother's legend—or outdo it. Whatever the cause, Kennedy plunged into the currents of change that were swirling through America in the mid-1960s, currents that were altering the perspective of liberalism and passing Johnson by. Kennedy opened a running dialogue with students, made a friend of Tom Hayden, felt the yearnings of the poor and the black for power and dignity, and took unnecessary political risks. Blood donations for the Vietcong? Burial for a Communist war hero in Arlington Cemetery? Why not? he asked. Kennedy went to South Africa in mid-1966 to aid the opponents of apartheid. He attacked administration witnesses at Senate hearings in August for unresponsiveness to the poor. He flew to California to stand with Cesar Chavez in his fight to unionize the grape pickers. A man who risked his life scaling mountains and defying tropical storms on the Amazon, Kennedy was becoming an existentialist in politics, defining himself in action and moving where his heart told him to go.

As Kennedy and Johnson edged closer toward political combat, their personal relations worsened. In February 1967 *Newsweek* erroneously reported that Kennedy had brought back from a recent trip to Paris a peace feeler from Hanoi. The story enraged Johnson, who, believing it was planted by Kennedy, called him to the White House for a tongue lashing. According to *Time*'s colorful account, Johnson told Kennedy, "If you keep talking like this, you won't have a political future in this country within six months," warned him that "the blood of American boys will be on your hands," and concluded, "I never want to see you again." Uncowed, Kennedy called Johnson an s.o.b and told him, "I don't have to sit here and take that—." Whether Kennedy really used vulgarity was a matter of some dispute, but there was no doubt that the gist of the conversation had been accurately reported. Less than a month later (March 2, 1967) Kennedy gave a major Senate speech calling for a halt to the bombing and a compromise settlement through negotiations. A few party malcontents, especially in the liberal wing, permitted themselves a small hope that maybe the crown prince of the Democratic party would claim his inheritance sooner than expected.

In the summer of 1967 gloom descended on the camp of the liberals. In August Johnson sent 45,000 more troops to Vietnam and asked for higher taxes to finance the war. And, though Defense Secretary Robert McNamara himself voiced public criticism of the bombing, day after day the bombs continued to fall. Liberals who had once viewed it merely as politically stupid watched in horror as the carnage mounted and now pronounced the war morally wrong as well. Meanwhile domestic insurrectionaries were gutting great American cities, the War on Poverty was bogging down, and the long-awaited white backlash finally arrived. Among those surrendering to despair that summer was Senator Fulbright. Speaking to the American Bar Association in August, he said, "How can we commend democratic social reform to Latin America when Newark, Detroit, and Milwaukee are providing explosive evidence of our own inadequate efforts at democratic social reform? How can we commend the free enterprise system to Asians and Africans when in our own country it has produced vast, chaotic, noisy, dangerous and dirty urban complexes while poisoning the very air and land and water?" Fulbright called the war "unnecessary and immoral" and blamed it for aggravating grave domestic problems. The country "sickens for lack of moral leadership," he said, and only the idealistic young may save us from the "false and dangerous dream of an imperial destiny."

Fulbright's charges about the damage done at home by the war were confirmed in the autumn. Driven by hatred of the war, new left students began acting out their guerrilla fantasies, and major campuses were threatened by chaos. No less disturbing to liberals was the fever of discontent rising in intellectual circles. Some of the nation's most brilliant writers and artists were concluding, as had their counterparts in France during the Algerian war, that they now had no choice but to resist the state.

From the beginning a minority of the nation's intellectual elite—call them radicals—saw the war as more than a blunder in judgment. Most of these radicals had life histories punctuated by episodes of dissent but had stayed aloof from politics during the Cold War. Vietnam brought them back to political awareness and gave focus to their inchoate alienation. To people like the novelists Norman Mailer and Mary McCarthy, the critics Susan Sontag and Dwight Macdonald, *New York Review of Books* editor Robert Silvers, the linguist Noam Chomsky, the anarchist writer Paul Goodman, and the poet Robert Lowell, America appeared to be in the hands of a technological elite that was debauching the American landscape and lusting after world dominion. Morally revolted by the imperial war against the peasants of Vietnam, the radicals found traditional politics insufficient to express their opposition. The war was a matter of conscience, and good men would act accordingly.

Their first impulse was to avoid complicity with the crime. Thus when Johnson invited a group of writers and artists to participate in a White House Festival of the Arts in June 1965, Robert Lowell refused to come. Scion of a distinguished American family, perhaps the best of living American poets, and a draft resister in World War II, Lowell sent a letter to the president, saying, "Every serious artist knows that he cannot enjoy public celebration without making subtle public commitments. . . . We are in danger of imperceptibly becoming an explo-

sive and suddenly chauvinistic nation, and we may even be drifting on our way to the last nuclear ruin. . . . At this anguished, delicate and perhaps determining moment, I feel I am serving you and our country best by not taking part." Robert Silvers took the lead in circulating a statement in support of his friend Lowell and in two days attracted the signatures of twenty of the nation's most prominent writers and artists, among them Hannah Arendt, Lillian Hellman, Alfred Kazin, Dwight Macdonald, Bernard Malamud, Mary McCarthy, William Styron, and Robert Penn Warren. Johnson was so angry at "these people," these "sonsofbitches" that he almost canceled the festival.

By 1967 the radicals were obsessed by the war and frustrated by their impotence to affect its course. The government was unmoved by protest, the people were uninformed and apathetic, and American technology was tearing Vietnam apart. What, then, was their responsibility? Noam Chomsky explored this problem in February 1967 in the *New York Review*, which had become the favorite journal of the radicals. By virtue of their training and leisure, intellectuals had a greater responsibility than ordinary citizens for the actions of the state, Chomsky said. It was their special responsibility "to speak the truth and expose lies." But the "free-floating intellectual" who had performed this function in the past was being replaced by the "scholar-expert" who lied for the government or constructed "value-free technologies" to keep the existing social order functioning smoothly. Chomsky not only enjoined the intellectuals once again "to seek the truth lying behind the veil of distortion"; he concluded by quoting an essay written twenty years before by Dwight Macdonald, an essay that implied that in time of crisis exposing lies might not be enough. "Only those who are willing to resist authority themselves when it conflicts too intolerably with their personal moral code," Macdonald had written, "only they have the right to condemn." Chomsky's article was immediately recognized as an important intellectual event. Along with the radical students, radical intellectuals were moving "from protest to resistance."

The move toward resistance accelerated through 1967. Chomsky announced in the *New York Review* that for the second consecutive year he was withholding half his income taxes to protest the war. Paul Goodman invited federal prosecution by acknowledging his efforts to aid and abet draft resistance. Mary McCarthy, back from a trip to Vietnam, said that "to be in the town jail, as Thoreau knew, can relieve any sense of imaginary imprisonment." On the cover of its issue of August 24, 1967, the *New York Review* put a diagram of a Molotov cocktail, while inside Andrew Kopkind, in the midst of dismissing Martin Luther King for having failed to make a revolution, wrote, "Morality, like politics, starts at the barrel of a gun." (Some intellectuals never forgave the *New York Review* for that one.) On October 12, 1967, the *New York Review* published a statement signed by 121 intellectuals and entitled "A Call to Resist Illegitimate Authority." The statement denounced the war on legal and moral grounds and pledged the signers to raise funds "to organize draft resistance unions, to supply legal defense and bail, to support families and otherwise aid resistance to the war in whatever ways may seem appropriate."

A few days later Stop the Draft Week began. This was an event whose possibilities excited radical intellectuals as well as radical students. Paul Goodman kicked the week off with a speech at the State Department before an audience of big business executives. "You are the military industrial of the United States, the most dangerous body of men at the present in the world," Goodman declaimed. On Friday, October 20, 1967, Lowell and Mailer spoke on the steps of the Justice Department prior to the efforts of the Reverend William Sloane Coffin to deliver to the government draft cards collected from draft resisters across the country earlier in the week. (This occasion provided evidence for later federal charges of criminal conspiracy against Coffin, Dr. Benjamin Spock, and three other antiwar activists.) Saturday began with speeches at the Lincoln Memorial ("remorseless, amplified harangues for peace," Lowell called them), and then the march across the bridge toward the Pentagon. Lowell, Mailer, and Macdonald, described by Mailer as "America's best poet? and best novelist??, and best critic???," walked to the battle together. Lowell wrote of the marchers that they were

> . . . like green Union recruits
> for the first Bull Run, sped by photographers,
> the notables, the girls . . . fear, glory, chaos,
> rout . . .
> our green army staggered out on the miles-long
>   green fields,
> met by the other army, the Martian, the ape, the
>   hero,
> his new-fangled rifle, his green new steel helmet.

At the Pentagon Mailer was arrested, much to his satisfaction, but Lowell and Macdonald failed of their object. Noam Chomsky, also present, had not intended to participate in civil disobedience, feeling its purpose in this occasion too vague to make a point. Swept up by the events of the day, Chomsky found himself at the very walls of the fortress, making a speech. When a line of soldiers began marching toward him, he spontaneously sat down. Chomsky spent the night in jail with Mailer.

In his brilliant book *The Armies of the Night*, Mailer probed for the meaning of these apocalyptic events. For him the siege of the Pentagon was a rite of passage for the student rebels, for the intellectuals, for himself. The few hundred fearful youths who sat on the Pentagon steps till dawn on Sunday were a "refrain from all the great American rites of passage when men and women manacled themselves to a lost and painful principle and survived a day, a night, a week, a month, a year." The battle at the Pentagon was a pale rite of passage, he thought, compared to that of the immigrants packed in steerage, Rogers and

Clark, the Americans "at Sutter's Mill, at Gettysburg, the Alamo, the Klondike, the Argonne, Normandy, Pusan." But it was a true rite of passage nonetheless, the survivors having been reborn and rededicated to great purpose. On departing from jail Sunday morning, Mailer felt as Christians must "when they spoke of Christ within them." For Mailer and many other radical intellectuals, American institutions seemed so illegitimate that a moral man could find redemption only in resisting them. As for the liberals, they could only wonder what would happen to America if Lyndon Johnson was not stopped.

Signs of a liberal revolt against Johnson's renomination were plentiful in the fall of 1967. Reform Democrats in New York, the liberal California Democratic Council, party factions in Minnesota, Michigan, Wisconsin, and elsewhere were preparing to oppose him. In late September the ADA national board implicitly came out against him by promising to back the candidate who offered "the best prospect for a settlement of the Vietnam conflict." The *New Republic* explicitly rejected his candidacy in an editorial that same week. And Allard Lowenstein, thirty-eight-year-old liberal activist and ADA vice-chairman, opened an office in Washington and began organizing a movement on campuses, in the peace movement, and among dissident Democratic politicians to "dump Johnson."

Lowenstein wanted Robert Kennedy to be his candidate. And the existentialist Bobby was tempted. Kennedy worried about the frustration building up in the antiwar movement and had himself come to view the war as morally repugnant. "We're killing South Vietnamese, we're killing women, we're killing innocent people because we don't want to have the war fought on American soil, or because they're 12,000 miles away and they might get 11,000 miles away," he said on *Face the Nation* late in November 1967. But Bobby the professional hated losing, and in his view he could not defeat Johnson in a fight for the nomination, and neither could anybody else. On that same

TV program he stated flatly that he would not be a candidate. If he were, he said, "it would immediately become a personality struggle," and the real issues would be obscured. Asked about some other Democrat, such as Senator Eugene McCarthy of Minnesota, taking on the president, Kennedy replied, "There could be a healthy element in that." He would endorse neither Johnson nor McCarthy but support whoever was the eventual party nominee.

Eugene McCarthy had become convinced that someone would have to raise the issue of the war in the party primaries in 1968. When Kennedy and other leading doves rejected Lowenstein's pleas to be the candidate, McCarthy agreed to run. Explaining his purpose at a press conference on November 30, 1967, he said, "There is growing evidence of a deepening moral crisis in America—discontent and frustration and a disposition to take extralegal if not illegal actions to manifest protest. I am hopeful that this challenge . . . may alleviate at least in some degree this sense of political helplessness and restore to many people a belief in the processes of American politics and of American government." In other words, McCarthy was offering his candidacy as an alternative to radicalism.

Only an unusual politician would undertake what no one else would dare. In truth McCarthy, who had spent eight months of his youth as a novice in a Benedictine monastery, was in the political world but not of it. He was a senator bored by the Senate, an office seeker who distained intrigue and self-advertisement, a professional who valued honor more than influence. In recent years he had seemed more interested in Thomistic theology and writing poetry than in the business of government. His career, it appeared, would not fulfill its early promise. But the political crisis in the United States in late 1967 provided McCarthy with an opportunity perfectly suited to his self-conception. Like his hero Thomas More, he would play the martyr in a historic confrontation between conscience and power.

McCarthy's candidacy prospered beyond anyone's expectation, even his own. Though Johnson's rating on the Gallup poll was only 41 percent in November, the professionals were mesmerized by the cliché that no president could be denied renomination by his own party. The war was the biggest cause of Johnson's unpopularity. Hawks and doves disagreed on how best to end the war but otherwise had much in common: both disliked the war, wanted its early termination, and tended to blame Lyndon Johnson for dragging it on. It was the public's declining confidence in Johnson's ability to conclude the war that made him vulnerable to McCarthy's candidacy.

What little confidence still existed in the president's war leadership was shattered on January 31, 1968, when the Vietnamese Communists launched a massive attack in the midst of a truce called for the Tet holiday. Sixty-seven thousand enemy troops invaded more than one hundred of South Vietnam's cities and towns. The allies recaptured most urban areas after a few days and inflicted huge casualties on the attackers. But the Tet Offensive had astounded military men by its scope and daring. It showed that no place in South Vietnam was secure, not even the American embassy, whose walls had been breached in the first hours of the attack. And it temporarily derailed the pacification program in the countryside by drawing allied troops into the cities. Coming after recent administration assurances that the war was being won, the Tet Offensive dealt Johnson's credibility its crowning blow. When he and the U.S. commander in Vietnam, General William Westmoreland, issued victory statements after the offensive ended, few took them seriously, though militarily they were right. The chief political casualty of the Tet Offensive, therefore, was Lyndon Johnson.

In the six weeks after Tet, such pillars of establishment opinion as Walter Cronkite, *Newsweek*, the *Wall Street Journal*, and NBC News gave way and called for de-escalation. High officials in the government finally dared express their private doubts about the war to the president. The Gallup poll reported a seismic shift in public opinion: in February self-described hawks had outnumbered doves 60 percent to 24 percent; in March it was hawks 41 percent, doves 42 percent. And on March 10, two days before the New Hampshire primary, the *New York Times* set off waves of national anxiety by reporting a secret request from the generals to the president for 206,000 more troops for the war.

Meanwhile, in New Hampshire, the first primary state, McCarthy was proving an eccentric candidate. A lazy campaigner, he often did not return phone calls, would not court potential contributors, and avoided local politicians. His manner on the stump was uninspired, and even his references to the war were low-key. (McCarthy opposed unilateral withdrawal and advocated a negotiated settlement.) But McCarthy had an insight denied to his detractors: he mattered less in this campaign than the movement he represented. At the climax of the campaign there were so many student volunteers in the tiny state (3,000, or one for every 25 Democratic voters) that McCarthy's lieutenants begged potential workers to stay home. Scrubbed and shaven, the students ran a canvassing operation that was the envy of the professionals. Even McCarthy's peculiar style proved to be an asset. At a time when the country was fed up with politicians, shrill voices, and the hard sell, there was something reassuring in McCarthy's unhurried, dignified manner. He did not frighten people. He seemed safe.

Governor John W. King, one of the inept managers of Johnson's write-in campaign in New Hampshire, said in the beginning that McCarthy would get 5 percent of the vote. McCarthy himself predicted 30 percent. On March 12, 1968, 49 percent of New Hampshire's Democratic voters wrote in the name of the president of the United States, and 42 percent marked their ballots for a senator of whom days before few had heard. Poll data showed that more McCarthy voters in

New Hampshire were hawks than doves. McCarthy's remarkable showing, then, was not a victory for peace, merely proof that Lyndon Johnson, who could neither pacify the ghetto, speak the plain truth, lick inflation, nor above all end the war, was a mighty unpopular president indeed.

McCarthy had done more than demonstrate Johnson's vulnerability. As he had hoped, his candidacy drained off some of the discontent flowing into illegal protest. Thousands of students who might otherwise have joined SDS got "clean for Gene." Intellectuals who had flirted with resistance a few months before became the senator's avid fans. McCarthy's traveling companion through much of New Hampshire was Robert Lowell—a symbolic relationship whose significance was probably lost on neither of these famous poets.

It had been a hard winter for Robert Kennedy. He realized after the Tet Offensive that his refusal to run had been a mistake. Throughout February 1968, while McCarthy's New Hampshire campaign was getting started, Kennedy and his advisers wrestled again with the problem of his candidacy. Kennedy was ready to go early in March and set in motion machinery for a campaign. But still he found reason to delay a public announcement. By the time he declared on March 16, 1968, the results of the New Hampshire primary had already electrified the country. Much of the constituency that would have been his now belonged to McCarthy. Lyndon Johnson, however, took Kennedy's candidacy more seriously than McCarthy's. He knew, even if the students did not, that Kennedy was the one man in the party who might beat him.

McCarthy refused to set aside for Kennedy and moved on to the Wisconsin primary, whose date was April 2. Early in March the president's men in Wisconsin had been confident of victory. But McCarthy arrived with more students, money, and prestige than he had had in New Hampshire, and by mid-month the Johnson managers knew their man was in trouble. On March 28 Postmaster Larry O'Brien,

an old political pro, returned from a look around the state to tell Johnson that his cause there was hopeless.

While the political storms raged around them, Johnson and his advisers were deep into a momentous review of war policy. General Earl Wheeler, chairman of the Joint Chiefs of Staff, had blundered in late February when he privately requested 206,000 additional troops for Vietnam. Since General Westmoreland was in no danger of being overrun, there was never much chance that Johnson would dispatch massive reinforcements. The tax money to pay for escalation was not there, and neither was the political support. Wheeler's request had one unintended result. By asking so much, it forced policy makers to resolve the basic ambiguity that had characterized America's policy since 1965. Militarily, Johnson had been seeking victory over the Vietcong. Diplomatically, he paid lip service to a negotiated settlement, which implied compromise. Since his generals were in effect telling him that they needed more troops than he could furnish to win, Johnson had no choice now except to opt for negotiation. Accounts differ on how Johnson reached this conclusion in March 1968. But in the end those of his advisers urging some steps in the direction of de-escalation prevailed. On March 31 Johnson went on television to announce that he was stopping the bombing over most of North Vietnam and would end it entirely if Hanoi demonstrated comparable restraint. Johnson called on the North Vietnamese to respond to his partial bombing halt by accepting his invitation to negotiate. A few days later they did so.

Johnson announced another decision in this speech. For some time he had been dropping hints among friends and advisers that he might not run in 1968. Only at the last minute did he determine not to make his 1968 State of the Union Message the occasion for announcing his retirement. But his mood seemed to change after that, and he took steps to organize a re-selection campaign. Even after the ambush in New Hampshire, Johnson authorized Larry

O'Brien to meet with cabinet officers and give them marching orders for the political battle ahead.

Though most Johnson intimates believed he would run, he had compelling reasons not to. Exhausted, haunted by fear of another heart attack, bitter at the vilification he had suffered, the man had had enough. "The only difference between the [John F.] Kennedy assassination and mine," he said in this period, "is that I am alive and it has been more tortuous." There were other reasons too. Politically he faced a Congress opposed to his programs, a public that had lost confidence in his leadership, a defeat at the hands of McCarthy in the Wisconsin primary, and an uncertain contest with Robert Kennedy. On the diplomatic front, he wished to take a step toward peace, which his opponents, domestic and foreign, would probably dismiss as insincere if he remained a potential candidate. In his speech of March 31, Johnson spoke of "division in the American house" and declared his intention to keep the presidency above partisanship in this election year. "Accordingly," he told a stunned nation, "I shall not seek, and I will not accept, the nomination of my party for another term as your President." The liberals, with an assist from the peace movement, the attackers of Tet, and war-weariness, had dumped Johnson.

GLOSSARY

Nikita Kruschchev: Soviet leader during the early to mid-1960s.

Sino-Soviet split: The rift between Chinese and Soviet communism in the late 1940s and early 1950s that led both nations to adopt separate national and international policies.

Gulf of Tonkin Resolution: A 1964 Congressional resolution authorizing military action in southeast Asia, the legal basis for the escalation of the Vietnam War.

IMPLICATIONS

In this essay, Matusow shows how the Vietnam war marked the downfall of Johnson and his Great Society program of domestic reform. How do you explain Johnson's increasingly inflexible commitment to the Southeast Asian war when it meant the destruction of his domestic reform program?

Past Traces

The passage of the Civil Rights and Voting Rights Acts in 1964 and 1965 mandated an end to racial discrimination in the United States. But social practice ran well behind the law in the United States during the 1960s and 1970s. In education, for example, public schools reflected the segregated nature of the neighborhoods from which they drew their students. Determined to correct this situation, federal courts ordered the busing of students to equalize the racial makeup of local schools. Responding to the prospect of having their children transported to distant schools, many parents aggressively protested the very idea of school busing. This essay is introduced by an account of life inside a local school during one of the most vocal and dramatic of these protests—that in South Boston, Massachusetts, in 1975. Written from the perspective of teachers and administrators, it reveals the tensions and anxieties associated with readjusting the racial balance in America.

Ione Malloy, *Southie Won't Go (1975)*

From my homeroom window I watched the school buses empty one by one, while an administrator, Mr. Gizzi, checked each student's class program to see whether the student belonged at the high school. As I watched, a girl's piercing screams rose from the front lobby. Troopers began running toward the building. Trooper squad cars blocked off G Street down the hill so the buses couldn't move. Mr. Gizzi stayed with the buses. Over the intercom the secretary's voice cried, "We need help here on the second floor. Please send help to the office." Isolated on the second floor in the front corner of the building, in a small room attached to two adjoining rooms, I again felt the terror of not knowing what was coming from what direction, feeling unable to protect myself or the students from an unidentified danger.

I have never had a desire to flee, just to protect the students, though I don't like the feeling of being trapped. I closed the door, turned out the lights, and told my homeroom students we would stay there and help each other. We waited—two white girls, Kathryn and Becky; James, a small, long-haired white boy; and Jeffrey, a black. In a few minutes the door opened. The gym teacher, carrying an umbrella, stood there with a trooper, their faces anxious. "Have you seen Jane?" they asked, then hurried away. What had happened? Why was the teacher carrying an umbrella? Who was Jane, and where might she have gone, we wondered, but there was no chance to ask. They had already shut the door behind them.

Then came a call for all teachers not assigned to homerooms to report to the front lobby. The call was repeated several times.

About forty minutes later, I was amazed when, from my window, I saw the last bus empty. Several minutes later the intercom announced that the school day would begin. Students should proceed to their first class. Instead, everyone just sat, afraid to move, paralyzed by the unknown.

There were only twenty minutes left in the first class, senior English. The seniors were upset. There had been fights in the South Cafeteria, in the third floor lavatory, and in room 303 on the third floor down the hall, they told me. Because the fights had broken out simultaneously, the seniors felt they had been planned. Just then the intercom requested custodians to report to the third floor lavatory and to the South Cafeteria. "To clean up the blood," the seniors explained.

Although the seniors wanted to discuss the fights, I said we would first take a quick, objective, one-word test. I was a little angry. It was better to get their minds focused on something else. In the few remaining minutes, I let them take the Luscher color preference test and talk about the correlation of color with personality. Most of them chose yellow, red, or blue in their color preference. They are a good class.

When I passed room 303 a few minutes later, the students were pushing at the door to get out. A trooper was holding them in. I told two boys at the door to go in and help their teacher. They asked, "Help *her*?" It hadn't occurred to them that she might need their help. Jack Kennedy, administrator, passed me in the corridor, his face white and drained. I stopped in the teachers' room

to comb my hair. My face in the mirror looked ghastly. It must take the body time to recover its equilibrium, even after the mind has composed itself.

As I walked around the school, and felt the mood of the school, I thought, "This school is DEATH. The mood of the school is black."

The troopers were happy, however, I was surprised to see. One said, "This is more like it. It gets the old adrenalin going."

My sophomores, a mixed class of black and white students, also wanted to talk about the incidents. They explained how the fight before school had started at the front lobby door. A black girl and a white boy were going through the front lobby—the boy first. He let the door slam on her. She screamed; a black male jumped to her defense, and the fight was on. A trooper pushed a white boy back over a desk and dislocated his shoulder. A black student on the stairs started screaming insults at the white students—among them Michael Faith—and Faith lunged for him. Fights broke out everywhere in the lobby. Students rushed down from the classrooms, or out of their homerooms to aid the secretaries when they called for help on the intercom.

Anne was upset because a trooper in the cafeteria had grabbed a black girl and called her "nigger." "Nobody calls me 'nigger.'" Anne said. "My friend got her comb and got a piece of his red meat."

I played dumb and, for the benefit of white students, said, "But I hear black kids call each other 'nigger,' and they don't seem to mind." Anne said, "Nobody's called me 'nigger.' I don't care who he is." Louis, a black student who has come to school regularly in a taxi even when Atkins called for a boycott, sat back confidently in his fine pressed suit and said, "It's all right when another black person calls me a 'nigger,' but not a white person. Then it's an insult. If I don't know a person and he calls me 'nigger,' I don't say anything until I find out how he feels about me."

Anne said, "I hate this school. I don't never want to come back."

I concluded, "We all need more understanding." . . .

There was a faculty meeting after school. Dr. Reid took the toll of casualties and names involved in fights. Unconsciously he wiped his brow with the classic tragic sweep of his hand and said, "I don't know what we can do. We were all at our posts doing our jobs. But if a youngster will insult and another responds with his fists, there's nothing we can do—except encourage them to watch their mouths and language."

Dr. Reid announced he would like to have an honor roll assembly for sophomores. Mrs. Marie Folkart, the oldest, most respected member of the faculty, raised her hand: She hoped he wouldn't have an assembly. Usually very deferential to her, he disagreed, "I don't know about that. I think maybe we should."

The assembly, the first this year, is scheduled for Friday, a day when attendance is the lowest. . . .

The sophomore assembly convened as planned. Classes filed to assigned seats room by room without incident. Troopers lined the auditorium. The mood was ugly.

Dr. Reid entered from the rear of the hall. As he moved down the center aisle to the stage, he urged the students to stand. He stopped at my class. Martin

wouldn't stand because Siegfried, behind him, wouldn't. Then James sat down—later, he told me, because the black kids—Martin and Siegfried— wouldn't stand. Dr. Reid insisted, and I insisted, but Martin refused. Dr. Reid proceeded on. Again I thought, "This school is death."

After the pledge of allegience to the flag, Dr. Reid lectured on the courtesy of standing when a guest comes to one's home. A few students snickered. When he alluded to the troopers, the black boys in the row behind me yelled, "Get them out." Then Dr. Reid outlined the sports plan for the winter and told the assembly, "We will be together for the year. After that I don't know. But we're here, and we had better make the best of it. And let's have a little courtesy toward one another. Let's treat each other with respect and watch what we say to one another—treat each other with a little kindness. A smile goes a long way if someone accidentally bumps you, instead of pushing back." The students listened respectfully.

Then, as both black and white students crossed the stage to accept their honor roll cards from Dr. Reid, the assembly applauded.

Students left the auditorium room by room.

During the day, girl students traveled the school in roving gangs of blacks and whites, bursting out of classes at any provocation, spreading consternation among the police. "They're in holiday mood," I told the police, dismayed at the prospect of chasing pretty girls back to classrooms.

At the end of the day in homeroom, I told Martin, "Dr. Reid has put his life on the line about desegregation because it is the law. His house in South Boston is guarded. Then he asks you to stand in the assembly, and you refuse. He is your friend, the friend of all of us, and you should know that." James said to Martin, "That's right, Dr. Reid has guards."

A neighborhood crowd chanted at Dr. Reid outside the school this morning. . . .

A librarian at the Boston Public Library in Copley Square told me there are enough kids in the library all day to have school there. He doesn't know where they come from. . . .

The number of troopers in the building was increased instead of decreased, contrary to what the troopers had anticipated Friday when I talked to them.

The two black boys—Martin and Jeffrey—and one white girl, Kathryn, were present in my homeroom today. Expecting a boycott, I was surprised to see any white students in school until I learned that a walkout of white students was anticipated at 9:45 A.M., when the parents, now gathering on the sidewalk, planned to walk in to protest the presence of steel combs in the school.

Walkers (or white students) were permitted to leave by the side doors, if they preferred, so as not to be identified and, perhaps, intimidated by the now divided community. In South Boston families once friends are now enemies, since half support the antibusing boycott and the other half feel they have to educate their children.

Television cameras recorded Dr. Reid facing the protesters outside the building in the morning sunshine. He told them, "The black parents have elected no biracial council; the white students have elected none; the white parents have elected none. And frankly, the number of fights last week made me afraid."

In class Anne described the walkout. "The white kids said, 'See you Tuesday, niggers.' If the black kids had a walkout, I'd go, too. The white kids have to go, or they'll get beaten up." Gretchen, a diligent and intelligent white student, who had attended the advanced classes of the New York public schools, listened. I give her extra reading and reports because she is highly motivated. Besides Gretchen, there were five black students in the class.

I left school at the end of the day by the front lobby staircase, passing the Greek frieze laboriously painted by the art teachers in neutral dark brown last September before school began. The frieze had been nightly mutilated with spray paint and daily repaired by the art department, until finally they gave up. The frieze is now hideous: The faces are black blobs, or white blobs, or faceless with black holes for eyes. Looking at them, one teacher shuddered, "The hatred is getting to me."

17

After Civil Rights: The African American Working and Middle Classes

Robin D. G. Kelley

The passage of civil rights legislation in the mid-1960s signaled the end of racial segregation that had been a fact of American life since the Civil War. With comprehensive voting and civil rights legally secured, most white Americans congratulated themselves for having solved the nation's long-standing "race problem." All Americans, they felt, now had equal opportunities for education, employment, advancement, and success. As the 1970s progressed and passed into the 1980s, mainstream America became much more concerned about the faltering economy than about the condition of its African American counterparts.

But while federal legislation was a crucial step forward, it failed to bring about immediate changes in African American economic life. By the mid-1970s, it had become increasingly obvious to many observers that the economic conditions of African American life had changed but little. While a small middle class had benefited from antidiscriminatory legislation and had gained educations and well-paying jobs during the 1970s and 1980s, the majority of African Americans continued to find themselves frozen into low-status and low-paying jobs with little security. During the 1970s and 1980s, for example, the unemployment rate of black teens was more than twice that of whites.

Making conditions even worse, the late 1970s and early 1980s witnessed the end of America's post–World War II economic boom. Foreign competition and the increasing use of cheap, overseas labor joined with the mounting costs of the Vietnam war and the nation's burgeoning welfare state to drive the American economy into a downward spiral that, by the 1980s, would find it at its lowest point since the Great Depression. This economic downturn had an especially detrimental impact on the African American working class, as Robin D.G. Kelley demonstrates in this essay.

From *To Make Our World Anew: A History of African Americans* edited by Robin D.G. Kelly and Earl Lewis (New York: Oxford University Press, 2000). Copyright © 2000 by Oxford University Press, Inc. Reprinted by permission of the publisher.

Despite affirmative action policies that had placed black workers on many payrolls for the first time, when layoffs began, as the last hired, African Americans became the first fired. Even middle-class blacks discovered that their access to education seldom took them as far as their white counterparts. As Kelley notes, by the 1980s, it was apparent to African American leaders that "a new freedom movement was needed."

INNER CITY BLUES: URBAN POVERTY IN THE SEVENTIES

North Lawndale was once a thriving Chicago community made up of European immigrants and U.S.-born whites and blacks. A community of working-class neighborhoods, North Lawndale before 1970 was home to people who worked for International Harvester, Western Electric, Sears Roebuck, Zenith, Sunbeam, or any one of several other factories and retail outlets in the area. By 1980, most of these firms had closed up shop, leaving empty lots and burned-out buildings in their wake. The dominant retail outlets by the early eighties were bars and liquor stores. In less than a generation, North Lawndale's economy had evaporated, leaving fifty-eight percent of its able-bodied workers unemployed and half of its population on welfare. As jobs disappeared, so did most of the white and black middle-class residents. Once a thriving industrial hub, North Lawndale became one of the poorest black ghettos in Chicago.

The story of North Lawndale was repeated in almost every major city in the United States after 1970. What are the reasons for such economic devastation? Why has the collapse of the urban economy had such a profound impact on African Americans? To answer these questions, we need to first acknowledge that the economies under the free enterprise system have always had their ups and downs. Sometimes manufacturers produce more than the market can absorb, which not only results in lower prices but leads many companies to fire excess workers. Other times new technology intended to make production faster and more efficient leads to layoffs or reduced wages because new machinery often requires workers with less skill. These and other worldwide economic conditions have caused the U.S. economy to swing between economic surges and periods of economic recessions or outright depressions. And in virtually every case of recession, African-American workers were the "last hired and first fired."

But by the mid-seventies, parts of the U.S. economy appeared to be in a permanent crisis. Ironically, just as programs were being implemented to correct racial imbalances in the workplace, and laws barring discrimination in hiring were being enforced a little more vigorously than before, much of the manufacturing part of the economy began a downward cycle from which it never seemed to recover. Even if protection for black workers improved slightly, changes in the global economy created massive unemployment and led to an expansion of poverty among African Americans not seen since the Great Depression of the thirties.

A series of events and policies during the early seventies contributed to the decline of the U.S. economy, especially its heavy industry—steelmaking and the manufacture of automobiles, tires, textiles, and machines of various kinds. In 1973, the Organization of Petroleum Exporting Countries (OPEC), an alliance of mostly Arab oil-producing countries that joined together in 1960 to reduce competition and set higher oil prices, declared an embargo on oil shipments to the United States and Western Europe to protest Israel's war with its Arab neighbors. Because the United States had become dependent on foreign oil supplies, the embargo had a devastating impact on the economy, making it difficult for individual consumers and big business to obtain inexpensive fuels. Plants shut down in large numbers. In 1974 alone, sales and manufacturing of American automobiles declined drastically, unemployment nearly doubled, and inflation more than doubled. Over the next ten years the economy never really recovered; the value of imported manufactured goods from places like Japan and Western Europe grew from less than fourteen percent of the U.S. domestic economy in 1970 to almost forty percent in 1979, while at the same time inflation sharply increased. With increased inflation came a steady loss in the standard of living for all Americans.

President Nixon tried to control inflation, but his policies actually made matters worse, especially for the poor. First, in August 1971 he temporarily froze wages, prices, and rents. But because prices and rents were already high, those earning low wages found themselves in the same situation as before. Second, Nixon placed a tariff on Japanese-made cars. This was intended to reduce competition between Japanese auto manufacturers and American manufacturers, but all it did was increase the price of otherwise affordable Japanese economy cars. American-made cars, for the most part, were still rather expensive and tended to use more gas than foreign cars. And in an economy in which oil prices were rising faster than just about any other item, cars that required less gas continued to be popular in the United States.

In spite of Nixon's measures, inflation continued to rise rapidly and low wages and growing unemployment made it impossible for large numbers of consumers to buy American products, no matter how much the government tried to protect the market with tariffs. Moreover, massive military spending exacerbated the country's economic woes. It dramatically increased the national debt and redirected much-needed investment away from roads, schools, and industries unrelated to the military buildup. Just months before President Nixon signed a peace agreement withdrawing U.S. troops from Vietnam, the national deficit had grown to $40 billion.

President Gerald Ford continued Nixon's economic policies, and when Democrat Jimmy Carter took over the Presidency in 1976, the situation for African Americans improved only slightly. He appointed Patricia Harris, an African-American woman, as Secretary of Housing and Urban Development, and Andrew Young, a black veteran of the civil rights movement, as ambassador to the United Nations. The Carter administration did little to lessen unemployment, and the jobless rate for African Americans increased during his first two years in office. Like the Republican presidents before him, Carter gave corporations a big tax cut, reduced financial aid to black colleges and universities, provided minuscule support for the nation's declining cities, and slashed federal spending for social programs—notably welfare, free lunch programs for children, and health, services. He even backpedaled on his promise to reduce defense spending: the military budget for 1978 reached $111.8 billion, the highest level in U.S. history up to that point.

The creation of multinational corporations in the post–World War II era was the most important change in the new global economy. These multinational corporations no longer had a stake in staying in a particular country or region. Instead, they moved their firms wherever labor and taxes were cheaper, pollution laws were less stringent, and labor unions were either weak or nonexistent. Some manufacturers moved from the Midwest and Northeast to the southern United States in search of cheaper labor with weaker unions, although the South hardly experienced an economic boom during the seventies. The more common trend was for big companies to set up shop in countries like Mexico, Brazil, and South Africa, leaving in their wake empty American factories and huge numbers of unemployed workers. By 1979, for example, ninety-four percent of the profits of the Ford Motor Company and sixty-three percent of the profits from Coca-Cola came from overseas operations. Between 1973 and 1980, at least four million U.S. jobs were lost when firms moved their operations to foreign countries. And during the decade of the seventies, at least 32 million jobs were lost as a result of shutdowns, relocations, and scaling-back operations.

The decline of manufacturing jobs in steel, rubber, auto, and other heavy industries had a devastating impact on black workers. Although black joblessness had been about twice that of whites since the end of World War II, black unemployment rates increased even more rapidly, especially after 1971. During these economic downturns, white unemployment tended to be temporary, with a higher percentage of white workers returning to work. For blacks, layoffs were often permanent. While the number of unemployed white workers declined by 562,000 between 1975 and 1980, the number of black unemployed *increased* by 200,000 during this period—the widest unemployment gap between blacks and whites since the government started keeping such statistics.

The loss of well-paying industrial jobs affected not only African Americans but the entire working class. Some workers looked to labor unions affiliated with the AFL-CIO to battle factory closures and wage reductions. At the height of the recession in the seventies, however, most labor unions were on the defensive, fighting desperately to hold on to the gains they had made a decade earlier. To make matters worse, many black industrial workers felt that white labor leaders were not very responsive to their needs. These leaders did not actively promote African Americans to leadership positions within the unions. In 1982, for example, the AFL-CIO's thirty-five member Executive Council had only two black members, a figure that fell far short of representing actual black membership. Indeed, African Americans tended to have higher rates of participation than whites in union activities: by 1983, more than twenty-seven percent of black workers were union members, compared to about nineteen percent of white workers.

Politically, the AFL-CIO leadership took stands that openly went against the interests of the majority of black workers. In 1972 George Meany supported Nixon's bid for the Presidency, which was interpreted by black rank-and-file members as a clear sign that the AFL-CIO was deserting African Americans. In response, a group of black trade union activists formed the Coalition of Black Trade Unionists (CBTU) in 1972. Under the leadership of veteran labor organizer William Lucy, secretary-treasurer of the American Federation of State, County, and Municipal Employees (AFSCME), the CBTU not only condemned the Nixon administration for what it felt were racist policies but also attacked AFL-CIO president George Meany for endorsing Nixon. The CBTU also issued a statement critical of union leaders who did not actively oppose discrimination and support minority and rank-and-file efforts to have a greater voice in the affairs of the union.

The loss of manufacturing positions was accompanied by an expansion of low-wage service jobs. The more common service jobs included retail clerks, janitors, maids, data processors, security guards, waitresses, and cooks—jobs with little or no union representation. Not everyone who was laid off in the seventies and eighties got these kinds of jobs, and those who did experienced substantial reductions in their income. Many of these new service jobs paid much less than manufacturing jobs. They tended to be part-time and offered very little in the way of health or retirement benefits.

Black men and women who were laid off from auto plants and steel mills in the Midwest and South suddenly found themselves working at fast food and sanitation jobs to make ends meet. Young people entering the job market for the first time quickly discovered that the opportunities their parents once had were fading quickly. Many African-American youths without the option to go to college chose the military as an alternative to low-wage service work. As the United States pulled out of Vietnam, the military became one of the biggest employers of African Americans: the percentage of blacks in the armed forces rose from eighteen percent in 1972 to thirty-three percent in 1979.

These dramatic changes in the economy meant greater poverty for African Americans. One of the most striking features of the seventies was the widening income gap between blacks and whites. At the beginning of the decade, African Americans in the northeastern United States made about seventy-one cents for every dollar whites made; by 1979 that ratio dropped to fifty-eight cents. In 1978, 30.6 percent of black families earned income below the official poverty line, compared with 8.7 percent of white families.

Black women and children were the hardest hit by the economic crisis. Hemmed in by limited job opportunities, more and more working-class black women found themselves having to raise children without the benefit of a spouse to help pay the bills or participate in child care. The number of black homes without male wage earners rose from twenty-two percent in 1960 to thirty-five percent in 1975. Since black women, especially those in their teens and twenties, were the lowest paid and had the highest unemployment rate, it is not an accident that black single-mother households headed the list of families below the poverty line. In 1969, fifty-four percent of all black families below the poverty line were headed by women; in 1974 this figure rose to sixty-seven percent.

Several politicians arid academics blame the rising number of "female-headed households" for the decline of inner cities and the rise of black crime and violence. This crisis of the black family, they argue, is new and unprecedented. They insist that the inability of single mothers to control and discipline their children, combined with the lack of male role models, has led to a whole generation of out-of-control youth. But a lot of these claims are based on misinformation. First of all, single-mother families are not a uniquely "black" crisis; between 1970 and 1987 the birth rate for white unwed mothers rose by seventy-seven

percent. Second, out-of-wedlock births are not entirely new to African-American communities. Studies have shown that at least since the days of slavery black women are more likely than white women to bear children outside of marriage and to marry at later ages, after becoming mothers. Part of the reason has to do with the fact that black families have tended not to ostracize women for out-of-wedlock births.

Why have the number of female-headed households grown, and what impact has it had on the social and economic fabric of black communities? First, the declining number of employed black men has contributed to the growth of single-parent households. Aside from a rapid increase in permanently unemployed black men who suddenly cannot support their families as they had in the past, black men have a higher chance of dying young than any other male population in the United States. They are more often victims of occupational accidents, fatal diseases, and homicides than other men. And throughout the seventies and eighties, the black male prison population increased threefold; by 1989, twenty-three percent of black males ages twenty to twenty-nine, or almost one out of every four, were either behind bars or on legal probation or parole. Another important factor is that African Americans have a higher divorce and separation rate than whites. High unemployment for black males certainly contributes to marital instability among poor families, but welfare policies also play a major role. In at least twenty-five states, two-parent families are ineligible for Aid to Families with Dependent Children (AFDC), and in many cases black men have to leave the household in order for the women and children to have access to welfare and Medicaid.

Although single-parent families (including those run by males) tended to suffer more than two-parent families because they lacked a second wage earner, the structure of the family was not the *cause* of poverty. Most of these households were poor not because the women were unmarried but because of the lack of employment opportunities for women, lower levels of education, and the gross inequality in wages as a result of race and sex discrimination. One study shows, for example, that while seventy-five percent of unemployed black women heading families were poor in 1977, only twenty-seven percent of employed black women heading families were poor. Besides, the vast majority of women who ended up as single parents were poor *before* they had children or experienced divorce, separation, or the death of their husband.

Finally, single-parent families are not always the product of economic deprivation. Oftentimes they reflect the efforts of black women to escape abusive situations and to raise their children in a more supportive environment. As Barbara Omolade, an African-American scholar and activist, explained it: "My children and other children of Black single mothers are better people because they do not have to live in families where violence, sexual abuse, and emotional estrangement are the daily, hidden reality. . . . In a society where men are taught to dominate and women to follow, we all have a lot to overcome in learning to build relationships, with each other and with our children, based on love and justice. For many Black single mothers, this is what the struggle is about."

Because many families headed by single women are poor, they frequently must turn to welfare to survive. The amount of financial support available to welfare recipients in most states barely allowed families to make ends meet. In a recent study of welfare in the eighties, for example, one researcher met a divorced mother of two whose combined cash aid and food stamps amounted to a mere twelve dollars per day. "This is probably about the lowest point in my life," she admitted, "and I hope I never reach it again. Because this is where you're just up against a wall. You can't make a move. You can't buy anything that you want for your home. You can't go on vacation. You can't take a weekend off and go see things

because it costs too much." The stigma attached to welfare made matters worse. Using food stamps often brought stares and whispers of disgust from clerks and consumers standing by.

The majority of single black mothers who received welfare during the eighties, however, did so for an average of only six months, and most had to supplement aid with odd jobs in order to make ends meet. Besides, not all poor African Americans received public assistance, nor were they the primary beneficiaries of welfare. In 1991, sixty-one percent of all people on welfare were white. Blacks, by comparison, made up only thirty-three percent of welfare recipients. And many who did qualify for some form of public assistance did not always receive it. A 1979 study revealed that seventy percent of all unemployed blacks never received any unemployment benefits; more than half of all poor black households received no AFDC or General Assistance; half of all black welfare households received no Medicaid coverage and fifty-eight percent of all poor black households received benefits from only one or two of the seven income programs available to assist the poor. There are many reasons why a substantial number of poor people did not receive full benefits. In some cases, the lengthy application process discouraged applicants; in other instances, computer errors, misplaced files, or unsympathetic or ill-informed case workers were to blame. But in many cases, black men and women living below the poverty line were simply too proud to accept welfare.

LIVING THE DREAM? THE BLACK MIDDLE CLASS

To the residents of Philadelphia, July 1976 must have felt like the hottest month in that city's history. Throngs of people from all over the country and throughout the world invaded the "City of Brotherly Love" to celebrate the 200th birthday of the Declaration of Independence. Waving overpriced flags and wearing red, white, and blue outfits, they came to examine the famous crack in the Liberty Bell and see firsthand the document that announced the beginning of this country's democratic journey.

In the neighborhoods just north, west, and south of the celebrations, a growing number of jobless and working-poor African Americans were fighting to survive. While the patriotic celebrations of the moment cast a shadow over Philadelphia's dark ghettos, hiding much of the recent devastation that would characterize the next two decades, a group of African-American leaders was trying to get the bicentennial committee to acknowledge the black presence in the past two hundred years of history. The fact that the majority of Africans in America were still slaves when the Declaration of Independence was signed made many bicentennial organizers uncomfortable. Instead, they tried to integrate the celebrations by highlighting black achievement in business, politics, the arts and entertainment, sciences, and education.

By emphasizing black achievement and paying less attention to the crumbling ghettos in earshot of the Liberty Bell, the organizers of the bicentennial were not being entirely dishonest. Just as the majority of African Americans experienced immense poverty, segregation, violence, and rising racism, some black professionals and entrepreneurs were reaping the fruits of integration. Of course, there had always been middle- and upper-class blacks, but in the past they succeeded in a segregated economy, lived in segregated neighborhoods, and had to operate in an atmosphere of outright racial discrimination. Although discrimination did not disappear entirely, the civil rights struggles of the previous two decades helped usher in affirmative action programs that gave minorities and women preference in hiring and college admission to compensate for past and present discrimination.

"We were all . . . children of the civil rights movement: the nation had changed its laws and, in some respects, its ways during our childhoods and adolescences. We were living the opportunities for which generations of black folk had fought and died. Walking paths wet with the blood of our martyrs, we felt an uneasy fear that taking advantage of those opportunities was changing us."

These words were written in 1991 by Yale law professor and best-selling author Stephen L. Carter. Carter exemplifies what it meant for a generation of young people to live the American Dream. A graduate of Yale Law School, Carter turned out to be a gifted legal scholar and talented writer. In another era, a black person of his considerable talents might not have had the chance to attend Yale or to accept a major professorship at his alma mater. But affirmative action policies and an aggressive recruitment effort to attract African Americans to the school opened doors for him that had been closed to previous generations. He is clearly one of those who "made it." Between his salaries, royalties on his book sales, and fees for speaking engagements, Professor Carter makes more than enough money to live a comfortable middle- or upper-middle-class existence.

And yet, Carter is somewhat ambivalent about how his success and the particular road he had to take to achieve it has changed him and other black professionals. Everywhere he turned, his white colleagues hinted that he did not make it on his own merit; that every college and every law firm opened doors to him because he was black, not because he was good. Some days he believed this argument. Other days he felt enraged that so many of his colleagues viewed him as the representative of a race rather than as an individual. Occasionally he convinced himself that his success was entirely the result of his own initiative and hard work. Indeed, there were moments when Carter believed that the old racial barriers of the past had been completely destroyed. But just when life seemed good, the handsomely attired and articulate scholar would be reminded of his race. "When in New York, for example, if I am traveling with a white person, I frequently swallow my pride and allow my companion to summon the taxi as I hang back—for to stand up for my rights and raise the arm myself would buy only a tired arm and no ride. For a black male, blue jeans in New York are a guarantee of ill-treatment. There are the jewelry-store buzzers that will not ring, the counter clerks who will not say 'Sir,' the men's departments with no staff to be found."

Carter's mixed feelings about his success are characteristic of a rapidly expanding class of black urban and suburban professionals who came of age during the fifties and sixties. Their numbers increased substantially during the seventies. In 1970, 15.7 percent of black families had incomes over $35,000; by 1986 the percentage had grown to 21.2 percent. Likewise, black families earning more than $50,000 almost doubled, increasing from 4.7 percent in 1970 to 8.8 percent in 1986. And like Carter, their rapid success can be partially attributed to antidiscrimination laws and affirmative action programs first established in the sixties and expanded under President Jimmy Carter during the mid- to late-seventies.

The roots of recent affirmative action policies can be traced to the Civil Rights Act of 1964 and the establishment of the Equal Employment Opportunity Commission (EEOC) and the Office of Federal Contract Compliance (OFCC). Both of these agencies were created to monitor employment discrimination and enforce the law. Unfortunately, the staff at the EEOC and the OFCC was small relative to the number of cases it received each year.

While lack of personnel within these institutions has led to a huge backlog of cases and limited their effectiveness, the EEOC, especially, has put pressure on firms to hire more women and minorities. For example, in 1973 the EEOC successfully sued the U.S. Steel Corporation for failing to promote black workers at its Fairfield, Alabama, plant. The court ordered U.S. Steel to expand job opportunities for its African-American workers. The EEOC discovered blatant incidents of white workers with less seniority being promoted

to better jobs—mainly skilled machinist, clerical, technical, and managerial occupations. The court ruling required equal hiring of black and white apprentices and black and white clerical and technical employees until African Americans held about a quarter of these jobs.

Soon thereafter, the Detroit Edison Company was fined $4 million in punitive damages for discriminating against African-American employees, and a Detroit union local of the Utility Workers of America (UWA) was slapped with a $250,000 fine. The suit was initiated by a group of black Detroit Edison workers after the UWA and the International Brotherhood of Electrical Workers refused to file their grievance for them. Their primary complaint was that Detroit Edison employed very few black workers, turned down a large number of qualified black applicants, and kept blacks in the lowest-paid jobs. The judge in the case ordered the company to increase the proportion of black employees from eight percent to thirty percent and to set hiring guidelines that would ultimately place more black workers in higher-paying jobs with more authority.

Affirmative action policies were also responsible for briefly increasing black enrollment at major colleges and universities starting in the late sixties. Black enrollment rates rose from twenty-seven percent in 1972 to thirty-four percent in 1976, before dropping steadily during the next decade. Many leading black scholars and corporate leaders who came of age in the 1950s and sixties benefited from affirmative action initiatives. Because such policies were more strongly enforced at the federal, state, and municipal levels, African Americans employed in the public sector gained the most. By 1970, twenty-eight percent of all employed African Americans held government jobs, and approximately sixty percent of all black professional workers were employed by governmental bodies. This is particularly striking when we consider that in 1970 African Americans held only one percent of the managerial and administrative jobs in manufacturing. Thus, the expansion of public sector jobs for minorities has been largely responsible for the growth of the black middle class.

However, the inclusion of African Americans in public sector jobs and managerial positions did not always translate into big salary increases. Many black families reporting middle-class incomes were often the result of two parents working full-time for fairly low or moderate wages. Besides, in 1979, eighteen percent of all black female managers and thirteen percent of all black male managers actually earned wages below the poverty line. Many middle-class black families who had purchased suburban homes during the seventies lived from paycheck to paycheck; one layoff could mean the loss of their home. In fact, all economic indicators show that middle-class blacks, on average, possess substantially less "wealth" (savings, money invested in buying a home, stocks, bonds, retirement accounts, etc., minus debts) than middle-class whites who earn the same income.

Much of African-American wealth is concentrated in the hands of independent entrepreneurs, some of whom also benefited from affirmative action initiatives to provide more minority firms with government contracts and loans. The purpose of such programs was not to provide a handout to struggling businesses. Rather, they sought to rectify policies that had kept minority firms from obtaining government contracts in the first place and to improve the economic status of all African Americans by establishing a strong foundation for "black capitalism." The Nixon administration, for example, created several subsidy programs to assist black businesses, including the Office of Minority Business Enterprise, the Manpower Development and Training Program, and the Minority Enterprise Small Business Investment Company. Although these programs might have been effective if properly funded, they were never given much of a chance: after Ronald Reagan was elected

President in 1980, virtually all of these programs were cut back.

Between 1972 and 1977, the number of black-owned firms and their proportion of total industry revenue declined for the most part. The number of black-owned auto dealerships fell by twenty-four percent; black-owned hotel and lodging facilities dropped by twenty-one percent; and the number of food and eating establishments declined by ten percent. In 1977, black-owned firms made up only three percent of all businesses in the country. By 1980, more than eighty percent of all black-owned firms did not have a single paid employee aside from the owner, and at least one-third of these firms failed within twelve months of opening.

Competition with other businesses only partly explains the failure of certain black-owned ventures. Black entrepreneurs have had more difficulty securing loans for their businesses than their white counterparts. A recent survey of five hundred black entrepreneurs with an annual revenue of $100,000 or more revealed that ninety percent had been turned down by banks when they applied for business loans. Of those surveyed, seventy percent had to rely on personal savings to finance their business. Often, black business people have to turn to black-owned community banks for help.

Not all black business suffered during the seventies recessions and Reagan-era cutbacks. On the contrary, the last decades of the twentieth century are filled with remarkable stories of black entrepreneurship. One rising corporate star during the seventies was Naomi Sims, a high-fashion model originally from Oxford, Mississippi. After earning a degree in psychology from New York University and studying at the Fashion Institute of Technology, Sims quickly emerged as one of the most popular black women models in the country, making several magazine-cover and television appearances. In 1973, she helped develop a new fiber for a line of wigs and founded the Naomi Sims

Collection, selling cosmetics and hair-care products nationwide. By 1977, her firm reported annual revenues of about four million dollars.

Reginald F. Lewis's road to success was a bit more traditional. Born in Baltimore, Maryland, Lewis was helped by affirmative action policies that enabled him to earn a law degree from Harvard in 1968. After working for one of New York's most prestigious corporate law firms, Lewis, with fellow attorney Charles Clarkson, started his own law firm on Wall Street in 1970. His firm helped minority-owned businesses obtain financing and structure deals. In 1983, Lewis launched the TLC Group, an aggressive investment firm with the specific purpose of acquiring companies. And acquire he did: in 1984 TLC bought McCall's Pattern Company (a manufacturer of sewing patterns) for $25 million—and sold it for $90 million three years later. Then in 1987, the TLC Group made history by purchasing BCI Holdings, the former international division of the Chicago-based Beatrice Foods. Comprised of sixty-four companies operating in thirty-one countries, BCI Holdings manufactured and distributed a wide range of food products, including ice cream, meats, chocolates, and soft drinks. Lewis's firm paid $985 million for BCI Holdings, making it the largest leveraged buyout of an overseas operation in the history of American business up to that time.

The year before Lewis's death in 1993, TLC Beatrice had revenues of $1.54 billion and Lewis himself had amassed assets of more than $300 million, making him the wealthiest African American in U.S. history.

Perhaps the best-known black millionaire is publishing magnate John H. Johnson, founder of *Ebony* and *Jet* magazines. Born in Arkansas in 1918, he migrated to Chicago with his mother at age fifteen. While working for the black-owned Supreme Liberty Life Insurance Company in 1942, twenty-four-year-old Johnson decided to launch *Negro Digest*, a small magazine summarizing longer articles for

and about African Americans. Raising the money was hard. "Most people had seen *Reader's Digest* and *Time*," he recalled, "but nobody had seen a successful black commercial magazine. And nobody was willing to risk a penny on a twenty-four-year-old insurance worker." That is, except for the Citizens Loan Corporation of Chicago, one of the few financial institutions willing to loan money to African Americans. They loaned him $500, but only after Johnson's mother offered to put up all of her new furniture as collateral. It was a good investment, for within eight months of its founding *Negro Digest* was selling fifty thousand copies a month nationally. Three years later, Johnson launched *Ebony* magazine, a photo magazine modeled after *Life*. By 1991, the Johnson companies reported total gross sales of $252 million. According to *Forbes* magazine, Johnson headed one of the four hundred richest families in the United States.

The combination of higher incomes and the dismantling of legal segregation enabled many rising middle-class black families to flee collapsing ghettos and move out to the suburbs or to lavish townhouses and brownstones in wealthy urban communities. The trend is reflected in the rapid suburbanization of the African-American population during the seventies and eighties: between 1970 and 1986, the black suburban population grew from 3.6 million to 7.1 million. Although they often left behind deteriorating neighborhoods, a growing drug economy, and a rapidly expanding army of unemployed men and women, most blacks could not escape bigotry. To their surprise, some middle-class black families who moved into predominantly white suburbs discovered burning crosses on their lawns, hate mail, and letters from property owners' associations concerned that their presence would lower property values.

Potential black homebuyers also had to deal with real estate agents who deliberately steered them to poorer, predominantly black neighborhoods, and with financial institutions that blatantly discriminated against African Americans. The evidence of discrimination against African Americans in housing is over-whelming. Numerous studies conducted in major metropolitan areas since the sixties demonstrated that real estate agents frequently showed black home buyers different properties, withheld information, or simply lied about the status of the property in question. This practice of steering black home buyers toward non-white neighborhoods is a form of discrimina-tion known as "redlining." Similarly, a massive study of ten million applications to savings and loan associations between 1983 and 1988 revealed that the rejection rate for blacks applying for home mortgages was more than twice that of whites, and that high-income African Americans were rejected more than low-income whites.

What is clear from such stories of discrimi-nation is that the dismantling of legal barriers to segregation has not been completely effec-tive. Indeed, by some measures racial segrega-tion has increased in the urban North during the last three decades. Despite evidence that middle- and upper-income African Americans were the greatest beneficiaries of integration, it is interesting to note that in some major cities African Americans earning more than $50,000 were as segregated as those making less than $2,500 annually. Of course, in a few cases middle-class blacks have chosen predominantly black suburban enclaves in well-to-do com-munities such as Prince George's County, Maryland (just outside of Washington, D.C.), or sections of Westchester County, a commu-nity north of New York City. Their decision is understandable given the history of vio-lence and discrimination directed at African Americans who try to integrate all-white subur-ban communities. But fear of racist attacks and the desire for respectful neighbors indicate the narrowness of choices that are offered to blacks compared to whites.

School integration, another component of African Americans' desire to reach for the American Dream, quickly became one of the most contested racial battlefields during the post–civil rights era. A quarter of a century after the landmark case of *Brown v. Board of Education of Topeka, Kansas* (1954), the nation's public schools looked as segregated as they had ever been. Although black children made up about one-fifth of the total public school enrollment, almost two-thirds went to schools with at least fifty percent minority enrollment. This pattern is even more striking in major cities, where African-American children attended underfunded public schools while many white students, often the children of urban professionals, have deserted the public school system for private institutions. By 1980, for example, whites made up only four percent of public school enrollment in Washington, D.C., eight percent in Atlanta, nine percent in Newark, and twelve percent in Detroit.

Drastic measures were needed to remedy this situation, especially since middle-class fam-ilies who had migrated to the suburbs took pre-cious tax dollars needed to run city schools. With fewer well-paid, property-owning fami-lies living in urban areas, the property taxes so essential to funding education and other city services declined considerably. Under pressure from black families who wanted to send their children to better-funded schools in the suburbs and civil rights groups that believed the nation should live up to the *Brown* decision, school boards across the country tried to achieve racial balance by busing students to schools in different neighborhoods.

The nation was sharply divided over the issue of busing. President Nixon vehemently opposed court-ordered busing, officials in the Department of Health, Education and Welfare thought it was a good idea, and the Supreme Court remained unsure whether it was consti-tutional or not. The clearest expression of resis-tance to mandatory busing came from white parents who believed the addition of black children from the inner city would bring down the quality of education. Indeed, in some cities busing programs were met with militant protests that frequently led to violence. Throughout the early to mid-seventies, organized resistance erupted in cities throughout the country, including Pontiac, Michigan; Louisville, Kentucky; Pasadena, California; and Kansas City, Missouri. The best-known clashes were in Boston, where most public schools had been racially segregated until an NAACP-led campaign won a court order in 1975 to bus children from predominantly black and poor Roxbury to Charlestown, a largely working-class Irish community. Over the course of the next three years, Boston police were called in to protect black children from white mobs screaming racial epithets and occasionally throwing bricks and fists.

The Boston busing controversy died down by the early eighties, partly because liberal black and white politicians created a coalition that elected more supporters of integration to the city council and to the Board of Education. Besides, proponents of school integration could hardly claim a victory. By 1980, white flight to the suburbs and a decrease in the use of busing by conservative judges caused a resegregation of most big city school systems.

In the area of higher education, the backlash against affirmative action policies and financial aid for minorities took on many forms. During the late seventies and through the eighties, the number of reported racial assaults and acts of intimidation against blacks on college campuses showed a marked increase. The specific cases are chilling.

At Wesleyan University in 1981, black students found racist graffiti and flyers riddled with epithets and threats, including a leaflet advertising a fraternity "dedicated to wiping all goddamned niggers off the face of the earth." Ten years later, a white sorority at the University of Alabama hosted a party at which pledges painted their faces black and dressed as pregnant welfare mothers. Usually white backlash is much more subtle. One black college administrator vividly described the attitudes of white freshmen toward African Americans at

his university: "Somebody will have the idea that the dorm is exclusively theirs, so therefore we can't have these 'germy, diseasey, dirty, filthy,' black kids live in their dormitory. . . . Black kids are seen as a gang now. They must be on drugs or crazy or something."

By far the most devastating form of white backlash in higher education was the partial dismantling of affirmative action initiatives. In the case of *Regents of the University of California v. Bakke* (1978), Allan Bakke, an unsuccessful white applicant, claimed that he was discriminated against because the University of California, Davis, admitted African Americans with lower test scores than his in order to meet their quota of minority students. The Supreme Court ruled that Bakke had been unfairly denied admission to the medical school. The court did not overturn all forms of affirmative action, but it did argue that quotas—setting aside a specific number of slots for designated groups—were unconstitutional. The medical school's denial of admission to Bakke in order to increase the number of minority students was regarded by the court's majority opinion as "reverse discrimination."

Although Bakke won the case, the unspoken facts behind U.C. Davis's admissions policy call into question the court's opinion that he was a victim of reverse discrimination. First, the sons and daughters of influential white families—potential donors or friends of the dean of the medical school—were also admitted over Bakke despite lower test scores. As had been the case historically, the dean controlled a handful of slots to admit special cases. Second, most minority applicants had higher scores than Bakke. This is an important fact, for the Bakke case left many observers with the incorrect impression that U.C. Davis admitted unqualified minorities. Most importantly, the decision was a major setback for efforts to achieve racial equality through social policy. Justice Thurgood Marshall, the first African American to serve on the Supreme Court, dissented from the majority opinion. Marshall, who viewed the Bakke decision as a tragedy, did not believe that America was even close to becoming a color-blind society. "The dream of America as a great melting pot," he wrote in his dissenting opinion in the Bakke case, "has not been realized for the Negro; because of his skin color he never even made it into the pot."

Most African Americans who stood at the threshold of the Reagan era knew they had entered the worst of times. *Equal opportunity*, *welfare*, *civil rights*, and *Black Power* became bad words in the national vocabulary. Most white Americans believed they had given all they could give, and that any form of government support would be nothing more than a handout. A small but growing contingent of black conservatives agreed. And if this was not enough, the crumbling cities that African Americans and other minorities had inherited turned out not to be the utopia they had hoped for. They were dangerous, difficult places where racist police officers still roamed and well-paying jobs fled the city limits. Despite the rising number of black mayors, it became clear by the eighties that a new freedom movement was needed.

GLOSSARY

AFL-CIO:	American Federation of Labor and Congress of Industrial Organizations, the nation's largest union organization.
George Meany (1894–1980):	American labor leader who exerted great political influence as the first president of the American Federation of Labor and the Congress of Industrial Organizations (1955–1979).
Aid to Families with Dependent Children:	A federally sponsored welfare program.

IMPLICATIONS

In this essay, Kelley discusses the differing impacts that the civil rights "revolution" of the 1960s and the economic dislocations of the 1970s had on African American life. Do you think that passage of the Civil Rights Acts solved the problems of race in America? What do you think civil rights legislation accomplished?

Past Traces

The economic boom of the late 1980s combined with greatly increased access to higher education to create a new phenomenon: young urban professionals, or Yuppies. Commanding substantial salaries, yuppies developed a distinctive, fast-paced lifestyle focused around high-priced and prestigious consumer goods. This essay is introduced by an early account of the new yuppie lifestyle.

Patricia Morrisroe, *Yuppies—The New Class (1985)*

It's a Saturday night at 96th and Broadway. Inside the new Caramba!!! everybody's drinking frozen maragaritas and talking real estate, while outside on the traffic strip, a derelict swigs Wild Turkey and shouts obscenities. By 11 P.M., he's sound asleep on the bench, but the crowd at Caramba!!! is still going strong.

"These are the most lethal maragaritas in Manhattan," says a man in a blue pinstriped suit by Polo. He staggers out of the restaurant and into David's Cookies next door. "Get the double-chunk chocolate chip," says his girlfriend, who is window-shopping at Pildes Optical.

At the newsstand across the street, a middle-aged woman buys the Sunday *Times* and looks at the dozens of young professionals spilling out of Caramba!!! "Yuppies," she shouts. "Go home!"

But they are home. Ads in the *Times* tout the Upper West Side as "Yuppie Country," and Amsterdam is being called "Cinderella Avenue." According to a study of the years 1970 through 1980 by New York's Department of City Planning, 7,500 people between the ages of 25 and 44 flooded the area between West 70th and 86th Streets. That age-group now makes up 47 percent of the population there. At the same time, the number of singles went up by 31 percent, while the number of families dropped 24 percent. "You want to know who's moving into the West Side?" says a woman who owns an antiques store on Amsterdam Avenue. "It's the young, the rich, and the restless."

Some older West Siders blame the newcomers for the skyrocketing rents and the uprooting of local merchants. They deplore the cuteness of Columbus Avenue and the hordes of tourists who congest the sidewalks. They worry that the neighborhood's solid middle class values will be replaced by the yuppie version of the West Side Dream: a pre-war apartment with a Food Emporium around the corner.

They can't relate to the 30-year-old on Central Park West who takes her husband's shirts to the East Side because she can't find a "quality" laundry in the neighborhood. Or to the tenants at the Sofia on West 61st Street, 50 percent of whom bought their apartments after seeing a model of the bathroom. ("They're big and very Deco," says Richard Zinn, the building's director of sales.)

The Columbia, a condominium on West 96th Street, has been called the "Yuppie Housing Project" by locals who can't believe anyone would *pay* to live on Broadway. "Didn't anyone tell these people it's a *commercial* street?" says an elderly man who is buying Rice Krispies at the Red Apple on the corner. "If I had the money for a condo, I'd move to Florida."

One third of the Columbia's units were bought by lawyers; the average income per apartment is $100,000. "It's a nice first home for couples on their way up," says developer Arthur Zeckendorf, who worked with his father, William, to build the Columbia. Once they've made it, they can move to the Park Belvedere, a condominium on West 79th Street also built by the Zeckendorfs. Sold for an average of $400 per square foot, it has attracted a better-off buyer. "I looked at the Columbia," says a 27-year-old Wall Street bond trader, "but the neighborhood was just too borderline for me." So he bought an apartment in one of the Belvedere's towers and persuaded a friend to buy one, too. "It's a great deal," he says of his $400,000 one-bedroom.

Many West Side co-ops are besieged by Wall Street financiers who use their bonuses to make down payments.

"The last five apartments in my building went to investment bankers," says a woman who owns a co-op on West End Avenue. "I want to protect my property, so it's good to have people with money move in. But I worry about the population in the next ten years. Are you going to need an MBA to get into Zabar's?" . . .

Yet for all the money being poured into the neighborhood, some of the new West Siders have a decidedly old-fashioned point of view. For every yuppie who dreams about moving from Broadway to Central Park West there are others who chose the West Side because it seemed unpretentious. "I always hated everything the East Side represented," says 33-year-old Joe Powers in between feeding mashed carrots to his five-month-old son, Mark. "The West Side always seemed to have less airs about it. To me, it's Zabar's and Fairway. Not Rúelles and Pasta & Cheese." . . .

Ten blocks uptown, 31-year-old Richard Conway is setting up his VCR to tape Jacqueline Bisset in *Anna Karenina*. A vice-president at a Wall Street investment firm, Conway recently bought a twelfth-floor five-room co-op at 106th Street and Riverside Drive. In the past fifteen years, Conway has moved from Greenwich to Harvard to Third Avenue to Yale to Chelsea, and now to Duke Ellington Boulevard.

"This is not a yuppie neighborhood," says Conway, uncorking a bottle of white wine. "That's what I like about it. In my building, we have a wonderful mix of people. The head of the co-op board is a musical director, and we've got artists and writers and movie producers."

When Conway decided to buy a co-op, he wanted to look only north of West 96th Street. "I think a lot of the glamour is gone from the East Side," he says. "Besides, I considered it boring and staid, too much like Greenwich. I like living in a neighborhood that's ethnically diverse. Broadway has a lot of bodegas and mom-and-pop stores. To me, that's nice."

From his living room, Conway has a spectacular view of the Hudson. From the opposite end of the apartment, in the dining room, he can see a cityscape of charming turn-of-the-century brownstones. "I wonder how long they'll last," he says. "It's ironic, but everything I like about the neighborhood will probably disappear. And unfortunately, the reason is that people like me are moving into it." . . .

[Lawyer Jay] Zamansky, who grew up in Philadelphia, now makes his home in a renovated SRO next door to the Salvation Army senior citizen's home on West 95th Street. "I really wanted a place where I could establish roots," he says. Constructed around the turn of the century, the building has 30 apartments, most of which are inhabited by young professionals. "We're a real unique building," he explains. "In the summer, we have barbecues, and when our first co-op baby was born, everybody was thrilled."

Zamansky bought this apartment, a duplex with a roof garden, for a little over $100,000. "I'm real proud of it," he says. "It's the consummate bachelor pad." The ceiling is painted black, with lots of track lighting. "I met an interior designer at the Vertical Club," he explains, "and she helped me with the overall concept."

But Zamansky says he doesn't want to be the kind of person who does nothing but "work, eat at restaurants, and go to a health club. I really want to be a part of this neighborhood," he says. "I

attend community-board meetings, and I registered voters in front of Zabar's. I even went into the Salvation Army's old people's home and registered senior citizens. They were just so glad to see a young face that I don't think they cared how they voted. By the way, I'm a Republican. I think it's important to put that in the article.

"I'm also very pro-development," he adds. "It makes me angry when people criticize a lot of the changes. The displacement is unfortunate, but where are we supposed to live? We have rights. We pay taxes. Whether people realize it or not, we're real assets to this community."

Twenty-nine-year-old Paula Handler, who lives with her husband in a three-bedroom apartment in the Eldorado on Central Park West between 90th and 91st Streets agrees. "These big pre-war buildings need young blood," she says. "The old people can't maintain their apartments. They resist everything, from redoing the lobby to putting in new windows. The problem is they can't switch their rental mentalities into a co-op mode."

The Handlers moved from the East Side to the Eldorado a year ago. "Frankly, I didn't know anything about Central Park West," says Paula. "I mean, I knew the Dakota, but the Eldorado? What? All I knew was that I wanted space, and I wanted old. Old is chic."

"Originally, I said no to the West Side," says Scott, a quiet man who is involved in commercial real estate.

"That's right, he did," Paula says. "He didn't like it because it was dirty and nobody we knew lived there. But I fell in love with this apartment. It was a total wreck, but it was me. We gave them an offer the minute we saw it. We even offered more than they asked because we wanted it so much."

The Handlers put in two new bathrooms and a new kitchen, and redid the plumbing and wiring. Today, the apartment, which faces the park, is completely renovated. "See what I mean about new blood?" Paula says. "It doesn't take money. It just takes creativity."

Six floors above the Handlers, Linda and Mark Reiner also had to redo their apartment completely. "It was considered the worst disaster in the building," Linda says. "The walls, which were painted magenta, royal blue, and orange, were falling down. But we really wanted to live here. We recognized how the West Side was growing, and we wanted to be a part of that."

Two years ago, they moved from a house in Hewlett Harbor, where Mark Reiner had a medical practice. "It was a risk giving up everything," he says, "but Hewlett Harbor was very sterile and uniform."

"That's why we didn't want the East Side," adds Linda, who until recently was a practicing psychologist. "Now I sell real estate," she says. "I became addicted to it while we were looking for this apartment." The au pair brings their two-year-old son into the living room to say good night. "You wouldn't believe the children's playground in the park," Linda says. "You can barely get a place for your kid in the sandbox."

"Everybody wants to come here," says Mark. "There's nothing more exciting than living in a neighborhood in transition. It's sad, because a lot of people who live here can't afford to shop in the stores. But they're being pushed out of Manhattan, not just the West Side."

"The West Side makes you feel the difference between the haves and the have-nots," says Linda, who is dressed in a silk Chanel shirt, black pants, and pumps. "Right in our building, there's a real schism between the pre-conversion and post-conversion people. A new breed is taking over, and there's a lot of hostility. People are separated by age and economic class. The senior citizens got insider prices so low that there's a lot of resentment on all sides. At a recent meeting, one elderly person shouted, 'Well, I'm not rich like you.' But what can you do?"

"Basically, we're very optimistic," Mark says. "We feel good about the changes. The neighborhood is going to continue to improve."

Linda nods. "Definitely," she says. "For the West Side, there's no turning back."

18

The Insidious Cycle of
Work and Spend

Juliet B. Schor

Beginning in the 1980s and building to a fever pitch during the 1990s, Americans embarked on the largest spending spree in the nation's history. Taking advantage of easy credit, falling interest rates, two-income households, and rising wages, working- and middle-class men and women began to emulate the lifestyles of the wealthy and famous. No longer content with modest homes, people throughout the country began to purchase new and expensive houses that were designed to look like the mansions of the wealthy. Families leased prestigious cars and newly popular sport utility vehicles for fill their three-car garages. New and renovated shopping malls mushroomed everywhere, often anchored by high-end prestige stores, such as Nieman-Marcus, Lord and Taylor, and Saks Fifth Avenue, all catering to the newly developed upscale tastes of middle-class consumers. As the economy peaked in the late 1990s, advertising and television commercials made it appear that all Americans were striving to live like the rich and famous.

Although often portrayed by the media as a new phenomenon, this combination of materialism and consumerism had a long pedigree, stretching back at least to the 1920s. It was during the post–World War I era that businesses began to employ advertising to induce people to buy their products and created consumer credit to give Americans the means to pay for their purchases. Despite sometimes drastic swings in the national economy, consumerism has been a large part of American life ever since. In fact, today consumer indebtedness is at a record high and shows no signs of sub-siding. With consumer spending accounting for two-thirds of the nation's gross domes-tic product, middle-class consumption has literally driven the post-industrial economy.

This affluence has come at a price, however. As economist Juliet B. Schor shows in this essay, Americans have committed themselves to long working hours, little time for leisure and family life, and a frenetic pace of life in order to support their con-

From *The Overworked American: The Unexpected Decline of Leisure* by Juliet Schor. Copyright © 1991 by Basic Books, Inc. Reprinted by permission of the publisher.

sumption-driven lifestyles. As Schor notes, the more Americans become committed to consumerism, the more difficult it becomes for them to choose other ways of life.

....

SHOP 'TIL YOU DROP

We live in what may be the most consumer-oriented society in history. Americans spend three to four times as many hours a year shopping as their counterparts in Western European countries. Once a purely utilitarian chore, shopping has been elevated to the status of a national passion.

Shopping has become a leisure activity in its own right. Going to the mall is a common Friday or Saturday night's entertainment, not only for the teens who seem to live in them, but also for adults. Shopping is also the most popular weekday evening "out-of-home-entertainment." And malls are everywhere. Four billion square feet of our total land area has been converted into shopping centers, or about 16 square feet for every American man, woman, and child. Actually, shopping is no longer confined to stores or malls but is permeating the entire geography. Any phone line is a conduit to thousands of products. Most homes are virtual retail outlets, with cable shopping channels, mail-order catalogues, toll-free numbers, and computer hookups. We can shop during lunch hour, from the office. We can shop while traveling, from the car. We can even shop in the airport, where video monitors have been installed for immediate on-screen purchasing.

Some of the country's most popular leisure activities have been turned into extended shopping expeditions. National parks, music concerts, and art museums are now acquisition opportunities. When the South Street Seaport Museum in New York City opened in the early 1980s as a combination museum-shopping center, its director explained the commercialization as a bow to reality: "The fact is that shopping is the chief cultural activity in the United States." Americans used to visit Europe to see the sights or meet the people. Now "Born to Shop" guides are replacing Fodor and Baedeker, complete with walking tours from Ferragamo to Fendi. Even island paradises, where we go "to get away from it all," are not immune: witness titles such as *Shopping in Exciting Australia and Papua New Guinea*.

Debt has been an important part of the shopping frenzy. Buying is easier when there's no requirement to pay immediately, and credit cards have seduced many people beyond their means: "I wanted to be able to pick up the tab for ten people, or take a cab when I wanted. I thought that part of being an adult was being able to go to a restaurant, look at the menu, and go in if you like the food, not because you're looking at the prices." This young man quickly found himself with $18,000 of credit card debt, and realized that he and his wife "could have gone to Europe last year on [the] interest alone." For some people, shopping has become an addiction, like alcohol or drugs. "Enabled" by plastic, compulsive shoppers spend money they don't have on items they absolutely "can't" do without and never use. The lucky ones find their way to self-help groups like Debtors Anonymous and Shopaholics Limited. And for every serious compulsive shopper, there are many more with mild habits. Linda Weltner was lucky enough to keep her addiction within manageable financial bounds, but still her "mindless shopping" grew into a "troubling preoccupation . . . which was impoverishing [her] life."

The "shop 'til you drop" syndrome seemed particularly active during the 1980s, a decade popularly represented as one long buying spree. In the five years between 1983 and 1987, Americans purchased 51 million microwaves, 44 million washers and dryers, 85 million color televisions, 36 million refrigerators and freezers, 48 million VCRs, and 23 million cordless telephones—all for an adult population of only 180 million.

Much has, with some justification, been made of the distinctiveness of the decade. The rich made an important social comeback. Not since the 1920s had the country been so tolerant of unrestrained materialism and greed. But in other ways the 1980s were not unique. The growth of personal consumption—the hallmark of 1980s culture—is nothing new. Modern consumerism harkens back to at least the 1920s. The growth of expenditures was temporarily derailed by the Depression and the war but was on track again by the 1950s. Since then, the nation has been feeding on a steady diet of single-family houses, cars, household appliances, and leisure spending. The average American is consuming, in toto, more than twice as much as he or she did forty years ago. And this holds not only for the Gucci set but all the way down the income scale. Nearly everyone participated in the postwar consumption boom. Compared with forty years ago, Americans in every income class—rich, middle class, and poor—have about twice as much in the way of income and material goods.

Of course, the consumer boom of the 1980s *has* been different from the earlier decades in one important way—consumerism has been far more an affair of the affluent—the top 20 or 40 percent of the population. Income became far less equally distributed during this decade, and many people, especially those in the bottom quarter of the population, have experienced substantial declines in their standard of living. Others have maintained their incomes only by working longer hours. Had hours not risen, the average American worker's annual earnings would have been lower at the close of the decade than when it began. Still, declining wages have been mainly a phenomenon of the last ten years. From the longer vantage point of the "golden age" of the 1950s, 1960s, and 1970s, the depth and breadth of American affluence comes clearly into view.

Housing expenditures—the largest item in most family budgets—clearly reflect the country's growing wealth. In the 1950s, when developer William Levitt created Levittowns for ordinary American families, his standard house was 750 square feet. In 1963, the new houses were about twice as large; and by 1989, the average finished area had grown to almost three times the Levittown standard—2,000 feet. At the same time, fewer people were living in these dwellings. The typical 1950s family of four has shrunk to an average of 2.6 persons, so that each individual now has as much space as an entire family of four occupied in 1950. Fifty years ago, only 20 percent of all houses had more rooms than people living in them; by 1970, over 90 percent of our homes were spacious enough to allow more than one room per person. The size and quality of the American housing stock has not been replicated anywhere else on earth.

Houses are not only bigger, they are also more luxuriously equipped. As late as 1940, 30 percent still had no running water, and 40 percent were without flush toilets. Today virtually all houses have both, and three-quarters of single-family dwellings have two or more bathrooms. In 1940, less than 45 percent of homes had electric refrigerators. Now all do. Americans also acquired vacuum cleaners, toasters, irons, radios, and washing machines. Forty years ago, fewer than 5 percent of U.S. homes had air-conditioners, dishwashers, and clothes dryers. Now two-thirds have air-conditioning (a majority with centralized systems), microwaves, and dryers, and almost half have dishwashers. Only a quarter of homes had kitchen ranges in 1953; now all do.

More of us also own our own homes. The difficulties young people have had buying houses in the 1980s notwithstanding, overall rates of home ownership have risen impressively—from 44 percent in 1940, to 55 percent in 1950, to 64 percent in 1989. Homeownership rates for two-person households are even higher—just over 70 percent. Ownership of motor vehicles has also grown: in 1935, 55 percent of families had a car; today, 88 percent of households have a motor vehicle, and the average number of vehicles per household is two. Over 90 percent of all households also have color televisions and 80 percent have VCRs. In addition to VCRs and microwaves, Americans are buying many more services—like foreign travel, restaurant meals, medical attention, hair and skin care, and products of leisure industries such as health clubs or tennis lessons. Overall, per-capita service expenditures have risen 2.6 times since 1950—even more than consumer expenditures as a whole.

The consumerism of the postwar era has not been without its effects on the way we use our time. As people became accustomed to the material rewards of prosperity, desires for leisure time were eroded. They increasingly looked to consumption to give satisfaction, even meaning, to their lives. In both the workplace and the home, progress has repeatedly translated into more goods and services, rather than more free time. Employers channel productivity increases into additional income; housewives are led to use their labor-saving appliances to produce more goods and services. Consumerism traps us as we become habituated to the good life, emulate our neighbors, or just get caught up in the social pressures created by everyone else's choices. Work-and-spend has become a mutually reinforcing and powerful syndrome—a seamless web we somehow keep choosing, without even meaning to.

THE CREATION OF DISCONTENT

I never knew how poor I was until I had a little money.

—*a banker*

There is no doubt that the growth of consumption has yielded major improvements in the quality of life. Running water, washing machines, and electrical appliances eliminated arduous, often backbreaking labor. Especially for the poor women who not only did their own housework, but often someone else's as well, the transformation of the home has been profoundly liberating. Other products have also enhanced the quality of life. The compact disc raises the enjoyment of the music lover; the high-performance engine makes the car buff happy, and the fashion plate loves to wear a designer suit.

But when we add up all the items we consume, and consider the overall impact, rather than each in isolation, the picture gets murkier. The farther we get from the onerous physical conditions of the past, the more ambiguous are the effects of additional commodities. The less "necessary" and more "luxurious" the item, the more difficult it is automatically to assume that consumer purchases yield intrinsic value.

We do know that the increasing consumption of the last forty years has not made us happier. The percentage of the population who reported being "very happy" peaked in 1957, according to two national polls. By the last years these polls were taken (1970 and 1978), the level of "very happy" had not recovered, in spite of the rapid growth in consumption during the 1960s and 1970s. Similar polls taken since then indicate no revival of happiness.

Despite the fact that possessions are not creating happiness, we are still riding the consumer merry-go-round. In fact, for some Americans the quest for material goods became more intense in the last decade: according to the pollster Louis Harris, "by the mid-1980s, the American people were far more oriented toward economic growth and materialism than before. Most significant, young people were leading the charge back to material values."

Materialism has not only failed to make us happy. It has also bred its own form of discontent—even among the affluent. Newspaper and magazine articles chronicle the dissatisfaction. One couple earning $115,000 tallied up their necessary expenses of $100,000 a year and complained that "something's gone terribly wrong with being 'rich.'" An unmarried Hollywood executive earning $72,000 worried about bouncing checks: "I have so much paid for by the studio—my car, my insurance, and virtually all food and entertainment—and I'm *still* broke." Urbanites have it especially hard.

As one New York City inhabitant explained, "It's incredible, but you just can't live in this city on a hundred thousand dollars a year." According to the *New York Times*, the fast lane is not all it's cracked up to be, and Wall Streeters are "Feeling Poor on $600,000 a Year." "When the Joneses they are keeping up with are the Basses . . . $10 million in liquid capital is not rich."

Whatever we think of these malcontents—whether we find them funny, pathetic, or reprehensible—we must acknowledge that these feelings are not confined to those in the income stratosphere. Many who make far less have similar laments. Douglas and Maureen Obey earn $56,000 a year—an income that exceeds that of roughly 70 percent of the population. Yet they complain that they are stretched to the breaking point. Douglas works two jobs "to try to keep it all together. . . . I feel I make a fairly good income that should afford a comfortable lifestyle, but somehow it doesn't. . . . [I'm] in hock up to my eyeballs." The Obeys own their home, two cars, a second rental property, and a backyard pool.

Complaints about life style have been particularly loud among the baby-boom generation. One writer explained a state of mind shared by many in her generation: she was convinced she would not achieve the comfortable middle-class life style enjoyed by her parents (four-bedroom house, two-car garage, private schools for the children, and cashmere blankets at the bottom of the beds): "I thought bitterly of my downward mobility . . . and [had] constant conversations with myself about wanting . . . a new couch, a weekend cottage, a bigger house on a quieter street." Eventually she realized that more money was not the answer, her needs were satisfied. As she acknowledged: "Discontent was cheating me of the life I *had*."

CAPITALISM'S SQUIRREL CAGE

This materialism (and its attendant discontent) is taken for granted. It is widely believed that our unceasing quest for material goods is part of the basic makeup of human beings. According to the folklore, we may not like it, but there's little we can do about it.

Despite its popularity, this view of human nature is wrong. While human beings may have innate desires to strive toward something, there is nothing preordained about material goods. There are numerous examples of societies in which *things* have played a highly circumscribed role. In medieval Europe, there was relatively little acquisitiveness. The common people, whose lives were surely precarious by contemporary standards, showed strong preferences for leisure rather than money. In the nineteenth- and early twentieth-century United States, there is also considerable evidence that many working people exhibited a restricted appetite for material goods. Numerous examples of societies where consumption is relatively unimportant can be found in the anthropological and historical literature.

Consumerism is not an ahistorical trait of human nature, but a specific product of capitalism. With the development of the market system, consumerism "spilled over," for the first time, beyond the charmed circles of the rich. The growth of the middle class created a large group of potential buyers and the possibility that mass culture could be oriented around material goods. This process can be seen not only in historical experiences but is now going on in places such as Brazil and India, where the growth of large middle classes have contributed to rampant consumerism and the breakdown of longstanding values.

In the United States, the watershed was the 1920s—the point at which the "psychology of scarcity" gave way to the "psychology of abundance." This was a crucial period for the development of modern materialist culture. Thrift and sobriety were out; waste and excess were in. The nation grew giddy with its exploding wealth. Consumerism blossomed—both as a social ideology and in terms of high rates of real spending. In the midst of all this buying, we can discern the origins of modern consumer discontent.

This was the decade during which the American dream, or what was then called "the American standard of living," captured the nation's imagination. But it was always something of a mirage. The historian Winifred Wandersee explains:

> It is doubtful that the average American could have described the precise meaning of the term "American standard of living," but nearly everyone agreed that it was attainable, highly desirable, and far superior to that of any other nation. Its nature varied according to social class and regional differences, but no matter where a family stood socially and financially, it was certain to have aspirations set beyond that stance. This was the great paradox posed by the material prosperity of the twentieth century: prosperity was conspicuously present, but it was always just out of reach, for nearly every family defined its standard of living in terms of an income that it hoped to achieve rather than the reality of the paycheck.

The phenomenon of yearning for more is evident in studies of household consumption. In a 1928 study of Yale University faculty members, the bottom category (childless couples with incomes of $2,000) reported that their situation was "life at the cheapest and barest with nothing left over for the emergencies of sickness and childbirth." Yet an income of $2,000 a year put them above 60 percent of all American families. Those at the $5,000 level (the top 10 percent of the income distribution) reported that they "achieve nothing better than 'hand to mouth living.'" At $6,000, "the family containing young children can barely break even." Yet these were the top few percent of all Americans. Even those making $12,000—a fantastic sum in 1928—complained about items they could not afford. A 1922 Berkeley study revealed similar sentiments of discontent—despite the facts that all the families studied had telephones, virtually all had purchased life insurance, two-thirds owned their own homes and took vacations, over half had motor cars, and nearly every family spent at least a little money on servants or house-cleaning help.

The discontent expressed by many Americans was fostered—and to a certain extent even created—by manufacturers. Business embarked on the path of the "hard sell." The explosion of consumer credit made the task easier, as automobiles, radios, electric refrigerators, washing machines—even jewelry and foreign travel—were bought on the installment plan. By the end of the 1920s, 60 percent of cars, radios, and furniture were being purchased on "time." The ability to buy without actually having money helped foster a climate of instant gratification, expanding expectations, and, ultimately, materialism.

The 1920s was also the decade of advertising. The admen went wild: everything from walnuts to household coal was being individually branded and nationally advertised. Of course, ads had been around for a long time. But something new was afoot, in terms of both scale and strategy. For the first time, business began to use advertising as a psychological weapon against consumers. "Scare copy" was invented. Without Listerine, Postum, or a Buick, the consumer would be left a spinster, fall victim to a crippling disease, or be passed over for a promotion. Ads developed an association between the product and one's very identity. Eventually they came to promise everything and anything—from self-esteem, to status, friendship, and love.

The psychological approach responded to the economic dilemma business faced. Americans in the middle classes and above (to whom virtually all advertising was targeted) were no longer buying to satisfy basic needs—such as food, clothing and shelter. These had been met. Advertisers had to persuade consumers to acquire things they most certainly did not need. In the words of John Kenneth Galbraith, production would have to "create the wants it seeks to satisfy." This is exactly what manufacturers tried to do. The normally staid AT&T attempted to transform the utilitarian telephone into a luxury, urging families to buy "all the telephone facilities that they can conveniently use, rather than the smallest amount they can get along with." One ad campaign targeted fifteen phones as the style for an affluent home. In product after product, companies introduced designer colors, styles, even scents. The maid's uniform had to match the room decor, flatware was color-coordinated, and Kodak cameras came in five bird-inspired tints—Sea Gull, Cockatoo, Redbreast, Bluebird, and Jenny Wren.

Business clearly understood the nature of the problem. It even had a name—"needs saturation." Would-be sellers complained of buyers' strike and organized a "Prosperity Bureau," urging people to "Buy Now." According to historian Frederick Lewis Allen: "Business had learned as never before the importance of the ultimate consumer. Unless he could be persuaded to buy and buy lavishly, the whole stream of six-cylinder cars, super heterodynes, cigarettes, rouge compacts, and electric ice boxes would be dammed up at its outlets."

But would the consumer be equal to her task as "the savior of private enterprise"? The general director of General Motors' Research Labs, Charles Kettering, stated the matter baldly: business needs to create a "dissatisfied consumer"; its mission is "the organized creation of dissatisfaction." Kettering led the way by introducing annual model changes for GM cars—planned obsolescence designed to make the consumer discontented with what he or she already had. Other companies followed GM's lead. In the words of advertising historian Roland Marchand, success now depended on "the nurture of qualities like wastefulness, self-indulgence, and artificial obsolescence." The admen and the businessmen had to instill what Marchand has called the "consumption ethic," or what Benjamin Hunnicutt termed "the new economic gospel of consumption."

The campaign to create new and unlimited wants did not go unchallenged. Trade unionists and social reformers understood the long-term consequences of consumerism for most Americans: it would keep them imprisoned in capitalism's "squirrel cage." The consumption of luxuries necessitated long hours.

Materialism would provide no relief from the tedium, the stultification, the alienation, and the health hazards of modern work; its rewards came outside the workplace. There was no mystery about these choices: business was explicit in its hostility to increases in free time, preferring consumption as the *alternative* to taking economic progress in the form of leisure. In effect, business offered up the cycle of work-and-spend. In response, many trade unionists rejected what they regarded as a Faustian bargain of time for money: "Workers have declared that their lives are not to be bartered at any price, that no wage, no matter how high can induce them to sell their birthright. [The worker] is not the slave of fifty years ago. . . . he [sic] reads . . . goes to the theater . . . [and] has established his own libraries, his own educational institutions. . . . And he wants time, time, time, for all these things."

Progressive reformers raised ethical and religious objections to the cycle of work-and-spend. Monsignor John A. Ryan, a prominent Catholic spokesman, articulated a common view:

> One of the most baneful assumptions of our materialistic industrial society is that all men should spend at least one-third of the twenty-four hour day in some productive occupation. . . . If men still have leisure [after needs are satsfied], new luxuries must be invented to keep them busy and new wants must be stimulated . . . to take the luxuries off the market and keep the industries going. Of course, the true and rational doctrine is that when men have produced sufficient necessaries and reasonable comforts and conveniences to supply all the population, they should spend what time is left in the cultivation of their intellects and wills, in the pursuit of the higher life.

The debates of the 1920s clearly laid out the options available to the nation. On the one hand, the path advocated by labor and social reformers: take productivity growth in the form of increases in free time, rather than the expansion of output; limit private consumption, discourage luxuries, and emphasize public goods such as education and culture. On the other hand, the plan of business: maintain current working hours and aim for maximal economic growth. This implied the encouragement of "discretionary" consumption, the expansion of new industries, and a culture of unlimited desires. Production would come to "fill a void that it has itself created."

It is not difficult to see which alternative was adopted. Between 1920 and the present, the bulk of productivity advance has been channeled into the growth of consumption. Economist, John Owen, has found that between 1920 and 1977, the amount of labor supplied over the average American's lifetime fell by only 10 percent; and since 1950, there has even been a slight increase. The attitude of businessmen was crucial to this outcome. As employers, they had strong reasons for preferring long hours. As sellers, they craved vigorous consumption to create markets for their products. Labor proved to be no match for the economic and political power of business.

Finally, we should not underestimate the appeal of consumption itself. The working classes and the poor, particularly those migrating from Europe or the rural United States, grew up in conditions of material deprivation. The array of products available in urban America was profoundly alluring, at times mesmerizing. For the middle classes, consumption held its own satisfactions. Designer towels or the latest GM model created a sense of privilege, superiority, and well-being. A Steinway "made life worth living." Once the Depression hit, it reinforced these tendencies. One of its legacies was a longlasting emphasis on finding security in the form of material success.

THE PITFALLS OF CONSUMERISM

The consumerism that took root in the 1920s was premised on the idea of *dis*satisfaction. As much as one has, it is never enough. The implicit mentality is that the next purchase will

yield happiness, and then the next. In the words of the baby-boom writer, Katy Butler, it was the new couch, the quieter street, and the vacation cottage. Yet happiness turned out to be elusive. Today's luxuries became tomorrow's necessities, no longer appreciated. When the Joneses also got a new couch or a second home, these acquisitions were no longer quite as satisfying. Consumerism turned out to be full of pitfalls—a vicious pattern of wanting and spending which failed to deliver on its promises.

The inability of the consumerist life style to create durable satisfaction can be seen in the syndrome of "keeping up with the Joneses." This competition is based on the fact that it is not the absolute level of consumption that matters, but how much one consumes relative to one's peers. The great English economist John Maynard Keynes made this distinction over fifty years ago: "[Needs] fall into two classes—those which are absolute in the sense that we feel them whatever the situation of our fellow human beings may be, and those which are relative only in that their satisfaction lifts us above, makes us feel superior to, our fellows." Since then, economists have invented a variety of terms for "keeping up with the Joneses": "relative income or consumption," "positional goods," or "local status." A brand-new Toyota Corolla may be a luxury and a status symbol in a lower-middle-class town, but it appears paltry next to the BMWs and Mercedes that fill the driveways of the fancy suburb. A 10-percent raise sounds great until you find that your co-workers all got 12 percent. The cellular phone, fur coat, or _ (fill in the blank) gives a lot of satisfaction only before everyone else has one. In the words of one 1980s investment banker: "You tend to live up to your income level. You see it in relation to the people of your category. They're living in a certain way and you want to live in that way. You keep up with other people of your situation who have also leveraged themselves."

Over time, keeping up with the Joneses becomes a real trap—because the Joneses also keep up with you. If everyone's income goes up by 10 percent, then relative positions don't change at all. No satisfaction is gained. The more of our happiness we derive from comparisons with others, the less additional welfare we get from general increases in income—which is probably why happiness has failed to keep pace with economic growth. This dynamic may be only partly conscious. We may not even be aware that we are competing with the Joneses, or experience it as a competition. It may be as simple as the fact that exposure to their latest "life-style upgrade" plants the seed in our own mind that we must have it, too—whether it be a European vacation, this year's fashion statement, or piano lessons for the children.

In the choice between income and leisure, the quest for relative standing has biased us toward income. That's because status comparisons have been mostly around commodities—cars, clothing, houses, even second houses. If Mrs. Jones works long hours, she will be able to buy the second home, the designer dresses, or the fancier car. If her neighbor Mrs. Smith opts for more free time instead, her two-car garage and walk-in closet will be half empty. As long as the competition is more oriented to visible commodities, the tendency will be for both women to prefer income to time off. But once they both spend the income, they're back to where they started. Neither is *relatively* better off. If free time is less of a "relative" good than other commodities, then true welfare could be gained by having more of it, and worrying less about what the Joneses are buying.

It's not easy to get off the income treadmill and into a new, more leisured life style. Mrs. Smith won't do it on her own, because it'll set her back in comparison to Mrs. Jones. And Mrs. Jones is just like Mrs. Smith. They are trapped in a classic Prisoner's Dilemma: both would be better off with more free time; but without cooperation, they will stick to the long hours, high consumption choice. We also know their employers won't initiate a shift to more leisure, because they prefer employees to work long hours.

A second vicious cycle arises from the fact that the satisfactions gained from consumption are often short-lived. For many, consumption can be habit forming. Like drug addicts who develop a tolerance, consumers need additional hits to maintain any given level of satisfaction. The switch from black and white to color television was a real improvement when it occurred. But soon viewers became habituated to color. Going back to black and white would have reduced well-being, but having color may not have yielded a permanently higher level of satisfaction. Telephones are another example. Rotary dialing was a major improvement. Then came touch-tone, which made us impatient with rotaries. Now numbers are preprogrammed and some people begin to find any dialing a chore.

Our lives are filled with goods to which we have become so habituated that we take them for granted. Indoor plumbing was once a great luxury—and still is in much of the world. Now it is so ingrained in our life style that we don't give it a second thought. The same holds true for all but the newest household appliances—stoves, refrigerators, and vacuum cleaners are just part of the landscape. We may pay great attention to the kind of automobile we drive, but the fact of having a car is something adults grew accustomed to long ago.

The process of habituation can be seen as people pass through life stages—for example, in the transition from student life to a first job. The graduate student makes $15,000 a year. He has hand-me-down furniture, eats at cheap restaurants, and, when traveling long distances, finds a place in someone else's car. After graduation, he gets a job and makes twice as much money. At first, everything seems luxurious. He rents a bigger apartment (with no roommates), buys his own car, and steps up a notch in restaurant quality. His former restaurant haunts now seem unappetizing. Hitching a ride becomes too inconvenient. As he accumulates possessions, the large apartment starts to shrink. In not too many years, he has become habituated to twice as much income and is spending the entire $30,000. It was once a princely sum, which made him feel rich. Now he feels it just covers a basic standard of living, without much left over for luxuries. He may not even feel any better off. Yet to go back to $15,000 would be painful.

Over time, further increases in income set in motion another round of the same. He becomes dissatisfied with renting and "needs" to buy a home. Travel by car takes too long, so he switches to airplanes. His tastes become more discriminating, and the average price of a restaurant meal slowly creeps upward. Something like this process is why Americans making $70,000 a year end up feeling stretched and discontented.

Of course, part of this is a life-cycle process. As our young man grows older, possessions like cars and houses become more important. But there's more to it than aging. Like millions of other American consumers, he is becoming addicted to the accoutrements of affluence. This may well be why the doubling of per-capita income has not made us twice as well off. In the words of psychologist Paul Wachtel, we have become an "asymptote culture . . . in which the contribution of material goods to life satisfaction has reached a point of diminishing returns. . . . Each individual item seems to us to bring an increase in happiness or satisfaction. But the individual increments melt like cotton candy when you try to add them up."

These are not new ideas. Economists such as James Duesenberry, Edward Schumacher, Fred Hirsch, Tiber Scitovsky, Robert Frank, and Richard Easterlin have explored these themes. Psychologists have also addressed them, providing strong support for the kinds of conclusions I have drawn. My purpose is to add a dimension to this analysis of consumption which has heretofore been neglected—its connection to the incentive structures operating in labor markets. The consumption traps I have described are just the flip side of the bias toward long hours embedded in the production system. We are not merely caught in a pattern of spend-and-spend—the problem identified by many critics of consumer culture. The whole story is that we work, and spend, and work and spend some more.

CAUSES OF THE WORK-AND-SPEND CYCLE

The irony in all the consuming Americans do is that, when asked, they reject materialist values. The Gallup Poll recently asked respondents to choose what was most important to them—family life, betterment of society, physical health, a strict moral code, and so on. Among a list of nine, the materialist option—"having a nice home, car and other belongings"—ranked *last*. In a second survey, respondents ranked "having nice things" twenty-sixth in a list of twenty-eight. (Only opposing abortion and being free of obligations were less popular.) Over two-thirds of the population says it would "welcome less emphasis on money." Yet behavior is often contrary to these stated values. Millions of working parents see their children or spouses far less than they should or would like to. "Working" mothers complain they have no time for themselves. Volunteer work is on the decline, presumably because people have little time for it. Employed Americans spend long hours at jobs that are adversely affecting their health—through injury, occupationally induced diseases, and stress. My explanation for this paradoxical behavior is that people are operating under a powerful set of constraints: they are trapped by the cycle of work-and-spend.

Work-and-spend is driven by productivity growth. Whether the annual increment is 3 percent, as it was for much of the postwar period, or less, as it has been in recent years, growth in productivity provides the chance either to raise income or to reduce working hours. This is where the cycle begins, with the employer's reaction to the choice between "time and money." Usually a company does not offer this choice to its employees but unilaterally decides to maintain existing hours and give a pay increase instead. As we have seen, for forty years, only a negligible portion of productivity increase has been channeled into free time. Using productivity to raise incomes has become the firmly entrenched "default option."

One might imagine that where wages are set by collective-bargaining agreements employees would have more of a say in the choice between income and time. But less than 20 percent of the workforce is unionized. Furthermore, as union negotiators will attest, employers are frequently fiercely resistant to granting concessions on hours and jealously guard the authority to set schedules. But even if a firm is willing, the reduced worktime option it offers will often be worth less (in dollar terms) than a straight pay increase, because of the extra costs incurred, such as additional fringe benefits for new employees. The company will try and force the employees to bear the expenses associated with shorter working hours. So even with collective bargaining, the choice will be skewed against shorter hours.

Once a pay increase is granted, it sets off the consumption cycles I have described. The additional income will be spent. (The personal savings rate is currently only 4.5 percent of disposable income.) The employee will become habituated to this spending and incorporate it into his or her usual standard of living. Gaining free time by *reducing* income becomes undesirable, both because of relative comparisons (Joneses versus Smiths) and habit formation. The next year, when another increase in productivity occurs, the process starts again. The company offers income, which the employee spends and becomes accustomed to. This interpretation is consistent with the history of the last half-century. Annual productivity growth has made possible higher incomes or more free time. Repeatedly, the bulk of the productivity increase has been channeled into the former. Consumption has kept pace.

What drives this cycle of work-and-spend? One view—that of neoclassical economic theory—contends that it is motivated by the choices of workers. Workers have prior (and

fixed) attitudes about how valuable income is to them and how much they dislike work. On the basis of these attitudes they select the number of hours they want to work. Firms are passive and willing to hire workers for whatever quantity of hours they choose. By this account, if factory workers in the nineteenth century toiled twelve, fourteen, or sixteen hours a day, it was because they "preferred" this schedule above all others. If U.S. workers have added a month onto their annual worktime, it is because they want the extra income. Attempts to limit hours of labor will make employees worse, not better off. Invariably, *workers get what they want.*

I turn the neoclassical analysis on its head, arguing that *workers want what they get*, rather than get what they want. My starting point is firms rather than individual workers. Firms set the hours they require of their employees. Associated with those hours is a level of income that determines workers' consumption level. As a result of habit formation and relative status considerations, people develop preferences to accommodate that level of spending. Attitudes toward consumption are not preordained but are actually formed in the process of earning and consuming itself. These two interpretations—workers get what they want or want what they get—are the polar cases. According to neoclassical theory, attitudes toward consumption are independent of the actual experience of spending, and firms are passive. In my interpretation, firms set hours and workers do most of the adjusting.

ASSESSING THE NEOCLASSICAL VIEW

The crux of the neoclassical story is that workers determine hours. But do they? Not according to the evidence. Every study I have seen on this topic has found that workers lack free choice of hours. They are limited in both how much and how little they can work. In one survey of male heads of households, 85 percent reported that they did not have free choice of hours. A second study (of married men) again found that 85 percent were faced with the choice of either no job or a job at hours that were not those they would choose. The men wanted shorter hours, but all the jobs were full-time. The other existing studies report consistent results: workers face constraints on their hours of work. Indeed, institutionalist labor economists (oriented to the "real world") have long maintained that firms choose hours, giving employees a take-it-or-leave-it option. Now this institutionalist view is backed up by statistical evidence.

These findings do not imply that workers have *no* freedom in the matter of working hours. Moonlighting and retirement are options. And hours differ across occupations and industries, so that workers can quit their jobs to find alternate schedules. But the research shows that for most workers these adjustments are not sufficient to eliminate *binding* constraints on hours. As the economist Paul Samuelson noted years ago: "In contrast with freedom in the spending of the money we earn, the modern industrial regime denies us a similar freedom in choosing the work routine by which we earn those dollars." The failure of the neoclassical approach is rooted in its assumption that there is always full employment and that workers' choices are sovereign. As I have argued, this characterization is mistaken. Competition in labor markets is typically skewed in favor of employers: it is a buyer's market. And in a buyer's market, it is the sellers who compromise. Competition for labor is not strong enough to ensure that workers' desires are always satisfied. This is part of why firms are able to set working hours, even when they entail binding constraints on workers.

The second major point of difference between my approach and the neoclassical involves the nature of preferences. Neoclassical economists point to worker attitudes as evidence that the market is delivering the hours they want. Results from a 1985 survey are typical: asked whether they would prefer more,

fewer, or just the hours they were currently working, accompanied by commensurate changes in income, about two thirds of workers reported satisfaction with their current hours/income choice.

This evidence may sound compelling. But imagine, for a moment, what the responses would be like in the light of my interpretation, and workers want what they get. *The results would look just the same*, in the sense that majorities would express satisfaction with their current hours. The standard survey evidence is perfectly consistent with both views.

A great deal of psychological evidence casts doubt, however, on the neoclassical interpretation. Psychologists find that people tend to "adapt" to their environments: that is, their preferences adjust over time. The fact that large numbers of people say they are contented with their working hours (or job conditions) may reveal that they are tractable, not that their deeper desires have been fulfilled.

One type of evidence that can differentiate between the two interpretations is forward-looking surveys—questions about trading off future income for leisure. Here workers express markedly different views. In a 1978 Department of Labor study, 84 percent of respondents said that they would like to trade off some or all of future income for additional free time. Nearly half (47 percent) said they would trade *all* of a 10-percent pay raise for free time. Only 16 percent opted for the money with no increase in time off.

These findings support a key feature of the work-and-spend cycle—the difference in attitudes toward current and future income. As with all the previous surveys, this group was unwilling to give up its current income (only a small percentage chose that option). Presumably they had become materially or psychologically attached to their existing standard of living. But the desire to consume out of future income was far less compelling, a fact consistent with recent psychological research. In the neoclassical interpretation, there is no explanation for this asymmetry.

Because this study was conducted over ten years ago, we can check to see whether the stated preferences were actually validated. Did 84 percent of the population gain the free time they said they wanted? As we know, they did not. In fact, they lost free time. Of course, what has happened since 1978 is complicated. Some workers, particularly younger less-educated men, have lost purchasing power since 1978. Others have had stagnant incomes. But leisure time did not even increase among those with gains in income. In fact, hours increased substantially for those groups who both did well in the labor market and expressed the strongest desires for more time off—women and people in the higher-paid occupational categories. In 1989, when a similar survey was taken, the results indicated that forward-looking preferences for leisure are still strong. Eight out of ten Americans declared that they would sacrifice career advancement in order to spend more time with their families.

This evidence hardly settles the issue. Many more studies and surveys are necessary, particularly to track working hours and preferences over time. However, the findings do cast doubt on the sanguine view of labor/leisure choices which dominates the economic discourse. It is clear that we can no longer rely on the simple assumption that labor and product markets provide optimal outcomes, in response to what people want and need. The interaction between what we want and what we get is far more complicated.

THE SOCIAL NATURE OF WORK-AND-SPEND

Part of the power of the work-and-spend cycle is its social pervasiveness. Although individuals are the proximate decision makers, their actions are influenced and constrained by social norms and conventions. The social character of the cycle of work-and-spend means that individuals have a hard time breaking out of it on their own. This is part of why, despite evidence of growing desires for less demanding jobs and disillusionment with "work-and-spend," hours are still rising.

To see the difficulties individuals have in deviating from the status quo, consider what would happen to an ordinary couple who have grown tired of the rat race. John and Jane Doe, like nearly half of all Americans, want more time to spend with their children and each other. What will happen if they both decide to reduce their hours by half and are willing to live on half their usual earnings?

The transition will be most abrupt for John. Few men work part-time, with the exception of teens, students, and some seniors. Among males aged twenty-five to forty-four, virtually none (a meager 2.5 percent) voluntarily choose part-time schedules. Most report that they are not able to reduce their hours of work at all. And of those who do have the freedom to work fewer hours, it is likely that only a small percentage can reduce hours by as much as half. Unless John has truly unusual talents, his employer will probably refuse to sanction a change to part-time work. Chances are he'll have to find a new job.

Given the paucity of part-time jobs for men, John's choices will be limited. It will be almost impossible to secure a position in a managerial, professional, or administrative capacity. Most part-time jobs are in the service sector. When he does land a job, his pay will fall far short of what he earned in full-time work. The median hourly wage rate among male workers is about $10.50, with weekly earnings of $450. As a part-time worker paid by the hour, his median wage will be about $4, or $80 a week. He will also lose many of the benefits that went with his full-time job. Only 15 percent of part-time workers are given health insurance. The total income loss John will suffer is likely to exceed 80 percent. Under these conditions, part-time work hardly seems feasible.

The social nature of John's choice is revealed by the drama of his attempt to go against the grain. Since few adult men choose part-time work, there is almost none to be had. The social convention of full-time work gives the individual little choice about it. Those who contemplate a shift to part-time will be deterred by the economic penalty. There may even be many who would prefer shorter hours, but they will exert very little influence on the actual choices available, because their desires are latent. Exit from existing jobs—one channel for influencing the market—is not available, because they cannot find part-time jobs to exit to. Unless people begin to speak up and collectively demand that employers provide alternatives, they will probably remain trapped in full-time work.

Jane's switch to part-time will be less traumatic. She will find more job possibilities, because more women work part-time. Her earnings loss will be less, because women are already discriminated against in full-time work. (The median hourly wage for women working part-time is almost three-quarters of the full-time wage, compared with one-half for men.) If Jane can get health insurance through John's employment, part-time work may be feasible. But a great deal depends on his earnings and benefits. Even under the best of assumptions, Jane will have to forgo a wide variety of occupations, including most of those with the best pay and working conditions. She will most likely be relegated to the bottom part of the female labor market—the service, sales, and clerical jobs where the majority of women part-timers reside. Social convention and the economic incentives it creates will reproduce inequalities of gender. Despite their original intentions, Jane, rather than John, will end up in part-time employment.

These are the obstacles on the labor market side—low wages, few benefits, and severe limitations on choice of occupations. The dominance of full-time jobs also has effects on the consumption side. Imagine that Jane and John still want to cut back their hours, even under the adverse circumstances I have described. Their income will now be very low, and they will be forced to economize greatly on their purchases. This will affect their ability to fit in socially. As half-time workers, they will find

many social occasions too expensive (lunches and dinners out, movies). At first, friends will be understanding, but eventually the clash in life styles will create a social gap. Their children will have social difficulties if they don't have access to common after-school activities or the latest toys and clothes. They'll drop off the birthday party circuit because they can't afford to bring gifts. We can even see these pressures with full-time workers, as parents take on extra employment to live up to neighborhood standards. After her divorce Celeste Henderson worked two jobs to give her children the things their schoolmates had. Ms. Henderson's daughter says her mother "saved her the embarrassment of looking poor to the other children." For a family with only part-time workers, the inability to consume in the manner of their peers is likely to lead to some social alienation. Unless they have a community of others in similar circumstances, dropping down will include an element of dropping out. Many Americans, especially those with children, are not willing to risk such a fate.

Even with careful budgeting, a couple like the Does may have trouble procuring the basics (housing, food, and clothing), because the U.S. standard of living is geared to at least one full-time income and, increasingly, to two. Rents will be high relative to the Does' income. In part, this is because of price increases in the last decade. But there is also a more fundamental impediment. As I have argued, contemporary houses and apartment are large and luxurious. They have indoor plumbing, central heating, stoves, and refrigerators. They have expensive features such as closets, garages, and individual bedrooms. In our society, housing must conform to legal and social conventions that define the acceptable standard of housing. The difficulty is that the social norm prevailing in the housing market is matched to a full-time income (or incomes). It is not only that the cost of living is high these days. It is also that barebones housing, affordable on only half a salary, is rare. Even if the Does were willing to go without closets, garages, and central heating in order to save money, they would be hard-pressed to find such a dwelling.

This problem is common to many goods and services. In an economy where nearly everyone works full-time, manufacturers cater to the purchasing power of the full-time income. There is a limited market for products that are desired only by those with half an income. A whole range of cheap products are not even available. Only the better-quality goods will be demanded, and hence only they will be produced. We can see this phenomenon in the continual upscaling of products. We've gone from blender to Cuisinart, from polyester to cotton, from one-speed Schwinn to fancy trail bike. Remember the things that were available forty years ago but have disappeared? The semiautomatic washing machine. The hand-driven coffee grinder. The rotary dial telephone. For those who are skeptical about this point, con-sider the markets of poor countries. In India, one can find very cheap, low-quality clothing— at a fraction of the price of the least expensive items in the United States. Semiautomatic washers and stripped-down cars are the norm. On a world scale, the American consumer market is very upscale, which means that Americans need an upscale income to partici-pate in it.

The strength of social norms does not mean that the nature of work cannot be changed. Part-time employment *could* become a viable option for larger numbers of people. But the existence of social norms suggests that change will not come about, as the neoclassical econo-mist predicts, merely through individuals exer-cising their preferences in the market. Where Prisoner's Dilemmas and vicious cycles exist, change requires intervention on a social level— from government, unions, professional associa-tions, and other collective organizations.

GLOSSARY

Tract house: One of numerous houses of similar design constructed on a tract of land.

John Kenneth Galbraith (1908–): Canadian-born American economist, writer, and diplomat who served as U.S. ambassador to India (1961–1963). His best-known works include *The Great Crash* (1955) and *The Affluent Society* (1958).

IMPLICATIONS

At a national level, the late 1980s and early 1990s witnessed near-record economic pros-perity in America. But, as Schor reveals, this prosperity was purchased at the price of dual wage-earning families, long working hours, and an often frantic pace of life. Why do you think so many Americans accepted the "squir-rel cage" existence that Schor describes? What do you think the personal and economic conse-quences would be if Americans worked fewer hours and spent less money on consumer goods?